Innovation and Growth

Innovation and Growth

From R&D Strategies of Innovating Firms
to Economy-Wide Technological Change

Edited by
Martin Andersson, Börje Johansson,
Charlie Karlsson, and Hans Lööf

OXFORD
UNIVERSITY PRESS

Great Clarendon Street, Oxford, OX2 6DP,
United Kingdom

Oxford University Press is a department of the University of Oxford.
It furthers the University's objective of excellence in research, scholarship,
and education by publishing worldwide. Oxford is a registered trade mark of
Oxford University Press in the UK and in certain other countries

© Oxford University Press 2012

The moral rights of the authors have been asserted

First Edition published in 2012

Impression: 1

British Library Cataloguing in Publication Data
Data available

Library of Congress Cataloging in Publication Data
Data available

ISBN 978–0–19–964668–5

Printed in Great Britain by
MPG Books Group, Bodmin and King's Lynn

Preface

This book is part of the outcome of a long-term project on innovation and growth, initiated by the Centre of Excellence for Science and Innovation Studies (CESIS) at the Royal Institute of Technology (KTH) and the Jönköping International Business School (JIBS). The project is financed by the Swedish Governmental Agency for Innovation System (VINNOVA). The first ideas for this project were communicated with VINNOVA as early as 2007 and we started to contact the contributing authors shortly after the project was decided.

We are happy that authors in this volume found the idea for this book interesting and we are proud of the outcome. We believe that this volume, which includes contributions by scholars from different disciplines, working with different types of data and methods, but centred on a core issue of innovating firms, heterogeneity, and economy-wide effects, will fill a gap in the literature. The set of contributing authors is composed of respected scholars with an internationally recognized expertise within specific contexts of the relationship between innovation and growth. The volume comprises contributions and perspectives from both economics and business scholars, working in particular in the fields of international business and business strategy. We maintain that innovation research is a field where these disciplines should and indeed do meet each other.

We have of course had a lot of support from our colleagues and home universities in this project. We primarily wish to thank Kerstin Ferroukhi at JIBS for all her help with administrative and organizational matters. We are also grateful to Pardis Nabavi Larijani at KTH for helping us to format the manuscript to fit the guidelines from Oxford University Press. Finally, we owe gratitude to Adam Swallow and Aimee Wright at Oxford University Press for all help and constructive comments on the book volume.

During this project we organized four workshops where the project participants (i.e. the contributing authors) met and presented chapter drafts, exchanged ideas and discussed various issues. A first workshop took place in Autumn 2009, and was hosted by the School of Public Policy, George Mason University, Fairfax VA, USA. We are grateful in particular to professors

Kingsley Haynes, Roger Stough, and David Hart for making this workshop possible at their institution and for all their help and support in the preparations. The second workshop was hosted by the Institute for Economic Geography and GIScience at the Vienna University of Business and Economics in Vienna, Austria, in April 2010. We wish to thank Professor Manfred Fischer for making this possible and Thomas Seyffertitz for helping us with all practical matters such as booking of hotel rooms, workshop rooms, and restaurants. The third workshop took place at the Guö Värdshus in Blekinge in June 2010. For this event we acknowledge administrative help from Eleonore Huang Vogel at the Blekinge Institute of Technology (BTH), and financial support from BTH Innovation and the School of Management at BTH. The last workshop was arranged at JIBS in Jönköping to coincide with the 50th European Congress of the Regional Science International, August 2010, and we here wish to thank Kerstin Ferroukhi for all her help in the preparations.

November 2011

Jönköping and Stockholm

Martin Andersson, Börje Johansson,

Charlie Karlsson, Hans Lööf

Contents

Contents

List of Figures

List of Figures

List of Tables

Abbreviations

CIS	Community Innovation Survey
GEM	Global Entrepreneurship Monitor
GMM	Generalized Method of Moments
MNC (or MNE)	Multinational Corporation
R&D	Research and Development

Notes on Contributors

Zoltan J. Acs is University Professor and Director of the Center for Entrepreneurship and Public Policy (CEPP) at the School of Public Policy, George Mason University in Washington, DC, and a visiting professor at Imperial College Business School, London, UK, former Chief Economist at the Office of Advocacy, US Small Business Administration, and Research Scholar at the Max Planck Institute of Economics. He developed the Global Entrepreneurship and Development Index (GEDI). The most recent edition was published in 2012 by Edward Elgar. He is also on the board of the World Entrepreneurship Forum, the Swedish Foundation for Small Business, the Corporate Research Board, and Eurasia Circle for Cultural Undestanding and Prosperity (EC-CUP). *Business Economics*. He has also served as Chief Economic Advisor at the US Small Business Administration (SBA). Currently Dr Acs is working with the Kauffman Foundation on developing public policies that promote an entrepreneurial economy. This policy initiative takes a broad view of public policy encompassing the individual, the economy, international aspects, the region, and social policy.

Paul Almeida is the Senior Associate Dean of Executive Degree and Non-Degree Programs and an associate professor of strategy and international business at the McDonough School of Business at Georgetown University. He is also the co-director of the Georgetown-ESADE Global Executive MBA program. He received his Ph.D. from the Wharton School of the University of Pennsylvania. Professor Almeida is the Area Editor for Strategy, Innovation, and Economic Geography for the *Journal of International Business Studies*. He is the past chair of the Technology and Innovation Management Division of the Academy of Management. He has been awarded Georgetown's Faculty Research Award and the Dean's Service Award.

Martin Andersson is Professor of Innovation Studies at the Centre for Innovation, Research and Competence in the Learning Economy (CIRCLE) at Lund University and is also affiliated to the School of Management at the Blekinge Institute of Technology (BTH). He is an economist by training and has a Ph.D. in economics from the Jönköping International Business School (JIBS). Before joining CIRCLE, Martin worked for several years as Research Coordinator of CESIS and Post-Doctoral Researcher at the Royal Institute of Technology (KTH) and JIBS. His research focuses on innovation, trade, and location, and their interplay, including non-linear relations and dynamics in innovation and learning processes.

Cristiano Antonelli holds the chair of Political Economy at the University of Torino and is a fellow of the Collegio Carlo Alberto where he guides BRICK (Bureau of Research on Innovation, Complexity and Knowledge). He is the Managing Editor of *Economics of Innovation and New Technology*. He has been Director of the Department of Economics 'Salvatore Cognetti de Martiis' at the University of Torino (2005–2010), Visiting Professor in the universities of Paris Sud, Paris XIII, Lyon Lumière, Nice, Paris-Dauphine, Aix-en-Provence, Manchester, Rio de Janeiro, Vice-President of the International Schumpeter Society (2000–2004), a Rockefeller Fellow at the Sloan School of the MIT in the years 1983–1985 and a junior economist at the OECD (1978 and 1979).

René Belderbos is a full Professor of Managerial Economics and Strategy at the University of Leuven and part-time Professorial Fellow at Maastricht University and UNU-MERIT (The Netherlands). He chairs the Department of Managerial Economics, Strategy, and Innovation research, and Economics, at the Faculty of Business. His research focuses on innovation strategies and international business strategies of multinational firms. His research has been published widely in international journals including the *Review of Economics and Statistics, Strategic Management Journal, European Economic Review, Economica, International Journal of Industrial Organization, World Development, Research Policy, Journal of International Business Studies, Journal of Product Innovation Management*, and *Journal of World Economics*.

Katarina Blomkvist is a researcher and lecturer at the Department of Business Studies at Uppsala University and has been affiliated with the International Business Research Group and the Entrepreneurship Research Group since 2005. She earned her Ph.D. in 2009 from Uppsala University. Dr Blomkvist's dissertation focused on the role of foreign subsidiaries of multinational corporations and their role as sources of new technological capabilities, with specific attention to subsidiary technological evolution and drivers of innovation diffusion. Currently, she is working in a new project regarding innovation development and transfer inside and outside multinational corporations. She worked for the European Parliament's Economic and Monetary Affairs Committee during 2010.

Pontus Braunerhjelm is Professor in economics at the Royal Institute of Technology (KTH) and Managing Director of the Swedish Entrepreneurship Forum. He earned his PhD in international economics at the Graduate Institute of International Studies, University of Geneva, in 1994, followed by a second dissertation at the International Business, School in Jönköping in 1999. Braunerhjelm has also held positions at Linköping University, as well as leading Swedish research institutes (IFN and SNS), and was also assigned Secretary General of the Swedish Government's Globalization Council 2007 to 2009. His scientific output comprises more than 200 publications.

John Cantwell is Distinguished Professor (Professor II) of International Business at Rutgers University in the USA. His main research areas are the analysis of corporate technological change and international business. He is the author of *Technological Innovation and Multinational Corporations* (1989), a book which helped to launch a new literature on multinational companies and international networks for technology creation, beyond merely international technology transfer, and which has a cumulative social science journal citation count of well over 250. Professor Cantwell is serving as the editor-in-chief of the *Journal of International Business Studies* from 2011 to 2013.

Tommy Høyvarde Clausen is a senior researcher at the Nordland Research Institute in Bodø (Norway). He has a Ph.D. degree in innovation studies from the University of

Oslo, Norway. His research interests are primarily within evolutionary organizational theory, innovation within firms, entrepreneurship, and innovation policy. He has published on these topics in journals such as *Technology Analysis and Strategic Management, Acta Sociologica*, and *Journal of Evolutionary Economics*.

Geert Duysters is a full Professor of Entrepreneurship and Innovation at Tilburg University and Eindhoven University of Technology. He act as the Scientific Director of the Barbant Center of Entrepreneurship. He has published many articles in journals like *Organization Science, Journal of International Business Studies, Research Policy, Organization Studies, Journal of Management Studies*, and so on. Previously he acted as a global board member of ASAP and he founded three Internet companies over the past decade.

David M. Hart is Professor at the School of Public Policy, George Mason University, and also Director of the Center for Science and Technology Policy. In 2011–2012, he served as assistant director for innovation policy at the White House Office of Science and Technology Policy. Professor Hart is the co-author (with Richard K. Lester) of *Unlocking Energy Innovation* (MIT Press, 2012). His current research focuses on high-skill immigration, with a particular focus on the role of foreign-born entrepreneurs in the U.S. high-tech industry.

Börje Johansson is Professor of Economics at the Jönköping International Business School (JIBS) and guest professor at the Division of Economics at the Royal Institute of Technology, Stockholm (KTH). At the same place he is also director of CESIS, the Centre of Excellence for Science and Innovation Studies. He received his Ph.D. at the University of Gothenburg in 1978. Dr Johansson is editor of the international journal *Annals of Regional Science* (Springer-Verlag). In Sweden he has carried out major projects on high-speed-train development and on transport policies for the National Swedish Road Authority.

Philip Kappen is a Researcher and Lecturer of International Business and Entrepreneurship at Uppsala University's Department of Business Studies. He defended his doctoral thesis on technological evolution in foreign subsidiaries in 2009, which subsequently was awarded a prestigious Wallander scholarship from Handelsbankens research foundations. His research is concerned with the management of innovation and innovation diffusion within established corporations, with a specific focus on the strategic role of the headquarters in the contemporary diversified firm. He has published in journals such as the *Journal of International Business Studies, Journal of World Business*, and *Research Policy*.

Charlie Karlsson is Professor of the Economics of Technological Change at JIBS, Guest Professor of Economics at University West, Trollhättan, Professor of Industrial Organization at Blekinge Technical University, Ronneby, and Associate Professor ('docent') in Regional Planning at the Royal Institute of Technology, Stockholm. At JIBS he is director of INA (the Institute of Industrial Research), CISEG (Centre for Innovation Systems, Entrepreneurship and Growth), and JIBS/CESIS (Centre of Excellence for Science and Innovation Studies). He holds a B.Sc. and an M.Sc. in economics from the University of Gothenburg and a Ph.D. in economics from Umeå University.

Alfred Kleinknecht (born 1951) has a degree in economics from the Free University of Berlin (1977) and a Ph.D. from the Free University of Amsterdam (1984). Since 1997 he has held the chair of Economics of Innovation at Delft University of Technology (TU Delft). He previously worked at the Berlin Wissenschaftszentrum, the University of Amsterdam, and the University of Maastricht. In the early 1990s he belonged to the team that developed the Community Innovation Survey.

Hans Lööf is a Professor of Economics at the Royal Institute of Technology in Stockholm. He is also deputy director of the Research Centre of Excellence for Science and Innovation Studies and programme manager for the Masters programme in the Economics of Innovation and Growth. He is a member of the editorial board of the *Annals of Regional Science*. Dr Lööf has worked as an expert on innovation for the Ministry of Industry in Sweden and participated in the OECD project on innovation strategy. He is also a member of the Statistics Sweden's programme council for R&D statistics.

Jacques Mairesse is a founding member of the Centre for Research in Economics and Statistics (CREST), the research centre of INSEE that was created in 1990. He is a senior researcher of the microeconometric laboratory at CREST and a research associate of the NBER (National Bureau of Economic Research) since 1980. Dr Mairesse is Professor of Applied Econometrics of Research, Innovation, and Productivity at Maastricht University and Professorial Fellow of UNU-MERIT since 2005. He has been engaged in various comparative studies, using firm micro data for France, the USA, and other countries, in particular to analyse research and development (R&D) activities and their effects on productivity.

Anu Phene is an Associate Professor of international business at the School of Business at George Washington University. Before joining GW, she was an associate professor of strategy at the University of Utah. She received her Ph.D. in international management from the University of Texas and her MBA from the Indian Institute of Management, Ahmedabad. Her research focuses on knowledge creation and transfer within and across firms, geographic boundaries of knowledge, multinational firm and subsidiary evolution, and alliance mechanisms. She has authored publications in the *Journal of International Business Studies*, *Organization Science*, *Strategic Management Journal*, *Management International Review*, and the *Journal of Management*.

Henk Jan Reinders (born 1987) has a degree in natural sciences from Utrecht University (2008), a degree in management of technology from Delft University of Technology (2011) and is currently pursuing a Masters in economics at the University of Amsterdam.

Stephane Robin is Associate Professor in Mathematical and Quantitative Methods at the Department of Business and Management of the University of Paris 1 Panthéon-Sorbonne. Prior to this, he was Associate Professor at the University of Strasbourg and researcher at BETA (Bureau of Theoretical and Applied Economics). His research focuses on the economics of innovation. His interests range from the economic determinants of innovation to the impacts of the different forms of innovation on productivity and employment. He has published his research in various international journals including *Research Policy*, the *Review of Industrial Organization,* and the *Journal of Technology Transfer.*

Anna Sabidussi is Associate Professor in the field of innovation and entrepreneurship at TiasNimbas Business School and Director of the Competence Centre on Innovation and Entrepreneurship. Dr Sabidussi has experience in lecturing in the fields of strategy, finance, innovation, and entrepreneurship and over the years has been nominated for and awarded the title of Best Lecturer. Before joining TiasNimbas, Dr Sabidussi has been Assistant Professor at Eindhoven University of Technology (TU/e) and associated with the Brabant Centre of Entrepreneurship (BCE). During her Ph.D. studies, Dr Sabidussi also worked as Assistant Professor at Wageningen University, and Research Centre while cooperating with the School of Economics, Utrecht University, on a joint project sponsored by the Netherlands Organization for Scientific Research (NWO).

Bart Verspagen is an economist specializing in the economics of technological change. His workplace is the Economics Department of Maastricht University, as well as the research institute UNU-Merit in Maastricht. At the university, he holds the chair of international economics. Verspagen's research interests are fairly broad. The central area is the process of economic growth, and its relation to technological change. This also brings him into areas such as international trade theory, industrial dynamics, economic and technology history, and applied econometrics, statistics, and mathematical modelling. With regard to the latter, he has mainly been applying evolutionary theory to economics. This includes simulation modelling of international economies.

Edward N. Wolff received his Ph.D. from Yale University in 1974 and is Professor of Economics at New York University, where he has taught since 1974, and a senior scholar at the Levy Economics Institute of Bard College. He is also a research associate at the National Bureau of Economic Research. He served as managing editor of the *Review of Income and Wealth* from 1987 to 2004 and was a visiting scholar at the Russell Sage Foundation in New York (2003–2004), president of the Eastern Economics Association (2002–2003), a council member of the International Input-Output Association (1995–2003), and a council member of the International Association for Research in Income and Wealth (1987–2004). He has acted as a consultant with the Economic Policy Institute, the World Bank, the United Nations, the WIDER Institute, and Mathematica Policy Research. His principal research areas are income and wealth distribution and productivity growth.

Ivo Zander is the Anders Wall Professor of Entrepreneurship at Uppsala University. Before moving into the area of entrepreneurship, he conducted research on regional agglomerations and the internationalization of research and development in multinational corporations, with a particular focus on how international innovation networks have changed the multinational's innovation capacity and innovation processes. His current research interests include corporate entrepreneurship, art entrepreneurship, and the entrepreneurial dynamics of accelerated internationalization. He teaches entrepreneurship, strategic management, and various aspects of growing and managing the international firm, including foreign market entry and penetration, and innovation and entrepreneurship in the multinational corporation.

Feng Zhang joined the Bill Greehey School of Business in 2010. She holds a doctorate in international business from Rutgers University and a Master of science in international management from the University of Reading, UK. Zhang has taught courses in the fields of international business, international marketing, and the Asian business environment. Her research interests include technological innovation of multinational corporations, knowledge-management strategies, intellectual-property-rights protection, and technological catch-up of firms in emerging markets. She has published articles in academic journals and conference proceedings, and she has contributed chapters in several books. Zhang is an active member of many professional associations such as the Academy of International Business, the Academy of Management, and the Society of Strategic Management.

Introduction

Innovation and Growth—From R&D Strategies of Innovating Firms to Economy-Wide Technological Change

Martin Andersson, Börje Johansson, Charlie Karlsson, and Hans Lööf

This volume aims to provide additional knowledge and understanding of firms' R&D and innovation strategies and their economy-wide consequences, thereby contributing to the literature on innovation and growth. The idea for the book springs from two basic observations. This first is that there are ambiguities and inconsistencies in the empirical research literature analysing the relationships between R&D, innovation, and growth. A representative statement describing the general state of this literature is the following one, which is taken directly from a background paper on R&D and productivity growth to the congress of the United States in 2005 (CBO, 2005: 2):

> The consensus view of the link between R&D and productivity is probably the correct one: it is quite likely that R&D has a positive impact on productivity, with a rate of return that is at least equal to the return on other types of investments.

The quite cautious wording in this statement sends the signal that results are far from clear-cut. Indeed, results are often context-specific and depend on the time-period, the type of data, the unit of analysis and the methodology employed (Wieser, 2005; Hall et al., 2010). In particular, there are no clear patterns in the returns to R&D and innovation efforts at various levels of observation. There are inconsistencies in results amongst micro as well as macro studies, and there is a general difficulty in mapping and reconciling firm-level results to macro outcomes, both conceptually and empirically.

The second observation is that there is a growing literature documenting persistent differences between firms, both with regard to their R&D and innovation strategies and with regard to their performance. Reviewing a large empirical literature, Dosi and Nelson (2010: 97) state that 'firms persistently differ over all dimensions one is able to detect', and with regard to innovation they maintain, 'differential degrees of innovativeness are generally persistent over time and often reveal a small 'core' of systematic innovators' (ibid.: 100). Moreover, innovating firms are not a homogeneous group, but employ different R&D and innovation strategies in the sense that they differ with regard to the kinds of R&D and innovation efforts they make. Even within narrowly defined sectors, firms differ at lot with regard to their innovation strategies. Srholec and Verspagen (2012) show, for instance, that industries do not account for a large fraction of the variance observed in firms' innovation strategies.

With these two basic observations as a general starting point, this book is based on the premise that differences in firm-level returns as well as economy-wide outcomes may be linked to the heterogeneous ways in which firms organize and undertake R&D and innovation activities. The approach is to go from the micro- to the macro-level, while adhering to the perspective that firms are different and employ different R&D and innovation strategies.

The purpose of this introductory chapter is to place the book and its chapter contributions in the context of the broad literature on innovation and growth and describe its motivation and contribution in more detail. The final chapter discusses the conclusions and implications of the chapter contributions in the book.

R&D, innovation and growth—a growing research field

R&D and innovation are generally regarded as the main drivers of the growth of nations and regions as well as firms. In view of a gradual shift of routine jobs towards developing countries, many governments of advanced OECD countries conclude that they need to stimulate knowledge-intensive activities as a means to specialize in activities where advantages are created in R&D and innovation processes. The reliance on R&D and innovation for prosperity is illustrated by the well-known Lisbon Agenda of the EU, which comprises a target level of R&D spending amounting to 3 per cent of GDP. This target remains in the new EU 2020 strategy, as set by the member states in their national reform programmes in April 2011. The EU 2020 growth strategy states that EU should be a smart, sustainable, and inclusive economy, and the target level of 3 per cent R&D spending is regarded as a key for innovation and smart growth.

That R&D and innovation efforts are vital for long-term growth is also a widely held position in the academic community, and there is a growing

Table 1. Number of hits in Econlit from a search on 'innovation', 'R&D', and 'growth', respectively and in combination, in the title

	Number of hits in Econlit 1969–1999 (30 years)	Number of hits in Econlit 2000–2011 (11 years)
'Innovation' in title	1 158	2 814
'R&D' in title	550	1 156
'R&D' and 'Innovation' in title	26	86
'Growth' and 'Innovation' in title	66	145
'Growth' and 'R&D' in title	39	114

Note: The numbers in the table report the number of hits in the ECONLIT system. The search was specified with the following criteria: only peer-reviewed publications in scholarly journals, written in English. The search producing the numbers in the table was undertaken in October 2011. Econlit is published by the American Economic Association and provides bibliographic coverage of a wide range of economics-related literature. More information may be found at the following webpage: http://www.aeaweb.org/econlit/index.php

interest in the 'R&D-innovation-growth nexus' amongst researchers. During recent decades, there has been an explosion in research on R&D, innovation, and growth. Table 1 illustrates this development. It presents the number of hits obtained in Econlit from a search on published peer-reviewed scholarly journal articles with 'innovation', 'R&D', and 'growth' (respectively and in combination) in the title.

The table reveals that the number of hits for all search combinations since the year 2000 exceeds the number of hits during the 30-year period 1969–1999. The increasing number of published works may of course partly be explained by the fact that the number of journals and the number of active researchers have both expanded. Yet, the 'R&D-innovation-growth nexus' represents a subject field with one of the largest increases in the amount of published works the last decades (Fagerberg, 2005). This development can be related to a large set of circumstances. The following are among them:

Globalization, outsourcing and off-shoring: Many developed countries have experienced a gradual reallocation of labour-intensive manufacturing and service activities towards developing areas (e.g. South-East Asia, Eastern Europe) where firms capitalize on low labour costs and free-trade zones. Against such a development pattern, it is typically maintained that developed countries need to specialize in knowledge-intensive activities where comparative advantages develop in R&D and innovation processes to ensure long-term growth.

Faster innovation pace: Information and communications technology (ICT), flexible machine tools, and programmable multi-task production equipment are examples of new technologies which have increased flexibility, lowered costs of introducing new product varieties and expanding (updating) product lines, and stimulated knowledge and information flows. Consequently, product cycles have shortened in many industries, and firms need to adapt to new market conditions at a faster rate to remain competitive. In-house R&D, access to skilled workers, knowledge, and information about the technology frontier, and presence on 'lead' markets are frequently advanced as important for firms' capacity to survive in such an environment. In the 'knowledge economy', creativity, knowledge creation, and innovation are key driving forces.

Theoretical advancements in growth theory: The 1980s witnessed a revival in growth theory. The 'new growth theory' provided researchers with a coherent framework for analysing linkages between R&D, innovation, and growth, acknowledging the non-rival character of ideas and knowledge. The role played by the accumulated stock of knowledge and human capital in growth processes became clarified and highlighted. The new models incorporating increasing returns provided guidelines for theoretical and empirical research on a broad range of topics, such as international trade, technology diffusion and growth, agglomeration, and knowledge flows and growth. Evolutionary theories of technological change also acted as a catalyst for research on innovation, in particular the contribution by Nelson and Winter (1982).

Availability of micro-level data: During the 1990s, several micro-level data sets on firms' innovation activities became available to researchers. For example, partly as a response to increased policy interest, EU member states initiated the Community Innovation Survey (CIS), which serves as a statistical basis for policy guidelines. Availability of these and other data has stimulated research on linkages between R&D investments, human capital, patents, innovation, and growth at the level of individual firms.

Concerns about R&D and innovation 'paradoxes': Concerns have been raised about what seems to be a paradox. Several OECD countries display relatively high R&D expenditures combined with moderate economic growth.

Inconsistencies and ambiguities in results

In his detailed survey of fifty years of empirical studies of innovative activity and performance, Cohen (2010), gives the overall conclusion from the literature that the capacity of a firm, industry, or nation to progress technologically underpins its long-run economic performance. In contrast to the broad agreement that R&D and innovation are crucial drivers of long-term growth, research shows significant variations in the correlation between (1) R&D and innovation, (2) R&D and productivity, and (3) innovation and productivity. The results also differ depending on whether the studies relate to a cross-section of companies at one point in time or across time for a given firm. Moreover, the literature shows significant differences in the relationship between R&D and innovation on the one hand and productivity on the other, depending on whether you measure in terms of the level or growth rate. The presence of knowledge spillovers and the potential for capturing the impact of both internal and external R&D makes the correlation and causality even more complex.

Some of the most robust results in terms of innovation at the firm level are the following: difference in R&D intensity across firms is highly persistent; R&D and productivity are positively related; R&D and innovation are positively related; innovation and productivity are positively related.[1] However, there is no statistically strong link between R&D level and productivity growth, or R&D growth and productivity growth. The latter applies also at the level of the whole economy (GDP), and has sometimes been described as a paradox (as mentioned above).

It is not surprising that the empirical research literature on the 'R&D-innovation-growth nexus' does not provide a clear picture of the returns to R&D and innovation efforts. Results at the micro level are not easily translated into a macro context. Thus, there are inconsistencies in results amongst micro as well as macro studies, and there is a general difficulty in mapping firm-level results to macro outcomes, both conceptually and empirically (cf. Kortum, 2008). However, most evidence from plants suggests that differences in innovativeness and production efficiency result in increased output shares in high-productivity plants and decreasing shares of output in low-productivity plants (Dosi and Nelson, 2010). This is an essential part of Schumpeter's (1934) notion of creative destruction and an important driver to growth at various levels of aggregation.

Persistent heterogeneity in characteristics and performance

It is a stylized fact that firms are different, even in narrowly defined industries. Classic economic theory suggests that when they face similar external conditions (such as belonging to the same industry), they should be forced to behave alike over the long run, so that firm-level heterogeneity vanishes over time (at least within industries).

A source of firm heterogeneity can of course be the luck of the draw in uncertain R&D and innovation processes. R&D and innovation efforts are, however, traditionally modelled as having only transitory effects on firms' profitability and growth, in that they alter a firm's competitive position in the short-run. Innovation implies a temporary advantage (e.g. in the form of a monopoly over a new product), and imitation ensures that the temporary increase in market power disappears over time (see e.g. Grossman and Helpman 1991; Aghion and Howitt, 1992; Roberts 1999). Yet, the evidence is clear

---

[1] (Griliches, 1990 and 1998; Hall 1996; Johansen and Klette, 1998; Klette and Kortum, 2004; Link and Siegel, 2007; OECD, 2009; Hall et al., 2010; and others).

that firm-level differences are persistent. The fact that differences are persistent is, of course, important for how we think about heterogeneity, both with regard to its consequences and sources.

As an illustration of the sources of heterogeneity, consider a simple example where firms are assumed to undertake uncertain R&D and innovation efforts every year. Firms may be more or less successful in their efforts and we assume that the realization of a more successful R&D and innovation process is a high level of labour productivity and profits. If successfulness in R&D and innovation efforts is normally distributed, we would expect to observe an S-shaped cumulative distribution of firms according to labour productivity and profits.[2]

Figure 1 plots value added per employee and gross profits per employee against the cumulative fraction of value added for four different sector aggregates, using Swedish firm-level data in 2004. Distributions of this kind are

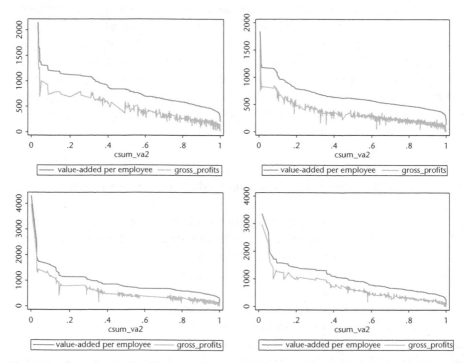

Figure 1. Cumulative distribution of firms according to value added per employee and gross profits per employee

Notes: a) Upper left panel—sector dominated by differentiated products, b) upper right panel—labour-intensive sector, c) lower left panel—scale-intensive sectors, d) lower right panel—resource-intensive sectors. The underlying information is Swedish firm-level data in 2004.

---

[2] An S-shaped cumulative distribution corresponds to a bell-shaped normal distribution.

known as Hotelling distributions (Hotelling, 1932). They are constructed by ranking all firms in an industry in descending order and then plotting labour productivity against the cumulative fraction of the sector's total value added. One observation in the figure thus represents a firm's labour productivity and its corresponding cumulative fraction of the sector's value added when all firms are ranked in descending order according to labour productivity. The cumulative fraction of the sector's total value added is thus by definition 1 for the firm with the lowest labour productivity in the sector.

The figure includes Hotelling distributions of four manufacturing-sector aggregates: (1) differentiated, (2) labour-intensive, (3) scale-intensive, and (4) resource-intensive sectors. As seen from the figure, the Hotelling distributions of all four sector aggregates resemble an S-shaped pattern. In addition, in line with expectations, the curve for gross profits per employee mimics the labour-productivity curve, when firms are ranked according to their productivity.

At every point in time, a Hotelling distribution may reflect differences in technical advantages, product and routine vintages, or technology adoption rates among firms within a given sector or industry. With strong 'homogeneity mechanisms' in the form of imitation of best-practice management, technology, or innovations, one would expect that the Hotelling distributions become flatter over time. Such a story corresponds to what is known as 'replicator dynamics' in evolutionary games, where imitation of neighbouring competitors may generate population distributions of agent behaviour (cf. Vega-Redondo, 2003). However, the shape of the Hotelling distributions is highly persistent over time.

The fact that this type of distribution is invariant over time is consistent with either a story where firm performance is truly stochastic (so that firms may change their positions in the distribution over time), or a story where firms display persistent differences in performance (firms keep their position in the distribution). Temporal examination of the data as well as a large empirical literature rejects the first story.

To illustrate, consider Table 2. Following Geroski (1998), this table decomposes the total variance in a panel of Swedish manufacturing firms over a ten-year period (1997–2006). It reports this breakdown for five variables: (1) sales, (2) value added per employees, (3) gross profits per employee, (4) knowledge intensity, and (5) patent applications. Knowledge intensity is measured as the fraction of employees with a long university education (> 3 years) and patent applications is the number of patents applied for at the Swedish Patent and Registration office.

'Between' variation reflects differences between firms which prevail on average over a period, whereas 'within' variation reflects variations in a variable of a typical firm over time. A large fraction of between variations suggests more or less permanent differences between firms over time.

Table 2. Within and between variance as a fraction of total variance

Variable	Within variance (% of total)	Between variance (% of total)
Sales	4	96
Value added per employee	30	70
Gross profits per employee	29	71
Knowledge intensity	13	87
Patent applications	16	84

Note: Numbers are based on a balanced panel of Swedish manufacturing firms (NACE 15–36) with a median number of employees of at least 10. The panel covers the period 1997–2006. Patent applications refer to the number of patent applications to the Swedish Patent and Registration Office. Knowledge intensity is measured as the number of employees with a long university education (> 3 years) as a fraction of the total number of employees.

The table reveals that it is indeed between variations that dominate with regard to all the variables. The fraction of between variations is also particularly high for sales, knowledge intensity, and patent applications. Hence, the dominant feature of the data suggests persistent differences between firms.

How can firms sustain such a persistent advantage? Under the assumption that firms attempt to imitate and catch up with the leading firms, one may distinguish between two basic interpretations. One is that top-performing firms sell unique goods and services that are difficult to imitate. A second is that the top performing firms have certain capabilities or characteristics that make them better equipped to constantly introduce new and improved products and services (so that imitators never catch up), and that it is these innovation capabilities that are difficult to imitate (not the products/services themselves).

The latter interpretation is consistent with the so-called resource-based view of the firm, which emphasizes durable and difficult-to-imitate resources (typically knowledge assets) as a key to competitive advantages (Wernerfelt, 1984; Barney, 1991). However, it is perhaps even more closely aligned with Teece et al.'s (1997) notion of 'dynamic capabilities'. The argument by Teece and his colleagues builds on the resource-based view of the firm, but they add that for sustained competitive advantage it is capabilities to continuously develop and orchestrate 'resource-bases' (again typically knowledge assets) to create new products, services, and markets that really matters. These capabilities are referred to as 'dynamic capabilities'.

Persistent performance differences amongst firms may be interpreted as reflecting persistent differences in innovation capacity where firms at the top of the distribution keep their position by persistently innovating to renew and expand their product and service portfolios (Andersson and Johansson, 2012). There are arguments that such innovation capacity is derived from dynamic capabilities, i.e. capabilities to develop and use resource-bases to adapt to a changing business environment. Teece (2010: 723) states that 'the particular (nonimitable) orchestration capacity of a business enterprise—its dynamic capabilities—is the irreducible core of the innovating firm'.

If the firms in the upper segments of (skewed) performance distributions sustain their position through continuous innovation, then we should also observe that the distribution of innovation across firms is not only skewed, but also persistent at the firm level. Going through stylized facts about innovating firms, Dosi and Nelson (2010) conclude that: (1) innovation is asymmetric, and a small set of firms in each sector is responsible for a large fraction of innovations (a similar asymmetry applies to adoption of innovations), and (2) heterogeneity in innovativeness tends to be persistent over time and often reveals a small core of systematic innovators. This pattern is indeed consistent with the arguments above, and we would certainly expect to find these innovating firms at the top of the performance distribution.

The issues and the volume's approach

The two preceding sections show that there is a need for reconciliation with regard to two basic issues. One is how innovation efforts cause growth when inspected with firm-level, sector-level, and aggregate level lenses. A second is the heterogeneity of firm productivity and its relation to differences in firms' innovation strategies. The contributions in this volume may be combined to shed some light on these matters, where phenomena that help to sustain permanent differences between firms can be linked to phenomena that affect inter-sector and hence economy-wide consequences of R&D investments.

We argue that it is important to consider the idea of time scales for change processes, which suggests that persistent differences between firms should be related to variables that change on a slow time scale. The set of slowly changing variables includes a firm's resource base, the economic environment of its location, and the networks for interaction and knowledge exchange that a firm establishes gradually over time. To the extent that a firm follows a long-term strategy, this strategy should comprise investments in its resource base and in networks as well as decisions about location.

The contributions in this volume indeed emphasize and illustrate that heterogeneity in, for example, innovation can be related to heterogeneity in intra-firm and extra-firm resources, where the latter comprise networks and the local/regional environment of the firm. At the same time, knowledge and other interaction links may extend over long distances and hence represent a possible substitute for the short-distance economic milieu of the firm (Johansson and Quigley, 2004).

An important consideration is of course that variables that operate on a slow time scale can generate lasting differences in firm performance. As discussed in several chapters, this may also point at feedback mechanisms such that an innovation strategy aiming at improved innovation capabilities may be rewarded by successful innovations, where success breeds success, making the arrival of innovation ideas a state-dependent process. One may also consider that the resource base of a firm is the outcome of two parallel processes. The first is deliberate goals for the firm's development and the second is a firm's gradually accumulated experiences. The latter may be thought of as a learning process that relates to Griliches' (1979) proposal of three areas of spillover phenomena: learning from product market rivals, learning from firms conducting a similar type of research, and learning from suppliers. We can add to this that firms in particular learn by accumulating experiences about how to organize routines for innovation activities.

In order to learn from the economic environment, however, a firm needs to have absorptive capacity, which may be the most critical component of the resource base of the firm, together with networks for knowledge flows from local as well as global sources. This conclusion relates to the new insights about economy-wide consequences of innovation efforts that this book offers. In this view, a firm's economic environment and networks are rather a synergistic complement than a substitute for its internal resource base, implying the possibility of super-additivity.

Organization and summary of chapter contributions

The volume is organized to go from the micro- to the macro-level. This structure reflects a premise that R&D, innovation, and growth refers to two interdependent perspectives. The first of these is micro-oriented and focuses on innovation processes of firms, where R&D activities and other innovation efforts give rise to consequences to the firm, such as a strengthening of resource bases, growth of sales and employment, patents, new products, increasing productivity and profits, and improved chances of survival. The second perspective comprises economy-wide effects in the form of overall technological change, growth in total factor productivity, and structural change processes, where certain sectors may benefit from new inputs from other sectors while others experience declining markets and reduced output.

Based on this, the book consists of three parts: (I) Understanding R&D and innovation strategies of the innovating firm, (II) Firm-level returns to R&D strategies, and (III) Beyond the firm: economy-wide effects. The first part focuses on the micro perspective and recognizes that R&D and innovation efforts do not represent a uniform type of investment. Firms employ a wide set of different R&D and innovation strategies, even in narrowly defined sectors. This leads to the conclusion that differences in firm-level returns to R&D and innovation efforts as well as economy-wide consequences may be due to differences in the underlying R&D and innovation strategies that firms employ. It follows that knowledge of alternative R&D and innovation strategies and which types of firms that employ them is critical.

The four contributions in the first part of the book all deal with R&D and innovation strategies of firms and illustrate the variety of strategies that firms employ. They all also address questions of the following type:

• What alternative strategies do firms actually employ and what are their drivers?
• How are we to understand heterogeneity in R&D and innovation strategies across firms in the same industry?
• What governs a firm's choice of R&D strategy?

In Part 1, Paul Almeida and Anu Phene apply a case-based approach and focus on the strategic aspects of innovation and knowledge processes within multinational corporations (MNCs). Their contribution illustrates how large MNCs that build their competitive advantages on knowledge assets actually go about managing knowledge sourcing and innovation efforts. The chapter by Tommy Clausen and Bart Verspagen uses Community Innovation Survey (CIS) data linked over time to identify innovation strategies and investigate which firm characteristics can be associated with the use of a particular strategy. They also introduce and apply a methodology that makes it possible to define the innovation strategy in a dynamic way. Katarina Blomkvist, Philip Kappen, and Ivo Zander take the role of foreign subsidiaries in the evolution of innovation capabilities of MNCs as their starting point, and focus on the long-term, evolutionary developments in advanced foreign subsidiaries, thus focusing on particular members of a corporation. Using two cases, they explore the origins and drivers of those foreign subsidiaries which over an extended period generate a significantly larger number of entries into new technologies than the average subsidiary of the MNC, and which over the long term will have a correspondingly larger influence on the MNC's technological and strategic development. The final chapter in part one by John Cantwell and Feng Zhang relates differences in innovative performance at the corporate level to the technological content and geographical pattern of firms' accumulation of technological knowledge. In so doing, they identify different strategies with regard to the breadth of firms' technological knowledge portfolios and the spatial pattern of their knowledge sources. The analysis generates important insights on how the accession and utilization of geographically dispersed technological knowledge affect the innovative performance of MNC groups at a corporate-level.

The second part of the book shifts attention to the returns to R&D strategies. A basic question here is whether heterogeneity in R&D and innovation strategies is reflected in heterogeneity in firm-level returns to R&D and innovation. Part two thus collects contributions that assess the returns to firms' R&D and innovation strategies, as well as contributions that provide methodological guidelines.

Jacques Mairess and Stephane Robin estimate returns to innovation strategies. They recognize that product and process innovation represent two different technological paths (or innovation strategies), and set-up an econometric model with three stages to estimate the returns to the two forms of innovation. The first stage deals with R&D activities, in terms of both propensity and intensity. The second stage represents the 'knowledge-production function', distinguishing between product and process innovation. The third and final stage identifies the impact of both types of innovation on labour productivity. The chapter by Alfred Kleinknecht and Henk Jan Reinders is a methodological contribution analyzing the correspondence between two often-employed measures of innovation, i.e. patents and product and process innovation. They use data from the German Community Innovation Survey (CIS) for an investigation of deviations between patent applications and innovation. This is an important issue as both measures are frequently employed, and any analysis of innovation strategies and their returns must ultimately decide on innovation indicators.

René Belderbos, Geert Duysters, and Anna Sabidussi focus on R&D collaboration, which is an important element of many firms' R&D and innovation strategy. They conduct a systematic overview of the findings in prior academic studies related to the relationship between R&D collaboration and innovative performance, identify knowledge gaps, and provide suggestions as to how the research frontier may be pushed forward. One of the results is that R&D cooperation is often beneficial for innovative performance, but that findings depend on the level of analysis and on the variable chosen to proxy (innovative) performance. The latter reinforces the importance of the contribution by Alfred Kleinknecht and Henk Jan Reinders. The last chapter by Martin Andersson, Börje Johansson, Charlie Karlsson, and Hans Lööf estimates returns to R&D strategies. They introduce the notion of R&D strategy as captured by the persistence of the firm's commitment to R&D as an alternative way to assess empirically the relationship between R&D and growth. Using a Swedish panel data set where firms in the Swedish CIS 2004 survey are followed over several years, they distinguish between three different R&D strategies: (1) no R&D, (2) temporary R&D, and (3) persistent R&D. The authors argue that these strategies may be important in explaining the phenomenon of persistent performance gaps between firms. Panel-data estimates of the relationship between the R&D strategy variables and productivity lend support for their argument.

The third part of the book is devoted to system effects of firm-level behaviour. It focuses on economy-wide impacts and centres on the following types of question:

- What are the economy-wide effects of firms' R&D and innovation strategies?
- To what extent do R&D and innovation activities spill over?
- Are spillovers intra- or inter-sectoral?
- What circumstances stimulate spillover effects?

Five contributions make up the third part.

The chapter by Cristiano Antonelli emphasizes that there are two forms of technological change generating efficiency gains: neutral and biased technological change. The author introduces the notion of technological congruence and argues that when technological change is biased, efficiency gains are obtained because of higher levels of congruence between the local factor markets and the output elasticity of production factors. Cristiano Antonelli's contribution illustrates that economy-wide efficiency gains from technological change brought about by firms' R&D and innovation strategies will depend on the matching between the relative abundance of production factors locally available and the factorial characterization of the technology used in the production. Chapter 10 by Edward Wolff analyzes the contribution of inter-sectoral R&D spillovers to industry productivity growth in the USA in the period 1958–2007. Spillovers constitute one way in which economy-wide effects of firms' R&D investments materialize. The author hypothesizes that technological spillover effects may have become more important over time as information technology (IT) penetrated the economy. The rationale is that IT may speed up the process of knowledge transfer and make these knowledge spillovers more effective. Input-output relations are confirmed as a source of R&D spillovers, and the results suggest a strengthening of the R&D spillover effect over time.

In Chapter 11, Zoltan Acs also emphasizes R&D spillovers but from a different angle. He describes the research literature leading up to knowledge-spillover theory of entrepreneurship (KSTE) and associated contributions. According KSTE, entrepreneurship is a response to opportunities created by investments in new knowledge that was not commercialized by incumbent firms, such that entrepreneurship becomes a conduit for knowledge spillovers. From this perspective, KSTE regards entrepreneurship as an important part of economy-wide consequences of (incumbent) firms' R&D behaviour. The contribution by Pontus Braunerhjelm provides a large-scale literature review of the mainstream endogenous growth models, focusing on their microeconomic foundation and the mechanisms that generate innovation, spillovers, and productivity, i.e. economy-wide technological change. He emphasizes the risk of drawing normative conclusions from a model based on simplifying assumptions and an excessively rudimentary microeconomic setting. Pontus Braunerhjelm argues that empirical support for many models is ambiguous at the aggregate level, but that the micro-economic modelling of the emergence and exploitation of innovative opportunities has improved considerably in the last decade. The last chapter by David Hart deals with framework conditions for high-potential entrepreneurship, i.e. circumstances which facilitate economy-wide technological change. Hart advances a set of 'framework conditions' that seek to explain variation in rates of high-potential entrepreneurship over time and across societies. These conditions are claimed to operate at three levels—the individual, the organization, and the society—and are interconnected, so that a society's capacity to generate high-potential entrepreneurship cumulates over time.

A first reflection

The last chapter in the book presents conclusions and reflects upon the volume's implications. We nevertheless wish to emphasize one reflection already at this point, although we will come back to it in the concluding chapter.

From Part III of this volume, we learn that the social returns to R&D are considerably higher than direct returns to R&D. A basic mechanism is that a buying firm receives embodied R&D via the input suppliers in other industries. R&D among suppliers affects the quality of equipment as well as current input flows, and these inflows embody the suppliers' innovations. This phenomenon corresponds to inter-industry spillovers. In line with Griliches' suggestions, there may also be intra-industry externalities such that innovation knowledge spills over from rival firms. However, the linkage between an industry and its suppliers appears to be the dominant factor in accounting for growth externalities. These impacts from inputs embodying R&D made in input-delivering industries also include inputs from abroad. This also implies that it matters which links to import sources that the firm manages to develop and re-arrange over time (Helpman, 2004). In this view, innovating firms will benefit from a local milieu with abundant knowledge flows that guide the search for import sources.

The above influences from input suppliers on an industry's performance are of course not homogeneous across alternative input suppliers. Each individual input supplier may have specific technical solutions, and this implies that inter-sector spillovers will vary across input buyers as their choice of supplier differs. For the spillover mechanism to be effective, the individual firm has to engage in search processes. Due to this, the absorptive capacity of each input buyer will affect the proportion of available opportunities that each firm manages to exploit. A similar conclusion applies to the buying firm's local economic milieu and its network for information and knowledge access.

The perplexing result is that our discussion leads to the suggestion that there is a core in which studies of firm-level analyses of returns to innovation efforts refer to more or less the same the same system features as do studies of economy-wide consequences and returns. In both cases, the returns are related to (1) intra-firm development efforts and absorptive capacity, and (2) the individual firm´s links to knowledge sources, links for input flows of intermediaries and equipment, and interaction opportunities in the local milieu. Economy-wide studies that employ inter-sector models of the economy attempt to capture the same phenomena on the industry level (Wolff, 1997). The message from economy-wide studies is that the growth impact from the firm´s environment in an industry is larger than the impact from the efforts of firms in the same industry. There is a lesson in this observation: it is a challenge to better decompose the conditions for firm performance into (1) intra-firm, and (2) extra-firm phenomena. Such an approach would recognize that economy-wide consequences are the result of networks and spatially localized spillovers. However, the same view applies to firm-level consequences, and regularities in contemporary findings are founded on the slow pace of change in these pre-conditions.

The networks for knowledge accession and R&D collaboration may be appreciated as the result of an innovating firm's strategy for developing pre-conditions that positively affect its innovation capability. This view follows similar development logic as the firm's investment in its resource base. For firms that belong to a multinational group we may also recognize the intra-group links between group members as a part of the individual firm's resource base. Thus, firms can develop and maintain their heterogeneity because of idiosyncratic resource bases, firm-specific networks, and the location of firms in economic milieus with very different knowledge sources. The lesson to be learned is that these two slowly changing pre-conditions for innovation efforts help to explain why heterogeneity should be appreciated as a generic phenomenon.

References

Aghion, P. and Howitt, P. (1992), 'A model of growth through creative destruction', *Econometrica*, 60(2): 323–351.

Andersson, M. and Johansson, B. (2012), 'Heterogeneous distributions of firms sustained by innovation dynamics—a model with empirical illustrations and analysis', *Journal of Industry, Competition and Trade*, forthcoming.

Barney, J. (1991), 'Firm resources and sustained competitive advantage', *Journal of Management*, 17: 99–120.

CBO (2005), 'R&D and Productivity Growth', Congressional Budget Office, Background Paper, Congress of the United States.

Cohen, W. (2010), Fifty years of empirical studies of innovative activity and performance'. In Hall, B. and Rosenberg, N. (eds), *Handbook of the Economics of Innovation*. Amsterdam: North-Holland.

Dosi, G. and Nelson, R.R. (2010), 'Technical change and industrial dynamics as evolutionary processes'. In Hall, B. and Rosenberg, N. (eds), *Handbook of the Economics of Innovation*. Amsterdam: North-Holland.

Fagerberg, J. (2005), 'Innovation: A guide to the literature'. In Fagerberg, J., Mowery, D. and Nelson, R.R. (eds), *The Oxford Handbook of Innovation*. Oxford: Oxford University Press.

Geroski, P. (1998), 'An applied econometrician's view of large company performance,' *Review of Industrial Organization*, 13(3): 271–294.

Griliches, Z. (1979), 'Issues in assessing the contributions of research and development to productivity growth,' *The Bell Journal of Economics*, 10: 92–116.

—— (1990), 'Patent statistics as economic indicators: A survey,' *Journal of Economic Literature*, 28(4): 1661–1707.

—— (1998), *R&D and Productivity: The Econometric Evidence*. NBER Books, National Bureau of Economic Research, Inc, number 98-1, July.

Grossman, G. and Helpman, E. (1991), *Innovation and Growth in the Global Economy*. Cambridge, Mass.: MIT Press.

Hall, B.H. (1996), The private and social returns to research and development. In Smith, B.R. and Barfield C.E. (eds), *Technology, R&D and the Economy*. Washington, DC: Brookings Institute.

——, Mairesse, J. and Mohnen, P. (2010), 'Measuring the returns to R&D', in Hall, B. and Rosenberg, N. (eds), *Handbook of the Economics of Innovation*. Amsterdam: North-Holland.

Helpman, E. (2004), *The Mystery of Economic Growth*. Cambridge, MA: Harvard University Press.

Hotelling, H. (1932), 'Edgeworth's taxation paradox and the nature of demand and supply functions', *Journal of Political Economy*, 40: 577–616.

Johansen, F. and Klette, T.J. (1998), 'Accumulation of R&D capital and dynamic firm performance: A not-so-fixed effect model,' *Annales d'Economie et de Statistique*, 49–50: 389–419.

Johansson, B. and Quigley, J. (2004), 'Agglomeration and networks in spatial economics', *Papers in Regional Science*, 83: 165–176.

Klette, T. and Kortum, S. (2004), 'Innovating firms and aggregate innovation', *Journal of Political Economy*, 112: 986–1018.

Kortum, S. (2008), 'Exploring innovation with firm-level data', The Conference Board, Economics Program Working Paper Series 08-11.

Link, A. and Siegel, D.S. (2007), *Innovation, Entrepreneurship and Technological Change*. Oxford: Oxford University Press.

Nelson, R.R and Winter, S.G. (1982), *An Evolutionary Theory of Economic Change*. Cambridge, MA: Belknap Press.

OECD (2009), *Innovation in Firms. A Microeconomic Perspective*. Paris: OECD.

Roberts, P.W. (1999), 'Product innovation, product-market competition and persistent profitability in the U.S. pharmaceutical industry', *Strategic Management Journal*, 20(7): 655–670.

Schumpeter, J.A. (1934), *The Theory of Economic Development. An Inquiry into Profits, Capital, Credit, Interest, and the Business Cycle*. Cambridge, MA: Harvard University Press.

Srholec, M. and Verspagen, B. (2012), 'The voyage of the Beagle into innovation: Explorations on heterogeneity, selection and sectors', *Industrial and Corporate Change*, 20, forthcoming.

Teece, D.J. (2010), 'Technological innovation and the theory of the firm'. In Hall, B. and Rosenberg, N. (eds), *Handbook of the Economics of Innovation*. Amsterdam: North-Holland.

——, Pisano, G. and Shuen, A. (1997), 'Dynamic capabilities and strategic management', *Strategic Management Journal*, 18: 509–533.

Vega-Redondo, F. (2003), *Economics and the Theory of Games*. Cambridge, UK: Cambridge University Press.

Wernerfelt, B. (1984), 'The resource-based view of the firm', *Strategic Management Journal*, 5(2): 171–180.

Wieser, R. (2005), 'Research and development productivity and spillovers—Empirical evidence at the firm level', *Journal of Economic Surveys*, 19: 587–621.

Wolff, E. (1997), 'Spillovers, linkages and technical change,' *Economic Systems Research*, 9(1): 9–23.

Part I
Understanding the R&D Strategies of the Innovating Firm

1

Managing Knowledge Within and Outside the Multinational Corporation

Paul Almeida and Anu Phene

1.1. Introduction

Knowledge has long played an important role in the theory of the firm. The emerging resource-based view of the firm focuses on knowledge as a key competitive asset and recognizes knowledge as the basis of firm growth (Grant and Baden Fuller, 1995). Kogut (1993) suggests that knowledge is not just a cornerstone of competitive advantage but the basis for sustainable advantage since it cannot be easily transferred or replicated. Firms that are adept at the development, transfer, and exploitation of knowledge are therefore most likely to succeed.

An organization cannot, however, develop within its boundaries all the critical knowledge needed to prosper and grow (Coase, 1937; Dussauge, Garrette and Mitchell, 1998). Technological dynamism, reflected in an environment punctuated by competence-destroying technologies, has forced firms to maintain a wide range of technological knowledge and skills (Tushman and Anderson, 1986). Very few firms can develop this wide range of knowledge internally (D'Aveni, 1994; Lane, Lyles and Salk, 1998). Consequently managers need to tap into external knowledge sources. Creating a broader knowledge base through external learning increases the flexibility of the firm, critical in a dynamic environment (Grant, 1996). Therefore managers need to be able to identify and isolate potential useful sources of knowledge that are external to the organization as well as those within the organization. They also need to be active in creating conduits to the external environment that permit knowledge flows to the firm and in building communication channels and routines within the firm that allow for intra-firm knowledge transfer.

However, recognition of, and access to vital knowledge alone does not ensure firm competitiveness in innovation and knowledge development. Managers must also foster capabilities that enable the firm to effectively utilize and integrate knowledge gained from multiple sources. They must exploit internal knowledge in conjunction with external knowledge to compete successfully, gain profitability, and grow. Yet which firm can claim to harness the potential of its knowledge fully and effectively? Which organization does not re-invent the wheel almost on a daily basis? Which organization thoroughly exploits its 'best practices' or rejects its 'worst practices'? Which firm can always find (within the organization or outside it) all the knowledge needed for innovation? Few, if any. Until the answers to all these questions are in the affirmative, there will always be opportunities for firms to increase their operational efficiency, manage risk, and learn, by further developing the capabilities to manage knowledge available within the organization or within their competitive environment.

Our study seeks to shed light on the innovation and knowledge-management process within the multinational firm from a managerial perspective. We build on prior research and on insights from field interviews with research personnel in the semiconductor industry to develop our model of the knowledge-management process for the multinational corporation (MNC). We focus on the multinational corporation since it allows us to explore knowledge management across business units, a process about which little is known, in a cross border setting, where the ability of the MNC and its subsidiaries to use knowledge for innovation is incompletely understood (Phene and Almeida, 2008). We build a model that unbundles this process and identifies the managerial abilities required at every stage in the process. The first stage explores how managers can identify critical sources of knowledge. The second stage examines how managers can build connections to knowledge sources.[1] Finally, it examines the mechanisms that managers can utilize to create innovations through integration and recombination of existing information. For managers it offers a comprehensive overview of the knowledge-management process with clear identification of the abilities they need to develop to maximize the value at each stage. Firms can develop these abilities in a complementary manner since investment in effective identification of knowledge sources is also likely to generate synergies and lead to the integration and recombination of existing information (McEvily, Eisenhardt and Prescott, 2004). Our study suggests that the identification of capabilities associated

---

[1] We adopt Kogut and Zander's (1996) distinction between knowledge and information. Information comprises that portion of knowledge that can be transmitted without loss of integrity. The other component of knowledge is know-how, which reflects accumulated expertise and skill.

with knowledge management is a first step for firms, and investments in the design and operation of organizational structures, management systems, and shared values and behavioural norms can facilitate knowledge development and transfer.

1.2. Identification of knowledge sources

The first phase of the knowledge-management process consists of the identification of suitable sources of knowledge. Research demonstrates that multinational firms typically rely on the internal firm environment, consisting of the headquarters and the network of multinational subsidiaries as well as the external host-country environment for valuable knowledge significant to innovation (Almeida and Phene, 2004). We explore the role that each of these environments plays in managers' search for knowledge.

MNC and knowledge: The resource-based view of the firm suggests that internal knowledge embodied within a firm's resources is an important source of competitive advantage (Wernerfelt, 1984; Barney, 1991). The firm is often the source of much of the knowledge used in innovation. During the last decade, as a result of theoretical and empirical research into international firms, the traditional view of how the multinational corporation (MNC) creates value from knowledge has evolved, and there has been a corresponding change in the view of the subsidiary. Central to Perlmutter's (1969) 'geocentric' firm, Bartlett and Ghoshal's (1989) 'transnational' corporation, and Hedlund's (1994) 'N-form' corporation is the idea that technical, market, and functional knowledge is generated continuously in all parts of a company, and shared across the organization. In this networked corporation, an important role in the innovative process (in terms of accessing, sharing, and creating knowledge) is played by the subsidiaries. These insights into the role of the MNC in generating and leveraging knowledge have stimulated research into the processes through which knowledge flows are managed and the mechanisms that underlie the creation of a knowledge network within the multinational (Gupta and Govindarjan, 2000). Although organizational processes and mechanisms link various units of the MNC, differentiation between the subsidiaries of the corporation also appears to be conducive to knowledge creation. Zander (1997) points to the tendency for overseas subsidiaries to specialize in developing particular technologies, while Nobel and Birkinshaw (1998) show that differentiated roles of international R&D units are associated with differentiated control and communication structures. Thus we see the MNC as a differentiated and yet integrated firm with a range of formal and informal linking mechanisms underlying the relationships between subsidiaries.

While the MNC serves as an important source of knowledge, few firms possess all the inputs required for successful and continuous innovation. Consequently, most organizations will develop a deficit within their boundaries as regards the critical knowledge needed to prosper and grow (Coase, 1937; Dussauge, Garrette and Mitchell, 1998). Thus, although a firm's own research efforts play an important role in innovation, firms must turn to external sources of knowledge to maintain their innovative processes. In the context of a multinational corporation, the host-country environment of the subsidiaries plays the role of a critical knowledge base.

The host country and knowledge flows: External learning from host-country locations can be a potent source of value creation for MNCs. As with the view of the MNC, the view of the host country has changed in the more recent literature concerning international strategy. While host countries were originally seen primarily as markets or as sources of cheap labour for the MNC, increasingly host-country regions are seen as potential sources for sourcing new knowledge. Common to Alfred Marshall's (1920) 'industrial districts' and Porter's (1990, 1998) localized industry 'clusters' is the idea that industry-specific knowledge develops in geographically concentrated locations. This phenomenon is true not only of traditional, craft-based industries, but also high-technology industries. Saxenian (1990) relates the dynamism and the vitality of Silicon Valley to the extensive networking both at the firm level (between firms and universities, buyers and suppliers, venture capitalists, etc.) and also between individuals within the region. Porter's (1990) description of the localized Italian ceramic tile industry points to close and repeated interactions between the various small businesses in the region. The presence of social, professional, and business networks characterizes many host-country regions that embody localized knowledge and expertise (Almeida and Phene, 2004).

An important advantage of the MNC is its potential to access local knowledge from such regions located in multiple host countries. Through the location of subsidiaries in technologically advanced regions, MNCs can gain access to knowledge embodied within them. Almeida (1996) has shown that the US subsidiaries of foreign MNCs draw heavily upon the technology of local companies in their knowledge building. Shan and Song (1997) found that in the biotechnology industry, foreign MNCs make equity investments in American biotechnology firms with high levels of patent activity, thus sourcing country-specific, firm-embodied technological advantages.

Managers of multinational corporations must recognize the importance of capable, innovative subsidiaries in the MNC network and dynamic, research-oriented host-country regions and their influence in determining firm competitiveness in innovation. Research suggests that subsidiaries who are leading innovators make use of host-country knowledge richness and diversity but are less likely to use knowledge from the multinational corporation (Almeida and Phene, 2004), pointing to limited interdependencies between the two kinds of knowledge sources. Responsibilities of managers should include continuous monitoring of the MNC network and the external environment to identify critical sources. Having identified the knowledge sources, managers need to be able to access the knowledge residing in these locations.

1.3. Building connections to access knowledge

Recognizing the importance of knowledge sources does not necessarily permit a firm to access and transfer knowledge. Nor does it completely explain which firms are best able to access knowledge or why firms are attentive to knowledge from certain sources and less attentive to other sources. The second stage of the knowledge-management process, building connections to access knowledge is an important component. To facilitate knowledge transfer, firms must develop linkages to sources of knowledge that act as conduits for knowledge transfer (Almeida, 1996; Dyer and Nobeoka, 2000; Gulati, Nohria and Zaheer, 2000). It is these conduits that channel the available knowledge, and determine which knowledge the firm actually uses in the innovative process.

1.3.1. *Internal knowledge*

Within MNCs a range of coordination and integration mechanisms are available to link various entities. Research has directed attention to the importance of informal and lateral structures and systems. Ghoshal et al. (1994) identify the important role of interpersonal networks among the subsidiary managers of Philips and Matsushita, while Gupta and Govindarajan (2000) also show how informal mechanisms promote knowledge flows within MNCs. Differentiation between the MNC country subsidiaries also appears to be conducive to knowledge transfers. There is evidence that subsidiaries of MNCs tend to become technologically specialized, leading to greater differentiation within the firm (Phene and Almeida, 2003). Zander (1997) points to the tendency for overseas subsidiaries to specialize in developing particular technologies, while Nobel and Birkinshaw (1998) show that differentiated roles of international R&D units are associated with differentiated control and communication structures. Kogut and Zander (1996) show that it is in transferring tacit knowledge that the advantages of the MNC are most apparent: the more complex, less codifiable, and less teachable the knowledge embodied within an innovation, the greater the likelihood that it is transferred overseas by direct investment.

1.3.2. *External knowledge*

Prior research suggests that firms use a number of mechanisms that enable them to create conduits to sources of useful external knowledge. Besides traditional supply arrangements, these mechanisms include the hiring of scientists and engineers (Zucker, 1998; Almeida and Kogut, 1999), the forming of strategic alliances (Mowery, Oxley and Silverman, 1996; Rosenkopf and Almeida, 2003), and the appropriation of informal networks in geographically proximate locations. (Liebeskind and Oliver, 1996; Almeida and Kogut, 1997; Rosenkopf and Tushman, 1998). Indeed, Rosenkopf and Almeida (2003) use patent-citation data to evaluate the three mechanisms of learning, and find that all three mechanisms play a role in facilitating external learning by semiconductor startups.

Alliances: A central idea in the literature on alliances is that they are useful mechanisms for knowledge acquisition and learning (Hamel et al., 1989). The explosive growth of strategic alliances over the years, especially in high-technology industries such as semiconductors or commercial aircraft, supports the view of the increasing importance of collaborative agreements in accessing and transferring external knowledge (Contractor and Lorange, 1988; Mowery, Oxley and Silverman, 1996; Dyer and Singh, 1998). Recent empirical research provides some support for the notion that the repeated use of alliances may result in increasing the capability of fims to learn from these mechanisms (Anand and Khanna, 2000). Powell et al. (1996) postulate the existence of 'networks of learning', and suggest that participation in networks of R&D alliances facilitates the growth of new biotechnology firms because these networks create access to knowledge.

In-depth case studies provide us with a rich illustration of learning between alliance or network partners demonstrating overall knowledge flows across networks. Doz (1996) explores how alliances may be construed as learning processes, where learning occurs in multiple dimensions—environment, task, process, skill, and partner goals—and the amount of learning is facilitated or constrained by initial conditions. Dyer (1996) suggests that the breadth and intensity of the relationship between alliance partners will grow over time. There is a considerable literature showing the relationship between learning and alliances and a few studies explicitly measure inter-firm knowledge transfers associated with alliances. In Stuart and Podolny's (1996) study of the major Japanese semiconductor firms, the authors suggest that Matsushita accomplished a technological transition through the strategic use of alliances. In two studies of alliances between multinational firms in 1985–1986, spanning a variety of industries, Mowery, Oxley and Silverman (1996, 1998) demonstrate that certain alliances are followed by rises in the cross-citation and common-citation patterns between the firms, suggesting some transfer of knowledge.

Mobility: Another mechanism for the transfer of knowledge across firm boundaries is the mobility of people. Several primarily descriptive studies suggest that people are an important conduit of inter-firm knowledge transfer (Malecki, 1991). However, most research does no more than suggests a connection between mobility and knowledge flows, offering at best indirect evidence. For instance, Markusen, Hall and Glasmeier (1986) find that regions with high concentrations of technical workers attract new high-technology investment. In technology-intensive industries as well, there are numerous descriptive studies of people carrying knowledge across firms (Hanson, 1982). In the semiconductor industry, interviews with engineers reveal many anecdotes of inter-firm knowledge flows associated with the mobility of engineers (Rogers and Larsen, 1984; Saxenian, 1990).

As was the case for research into alliances, the most direct evidence linking mobility of engineers to inter-firm knowledge transfers may be accomplished through patent records. Almeida and Kogut (1999) show that after a semiconductor firm hired a new engineer, there was a significantly greater tendency for the hiring firm to cite the prior patents of the newly employed engineer than would be expected given its technology profile. In addition, Song, Almeida and Wu (2001) demonstrate that during the early stage of development of Korean semiconductor firms, the practice of bringing US-educated and US-employed nationals back home led to similar patenting practices.

Informal mechanisms associated with geographic regions: Research points to the importance of geographically clustered social networks in facilitating the informal diffusion of knowledge across firms (Rogers and Larson, 1984). Localized knowledge sharing was common between firms in the steel industry in nineteenth-century England (Allen, 1983). Case studies of regional clusters in Italy (Piore and Sabel, 1984) and Baden-Wuerttemberg in Germany (Herrigel, 1993) indicate extensive knowledge flows through networks in these regions. Why does co-location matter to the transfer of knowledge? Industry-specific knowledge develops in geographically concentrated locations. This localization phenomenon applies for all sorts of industries, including high-technology industries. This in turn leads to greater knowledge transfers between firms, due to the similarity in their knowledge bases and due to the extensive linkages that develop within a region.

Although linkages between firms could develop across geographic distances, proximity enhances the development of complex networks (Graham, 1985; Almeida and Kogut, 1999). Locational proximity reduces the cost and increases the frequency of personal contacts which serve to build social relations between players in a network (Dorfman, 1987; Saxenian, 1990; Almeida and Kogut, 1997; Zucker, 1998) that can be appropriated for learning purposes.

Further proximity builds common institutional and professional ties that help build a context for knowledge transfers (Saxenian, 1990). As explained earlier in this chapter, there is a significant amount of research that offers evidence to the support this. Almeida and Kogut (1999) show that the flow of knowledge within many of the semiconductor regions within the United States is facilitated by the mobility of engineers across firms within the region.

Thus, management of knowledge accession requires distinctive mechanisms in sourcing external and internal knowledge. While internal sourcing depends on the MNC's organizational structure and a culture that ensures communication between subsidiaries, the external sourcing reflects the use of cooperative agreements, mobility, and physical location. Thus managers will have to adapt the choice of conduit depending on the source of knowledge. MNC access to knowledge sources within multiple subsidiaries within its own network and to different host-country environments through locational proximity constitutes a unique advantage that may not be available to domestic firms or multibusiness firms with operations in a single country.

1.4. Utilizing knowledge through integration and recombination

The final stage in gainfully using knowledge that has been determined to be useful and transferred within firm boundaries is its integration with knowledge existing in other parts of the firm, which results in innovation (Almeida, Phene and Grant, 2002). It was Schumpeter (1934: 65) who first pointed out that innovation takes place by 'carrying out new combinations'. Henderson and Clark's (1992) concept of architectural knowledge reinforces this idea, suggesting that a critical feature of a firm's innovative ability may be the broader managerial capability to determine the compatibility of knowledge and then to combine or link it together with other knowledge within the firm. Thus integration appears to be an important stage in the knowledge-management process since it results in value creation.

To shed some light on the knowledge-integration process, we discuss our insights from field interviews carried out by the authors with research personnel in semiconductor firms to obtain their views on the process of the integration of knowledge within the firm. We conducted interviews at eight companies—Philips, Siemens, National Semiconductor, Fujitsu, Texas Instruments, IBM, Intel, and Samsung—with two levels of employees. To gain direct input from the front-line personnel engaged in cross-border knowledge building, we contacted a sample of the engineers identified as 'inventors' in patent documents (in some cases these individuals referred us to colleagues). To gain a management-level perspective of the cross-border knowledge processes, we spoke to design managers and directors of technology development. The semi-structured interviews (usually with two or three experts at each level) concentrated upon three areas: the processes of knowledge management, the types of knowledge being managed, and the mechanisms for knowledge transfer.

The interviews with managers suggested that managers emphasized the integration stage of the knowledge-management process as opposed to the stages of knowledge search and transfer. The critical issue for each of our semiconductor firms was the integration of specialized knowledge from different parts of the company. This emphasis seems logical considering that the creation of value occurs only at this stage in the knowledge-management process. Thus, the former director of Texas Instruments' (TI) Tokyo R&D lab outlined the lab's role in accessing the knowledge bases of TI's Japanese customers, developing technologies where Japan was particularly strong (notably algorithms for image compression), and linking these technologies with ongoing research in Austin, Texas. Similarly, Fujitsu's 3D geometry processor was the result of closely integrated development involving both Fujitsu Laboratories in Japan and Fujitsu Microelectronics Inc. in San Jose, California. The need for integration of knowledge within the firm is a direct outcome of the increasing globalization of firm activity resulting in a dispersed knowledge base. This is evident in the case of National Semiconductor, where the firm explained how closeness to customers necessitated dispersion of semiconductor activity, with semiconductors for games machines being developed in Japan, computer processors in the USA, and digital wireless chips in Europe. Hand in hand with the dispersion of knowledge bases, there is increasing specialization of these bases. Siemens, Philips, Fujitsu, and National Semiconductor all noted that the increased specialization of knowledge in different parts of the firm has greatly increased the need to bring together specialist chip-design knowledge from multiple locations.

How do firms engage in integration? The processes by which this geographically distributed knowledge was brought together by the companies was very different from the continual, intense knowledge-sharing that has been advocated by some exponents of 'the learning company'. In relation to semiconductor design, our interviewees identified the key process as *integrating* specialized knowledge drawn from different locations—what Nonaka and Takeuchi (1995: 67–69) refer to as 'knowledge combination' to create 'systemic knowledge'. The key to efficient integration was the use of loosely coupled modular designs that permitted different individuals and groups to input their knowledge into the chip design without overloading the channels of communication and learning capacity of every other design unit. Fujitsu told us that its VLIW (Very Long Instruction Word) processor chip (used primarily for mobile phones, video compression, and other media-rich processing) was developed jointly by design teams in Tokyo, San Jose, and Frankfurt, but with each team working on specific modules and subsystems (these included a 16-bit instruction set, a 32-bit instruction set, a media instruction set, a digital-signal instruction set, and a floating-point instruction set). Hitachi reported that a similar modular architecture facilitated knowledge combination between its designers in Japan and California in its range of combined microcontroller and DSP (Digital Signal Processing) chips.

Segmented modular designs did not mean, however, that cross-border knowledge flows could be reduced to codified knowledge capable of electronic transmission. Engineers and managers whom we interviewed confirmed the importance of different types of knowledge in determining the pattern and effectiveness of cross-border knowledge integration. The critical characteristic was the codifiability of knowledge: technical information tends to be highly codifiable and its transmission can be reduced to mere data transfer. Certainly, computer-based information systems for transferring electronic data formed the backbone of the knowledge-management systems for all seven of the companies to whom we spoke.

However, our interviews with engineers emphasized that due to increasing chip densities (up to over a million transistors being packed into a single chip) and increasingly fine circuitry (approaching 0.1 microns), semiconductor design was pushing at the limits of physics. The result was that experience, intuition, creativity, and problem-solving became increasingly important. The design engineers spoke of chip design as a continual battle against the limits imposed by the materials used and the fabrication processes that required experience and scientific knowledge with the addition of intuition and creativity. Successful problem-solving required linking with multiple knowledge bases: with university researchers on fundamental science, with customers on the functional and technical requirements of new products, with manufacturing engineers over fabrication issues, with different design teams in order to access parallel experience and stimulate creative thinking. Most of these knowledge bases required accessing experience-based, intuitive knowledge of the tacit kind. The head of technology development at National Semiconductor pointed to the importance of integrating both explicit and tacit knowledge. A key characteristic of successful design teams was the ability to make full use of the form of computerized design tools and the company's library of designs, while exploring new opportunities through drawing upon the deeply-engrained know-how of seasoned engineers and the creativity and persistence of younger team members. Tacit knowledge is accumulated through experience and is inherently uncodifiable. Our interviews confirmed that the transfer of tacit knowledge depends not only upon trial-and-error imitation but also cultural and social context. This cultural and contextual knowledge is a function of socialization, often over a substantial period of time.

Our research revealed a wide range of media through which knowledge moves between the national units of the firm. All our interviewees put heavy emphasis on the importance of communicating internationally through electronic media. All the companies had invested considerably in information technology for the purposes of increasing the extent and efficiency of global knowledge management. In relation to semiconductor design, initiatives included standardized design tools and file formats, shared databases, common communications software, and design libraries, with users linked by company intranets. National Semiconductor's head of technology development explained how its integrated design system with common naming conventions, UNIX file structures, and design tools had been driven by the vision of concurrent chip design where design teams were capable of working closely together regardless of geographical separation. Similarly, Fujitsu's 'IP Highway', launched in 1998, was an Internet-based infrastructure allowing the transfer of intellectual property and design data across all Fujitsu's subsidiaries.

However, the very nature of the knowledge integration—whereby individual country units were engaged in simultaneously receiving, creating, transmitting, and integrating knowledge—revealed the limitations of electronic communication systems, especially in communicating experiential and intuitive know-how. At Siemens, engineers working on optoelectronic components explained that e-mails and file transfers only worked when supplemented by frequent telephone conversations, videoconferences, and personal visits to other labs. National Semiconductor pointed to the importance of company-wide desktop videoconferencing facilities and the authority given to individual engineers to make overseas visits to meet with colleagues without the need for supervisory or budgetary approvals. Our interviewees confirmed prior research concerning the need for 'rich' communication media to overcome the limits of electronic media with regard to complexity of language, flexibility of format, degree of personalization, and the extent of interactivity (Daft and Lengl, 1986).

Thus a manager's ability to transfer knowledge from the points of access, with the boundary spanners and gatekeepers (Allen, 1977), to other locations within the firm where this knowledge can be usefully exploited seems to be critical to innovation. How can managers develop this capability? The scale and scope of the firm's knowledge stock increase the potential for recombinations within the firm. However, to capitalize on this potential, firms need to develop internal mechanisms that enable recombinations. The role of internal communication systems (Cohen and Levinthal, 1989) is crucial in this regard. Zenger and Lawrence (1989) point out that the ability to communicate knowledge across organizational sub-units depends in part on the prevalence of a shared language and culture. But mere communication of knowledge may not be sufficient to ensure its exploitation. The nature of innovation, and the tacit and complex nature of knowledge may require that several sub-units interact actively across extended periods of time to build new products or processes (Westney and Sakakibara, 1986). To facilitate this knowledge-integration process, firms must establish intra-organizational mechanisms, processes, and systems to link various sub-units across time (Almeida, Grant and Song, 1998). Our field interviews suggested the firm's ability to ensure internal compatibility of information systems, sharing of intellectual property, and common software, protocols, and methodologies were viewed as significant in enabling knowledgeintegration within the firm.

Another mechanism to enhance integration was mobility within the organization. Field interviews indicated the extensive use by the companies of transfer of personnel, either for short visits or for longer-term assignments (several years in some cases), as a means by which deeply embedded tacit knowledge could be transferred and integrated within the firm. However, international personnel transfers also served to improve integration through two other methods. First, they contributed to internationalizing the company's culture, thereby overcoming some of the linguistic and cultural barriers that might inhibit cross-border knowledge integration. The semiconductor divisions of Hitachi, Fujitsu, and IBM put considerable emphasis of building collaborative company cultures and behavioural norms that transcended national differences. Second, international transfers helped to build informal cross-national mechanisms for knowledge integration. The engineers at Philips and Siemens and R&D managers at IBM gave considerable weight to the role of the interpersonal networks that employees established during their careers in a company.

1.5. Conclusion

We have examined the knowledge-management and creation process within the MNC from a managerial perspective. We believe our study sheds new light on this process by unbundling it into its components and offering specific prescriptions for managers at every stage of the process. The knowledge-management process consists of three related yet distinct sub-processes: identification of the critical sources of knowledge, building conduits to access knowledge, and finally utilization of knowledge through integration. We suggest that it may be worthwhile for managers in the MNC to study not just the processes but the firm-specific capabilities associated with each stage.

The capabilities associated with each stage of knowledge management (see Figure 1.1) become more complex as the process gets closer to culminating in value creation, progressing from simple monitoring abilities to more

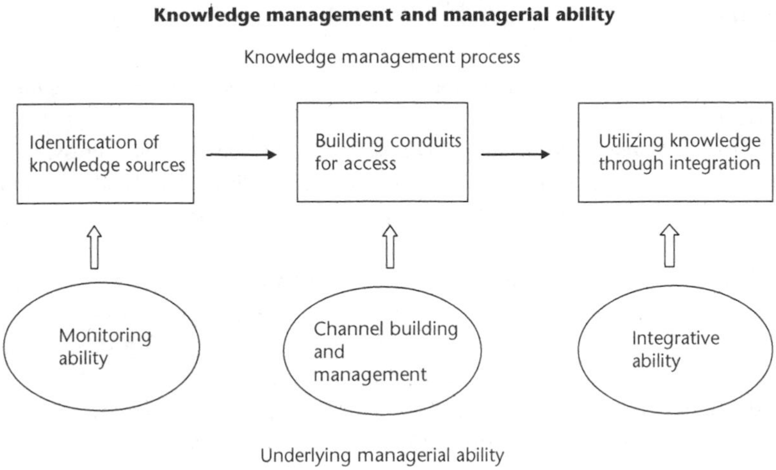

Knowledge management and managerial ability

Knowledge management process

Underlying managerial ability

Figure 1.1. Knowledge management and managerial ability

demanding conduit building and management ability and finally the most complex integrative ability.

The identification of each stage and the associated capabilities enables us to offer prescriptions to managers in developing capabilities that improve the overall knowledge-management capabilities of the firm. Better management of the knowledge-management process is a chief concern of most firms. All the companies we spoke to recognized the need to improve their handling of this process. Identifying the capabilities necessary to search for, transfer, and integrate knowledge is only a starting point. The critical issues for management practice relate to the design and use of these knowledge-management systems. Based on field research findings, we have argued that the knowledge-managing advantages of the MNC lie in its ability to use rules to standardized procedures and formats, directives to administer coordination between units, inter-personal relationships between employees, and a common culture to facilitate communication and cooperation. The design and choice of different mechanisms of knowledge transfer must take careful account of the nature of the knowledge-management process (e.g. the extent to which it seeks to replicate knowledge, to combine knowledge, or to create new knowledge through problem-solving) and the types of knowledge being transferred (in particular, the less codifiable the knowledge, the richer the communication medium needs to be). While firms have made huge strides in the use of IT to transfer information and support communication worldwide, the next level of knowledge management lies in the design and operation of organizational structures, management systems, and shared values and behavioural norms that can facilitate the movement of complementary knowledge types and link together the different modes of communication and knowledge transfer.

References

Allen, R.C. (1983), 'Collective invention'. *Journal of Economic Behavior & Organization,* 4(1): 1–24.

Allen, T. (1977), *Managing the Flow of Technology.* Cambridge, MA: MIT Press.

Almeida, P. (1996), 'Knowledge sourcing by foreign multinationals: Patent citation analysis in the U.S. semiconductor industry', *Strategic Management Journal,* Special Issue, 7: 155–165.

—— and Kogut, B. (1997), 'The exploration of technological diversity and the geographic localization of innovation', *Small Business Economics,* 9(1): 21–31.

—— —— (1999), 'The localization of knowledge and the mobility of engineers in regional networks', *Management Science,* 45: 905–917.

—— and Phene, A. (2004), 'Subsidiaries and knowledge creation: The influence of the MNC and host country innovation', *Strategic Management Journal,* 25(8/9): 847–864.

——, Grant, R. and Song, J. (1998), The role of international corporations in cross border knowledge transfer in the semiconductor industry. In Hitt, M.A., Costa, J. and Nixon, R.D. (eds), *Managing Strategically in an Interconnected World.* Chichester: John Wiley & Sons.

Phene, A. and Grant, R (2002), Innovation and knowledge management: Scanning, sourcing and intergration. In Easterby-Smith, M. and Lyles, M. (eds), *Handbook of Organizational Learning and Management.* Oxford: Blackwell.

Anand, B.N. and Khanna, T. (2000), 'Do firms learn to create value? The case of alliances', *Strategic Management Journal,* Special Issue: Strategic Networks 21(3): 295–315.

Barney J. (1991), 'Firm resources and sustained competitive advantage', *Journal of Management,* 17(1): 99–120.

Bartlett, C. and Ghoshal, S. (1989), *Managing Across Borders: The Transnational Solution.* Boston: Harvard Business School Press.

Coase, R.H. (1937), 'The nature of the firm', *Economica,* 4: 386–405.

Cohen, W. and Levinthal, D. (1989), 'Innovation and learning: The two faces of R&D', *The Economic Journal,* 99: 569–596.

Contractor, F. and Lorange, P. (1988), Why should firms cooperate? The strategy and economic basis for cooperative ventures. In Contractor, F. and Lorange, P. (eds), *Cooperative Strategies in International Business.* New York: Lexington.

Daft, R.L. and Lengl, R. (1986), 'Organizational information requirements, media richness and structural design', *Management Science,* 32: 554–571.

D'Aveni, R. (1994), *Hypercompetition: Managing the Dynamics of Strategic Maneuvering.* New York: Free Press.

Dorfman, N.S. (1987), *Innovation and Market Structure: Lessons from the Computer and Semiconductor Industries.* Cambridge: Ballinger.

Doz, Y. (1996), 'The evolution of cooperation in strategic alliances: Initial conditions or learning processes?', *Strategic Management Journal,* 17: 55–83.

Dussauge, P., Garrette, B. and Mitchell, W. (1998), Acquiring partners; capabilities: Outcomes of scale and link alliances between competitors. In Hitt, M.A., Costa, J. and Nixon, R.D. (eds), *Managing Strategically in an Interconnected World*. Chichester: John Wiley & Sons.

Dyer, J. (1996), 'Effective interfirm collaboration: How firms minimize transaction costs and maximize transaction value', *Strategic Management Journal*, 18: 535–556.

—— and Noboeka, K. (2000), 'Creating and managing a high performance knowledge sharing network: The Toyota case', *Strategic Management Journal*, 21: 345–367.

—— and Singh, S. (1998), 'The relational view: Cooperative strategy and sources of interorganizational competitive advantage', *Academy of Management Review*, 23: 660–679.

Ghoshal, S., Korine, H. and Szulanski, G. (1994), 'Interunit communications in multinational corporations', *Management Science,* 40(1): 96–111.

Graham, M. (1985), Industrial research in the age of big science. In Rosenbloom, R. (ed.), *Research on Technological Innovation, Management and Policy*. Volume 2. Greenwich: JAI Press.

Grant, R.M. (1996), 'Prospering in dynamically-competitive environments: Organizational capability as knowledge integration', *Organization Science*, 7: 375–387.

—— and Baden-Fuller, C. (1995), 'A knowledge-based theory of inter-firm collaboration', *Academy of Management Best Papers Proceedings*, 17: 109–122.

Gulati, R., Nohria, N. and Zaheer, A. (2000), 'Strategic networks', *Strategic Management Journal,* 21: 203–215.

Gupta, A. and Govindrajan, V. (2000), 'Knowledge flows within the multinational corporation', *Strategic Management Journal*, 21: 473–496.

Hamel, G., Doz, Y. and Prahalad, C. (1989), 'Collaborate with your competitors and win', *Harvard Business Review*, 67: 133–139.

Hanson, D. (1982), *The New Alchemists: Silicon Valley and the Microelectronics Revolution*. Boston: Little, Brown.

Hedlund, G. (1994), 'A model of knowledge management and N form corporation', *Strategic Management Journal*, 15: 73–90.

Henderson, R. and Clark, K. (1992), 'Architectural innovation: The reconfiguration of existing competencies', *Administrative Science Quarterly*, 35: 9–31.

Herrigel G. (1993), Large firms, small firms, and the governance of flexible specialization: The case of Baden Wurttemberg and socialized risk. In Kogut, B. (ed.) *Country Competitiveness: Technology and the Organizing of Work*. New York: Oxford University Press.

Kogut, B. (1993), Introduction. In Kogut, B. (ed.) *Country Competitiveness: Technology and the Organizing of Work*. New York: Oxford University Press.

—— and Zander, U. (1996), 'What firms do: Coordination, identity, and learning', *Organization Science*, 7: 502–518.

Lane, P., Lyles, M. and Salk, J. (1998), Relative absorptive capacity, trust and interorganizational learning in international joint ventures. In Hitt, M.A., Costa, J. and Nixon, R.D. (eds), *Managing Strategically in an Interconnected World*. Chichester: John Wiley & Sons.

Liebeskind, J.P. and Oliver, A. (1996), 'Social networks, learning, and flexibility: Sourcing scientific knowledge in new biotechnology firms', *Organization Science*, 7(4): 428–443.

McEvily, S.K., Eisenhardt, K.M. and Prescott, J.E. (2004), 'The global acquisition, leverage and protection of technological competencies', *Strategic Management Journal*, 25 (8/9): 713–722.

Malecki, E.J. (1991), *Technology and Economic Development*. New York: John Wiley.

Markusen, A., Hall, P. and Glasmeier, A. (1986), *High Tech America*. Boston: Allen and Unwin.

Marshall, A. (1920), *Principles of economics*. London: Macmillan.

Mowery, D.C., Oxley, J. and Silverman, B. (1996), 'Strategic alliances and interfirm knowledge transfer', *Strategic Management Journal*, Winter Special Issue, 17: 77–91.

—— —— —— (1998), 'Technological overlap and interfirm cooperation: Implications for the resource-based view of the firm', *Research Policy*, 27(5): 507–523.

Nobel, R. and Birkinshaw, J. (1998), 'Innovation in multinational corporations: Control and communication patterns in international R&D operations', *Strategic Management Journal*, 19(5): 479–496.

Nonaka, I. and Takeuchi, H. (1995), *The Knowledge Creating Company*. New York: Oxford University Press.

Perlmutter, H. (1969), 'The tortuous evolution of the multinational corporation', *Columbia Journal of World Business*, 4: 9–18.

Phene, A. and Almeida, P. (2003), 'How do firms evolve? The patterns of technological evolution of semiconductor subsidiaries', *International Business Review*, 12(3): 349–367.

—— —— (2008), 'Innovation in multinational subsidiaries: The role of knowledge assimilation and subsidiary capabilities', *Journal of International Business Studies*, 39(5): 901.

Piore, M. and Sabel, C. (1984), *The Second Industrial Divide: Possibilities for Prosperity*. New York: Basic Books.

Porter, M. (1990), *The Competitive Advantage of Nations*. New York: Free Press.

—— (1998), 'Clusters and the new economics of competition', *Harvard Business Review*, 76(6): 77–90.

Powell, W., Koput, K. and Smith-Doerr, L. (1996), 'Interorganizational collaboration and the locus of innovation: Networks of learning in biotechnology', *Administrative Science Quarterly*, 41: 116–145.

Rogers, E. and Larsen, J. (1984), *Silicon Valley Fever*. New York: Basic Books.

Rosenkopf, L. and Almeida, P. (2003), 'Overcoming local search through alliances and mobility', *Management Science*, 49(6): 751–766.

—— —— and Tushman, M. (1998), 'The coevolution of community networks and technology: Lessons from the flight simulation industry', *Industrial & Corporate Change*, 7(2): 311–346.

Saxenian, A. (1990), 'Regional networks and the resurgence of Silicon Valley', *California Management Review*, Fall, 32: 89–112.

Schumpeter, J.A. (1934), *The Theory of Economic Development*. Cambridge, MA: Harvard University Press.

Shan, W. and Song, J. (1997), 'Foreign direct investment and the sourcing of technological advantage: Evidence from the biotechnology industry', *Journal of International Business Studies*, 28(2): 267–284.

Song, J., Almeida, P. and Wu, G. (2001), Mobility of engineers and cross-border knowledge building: The technological catching-up case of Korean and Taiwanese semiconductor firms. In Chesbrough, H. and Burgelman, R. (eds), *Research in Technology and Innovation Management*. Bingley: Emerald Group Publishing.

Stuart, T. and Podolny, J. (1996), 'Local search and the evolution of technological capabilities', *Strategic Management Journal*, summer special issue, 17: 21–38.

Tushman, M. and Anderson, P. (1986), 'Technological discontinuities and organizational environments', *Administrative Science Quarterly*, 31: 439–465.

Wernerfelt, B. (1984), 'A resource-based view of the firm', *Strategic Management Journal*, 5(2): 171–181.

Westney, E. and Sakakibara, K. (1986), The role of Japan based R&D in global technological strategy. In Hurowitch, M. (ed.), *Technology in the Modern Corporation*. London: Pergamon.

Zander, I. (1997), 'Technological diversification in the multinational corporation: Historical trends and future prospects', *Research Policy*, 26(2): 209–227.

Zenger, T. and Lawrence, B. (1989), 'Organizational demography: The differential effects of age and tenure', *Academy of Management Journal*, 32(2): 353–377.

Zucker, L.G. (1998), 'Geographically localized knowledge: Spillovers or markets?' *Economic Inquiry*, 36(1): 65–86.

2

The Dynamics of Innovation Strategies

Bart Verspagen and Tommy Høyvarde Clausen

2.1. Introduction

Economists have traditionally considered innovation as a one-dimensional phenomenon that can usefully be described by an input-output relation (e.g. Crépon and Duguet, 1998, and other work on the 'innovation production function'). Research and Development (R&D) has been used as the main input indicator, and outputs have been proxied by such diverse indicators as productivity, patents, and innovation counts. The Community Innovation Survey (CIS) arose from the dissatisfaction of some economists with this state of affairs (Smith, 2004). These economists argued that innovation decisions of firms are not only concerned with how much effort to make, but especially with what kinds of innovation strategies to pursue. This followed on from early work by, among others, Freeman and collaborators at SPRU, who argued on the basis of qualitative evidence that firms could employ a diverse set of innovation strategies. For example, Freeman (1974) distinguished between six innovation strategies: offensive, defensive, imitative, dependent, traditional, and opportunistic.

The quantitative measurement of the strategic decisions that firms make with respect to innovation is severely limited by a paucity of data. For example, in the innovation surveys that are most frequently used in the literature, only a very limited part of Freeman's six strategies can be observed (specifically, the imitative aspect of product innovations). Thus, rather than starting from a theoretical analysis of innovation strategies, a part of the literature (e.g., Hollenstein, 2003; Leiponen and Drejer, 2007) has proceeded to define innovation strategies on the basis of the measurement scheme that the innovation surveys offer. This chapter follows in this tradition, applying methods that are similar to Srholec and Verspagen (2011) to identify innovation strategies in a dataset that covers two waves (2001 and 2004) of the CIS survey in Norway.

The aim of the chapter is to identify innovation strategies and investigate what characteristics of the firm—such as size, the industry in which the firm operates, and the geographical market scope of the firm—can be associated with the use of a particular strategy. Although we would be interested in the causal relationships between such variables and the decision to adopt a particular innovation strategy, the available data, which has only a limited panel dimension, does not allow us to identify such causal links. Therefore, we aim to find some statistical associations between the characteristics of a firm and the use of an innovation strategy that can guide further research into causal relationships when better databases become available.

A second aim of the chapter is to introduce and apply a methodology that makes it possible to define the innovation strategy in a dynamic way. The dominant approach to identifying innovation strategies is to focus on the innovation activities of the firm in a single year. However, such an approach ignores the issue of innovation persistence (e.g. Peters, 2009), which seems to be an important element of the strategic innovation patterns. The dynamic approach to innovation strategies that we implement depends on the joining of several waves of the innovation survey.

Since it has been put forward that diversity in the way that firms innovate can be explained by differences across sectors and/or countries (Pavitt, 1984; Nelson, 1993; Malerba and Orsenigo, 1995), part of our interest lies in investigating the explanatory power (in the pure statistical sense) of sectoral dummy variables for predicting the use of innovation strategies at the firm level. Srholec and Verspagen (2011), using a database in which firms were drawn from 13 countries rather than the single country, Norway, of this study, found that the sectoral dimension does not explain much of the variation in innovation strategies between firms. By reducing the number of countries, which is a 'by-product' of the dynamic measurement of the innovation strategies, the sectoral dimension may gain importance, because sectors within a single country may be more homogeneous than sectors between countries.

2.2. Innovation strategies: A review of theoretical and empirical work

It is a well-known fact from empirical strategic management studies (e.g. Rumelt, 1991; McGahan and Porter, 1997) that there is large heterogeneity in the performance of firms in markets. For example, Rumelt (1991) concludes that there are large so-called business unit effects, i.e. unobserved factors at the business-unit level that are the most important explanatory factors behind observed differences in profit rates. Such 'competitive heterogeneity' (Hoopes, Madsen and Walker, 2003) is likely to be related to long-run strategic factors that distinguish firms from each other, and innovation is one of those factors. However, before the so-called Community Innovation Surveys (CIS) that were launched in Europe in the 1980s, very little evidence existed on innovation activities at the firm level. Hence the links between 'competitive heterogeneity' and innovation remained, for a long time, beyond the scrutiny of quantitative microeconomic analysis.

Without sufficient microeconomic evidence on innovation, the dominating view was that sectors could be used as a way to harness heterogeneity of innovation. Pavitt (1984) proposed a taxonomy of innovation patterns that was based on such a sectoral view. In his taxonomy, four innovation patterns were introduced: supplier-based, scale-intensive, science-based, and specialized suppliers. Although the taxonomy was based on micro evidence from a database on innovations, the main point of the taxonomy seemed to be that innovation patterns differ between sectors. A lot of firm-level diversity may have been lost when adopting the sectoral level as the main focus of analysis. Users of the taxonomy have rarely returned to the question of heterogeneity of firms within sectors. In fact, Archibugi (2001) argues that sectoral taxonomies have been uncritically adopted as a classification tool in empirical research. The underlying assumption that sectors can be used to represent how firms innovate has only recently been questioned in this literature.

Studies based on data from early vintages of the CIS questionnaire, for example Cesaratto and Mangano (1993), Hollenstein (1996, 2003), de Jong and Marsili (2006), and Leiponen and Drejer (2007), showed that besides the traditional idea about 'science-based' innovation, many firms rely on 'market-oriented' and 'process, production, supplier-driven' strategies. Using evidence on organizational and marketing changes from the fourth round of CIS, Frenz and Lambert (2009) added what they call 'wider innovating' mode. Jensen et al. (2007), based on the Danish DISKO survey, highlighted two types of learning in firms labelled as 'science, technology, and innovation' and 'doing, using, and interacting' modes.

A crucial question that arises from these, and similar, studies is whether firms within the same sector tend to be homogeneous (Srholec and Verspagen, 2011). If they do, the findings derived from micro data call for a mere revision of the sectoral taxonomy. If they do not, however, the fundamental assumption made by Pavitt and his followers—that these patterns can be represented by sectors—needs to be revised. This is a first research question that will be investigated below. Following Srholec and Verspagen (2011), who show that firm heterogeneity within sectors indeed seems to be large, we suggest that in cases where sectors are not very much related to firm heterogeneity in innovation, the concept of innovation strategies is more appropriate than the idea of sectoral taxonomies. The term 'innovation strategy' then refers to differences between firms, irrespective of the sector they operate in.

Our other research questions concern the nature and backgrounds of the differences in innovation strategy that we observe to exist between firms. In line with Clausen et al. (2011), we use the term 'innovation strategy' to refer to long-run decisions that the firm makes with regard to the way in which it wants to innovate. This includes the type and quantity of resources that it devotes to innovation, the goals it wants to pursue with innovation, and the position and linkages with other organizations that the firm wants to develop. The long-run nature of these differences, and their (assumed) relationship to long-run differences in firm performance, are the main reasons for referring to them as 'strategic' differences.

Two related fields of literature, evolutionary economics and strategic management, that have influenced the recent discourse on innovation, suggest that such strategic considerations about innovation are indeed relatively invariant in the medium- to long run. Evolutionary economics portrays industrial dynamics as a process of variation, selection, and retention (Nelson and Winter, 1982; Aldrich, 1999). It argues that firms possess a set of semi-stable routines in which they store factors that affect innovation, as well as other strategic factors of the firm's behaviour. Although these routines are subject to change, this does not occur often, and generally, any such changes are often not radical (Cyert and March, 1963; Nelson and Winter, 1982; Levitt and March, 1988). Because the routines are not based on a decision-making model with rational expectations or full information, and because firms differ in respect of their predetermined knowledge and resources, they imply a relatively large degree of firm heterogeneity, which evolves only slowly under the pressure of market selection. In the words of Nelson and Winter (1982: 14), ' . . . routines play the role that genes play in biological evolutionary theory. They are a persistent feature of the organism and determine its possible behaviour'.

The strategic-management literature identifies competencies or capabilities as a crucial factor determining innovation patterns at the firm level (for example, see Penrose, 1959; Grant, 1996; Winter, 2003). Competencies related to innovation and change within a firm are sometimes referred to as dynamic capabilities (Teece et al., 1997). The theory states that firms need to create or acquire these dynamic capabilities in order to be able to innovate successfully in a changing competitive environment. Dynamic capabilities are 'higher level' competencies which enable the firm to renew its resource and knowledge base continually in order to keep up with the demands of the market and persistently innovate (Winter, 2003). Specific dynamic capabilities lead firms to pursue different innovation strategies. The stable nature of strategic firm behaviour is also stressed in the strategic-management literature (see Hoopes and Madsen, 2008, for a review). In this respect, the notion of inertia plays an important role. Similar to the idea of semi-stable routines, the concept of inertia is that a firm's strategy is stable, hard-to-change, and persistent at the firm level (for example, see Helfat, 1994; Stuart and Podolny, 1996).

Because of their long-run nature, innovation strategies are also related to the notion of innovation persistence (Clausen et al., 2011). A firm that has adopted an innovation strategy in which it commits resources in the long run may set up specialized departments, such as R&D, in which the innovation goals are pursued. The costs associated with these kinds of investments are largely sunk by nature of the activity (Sutton, 1991; Cohen and Klepper, 1996). R&D, for example, is not an activity which can be easily discontinued one year, and started again in the next year, because knowledge is embodied in the human capital of researchers. Thus, whether or not to invest in an R&D laboratory is a long-term decision, and once that decision has been taken, the firm is expected to have a constant flow of innovation.

Firms that see innovation, on the other hand, as a one-off event, may choose other ways of pursuing their innovation goals: for example, by relying on external knowledge. Thus, one innovation strategy may be to acquire the knowledge and means for innovation externally, possibly leading to a less persistent innovation pattern. Such a firm may, for example, implement an innovation once, and spend a longer period exploiting this innovation, without continuous investment in new innovations. It seems that not all innovation activities are associated with the same level of persistence as R&D. For example, buying a licence could be a one-off activity, leading to a single innovation, and the training of employees could relate to a single innovation project. When innovation or knowledge can be bought in the marketplace (Arora et al, 2001), persistence may also be low. On the other hand, strategic alliances in which knowledge is jointly developed between firms (Duysters and Hagedoorn, 1996; Vonortas, 1997), user–producer interactions (Von Hippel, 1988; Jensen et al., 2007), or cooperation with universities and public research institutes (Nelson, 1993; Mowery and Sampat, 2004) may have important sunk costs and may, therefore, be more durable.

Thus, persistence of innovation seems to be an important aspect of the innovation strategy of the firm, related to the choices made about what kind of innovation inputs to use (Clausen et al., 2011). But this aspect of innovation strategy has remained largely alien to the literature that tries to identify innovation strategies from the innovation-survey databases. The reason is that most of the existing work is based on a single wave of the survey, thus providing only a single observation per firm. Now that more waves of the innovation surveys have become available, it is possible to construct a panel dataset and address the dynamic aspects of innovation strategies. This leads to a second research question, i.e. what is the relationship between innovation strategies and persistence of innovation.

A final topic that will inspire our research questions is why heterogeneity in innovation, and firm performance in general, is persistent over time. The mainstream economic (neoclassical) theory of the firm states that competition will lead to the elimination of differences between firms. Only firms that adopt the single profit-maximizing routine will remain in business, hence no heterogeneity is to be expected in the long run. A useful assumption for this to happen is that firm capabilities and other factors (innovation strategies) that lead to differences in performance, can be imitated (either by entrants or incumbent firms), so that 'bad' firms will abandon their routines and adopt those of 'good' firms. In an evolutionary perspective, selection will operate on the heterogeneity in firm behaviour. One view of the outcome of such a selection process is that of Friedman (1953), who argues that economic evolution leads to the survival of firms that maximize profits only. In this case the mainstream profit-maximizing theory is adequate at least as an ex post description of the evolutionary process.

Such a view may be too simplistic a picture of the evolutionary process, as selection may actually lead to a stable heterogeneity of behavioural patterns, as well as the economic outcomes that are associated to them. This may happen when strategies are symbiotic, as would be the case, for example, when an offensive innovation strategy provides radical novelty in the form of a new design, and an imitative innovation strategy provides incremental improvements and a user-base for the basic design. In this case, the strategies feed upon each other and may co-exist in the market. Distinct innovation strategies may also co-exist in the face of selection if they serve different user niches, for example as based on competition with regard to quality, with different firms putting in different amounts of resources and different innovation activities to achieve various degrees of product quality. One may also imagine the co-existence of heterogeneous innovation strategies if higher-cost strategies would be associated with higher (gross) returns. Lippman and Rumelt's (1982) idea of 'uncertain imitability' states that because firm routines are unobserved to outsiders, they cannot be imitated perfectly, and hence even if there is a tendency for unsuccessful firms to imitate the routines of successful firms, this will not lead to perfect convergence of strategies and routines.

All of these are just examples of possible theoretical conceptualizations as to why heterogeneity of innovation strategies, and possibly associated to this, heterogeneity of firm performance, may persist in the long run, despite selection operating to winnow out some heterogeneity. This leads to our final research question, which is the following: which broad categories of factors can be associated with the persistent heterogeneity of innovation strategies?

Because we only have an imperfect dataset (which will be introduced below), we will have to limit ourselves to broad categories of factors to answer this research question. In particular, we will distinguish between demand-related factors on the one hand and supply-related factors, such as firm size, corporate structure, and industry effects, on the other hand.

2.3. Analysis and results

The dominant empirical strategy used to identify innovation strategies in the literature that was discussed in the previous section, is factor analysis (or principal-components analysis), possibly combined with cluster analysis. In the innovation-survey context, factor and cluster analysis is typically applied to the variables on which innovation activities (such as R&D, buying licences, marketing of new products, etc.) the firm invests in, to the variables on which goals the firm pursues with its innovation (product-related goals or process-related goals), and which knowledge sources it uses (such as universities, suppliers, and customers).

Most of the literature focuses on a pure cross-firm context, i.e. there is no temporal dimension in the data used. However, now that the innovation surveys (CIS) are available for a number of years, it is possible to create panel datasets, i.e. datasets where the same firm is followed for a number of years. Unfortunately, there is no obvious way in which factor analysis can be adapted to a panel context. Two simple empirical strategies may be considered, although they do not seem to suffice if one wants to fully exploit the dynamic nature of the data. First, one could run a separate analysis for each individual time period, thus creating multiple cross-firm perspectives, and compare how these evolve over time. Second, one could pool data from multiple time periods, and run a single analysis on the complete dataset, and interpret the resulting pattern as an average over time.

While these strategies may produce useful results, they do not actually take into account the dynamics of innovation strategies at the firm level. They look at changes in strategy at the population level, and ignore inter-temporal links at the actual micro level. The alternative method that we propose below addresses this issue explicitly.

The interpretation of any dynamic analysis in CIS is made somewhat difficult by the fact that the CIS panels are usually unbalanced. In most countries, including Norway, the CIS sample is redrawn every time the survey is run. Large firms tend to have a higher probability of being included in the sample (sometimes a probability equal to 1, implying that these firms are always in the sample), which means that especially for small firms, the probability that a firm has observations for all time periods is small.

Our proposed methodology starts from creating a balanced panel for a number (in the present case, two) of subsequent CIS-waves. We then reduce the dataset to a single observation per firm by creating lagged versions of the variables of interest. Thus, in our case of two time periods, the 'one-observation-per-firm' dataset contains all variables $X_{i,t-\tau}$, for $\tau = 0, 1, \ldots$. It encompasses the current observation, as well as the lagged versions.

We then simply include all these variables into a single factor analysis. The resulting factors will be 'mixtures' of two 'pure cases'. First, we may have variables from the same period load with each other. This indicates a correlation within the same time period, or, in terms of our research question, dimensions of an innovation strategy that are linked to each other. These correlations (loadings) are most easily compared to the results from a pure static (one time period) analysis.

Second, we may obtain high loadings between variables from different time periods (lag-orders). These are indicative of the inter-temporal relationships between innovation strategies, i.e. of persistence. A positive loading (or correlation) between lags of the same variable would indicate persistence of that element of the innovation strategy. Loadings between lags of different variables are indicative of more complex temporal relationships in innovation strategies.

The analysis is undertaken using the CIS-3 and CIS-4 waves in Norway. We focus on the sample of firms that are available in both waves (1955 firms), and exclude all firms that are available in only one of the two waves. This does mean that our sample is no longer a random one, since large firms have a higher probability to be present in the two waves than smaller firms. In order to obtain a relatively simple representation of innovation strategies, we focus exclusively on innovation activities, and leave innovation goals, knowledge sources, and other variables out of the analysis. Seven innovation activities are included in the first stage of the analysis, aimed at identifying dynamic innovation strategies (by factor analysis). One activity (design, prototyping, etc.) is excluded, because this is not available in the Norwegian CIS in a consistent way between the two waves of the survey that we use, and we add cooperation as an activity. We include firms that innovate, as well as firms that do not innovate. Although the latter category (non-innovators) does not answer the questions about innovation activities, we assign a zero value for them. These firms indicated that they had no innovation activities, either successful or unsuccessful, and either ongoing or completed. Therefore, we conclude that they, had they been asked the questions, would have answered 'no' to all of them.

All variables in this stage of the analysis are binary: they measure whether or not a firm has a certain activity. Table 2.1 gives the summary statistics for the seven activities. The two waves are marked '2001'and '2004', which are the

Table 2.1. Summary statistics (n = 1955) of innovation activities

	2004 (CIS-4)	2001 (CIS-3)
Internal R&D	0.371	0.313
External R&D	0.249	0.215
Machinery	0.155	0.182
Oth. Ext. Knowl.	0.107	0.097
Training	0.139	0.210
Marketing	0.084	0.143
Cooperation	0.233	0.242

Note: All variables are binary, values in cells give share of firms scoring 1 (Yes).

years in which the activities are measured. Internal R&D is the most common innovation activity in both time periods, although only about one third of all firms has this activity. Cooperation and external R&D are also common activities in both periods. Buying other external knowledge (such as licenses) and marketing are the least commonly observed activities. There seems to be some kind of persistence in the frequency of the activities between waves, but there are also differences (marketing being a marked case: it is much more frequent in the first time period).

We construct a tetrachoric correlation matrix between the 14 variables (the seven activities, multiplied by two periods). Tetrachoric correlation is used rather than the normal correlation coefficients to take account of the binary nature of the variables. The correlation matrix is used as an input into the factor analysis. We use principal-factors extraction in STATA to do this part of the analysis. Oblique rotation is applied to the raw results. The results of this analysis are presented in Table 2.2. We use a cutoff value of 1 for the

Table 2.2. Factor analysis results for innovation activities (rotated)

	Activity	F1	F2	F3
2004 (CIS-4)	Internal R&D	**0.545**	**0.617**	-0.100
	External R&D	**0.740**	0.322	-0.126
	Machinery	-0.002	**0.838**	0.070
	Oth. Ext. Knowl.	0.031	**0.796**	0.081
	Training	-0.082	**0.935**	0.082
	Marketing	0.020	**0.833**	0.073
	Cooperation	**0.703**	0.303	-0.139
2001 (CIS-3)	Internal R&D	**0.853**	-0.014	0.137
	External R&D	**0.916**	-0.132	0.146
	Machinery	0.056	0.087	**0.826**
	Oth. Ext. Knowl.	-0.107	0.059	**0.938**
	Training	0.096	0.038	**0.849**
	Marketing	0.212	0.078	**0.729**
	Cooperation	**0.688**	-0.110	0.396
R2 *cumulative*		0.54	0.17	0.09
			0.71	0.80

eigenvalues of the factors to determine the number of factors, and this yields three factors. Together, these factors account for 80 per cent of the total variance.

The table presents factor loadings that are larger than 0.5 (an arbitrary cutoff) in bold, and we focus on these in the interpretation of the factors. The first factor scores high on internal R&D, external R&D, and cooperation in both time periods. Thus, a firm that scores high on this dimension typically invests in R&D and has external links, and does so over both periods rather than just once. This factor therefore measures not only the type of activity (R&D and cooperation), but also the persistence of these activities. The second factor loads high only on variables for the last time period (2004). This includes all activities in that period, except external R&D and cooperation (which load high on the first factor). Therefore, the second factor measures a non-persistent dimension, focusing on the last time period only. It also has a much less exclusive focus on R&D than the first factor, which seems to indicate that the non-R&D activities are less persistent than R&D. This is confirmed by the third and final factor, which is similar to the second one, but with the crucial difference that it measures activities in the first time period (2001). One difference relative to the second factor is that internal R&D does not load high on the third factor. But the other innovation activities do (except external R&D and cooperation), which seems to indicate that buying machinery and external knowledge, as well as marketing and training, are less persistent innovation activities than R&D and cooperation with external parties.

We are now already in a position to answer a part of our second research question, which is about the relationship between innovation strategies and the persistence of innovation. The answer is that in our sample of Norwegian firms, some innovation activities, in particular R&D and external cooperation, are much more persistent, and therefore lead to more persistent innovation, than other innovation activities (marketing, buying equipment, training, and buying external knowledge). This accords well with the theoretical idea that R&D (apparently, even external R&D) and external cooperation involve a significant amount of sunk costs, while this is not so much the case for the other innovation activities.

The final step in identifying innovation strategies at the firm level is a cluster analysis on the factor scores calculated from Table 2.2. We use hierarchical cluster analysis (Ward's linkage method), and arbitrarily choose five clusters because this number offers the clearest theoretical interpretation of the clusters, as well as offering a clear contrast between the mean factor scores in the clusters. Table 2.3 presents the mean factor scores and standard deviations. The differences between the clusters are generally significant (1 per cent level) in a post-hoc test.

Table 2.3. Cluster analysis results for innovation activities

#	Label		F1	F2	F3	N
1	Non-innovators	Mean	−0.695	−0.466	−0.383	881
		Std. Deviation	0.104	0.048	0.084	
2	2004 non-persistent innovators	Mean	0.055	1.249	−0.217	310
		Std. Deviation	0.716	0.838	0.603	
3	Persistent innovators	Mean	1.091	−0.039	−0.398	408
		Std. Deviation	0.726	0.507	0.409	
4	Persistent and intensive inovators	Mean	1.108	0.539	1.773	211
		Std. Deviation	0.790	1.170	0.781	
5	2001 non-persistent innovators	Mean	−0.578	−0.514	1.330	145
		Std. Deviation	0.341	0.122	0.817	

Note: All means for the 3 factors are significantly different at 1% level (Tukey HSD post-hoc test) between all possible cluster pairs, except for clusters 1 and 5 (F1, F2), clusters 3 and 4 (F1), clusters 1 and 3 (F3).

The results in Table 2.3 can be used to interpret the nature of the clusters. The largest of the clusters is the first, which has a negative score on all three factors (remember that by construction, the mean values of all three factors over the 1955 firms are zero). This means that this cluster can be labelled as one of low innovation activity. We will label this cluster the 'non-innovators' cluster.

The second cluster scores particularly high on the second factor, which measures innovation in the second period. It has a near-zero value on the first factor (R&D, persistency), and a negative value on the third factor (measuring innovation activities in the first period). We therefore label this cluster the '2004 innovators' to indicate their non-persistent innovation activities.

The third cluster scores particularly high on the first factor, and negative on the second and third. The interpretation is therefore clear: these are 'persistent innovators', and mostly rely on R&D (not on other innovation activities, in either period).

The fourth cluster scores high (positive) on all factors, although the standard deviation on the second factor is relatively high. These firms are therefore persistent innovators, including the use of R&D (factor one) and also seem to use the range of innovation activities that are associated with the non-persistent strategies (i.e., non-R&D).

The final cluster has a positive score only for the third factor, which indicates non-persistent innovation in 2001. We label this cluster the '2001 innovators'.

The final step in the analysis addresses all three research questions. In order to do so, we ask which characteristics of the firm are correlated with the five innovation strategies (clusters) that were identified. In order to answer this question, we estimate a multinominal probit model. The explanatory variables are taken from the CIS-3, i.e. they refer to the same period as the first period in the factor analysis. Due to the nature and time-framing of the data (our explanatory variables do not precede the dependent variable), the analysis cannot claim to identify causality. Thus, the results of the analysis will point to correlations between the characteristics of the firm and innovation strategies.

The analysis is also hindered by a general lack of variables covering the characteristics of the firm in the CIS database. The variables that we can use are the size of the firm (natural log of employment in 2001), the market orientation of the firm (a set of binary variables indicating the main market in which a firm is active: local/regional, national, European, or rest of the world), whether or not the firm is part of a group (binary), a skill variable (highly skilled employees as a percentage of total employment in 2001), a dummy variable for whether the firm is located in a region that contains a large city (the large cities are Oslo, Bergen, Trondheim, and Stavanger),[1] and a set of sector 16 dummies. Table 2.4 presents the summary statistics for the explanatory variables.

For the binary variables, the values in Table 2.4 represent the fraction of the total sample in the given category. Thus, we see that almost two-thirds of all

Table 2.4. Summary statistics of the explanatory variables

	average	se
ln(empl)	4.332	1.203
Local/regional market	0.327	
National market	0.020	
European market	0.427	
Rest of the world market	0.225	
Group	0.281	
Independent	0.719	
Skill	24.839	26.072
Non-metropolitan	0.561	
Metropolitan	0.439	
Agriculture & fisheries	0.010	
Mining, oil refining	0.036	
Food	0.074	
Textiles, leather	0.032	
Wood & paper	0.050	
Chemicals, rubber, & plastic	0.047	
Basic & fabricated metals	0.069	
Machinery & transport eq.	0.114	
Electrical machinery	0.057	
Other manufacturing	0.111	
Utilities, construction	0.070	
Wholesale trade	0.048	
Transport	0.094	
Post & telecom	0.013	
Financial intermediation	0.060	
Computer services, R&D, other services	0.116	

[1] The four regions were also entered as separate dummy variables, but this did not yield any significant results.

firms are exporters, and the majority of these firms export to European countries rather than beyond Europe. About one-third of all firms operate mainly in the local or regional market. The group of firms that operates in the national market (as opposed to local/regional and international) is very small (only 2 per cent), and so we merge this category with the local/regional category. The variable 'Independent' shows that roughly 70 per cent of all firms are independent (30 per cent are part of a group). Slightly fewer than half of all firms are located in a region with a large city. The average skill intensity is about 25 per cent, but this variable has a high standard deviation. The average firm size in ln-terms is 4.3, which corresponds to about 75 employees.

In terms of the sectors, about 55 per cent of all firms are in manufacturing, about 33 per cent in services, about 5 per cent in primary sectors, and the rest in public utilities and construction. Within manufacturing, machinery and transport equipment and other manufacturing are the largest sectors. In services, transport and computer services, R&D, and other business services are the largest subsectors.

In the multinominal regressions, we use a firm in machinery & transport equipment that operates mainly in the local/regional/national market, in a non-metropolitan region, and which is part of a group as the baseline case. The regression is implemented with the non-innovators cluster, which is the largest, as the base category. Table 2.5 presents the estimated marginal effects for all five clusters. The marginal effects for the size variable (ln(empl)) and the skills variable are evaluated at the sample mean values of these variables (see Table 2.4). The other variables are all binary, and the documented marginal effect for these variables corresponds to a change from 0 to 1.

Firm size has a negative effect on the probability to be in the non-innovators cluster (i.e. larger firms tend to innovate more), which is an intuitive finding. Firm size has a positive effect on the probability of being in the two persistent innovators clusters. This effect is larger for the persistent innovators cluster, as opposed to the persistent and intensive innovators. Thus, larger firms tend to rely more on R&D alone. There is no significant effect of firm size on the probability of being a non-persistent innovator (both clusters). The interpretation of the size of the marginal effect is somewhat difficult due to the ln-form of this variable. A one–unit increase of ln(empl) actually corresponds to about 131 additional employees, which is closer to a tripling of the average firm size (75) than to a doubling.

Although, due to the non-linear nature of the probit model, the accuracy of such a calculation is low, we can express the marginal effects in terms of the number of employees necessary to generate a 1 per cent-point increase or decrease of the probability, as 0.01 divided by the observed marginal effect and multiplied by 131. For the non-innovators cluster, the addition of about 20 employees decreases the probability of being in this cluster by 1 percentage

Table 2.5. Multinominal probit estimations

Variable	Non-innovators			2004 innovators			Persistent innovators			Persistent and intensive innovators			2001 innovators		
	marg. effect	se		marg. effect	se		marg. effect	se		marg. effect	se		marg. effect	se	
ln(empl)	−0.065	0.012	***	−0.007	0.009		0.044	0.009	***	0.026	0.006	***	0.002	0.006	
European market	−0.120	0.028	***	0.037	0.021	*	0.046	0.024	*	0.044	0.018	**	−0.007	0.014	
Rest of the world market	−0.235	0.033	***	0.029	0.027		0.126	0.033	***	0.112	0.028	***	−0.032	0.016	**
Independent	−0.033	0.030		0.022	0.021		0.022	0.024		−0.013	0.018		0.002	0.015	
Skill	−0.0030	0.0007	***	−0.0001	0.0005		0.0012	0.0005	**	0.0016	0.004	***	−0.0003	0.0003	
Metropolitan	0.003	0.026		−0.003	0.019		0.000	0.021		0.003	0.014		−0.003	0.013	
Agriculture & fisheries	−0.001	0.126		−0.103	0.051	**	0.108	0.112		−0.064	0.033	*	0.059	0.108	
Mining, oil refining	0.192	0.072	***	−0.135	0.023	***	−0.052	0.049		−0.046	0.025	*	0.040	0.060	
Food	−0.051	0.057		−0.019	0.037		−0.025	0.042		0.000	0.030		0.096	0.057	*
Textiles, leather	−0.067	0.076		−0.020	0.048		0.047	0.067		−0.077	0.020	***	0.117	0.078	
Wood & paper	0.024	0.064		−0.016	0.041		−0.032	0.048		0.009	0.037		0.015	0.049	
Chemicals, rubber & plastic	−0.142	0.064	**	−0.017	0.043		0.013	0.053		0.065	0.045		0.081	0.065	
Basic & fabricated metals	−0.092	0.057		−0.037	0.035		0.073	0.052		−0.010	0.030		0.066	0.054	
Electrical machinery	−0.131	0.062	**	−0.052	0.036		0.078	0.056		0.044	0.040		0.062	0.059	
Other manufacturing	−0.053	0.052		−0.062	0.029	**	0.009	0.042		−0.019	0.025		0.126	0.055	**
Utilities, construction	0.140	0.061	**	−0.102	0.027	***	−0.092	0.038	**	−0.048	0.023	**	0.102	0.058	*
Wholesale trade	0.058	0.069		−0.043	0.039		−0.111	0.037	***	−0.052	0.022	**	0.148	0.070	**
Transport	0.305	0.051	***	−0.129	0.021	***	−0.147	0.026	***	−0.091	0.012	***	0.063	0.047	
Post & telecom	−0.170	0.112		0.039	0.087		−0.104	0.061	*	−0.025	0.043		0.260	0.129	**
Financial intermediation	−0.007	0.070		−0.120	0.025	***	−0.105	0.037	***	−0.050	0.022	**	0.283	0.080	***
Computer services, R&D, other services	−0.039	0.062		−0.007	0.042		0.021	0.050		0.026	0.006	***	0.049	0.049	

One, two, and three stars indicate significance at the 10%, 5%, and 1% level, respectively.

point. For the persistent innovators cluster, the addition of 30 employees will increase the probability of being in this cluster by 1 percentage point, and for persistent and intensive innovators, 50 extra employees are necessary to increase the probability to be in this cluster by 1 percentage point. Compared to the average firm size of about 75 employees, these are fairly large numbers, indicating that the marginal effects of firm size are relatively small.

The effects of market orientation appear to be larger, at least for non-innovators relative to the other clusters. The non-innovators cluster is associated with the baseline of local and regional markets, because all other categories are negative and highly significant. Even the smallest of these, European market orientation, lowers the probability of being in this category by 12 percentage points. The strongest effect is from exporting to non-European countries (rest of the world), which lowers the probability by almost 25 percentage points. In the two persistent innovators clusters, we see positive marginal effects associated with the two exporting categories, and there is not much difference between the elasticities of the two clusters. There is a weak positive effect associated with European markets in the 2004 non-persistent innovators cluster.

Corporate structure (Independent) is never significant, indicating that this variable does not seem to be linked to innovation strategies in the Norwegian case. The skills variable, on the other hand, is highly significant in general. It raises the probability of being in the two persistent innovators clusters, by roughly the same size, and lowers the probability of being in the non-innovators clusters. This latter effect is markedly stronger than the former effects. The skills-variable effect on the probability of being in the non-innovators group is significantly negative. The effect of being in a metropolitan region is not significant in any category.

With regard to our third research question, which asks what explains the persistence in heterogeneity of innovation strategies, we conclude that there is a mix of demand-side and supply-side variables that matters. On the demand side, whether the firm serves mainly local/regional/national markets or is an exporter is associated with the innovation strategy. On the supply-side, firm size and the skill-level of its employees lead to persistent differences in innovation strategies. Other supply factors, i.e. geography and corporate structure, do not seem to matter.

This leaves the role of sectors in the determination and persistence of innovation strategies to be explored, and for this we turn to the estimated effects of the sector dummies in Table 2.4. These are not significant more often than they are significant, but when they are significant, the marginal effects are relatively large, often of a comparable size to the market-orientation variable. The sectors that are associated with an elevated probability of being in the non-innovators cluster are mining and oil refining (20 percentage points), chemicals, rubber and plastic (–14 percentage points), electrical machinery (–13 percentage points), utilities and construction (14 percentage points), and transport (31 percentage points). This clearly identifies a number of non-manufacturing sectors (mining, utilities, construction, and transport) as relatively inclined to use the non-innovators strategy.

From the other significant sector effects in services and utilities/construction, all are negative, except for the 2001 non-persistent innovators category, which has positive and significant effects for most of these sectors. It is tempting to conclude that this is associated with ICT, for which investments in the early 2000s were peaking, and which is generally identified as a driving force for innovation in services. Between the two non-persistent innovators clusters (2001 and 2004), there may therefore be a large combined sectoral and temporal effect on innovation, with ICT-related innovation in services peaking in 2001, and strongly declining afterwards. Such an effect is not found for the manufacturing sectors, indicating the sectoral heterogeneity in innovation patterns between these large sectoral aggregates. Sectors do seem to matter somewhat (our first research question), but this is at the level of broad aggregates rather than at a refined level of disaggregation.

In summary, the most important effect on innovation persistence that we were able to identify comes from market orientation and broad sectors. Firms that mainly operate in foreign markets tend to have a much higher probability of being a persistent innovator than firms that operate in either local, regional, or national markets. Firm size and the skills level of employees are also positively associated with persistent innovation, but the effects of these variables are smaller. In terms of sectors, we mostly find negative effects (relative to machinery and transport equipment), and these negative sector effects are mostly found outside manufacturing.

2.4. Summary and conclusions

We have introduced a new method aimed at identifying the dynamic aspects of innovation strategies at the firm level. The method is based on factor analysis, and uses data from a panel version of the innovation survey database for Norway. We use the method on data for innovation activities of Norwegian firms, across a large spectrum of industries. We identify three major dimensions of the innovation strategy of firms. One of these is related to R&D and identifies this innovation activity as a persistent one, i.e. a strategy in which innovation is repeated in multiple time periods, rather than occurring once-and-for-all. This finding is in line with the literature on innovation persistence that argues that R&D costs are largely sunk in nature (Clausen et al., 2011).

The other two innovation strategy dimensions are less correlated to R&D, and, most importantly, identify activities in a single period only. This supports the idea that R&D is the most persistent of the innovation activities that we considered. Persistent innovators tend to rely on R&D, while non-persistent innovators may mostly resort to other innovation activities.

Our first research question asked how much sectors matter in the determination of innovation strategies. We find that there is some explanatory power of sectors, but this is mainly along the manufacturing/services divide, rather than at a finer level of disaggregation. The services sector tends to show a lower tendency for persistent innovation, and also seems to have a large temporal effect associated with the ICT boom in 2001.

Another of our research questions asks which firm characteristics are associated with the use of which innovation strategies. Although our ultimate interest is in causality, i.e. the question of what causes a firm to adopt a particular innovation strategy, the nature of the data only allows us to identify statistical correlations. Thus, we do not pretend that our results point out any particular causal chain.

We find that firm size, the skill level of the firm's employees, market orientation and the sectoral context are the variables that correlate with the use of particular strategies (including non-innovation). The geographical context and the corporate structure (ownership) of the firm do not seem to matter. Firms that do not innovate (i.e. which score low on all three dimensions of the innovation strategies that we identified) are typically small firms, with a small fraction of skilled employees, and who operate mainly in local, regional, or national markets. Increasing firm size, export orientation, and having more skilled employees increase the probability that the firm becomes a persistent innovator. On the other hand, these variables do not seem to influence the transition from being a non-innovator to being a non-persistent (one-off) innovator in a major way.

The effect of firm size is relatively small, and that of market orientation large. Firms whose main markets are abroad, especially outside of Europe, have a much higher probability of adopting a persistent innovation strategy. The sectoral context matters in a limited number of cases. First of all, there are a number of sectors, especially outside manufacturing, which seem inherently non-innovative. Being in such a sector (e.g. utilities and construction, mining, transport) is associated with an above average use of the non-innovation strategy. Persistent innovators are also less often found in service sectors such as trade and financial intermediation. All in all, the sector effects that are found to be significant do appear to be large. This somewhat contradicts the findings in Srholec and Verspagen (2011), who found that in a static analysis covering a broader set of countries, sectors do not matter much for innovation strategies.

References

Aldrich, H. (1999), *Organizations Evolving*. London: SAGE.

Archibugi, D. (2001),'Pavitt's taxonomy sixteen years on: A review article', *Economics of Innovation and New Technology*, 10: 415–425.

Arora, A., Fosfuri, A. and Gambardella, A. (2001), 'Markets for technology and their implications for corporate strategy', *Industrial and Corporate Change*, 10(2), 419–451.

Cesaratto, S. and Mangano, S. (1993), 'Technological profiles and economic performance in the Italian manufacturing sector', *Economics of Innovation and New Technology*, 2: 237–256.

Clausen, T.H., Pohjola, M., Sapprasert, K. and Verspagen, B. (2011), 'Innovation strategies as a source of persistent innovation', *Industrial and Corporate Change*, forthcoming.

Cohen, W. and Klepper, S. (1996), 'A reprise of size and R&D', *Economic Journal*, 106: 925–951.

Crépon, B. and Duguet, E. (1998), 'Estimating the innovation function from patent numbers: GMM on count panel data', *Journal of Applied Econometrics*, 12: 243–263.

Cyert, R.M. and March, J. (1963), *A Behavioural Theory of the Firm*. Englewood Cliffs: Prentice-Hall.

de Jong, J.P.J. and Marsili, O. (2006), 'The fruit flies of innovations: A taxonomy of innovative small firms', *Research Policy*, 35: 213–229.

Duysters, G. and Hagedoorn, J. (1996), 'Internationalization of corporate technology through strategic partnering: An empirical investigation', *Research Policy*, 25(1): 1–12.

Freeman, C. (1974), *The Economics of Industrial Innovation*. Harmondsworth: Penguin.

Frenz, M. and Lambert, R. (2009), Exploring non-technological and mixed modes of innovation across countries. In OECD (eds) *Innovation in Firms: A Microeconomic Perspective*. Paris: OECD.

Friedman, M. (1953), *Essays in Positive Economics*. Chicago: University of Chicago Press.

Grant, R.M. (1996), 'Toward a knowledge-based theory of the firm', *Strategic Management Journal*, 17: 109–22.

Helfat, C.E. (1994), 'Evolutionary trajectories in petroleum firm R&D', *Management Science*, 40(12): 1720–1747.

Hollenstein, H. (1996), 'A composite indicator of a firm's innovativeness. An empirical analysis based on survey data for Swiss manufacturing', *Research Policy*, 25: 633–645.

—— (2003), 'Innovation modes in the Swiss service sector: A cluster analysis based on firm-level data', *Research Policy*, 32: 845–863.

Hoopes, D.G. and Madsen, T.L. (2008), 'A capability-based view of competitive heterogeneity', *Industrial and Corporate Change*, 17: 393–426.

—— —— and Walker, G. (2003),'Guest editors' introduction to the special issue: Why is there a resource-based view? Toward a theory of competitive heterogeneity source', *Strategic Management Journal*, 24: 889–902.

Jensen, M.B., Johnson, B., Lorenz, E. and Lundvall, B.-A. (2007), 'Forms of knowledge and modes of innovation', *Research Policy*, 36: 680–693.

Leiponen, A. and Drejer, I. (2007), 'What exactly are technological regimes? Intra-industry heterogeneity in the organization of innovation activities', *Research Policy*, 36: 1221–1238.

Levitt, B. and March, J.G. (1988), 'Organizational learning', *Annual Review of Sociology*, 14: 319–340.

Lippman, S.A. and Rumelt, R.P., (1982), 'Uncertain imitability: An analysis of interfirm differences in efficiency under competition', *Bell Journal of Economics*, 13: 418–438.

Malerba, F. and Orsenigo, L. (1995), 'Schumpeterian patterns of innovation', *Cambridge Journal of Economics*, 19: 47–65.

McGahan, A.M. and Porter, M.E. (1997), 'How much does industry matter, really?', *Strategic Management Journal*, 18: 15–30.

Mowery, D.C. and Sampat, B.N. (2004), Universities in national innovation systems. In Fagerberg, J., Mowery, D.C. and Nelson, R.R. (eds) *The Oxford Handbook of Innovation*. Oxford: Oxford University Press.

Nelson, R.R. (1993), *National Innovation Systems: A Comparative Study*. Oxford: Oxford University Press.

—— and Winter, S.G. (1982), *An Evolutionary Theory of Economic Change*. Cambridge, MA: Harvard University Press.

Pavitt, K. (1984), 'Sectoral patterns of technical change: Towards a taxonomy and a theory', *Research Policy*, 13: 343–373.

Penrose, E. (1959), *The Theory of the Growth of the Firm*. New York: Wiley.

Peters, B. (2009), 'Persistence of innovation: Stylized facts and panel data evidence', *Journal of Technology Transfer*, 34(2): 226–243.

Rumelt, R.P. (1991), 'How much does industry matter?', *Strategic Management Journal*, 12: 167–185.

Smith, K. (2004), Measuring Innovation. In Fagerberg, J., Mowery, D. and Nelson, R.R. (eds), *The Oxford Handbook of Innovation*. Oxford: Oxford University Press.

Srholec, M. and Verspagen, B. (2011), 'The voyage of the *Beagle* into innovation: Explorations on heterogeneity, selection and sectors', *Industrial and Corporate Change*, forthcoming.

Stuart, T.E. and Podolny, J.M. (1996), 'Local search and the evolution of technological capabilities', *Strategic Management Journal*, Special Issue: Evolutionary Perspectives on Strategy, 17: 21–38.

Sutton, J. (1991), *Sunk Costs and Market Structure*. Cambridge, MA: MIT Press.

Teece, D.J., Pisano, G. and Shuen, A. (1997), 'Dynamic capabilities and strategic management', *Strategic Management Journal*, 18: 509–533.

Von Hippel, E. (1988), *The Sources of Innovation*. Oxford: Oxford University Press.

Vonortas, N.S. (1997), *Cooperation in Research and Development*. Boston: Kluwer Academic Press.

Winter, S.G. (2003), 'Understanding dynamic capabilities', *Strategic Management Journal*, 24(10): 991–995.

3

Superstar Subsidiaries of the Multinational Corporation: In Search of Origins and Drivers[1]

Katarina Blomkvist, Philip Kappen, and Ivo Zander

A long tradition of research has confirmed the importance of foreign subsidiaries for the evolution of the multinational corporation (MNC). Prior studies have highlighted the significant strategic and technological roles of foreign subsidiaries (e.g. Ronstadt, 1978; Pearce, 1989; Kuemmerle, 1997), and as a result the MNC has become known as a differentiated network of internationally dispersed units (Bartlett and Ghoshal, 1990; Nohria and Ghoshal, 1997).

In these differentiated networks, a select number of advanced foreign subsidiaries are known to take on significant strategic roles for the MNC as a whole (Bartlett and Ghoshal, 1989; Gupta and Govindarajan, 1991, 1994). Among these advanced subsidiaries, operations have shifted from knowledge exploitation to knowledge exploration, allowing them to generate new technology that is of significant importance for the development of the entire multinational group (Cantwell, 1989; Pearce, 1989; Dunning, 1994). These advanced subsidiaries have been described under various labels such as 'centres of excellence' (Holm and Pedersen, 2000) or 'competence-creating units' (Cantwell and Mudambi, 2005).

However, not all subsidiaries evolve into this advanced form and those that do still tend to contribute with innovations and new technologies at different paces. Recent findings suggest that there is significant variation in

[1] We would like to thank Fredrik Tell, KITE Group members, and researchers at Linköping University for stimulating seminar discussions and comments on the manuscript. Comments and suggestions from Ram Mudambi and researchers participating in the research seminar series at the Fox School of Business, Temple University, are also greatly appreciated. We further appreciate the insightful comments supplied by the CESIS workshop participants and the anonymous reviewers of earlier drafts. Financial support from The Bank of Sweden Tercentenary Foundation is gratefully acknowledged.

technological and strategic contributions even within the group of advanced foreign subsidiaries (Blomkvist, Kappen and Zander, 2010). Specifically, while several advanced foreign subsidiaries may be able to add new technologies to the MNC's overall technological portfolio, only a very small number of what may be termed 'superstar subsidiaries' seem to make it into an exclusive category that accounts for consistent and highly significant technological contributions to the multinational group.

While some of the factors that influence the likelihood that a foreign subsidiary will evolve into an advanced unit have been explored (Birkinshaw and Hood, 1998), there is still limited knowledge about what differentiates superstar subsidiaries from others in the multinational network, and in particular about the origins and underlying drivers of these differences. These are issues that have a bearing on our understanding of the nature and evolution of the MNC, and, as superstar subsidiaries appear to be those that can really influence and change the technological and strategic profile of the entire multinational group, they also come with managerial and strategic implications. The development of advanced and highly active foreign subsidiaries also has policy implications, especially in the light of their likely ability to create local spillovers and contribute to local business and technological development.

The primary ambition of this exploratory study is to identify the origins and drivers of such superstar foreign subsidiaries. It illustrates the evolution of two foreign subsidiaries of two Swedish multinationals—the German subsidiary of ball-bearing manufacturer SKF and the US subsidiary of agricultural-equipment producer Alfa Laval—and is a first attempt to come to grips with the phenomenon. A longitudinal investigation into their technological, business, and organizational development suggests that a number of factors need to coincide for a foreign subsidiary to develop superstar status, and that missing out on any of these individual factors will most likely hamper its ability to break out of the frame of the average foreign subsidiary. These factors include large and munificent local markets, high relative profitability, autonomy within the overall multinational group, as well as dynamic interrelationships between these factors.

The disposition of the chapter is as follows: the first of the following five sections reviews the literature that from various perspectives has addressed the development of advanced foreign subsidiaries of the MNC; it is followed by a presentation of the method applied in the study, which includes the use of background and descriptive patenting statistics as well as information derived from various secondary sources; the concluding sections contain a presentation and discussion of the main observations and findings, as well as a preliminary model which outlines the interrelated drivers of superstar subsidiaries. The concluding sections also include reflections about strategic and policy implications, and a more speculative note on what the observations might tell us about the fundamental nature of the MNC.

3.1. The drivers of advanced foreign subsidiaries of the MNC

Recent studies have indicated that the pace at which new technologies are introduced by advanced foreign subsidiaries of the MNC is modest, and that at the individual subsidiary level technological evolution is generally slow and time-consuming. Blomkvist et al. (2010) show that for the average advanced foreign subsidiary in a sample of 23 Swedish MNCs, and to the extent that it contributes any new technology to the multinational group at all, it takes some 17 years for the introduction of a significant new technology to occur. Among a total of 211 advanced foreign subsidiaries, the median number of new technologies introduced over the lifetime of subsidiary is two, and in technological terms most foreign subsidiaries have therefore been considered as 'average Joes' (Kappen, 2009).

However, there is conspicuous variation within this evolutionary theme. A very small number of advanced foreign subsidiaries enter into new technologies significantly more frequently than ordinary subsidiaries, suggesting that only a few specific subsidiaries develop the ability to significantly contribute to the renewal of the overall MNC's technological portfolio. This observation suggests that the technological influence from foreign subsidiaries on the overall multinational group can be narrowed down from the general level to what may be termed 'superstar subsidiaries'. These are subsidiaries which over an extended period of time enter a significantly larger number of new technologies than the average subsidiary of the MNC, and which over the long term will have a correspondingly larger influence on the MNC's growth and strategic development.

Nevertheless, relatively little is known about the longitudinal development of advanced foreign subsidiaries of the MNC, and the literature is yet to produce an explanation for why some and not all advanced foreign subsidiaries attain superstar status. There is relatively extensive knowledge about the various types of foreign subsidiaries that may exist within the multinational network, and also some evidence on the movements of foreign subsidiaries across the categories (e.g. Jarillo and Martinez, 1990; Molero and Buesa, 1993; Birkinshaw and Morrison, 1995; Taggart, 1997; Pearce and Papanastassiou, 1999, 2009). Some theoretical frameworks, such as Vernon's (1966) product life cycle and the Uppsala model of internationalization (Johanson and Vahlne, 1977: 1990) have outlined the mechanisms of changes of foreign units over time, but they fail to systematically account for the factors that may cause the formation of significant contributors to the technological and strategic development of the multinational group.

Birkinshaw and Hood (1998) address the issue of charter change in foreign subsidiaries and map out different pathways of development, but they consider a broad set of subsidiary charters and do not focus on the evolution of advanced foreign subsidiaries in particular. According to Birkinshaw and Hood (1998), three main factors influence the subsidiary's ability to gain and lose charters such as markets served, manufactured products, technologies, and functional area responsibilities: (1) local environmental factors, (2) subsidiary choice, and (3) head-office assignment. For a subsidiary to broaden its scope of charters, these factors are expected to co-evolve over time. Among other influencing factors, the likelihood of expanded subsidiary charters is assumed to be particularly high under conditions of local business dynamism, high-quality subsidiary–parent relationships, an entrepreneurial orientation of subsidiary management, and a high strategic importance of the host country for the overall development of the MNC. A strong track record of subsidiary activities and capabilities is expected to have a positive effect on the subsidiary's charter development, although the conceptual model is not specifically designed to account for longitudinal developments or repeat charter developments.

Blomkvist et al. (2010) develop a model that explains the long-term evolution of advanced foreign subsidiaries in particular, but it is a general model which does not account for variation in the relative pace at which individual foreign subsidiaries may develop. Their model considers three interrelated drivers of new technological contributions to the overall multinational group, including the subsidiary's gradually enhanced embeddedness in the local business environment, enhanced combinatory capabilities from involvement in a growing number of diverse technologies, and an increasing number of potential interconnections and sources of knowledge within the overall multinational group. Their prediction is an overall pattern of accelerated entry into new technologies in the group of advanced foreign subsidiaries, and the empirical findings indeed lend support for the existence of such a pattern. Yet, the model is unable to account for the fact that in their sample only a handful of advanced foreign subsidiaries bring about a significantly larger number of new technology contributions to their company group than most other subsidiaries, with up to 41 lifetime entries as opposed to the median number of two.

In sum, and while there is growing theoretical and empirical evidence on the development of foreign subsidiaries of the MNC, the literature is yet to account for the phenomenon of superstar subsidiaries and to produce an explanation for variation in the long-term development of subsidiaries that are capable of making significant technological contributions to the overall

MNC group. This effort appears particularly important in the light of the general view that foreign subsidiaries are and should be important contributors to the technological and strategic renewal of the MNC group (e.g. Hedlund, 1986; Bartlett and Ghoshal, 1989; Doz and Prahalad, 1991), and also on account of the fact that foreign subsidiaries may generate important knowledge spillovers in their respective local business environments.

3.2. Methodology

This study is based on longitudinal studies of the technological activity in two superstar foreign subsidiaries of SKF and Alfa Laval, two major Swedish MNCs which were established in 1907 and 1883 respectively. The opening part of the empirical examination draws upon the US patenting activity of these subsidiaries as registered over the time period 1890–2008, serving as an indicator of the evolution and significance of technological activity in the two subsidiaries.[2] We are particularly interested in instances where the foreign subsidiaries have entered classes of technology that represent new additions to the MNC's technology portfolio, serving as indications of more substantial contributions to the technological and strategic development of the entire multinational group. The definition of individual technologies follows the classification applied by the US Patent Office, including some 400 individual classes.[3]

This data is then complemented by information from a set of secondary sources and annual reports of the two firms, especially Wohlert (1982), Bondeson et al. (1983), Fritz (1983), Gårdlund (1983), Zander (1994), Zander and

---

[2] Blomkvist et al. (2010) investigated 211 foreign subsidiaries of Swedish MNCs and found that the German subsidiary of SKF and the US subsidiary of Alfa Laval accounted for a disproportionately large share of all entries into new technologies. The two superstar subsidiaries investigated in the current study were thus identified through their outstanding ability to break new technological ground, i.e. their outstandingly high degree of entry into new patent classes compared to other advanced subsidiaries.

[3] Patents are a frequently used technology indicator in the international business literature and elsewhere (Jaffe, 1986; Archibugi and Pianta, 1992; Almeida and Phene, 2004; Feinberg and Gupta, 2004; Gittelman, 2008; and they possess the specific advantage of providing consistent and comparable information over extended periods of time. For researchers interested in examining technological growth and development, patents offer several benefits (e.g. Schmookler, 1950; Pavitt, 1988; Mudambi and Navarra, 2004). First, by definition patents have an advantage in the study of knowledge-creation processes, as they are defined as inventions that are novel, useful and not obvious to people in the field (US Department of Commerce, 1992). Patenting has also been shown to correlate highly with alternative measures of technological activity and innovative performance, such as research and development expenditure and new-product introductions (Hagedoorn and Cloodt, 2003). One specific advantage of using US patenting data is that the patent records capture inventions deemed to be of comparatively high quality and that they reveal the nationality of the inventor rather than the nationality of ownership of the research unit. Assuming that inventors are typically based in research units in their home country, this makes it possible to identify where the research and development underlying the invention was performed.

Zander (1996), Åman (2003), and Fritz and Karlsson (2006). We use these sources to attempt to piece together what has caused the two foreign subsidiaries to assume such significant and important technological and strategic positions in their respective multinational groups. We particularly searched for conspicuous events and technological, business, and organizational developments that could explain the subsidiaries' unusual development and organizational status. Conceptual points of departure were offered by Birkinshaw and Hood (1998) and Blomkvist et al. (2010), but the search for explanatory factors remained broad throughout the empirical phase of the study.

As the material on the two subsidiaries was collected, we continuously probed different explanations for the development of superstar status across the two cases. Explanations that were contradicted by developments in either of the two cases were discarded, new ones were formulated, and eventually a set of key explanatory factors could be derived. As it turned out, and as is explained in more detail in the discussion, the result was an identified set of necessary but individually insufficient conditions for the development of superstar status within the multinational group.

We recognize the limitations associated with the methodological approach, especially the absence of comparisons with other foreign subsidiaries and especially those that did not develop superstar status, and therefore emphasize the exploratory nature of the current study. Although information on other subsidiaries within SKF and Alfa Laval was sought, information about less prominent subsidiaries was generally much scarcer in the historical accounts. To introduce a comparative perspective, we nevertheless included some of the available information in the discussion and conclusions, but the absence of full and detailed investigations into the development of contrasting foreign subsidiaries remains an important limitation and issue to be addressed by further studies.

3.3. Exploring the origins and drivers of superstar subsidiaries

As an initial point of departure, and against a background of generally limited numbers of entries into new technologies among advanced subsidiaries of similar MNCs (Blomkvist et al. 2010), let us consider the numbers of entry into new technologies displayed by SKF's German subsidiary and Alfa Laval's US subsidiary (see Figures 3.1 and 3.2).[4] Although the exact nature of these

---

[4] In the case of Alfa Laval, it is reasonable to believe that the US subsidiary had a relatively high propensity to patent in its 'home' market, making the importance of US technological activity appear greater than it actually was. Although the US subsidiary's entry into new technologies is probably inflated, the substantial technological contribution by the US subsidiary is unlikely to be explained by patenting propensity alone.

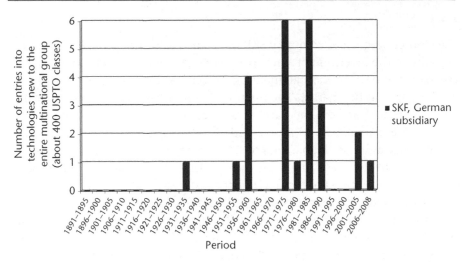

Figure 3.1. Number of entries into technologies new to the entire multinational group (USPTO classes)—SKF's German subsidiary

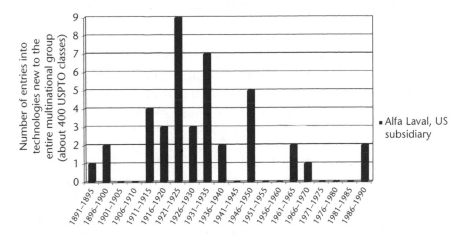

Figure 3.2. Number of entries into technologies new to the entire multinational group (USPTO classes)—Alfa Laval's US subsidiary

technological additions to the corporate portfolio remains unknown, they can be expected to serve as a good overall indicator of new-product introductions by the two units (Hagedoorn and Cloodt, 2003).

This type of significant deviation from the typical technological contribution by foreign subsidiaries warrants some attention and also calls for an explanation, and the section that follows sets out to explore the origins and drivers of technological activity in the two subsidiaries in more detail. What made it possible for the subsidiaries to break out of the frame and take on such prominent and important roles in their respective multinational groups?

3.3.1. *SKF*

The Gothenburg-based company SKF was founded in the spring of 1907, as a response to the invention of a new ball bearing by engineer Sven Wingqvist.[5] The new ball bearing was patented[6] and promised to be superior to existing ball bearings on the market. The main problem of ball bearings in use at the time was that they were rigid and tended to become overheated and break down if the machinery was misaligned. The new ball bearing offered better performance as it had double rows of self-aligning ball bearings with a spherical raceway in the outer ring, thus minimizing misalignment problems and reducing the likelihood of costly production stops.

Drawing upon this technological edge, and benefiting from a wave of industrialization in Europe, SKF went through a process of unusually rapid growth and internationalization, following the typical pattern of development and internationalization of Swedish firms at the time (Johanson and Vahlne, 1977). In 1908, SKF opened its first sales offices in Germany and France. Agents were also established in Finland, Switzerland, Denmark, Austria, and Australia. In the following year, a subsidiary was established in the United States. The first manufacturing subsidiary, however, was founded in 1910 in Luton in the United Kingdom. At the outbreak of the First World War, SKF had established sales representatives in 27 countries.

The expansion of SKF did not occur without competition. The main competitors were Hoffman in the United Kingdom, Fichtel & Sachs and Kugel-Fischer in Germany, and Timken in the United States. By the 1930s, SKF nevertheless had become the world's leading exporter of roller bearings and exported around 70 per cent of its production. In 1943, 75 per cent of the 38,000 employees were stationed outside Sweden. The German subsidiary was the largest, with 13,600 employees, followed by 7,200 employees in the United States and 4,000 in the United Kingdom.

Because of the politically sensitive nature of ball-bearing manufacturing, especially during wartimes, SKF de-emphasized foreign ownership of local subsidiaries and they were generally allowed to develop substantial organizational independence. In the early 1970s, a new system was introduced aimed at reducing the resulting duplication of production on the European market. At the same time, each subsidiary would be given global responsibility for sales regarding the specific bearings they produced. These rationalization efforts occurred between 1972 and 1977, during which time the plants in Sweden,

---

[5] Unless otherwise stated, the information about SKF in this and the following sections was obtained from Fritz and Karlsson (2006).

[6] A Swedish patent on the double-row spherical ball bearing was obtained on 6 June 1907. It was followed by patent rights granted in several major industrial countries. In 1912, SKF established a special patent department responsible for managing possible patent infringements.

Germany, France, Italy, and the United Kingdom were merged into one single division. Apart from enhanced coordination of production, the product mix was enlarged through an explicit diversification strategy which would continue into and throughout the 1980s.

3.3.2. The German subsidiary

Following the acquisition of half the share capital of the German ball-bearing factory Norma Compagnie in 1913, SKF undertook a number of acquisitions on the German market in the late 1920s, and ultimately achieved dominance over the German ball-bearings industry. It was also the German subsidiary that would develop into the single most important foreign contributor to the overall technological development of the SKF group.

While all of the manufacturing equipment was initially supplied by the headquarters in Gothenburg, both manufacturing and market development were local responsibilities. The main acquisition occurred in 1929 when Fichtel & Sachs in Schweinfurt, the main competitor with a 30 per cent market share, was acquired. Similar to the development and expansion of other Swedish MNCs of the time, notably ASEA/ABB (Zander, 2002), other local competitors such as Fries & Höpflinger, DWF, Riebe, and Rheinland were also acquired, and by 1929 all of these firms had been merged into a new unit with 9,000 employees: SKF Vereinigte Kugellagerfabrik AG (VKF).

The new unit's production was concentrated in production units in Schweinfurt and Canstatt, and the German head office was moved from Berlin to Schweinfurt. During the 1930s, the German subsidiary came to account for between two thirds and three quarters of the German domestic market for bearings. Because SKF was growing faster in Germany than at home, the Schweinfurt plant also came to have higher production and more employees than the factory in Gothenburg. The major competitor FAG Kugel-Fisher was also located in Schweinfurt, and there was thus a strong concentration of German ball-bearing production in Schweinfurt; just about 50 per cent of the ball bearings made in Germany were produced there.

As the Second World War commenced and continued, SKF's foreign subsidiaries to an increasing extent became part of national wartime administrations, and less connected with the headquarters in Gothenburg. That was also the case with the German subsidiary, which in 1942 was subordinated to the German war administration. Headquarters' desire to rationalize production was neglected, and in fact the foreign plants became more focused on the needs of their respective home markets and they produced the bearings locally. This resulted in increasing degrees of autonomy among the foreign subsidiaries as well as curtailed communication between headquarters and foreign subsidiaries. In some cases not even financial reports would reach headquarters. During the war the German influence over Europe was also paramount. The German subsidiary received massive deliveries from other foreign subsidiaries during the war. In particular, after the German occupation of France most of SKF's French production was delivered to Schweinfurt.

In the latter part of the war, the allied bombings more or less wiped out SKF's German plants, and the number of manufactured bearings fell by some 80 per cent to equal the volumes produced in France and the United Kingdom. SKF would ultimately lose all of its connections to and influence over the German subsidiary, as Philip Kessler was appointed separate Commissioner General for the German ball bearing industry.

After the war, with life slowly returning to normal and the withdrawal of the allied powers, the late 1940s saw the return of German operations and profitability. The German subsidiary experienced rapid growth from around 1950 and onward, with its manufacturing volumes again pulling away from the other main foreign subsidiaries. This expansion and growth was financed by the subsidiary itself, and in 1951 the German subsidiary returned a dividend to headquarters. Naturally, the German subsidiary was a part of the general upswing of the German economy, as reflected in steady increases in annual production. In 1953, the name of the subsidiary was changed to SKF Kugellagerfabriken GmbH, highlighting the fact that it was to be perceived as part of the SKF group.

For extended periods of time, the German subsidiary remained the largest and also the most profitable foreign unit within the SKF group, and it contributed the largest dividends to headquarters of all foreign subsidiaries. At certain times, the SKF plant in Schweinfurt produced bearings for export, and this was often the case when the factory in Gothenburg had more orders than it could handle. SKF continued to expand on the German market, although the plants that were added were considerably smaller than those in Schweinfurt and Canstatt, and personnel from the Schweinfurt plant were used to start up new manufacturing and educate the new workers.

Despite the fact that in the post-war period SKF was perceived as one single group, production was still very domestically oriented. As was typical among other foreign subsidiaries as well, the German subsidiary was producing mainly for its local market. In the 1960s, the organization of management and sales at SKF yielded an even higher degree of autonomy to the foreign subsidiaries. They became formally responsible for their own manufacturing priorities based on their local demand, and as long as they supplied dividends to headquarters they were allowed to operate independently. According to Lennart Johansson, Chief Executive Officer of SKF between 1971 and 1985, the heads of the companies out in Europe were like 'little kings' who had no desire to coordinate activities with other units.

In the 1960s, SKF Germany started to lose market share and showed diminishing aggregate profits. Towards the end of the decade, SKF Schweinfurt held a market share of about 36 per cent, compared to 45 per cent in the late 1950s. The problems were amplified as a consequence of the general recession in 1967, when the German automotive industry was hit particularly hard. SKF's two main customer segments were machinery and the automotive industry, and half of the output from SKF Germany was for the German automotive industry.

In the early 1970s, the integration of world markets and mounting international competition caused a revision of the traditional strategy of maintaining independent foreign subsidiaries. The global rationalizations at SKF that followed occurred during one of the company's weaker periods profit-wise, but in the end came to promote the German subsidiary's technological diversification. New areas of technology were investigated and acquired to spread risks and better handle economic cycles. It was during these years that the German subsidiary experienced a technological revival that even superseded the pre- and earlier post-war periods.

In the mid-1970s, diversification efforts were supported by the establishment of strategic global product centres. The aim was to draw upon and utilize the expertise residing in the SKF group, accomplish growth outside the area of roller bearings, and at the same time benefit from synergies in the international sales network. The different plants were to receive responsibility for areas such as product development, manufacturing, and marketing planning. SKF Germany became responsible for spherical, plain, and needle roller bearings, SKF France for all other non-standardized bearings, SKF Italy for bearings for aircraft engines, and SKF Sweden for hydrostatic shoe bearings. Clearly, the German operations gained responsibility for the largest and most profitable areas.

Moreover, in 1977 it was decided to build a central warehouse in Schweinfurt to rationalize distribution and avoid tying up capital in inventory. SKF Schweinfurt also had a specific organization for the development of new products, and already in 1978 it had managed to introduce several new, job-creating products and technologies. It was during this period of corporate diversification that SKF's German technological development picked up speed, especially in terms of entry into new technologies.

The diversification strategy continued into the 1980s and the German business areas came to include bearings, measuring equipment, and engineering products such as spring retaining rings and guidance systems, as well as textile-machinery components. Towards the end of the 1980s, and thus the most intensive period for SKF Germany in terms of developing new technologies, the SKF group began stressing core activities at the expense of further diversification.

3.3.3. *Alfa Laval*

The establishment and international growth of Alfa Laval is to a great extent connected to the firm's separator technology.[7] One of the founders, Gustaf de Laval, was experimenting with cream separators as early as in 1877, and joined forces with private investor Oscar Lamm Jnr in 1878. In 1883, after having performed much of the development work, the original firm was restructured and renamed AB Separator. The Alfa Laval name was not adopted until 1963, but will be used throughout the presentation for practical reasons.

While German and Danish manufacturers were responsible for much of the initial technological impulses and basic designs, development work at Alfa Laval was to a great extent associated with Swedish engineers, customers, research institutes, and component manufacturers. In addition, foreign research institutes were used for testing the Alfa Laval machines, as management believed positive evaluations were critical for gaining product acceptance in international markets.

A significant event, which also highlights the initial importance of foreign technological advancements, was Alfa Laval's acquisition of the Alfa patent from the German inventor von Bechtolsheim in 1888. Based on this patent, the Alfa hand separator was launched in the following year, opening up the segment of smaller separators used by individual farms. It also created a significant advantage over emerging competitors, and for a number of years allowed Alfa Laval to establish dominant positions at home as well as in international markets. By and large, it was the Alfa patent and the hand separator that made possible Alfa Laval's development into one of the leading firms in the industry. By 1913, the hand separator had come to account for 97 per cent of Alfa Laval's separator sales and about 70 per cent of total sales. It was to remain the company's most important product line until the Second World War and its production was accompanied by only gradual movements into other separation applications such as yeast separators (development work started in1890s), lubricant and mineral-oil separators (1890s), and slurry separators (1900s).

During the 1870s, and very much in the same way as SKF internationalized its operations, foreign agents were established in Denmark, Germany, France, the United Kingdom, and the United States. The first foreign subsidiary–De Laval Separator Co. or Lavalco—was established in New York in 1885, replacing an agent relationship which had been established in 1883. It was to be followed by additional foreign subsidiaries in Austria (1897), Denmark (1901),

---

[7] The information about Alfa Laval was primarily collected from Wohlert (1981), Gårdlund (1983), Fritz (1983), and Bondeson et al. (1983). A summary account and extended discussion of the company's technological development can be found in Zander (1994) and Zander and Zander (1996).

Germany (1901), Hungary (1902), France (1906), and Latvia (1910).[8] Early manufacturing units were established in Poughkeepsie in the United States (1892), Berlin and Hamburg in Germany (1902 and 1907), and Denmark (1909). A number of foreign sales subsidiaries followed in more peripheral markets throughout the 1920s, and the number kept growing until subsidiaries were found in 30 countries by the mid-1970s.

Over the years, Alfa Laval would become involved in milking machines and plate heat exchangers as two additional major product categories (entry into these two fields is accounted for in more detail in the presentation of developments in the US and German subsidiaries that follows). In the 1960s, the demand for separators, milking machines and plate heat exchangers stagnated and Alfa Laval answered by trying to build systems around these components. Some of these systems combined components according to specified customer needs, while others took the form of complete turnkey dairies and food processing plants. A more substantial broadening of Alfa Laval's technological portfolio took place in the following decade, through a series of major acquisitions with the specific aim of diversifying out of the traditional and mature businesses.

3.3.4. The US subsidiary, Lavalco

The United States rapidly became the most important market for separator sales. Initially, components, designs, blueprints, and qualified personnel were transferred from Sweden, but it appears that Lavalco had already taken over a substantial part of the development work at the turn of the century. A patent by Berrigan in 1899 supplied the US subsidiary with a significant technological advancement when the Alfa patent expired at the turn of the century. (Berrigan had been working on slurry separators in the Swedish unit before the turn of the century.) One specific application pioneered by the US subsidiary was industrial separators, especially for marine purposes. The US operations also came to include the development and manufacturing of turbine separators and steam turbines.

Already in 1885, US separator sales accounted for roughly one third of Alfa Laval's total separator sales. While the US separators were locally assembled, they were initially equipped with separator bowls that were imported from Sweden. Manufacturing was started in a plant in Poughkeepsie in the early 1890s. The factory was located very close to the 'Hartford Rectangle' and could draw upon the modern manufacturing and measurement methods emerging in that region. These modern methods would become transferred to the

---

[8] The exact times of establishment differs across publications, but not by more than one year.

Swedish home-country units, and in return full-scale manufacturing of the hand separator was allowed to move out to the US subsidiary (Wohlert, 1982: 104–105; Bondeson et al., 1983: 30–31). Although at the time the geographical location was dynamic in terms of the development of efficient measurement and manufacturing methods, technological progress specifically in the field of separators (at least initially) appears to have taken place in countries such as Denmark and Germany.[9]

The Lavalco subsidiary became very profitable early on and contributed substantially to Alfa Laval's total profits. In the period 1895–1914, the subsidiary supplied 46 million Swedish kronor in profits, which roughly equalled dividends paid by the parent company over the 1897–1914 period (Wohlert, 1982: 136). In the peak year of 1913, the US operations generated profits of $1,752,000 (Bondeson et al., 1983: 34), which coincided with a period of declining profitability of the parent corporation. In 1899, Lavalco also initiated its own internationalization by establishing an affiliated unit in Canada, which was transformed into a subsidiary in 1912 (The De Laval Dairy Supply Co. Ltd). In the early 1920s, substantial write-offs of Alfa Laval assets in Russia, Germany, and Austria were counterbalanced by an appreciation of the US operations.[10] Fritz (1983: 47) concludes that 'the fact that ABS [Alfa Laval] came through the crisis of the 1920s relatively intact was . . . because of the American companies'.

From an organizational perspective, the First World War meant that management of the US subsidiary management would become more independent from the Swedish headquarters. This independence then appears to have been maintained and even strengthened over several decades. According to Bondeson et al. (1983: 51), 'The increased self-sufficiency vis-à-vis the parent company was reflected in an almost negligible interest in technological exchange with other parts of the group.' Francis J. Arend would lead Lavalco's operations from 1895 to 1942,[11] and has been described as 'independent and incredibly self-

---

[9] It is difficult to pinpoint the relative positions of countries such as Denmark, Germany, and the United States in terms of offering dynamic environments for the development of the separator, and perhaps existing accounts of the early development of Alfa Laval reflect a European bias due to both accumulation and ease of access to company information. It appears, however, that in terms of patenting in the area of milk separators the most active locations were Germany and Denmark (Fritz, 1983: 378). In 1879, the only manufacturers of separators were found in Sweden (one manufacturer), Denmark (one), and Germany (three). In 1898, there were five manufacturers in both Sweden and Denmark, 13 in Germany, and now alongside six European manufacturers also six in the United States. In 1912, there were 16 manufacturers in Sweden, five in Denmark, 70 in Germany, and 25 in the United States. According to Bondeson et al. (1983: 60), in 1918 there remained 77 manufacturers of separators, nine of which were found in Sweden, 40 in Germany, and 19 in the United States.

[10] The American operations increased their proportion of the value of all foreign shares from 60 to 98 per cent, and their share of total Alfa Laval assets from 33 to 52 per cent (Fritz, 1983: 42).

[11] When Arend was succeeded by Ralph Stoddard in 1942, the parent company exercised an option to acquire Arend's 10 per cent of the Lavalco shares. In 1952, the parent company would also acquire Lavalco's shares in the Canadian subsidiary in Peterborough.

conscious' and 'something of a Caesar-type, to whom everyone—Wästfelt [Alfa Laval's CEO] not excluded—was very subservient' (Fritz, 1983: 124, 203). Fritz (1983: 203) also notes that Lavalco's special position within the group and Arend's self-consciousness were reflected in the fact that Arend never visited Europe. He concludes: Overall, it appears that Lavalco was little receptive to influences from Stockholm. Visiting administrative staff from ABS [Alfa Laval] reported how "Confidential information" laboriously developed at headquarters ended up unread in some archive. Lavalco's interest in Swedish production or the Swedish methods was extremely limited (Fritz, 1983: 205).

Having taken on a vital role in the development of hand separators, the US subsidiary also became actively involved in the milking-machine business. It appears that development work had started in Sweden in 1895 but was discontinued in 1912, and instead the technological breakthrough in milking machines took place in the United States. The US subsidiary introduced a promising design for the local market in 1917, and by 1928 milking machines had come to represent 16 per cent of the US subsidiary's sales. In the case of milking machines, it was a subsidiary of the Swedish parent that in 1921 acquired the rights to sell the new milking machines in all markets outside of the United States. The US subsidiary also pioneered marine separators, which achieved their breakthrough after the First World War as a result of significantly increased prices for lubricant oils and the expansion of the US Navy.

While at the aggregate level the Swedish units accounted for most of Alfa Laval's technological activity until about 1910, patenting data suggests that at that time the US subsidiary came to dominate technological development in the great majority of all technologies (although it is necessary to take into account the comparatively high patenting propensity of the US subsidiary).[12] In the early 1910s, the US subsidiary dominated technological activity in more than 50 per cent of all technologies, and it maintained its dominant position until the Second World War. From a technological point of view, Alfa Laval was a US rather than a Swedish firm throughout much of its infancy (Zander and Zander, 1996).

In 1913 Lavalco accounted for about one-third of all separator sales in the United States and posted a record profit for the year, but increasing competition and lowered margins would gradually diminish profits and dividends paid to the parent company. According to some accounts, development activity also lost momentum during the 1920s (Fritz, 1983: 126). The economic

---

[12] While the relative position of the US subsidiary may be exaggerated by looking only at numbers and relative proportions of US patents, Alfa Laval had proved it was capable of patenting in the United States before local operations were established. Collaboration with local patenting agencies and consultants was extensive when Alfa Laval first entered the US market.

crisis following the events of 1929 had a particularly severe impact on Alfa Laval's US operations. In the period 1929–1933, sales fell from $7 million to $2 million, net losses were recorded from 1930 and throughout the following three years, and dividends to Sweden were discontinued entirely over the 1930–1934 period (Bondeson et al., 1983: 38; Fritz, 1983: 506–507).

As the economic crisis following the 1929 events was more or less universal, the US subsidiary nevertheless maintained its leading position within the Alfa Laval group. In 1936, the United States accounted for 19 per cent of Alfa Laval's sales, and Germany for just below 14 per cent. Together with the Swedish units, which accounted for 23 per cent of total group sales, the US and German subsidiaries were by far the most important individual units in the group. The situation remained about the same for more than two decades, although the United States would increase and Germany decrease its share somewhat. (In 1960, the two subsidiaries accounted for 20 and 13 per cent of total group sales, respectively.)

The Second World War brought renewed expansion to Lavalco, in large part because of rapidly increasing demand for marine separators and steam turbines, but also because of the manufacturing of various products and equipment related to the wartime efforts. Profitability also returned over the period 1936–1945, and organizationally Lavalco remained independent from the Stockholm headquarters. Products were designed to meet the demand from US customers, and the subsidiary was '. . . rather disinterested in exchanging technical knowledge and believed that in this respect there was little to be gained from Sweden' (Fritz, 1983: 330). Results from research and development were sent only intermittently to Stockholm, and in connection with a conference held in Poughkeepsie in 1947 the Swedish participants were referred to as representatives of 'European De Laval', not Separator AB (Fritz, 1983: 330).

The 1950s meant a return to stagnation, and during the general economic upswing Lavalco's growth was 2 per cent as compared to an average of 10 per cent for other parts of the Alfa Laval group. Profitability remained low, and no dividends were paid to the parent company in the period 1956–1966. During this period, it also appears that research and development work started to shift back to Sweden and the European market. The US subsidiary kept the technological lead until the late 1940s, but after that most of the improvements were made in Sweden, which is also well-reflected in the number of patents of US and Swedish origin (Zander, 1994). The US subsidiary maintained a dominant share of technological activity in slightly more than 50 per cent of all technologies in the period 1946–1950, but after that its importance was continually diminished, and the overall foreign share of technological development declined to reach about 10 per cent in the period 1971–1975.[13]

In 1966, Alfa Laval acquired the last outstanding Lavalco shares (the Canadian subsidiary, partly for tax reasons, had been wholly incorporated in 1958). Eventually, the US subsidiary would carry out a number of local acquisitions, notably G&H Products Co., Jay-Ro Services, and Hercules Filter (1963) and American Tool & Machinery Co. and Contherm Corp. (1969).

3.4. Discussion

Focused research on the evolution of technological capabilities in foreign subsidiaries started more than 30 years ago, when Robert Ronstadt (1978) suggested that initial R&D investments in foreign subsidiaries may expand into significant capabilities in developing new and improved products for foreign or even global markets. He predicted the emergence of an increasing number of advanced foreign research and development subsidiaries in the MNC, capable of making substantial contributions to the technological and strategic renewal of the entire corporation. Although since then research has shown that as a collective foreign subsidiaries of the MNC indeed have come to make an increasingly significant contribution to its technological renewal (e.g. Cantwell, 1989; Pearce, 1989; Dunning, 1994) and that technological and strategic roles may differ across foreign subsidiaries (e.g. Jarillo and Martinez, 1990; Birkinshaw and Morrison, 1995; Taggart, 1997; Pearce and Papanastassiou, 1999), the literature on the subject contains limited information about differentiated evolutionary paths among foreign subsidiaries that have reached the advanced stages of development. Recent findings suggest the existence of a very small number of 'superstar subsidiaries' that are able to make significant technological and strategic contributions to the multinational group (Blomkvist et al., 2010), but the origins and drivers of these subsidiaries have not been explicitly addressed by the extant literature.

The two cases explored in the present study—SKF's German subsidiary and the US subsidiary of Alfa Laval—highlight a number of factors that could potentially explain the emergence and unusual capabilities of each of these superstar subsidiaries. First, they were both located in what would represent large, munificent, and important markets for the parent firms. Second, both subsidiaries were very successful financially, and this financial strength

---

[13] The shifting of technological activity from foreign subsidiaries to Sweden occurred in several important technological classes, starting at about the time of the Second World War. This involved increased technological activity in the parent firm, but also at the same time a reduction in foreign technological efforts.

appears to have had a significant influence on their ability to achieve and maintain superstar status over time. Third, both subsidiaries were highly autonomous. Finally, and from a dynamic point of view, the slack provided by high levels of profit and its dynamic interplay with the levels of innovation activity and autonomy in all probability contributed positively to the subsidiaries' ability to retain their superstar status over extended periods of time. Below, each of these factors and their interconnections will be examined and discussed in more detail.

Market size and munificence: It is clear that the two subsidiaries were located in large markets, not only in terms of absolute size but also in terms of relative proportions of sales of the respective multinational groups. In Alfa Laval, the US subsidiary almost from inception in 1885 and at least into the 1960s was the largest foreign subsidiary of the multinational group. In SKF, the German subsidiary became the largest foreign subsidiary in the group in the early 1930s and by the end of that decade had more employees and sales than any other SKF entity, including headquarters. The Second World War diminished the size of the German operations, but the subsidiary recovered to once again become the largest entity within the group by the 1960s. Being located in large markets also implies relatively broad technological and business opportunities for the two subsidiaries, which would imply a positive effect on their ability to successively enter into and add technologies that were new to the respective multinational groups.

A more intricate question concerns the extent to which the respective host locations offered unique and particularly dynamic environments for the upgrading of the types of products embraced by the two subsidiaries (Birkinshaw and Hood, 1998). In the case of SKF, the German subsidiary had the domestic automotive industry as an important and presumably sophisticated customer base and it was co-located with its main local competitors, both conditions which have been identified as significant drivers of innovation (Porter, 1990) and inter-firm knowledge spillovers (Maskell and Malmberg, 1999). In the case of Alfa Laval's US subsidiary, it does not seem that the local environment was particularly conducive to innovation in dairy separators (the most significant technological advancements took place in Denmark and Germany), and these were the primary source of superior profits in the early years of operation. However, there appears to have been distinctive demand for marine separators, an area in which the US subsidiary would develop particular strengths. The second 'big hit' of the US subsidiary, the milking machine, may have benefited from comparatively large herds of livestock in the United States, but it is unknown if the location offered a particularly dynamic environment for technological improvements. It further appears that the US subsidiary was located in a generally dynamic region of the United States, specifically in terms of the introduction of modern measuring and manufacturing processes.

In sum, large market size in both absolute and relative terms was a common denominator in the two cases, and the two locations appear to have represented generally munificent and dynamic environments for new technological advancements. The extent to which the subsidiaries could draw upon particularly strong cluster dynamics in their entries into new technologies and products nevertheless remains an open question, which cannot be effectively addressed on the basis of the collected data.

Profitability: Both of the examined subsidiaries—partly as a result of technological superiority, but in all probability also because of a number of additional but unknown capabilities and events—were able to achieve dominant positions in their respective local markets. The German subsidiary at one point held a dominant position in the German market for ball bearings (a 65–75 per cent market share), and carried out several local acquisitions to secure its market leadership. Even during times of market saturation and in more recent periods, the German operations consistently enjoyed a leading market position, with local market shares of 45 per cent in the late 1950s and 36 per cent in the late 1960s. In the early 1910s, Alfa Laval's US subsidiary accounted for about one-third of separator sales in the local market, twice as much as the largest competitor, and market shares were even higher in the previous decade.

Both of the examined subsidiaries were financially strong and supplied substantial dividends to their respective parent firms. SKF's German subsidiary was very profitable in the early years, became financially stronger than headquarters, and financed its expansion on the German market during the 1950s on its own. According to Fritz and Karlsson (2006: 147), 'SKF in Germany was not only the largest but also the most profitable company in the Group, and returned by far the largest dividend of any subsidiary to the parent company.' The financial strength of Alfa Laval's US subsidiary allowed it to supply dividends that were roughly equal to shareholder dividends paid by the Alfa Laval group over the period 1897–1914.

But it appears that profitability was not only a question of levels of return of investment, it was also one of relative contribution and being an important source of income for the parent and overall corporation.[14] This is especially true in the Alfa Laval case, where dividends from the US subsidiary appear to have been critical for the financial stability of the overall corporation, for example when other foreign subsidiaries foundered in the early 1920s.

Autonomy: For a number of reasons, including external events as well as strategic and organizational decisions taken by headquarters, the two subsidiaries tended to be very autonomous from their respective headquarters. Presumably, this autonomy made it comparatively easy to explore and enter into new technologies and product areas (Yamin, 2002).

---

[14] For example, Fritz and Karlsson (2006: 76) note that the smaller US operations returned 'good dividends to the parent company, with an average figure of 10 per cent for 1921–1933.'

Notably, one observation does not seem to be in line with prior assumptions about the drivers of charter change and expansion, specifically that subsidiary mandates are the product of a high-quality parent–subsidiary relationships (Birkinshaw and Hood, 1998). While there is limited information about the German subsidiary of SKF, the accounts of the US subsidiary of Alfa Laval convey a picture of ongoing tension and an anxiously monitored power balance rather than a dyadic relationship characterized by an amicable, trustful and collaborative atmosphere (Åman, 2003). One cannot help getting the impression that in this case the workings of the MNC were simple and, if you so wish, 'caveman-like'. The Lavalco case does not come across as a story about sophisticated interaction and knowledge exchange across geographically dispersed units, or one of benevolent orchestration on the part of corporate headquarters. Instead, it appears to have been a story of power emanating from the ability to produce profits (Forsgren, 2008). As long as subsidiary profits were coming in they conferred independence from any type of interference from headquarters or other units of the multinational group.

Independence, in turn, especially in the strong form developed and displayed by US subsidiary management, was not seen favourably by headquarters:

> What irritated top management in Stockholm was that in addition, and after a few more successful years in the mid-1930s, labor and general cost increases led to lower and lower profitability at Lavalco. (Fritz, 1983: 205)

While profitability and organizational autonomy do not preclude the exchange of knowledge with headquarters and other units of the international network, as indeed is illustrated by the US subsidiary's early trade of manufacturing techniques against product designs, it is clear from the Lavalco case that commercial success and profitability did not naturally translate into an increasing desire to interact with and help other units of the multinational network. At least in the case of Lavalco, it rather strengthened the inclination to carry out operations according to its own preferences and ambitions.[15]

Dynamic interrelationships: The financial success of the two subsidiaries is likely to have enabled them to invest in research and development and become even more innovative, and to contribute an unusual number of new technological entries and capabilities to the corporate group. It may also have

---

[15] This observation does not discard the existence of high-quality headquarters–superstar subsidiary relationships generally, at least during selective time periods. One of the more important Swedish executives recounts SKF's entry into Brazil, a large and potentially important market: 'There we sat for three years, with no contact with Gothenburg and headquarters. When we returned home after four years and were still operating in red, we were told: "Don't feel too bad. It usually takes seven years for a factory to break even". Those were the days!' (interview with Herbert Backlund, Fritz and Karlsson, 2006: 168).

been the case that high profits made it possible for the two subsidiaries to engage in research projects where results and commercial potential were highly uncertain, creating conditions for breakthrough innovations that in the long term counterbalanced maturing technologies and intensified competition in the original fields of activity.

It appears that both SKF Germany and Alfa Laval US accumulated critical funds and resources on which the respective parents became dependent, suggesting that the subsidiaries could use the associated power to retain their autonomy over extended periods of time (Pfeffer and Salancik, 1978). Especially in the case of SKF Germany, a strong position within the multinational group also seems to have been instrumental for securing technological responsibility and mandates during periods of internal reorganization. It can be easily envisioned how, as long as profits continued to flow into the parent company, headquarters took the implicit or even explicit decision not to 'rock the boat' by insisting on enhanced levels of operational control or tighter coordination of activities among leading subsidiaries of the international network.

There indeed appears to be an intimate connection between profitability and organizational autonomy. As for Alfa Laval, Fritz (1983: 236) writes:

> In the troubled period during the end of the 1930s the previously very independent company had to get used to increasing proposals and direction from Stockholm. During the war, relationships with Stockholm became very sporadic, and as Lavalco again was able to show good results self-confidence of course grew in the United States, fuelled by military and foreign policy successes. Technical development was carried out very independently. Shortly after the end of the war, a disillusioned visitor form the Stockholm office reported: 'We really have only superficial knowledge about (and did not have it either before the war) which separator types DeLaval manufacture and their knowledge about ours is possibly even smaller.'

A similar story holds for SKF's larger manufacturing units, which have been characterized as 'extremely independent' (Fritz and Karlsson, 2006: 197):

> In terms of the organization of manufacturing and sales, the SKF companies in Germany, the UK, and the USA and Italy . . . with a total together of two-thirds of the Group employees, were run with a great deal of autonomy. As long as they turned over the agreed portion of their profits to the parent company in Göteborg, they were allowed to proceed independently. (ibid.)

For the superstar subsidiary and probably also more generally, a relatively simple story shines through—as long as profits keep coming in autonomy is secured, but periods of weak profitability invite greater interference and control from headquarters.

Once in place, the three factors of market size and munificence, profitability, and power and autonomy are likely to have worked in mutually reinforcing ways, contributing positively to the two subsidiaries' ability to create and sustain their positions as advanced subsidiaries of superstar status. In the absence of significant changes in any of the three domains, a virtuous cycle seems to have been entered, securing unusual levels of productivity in terms of technological and strategic contributions to the overall multinational group.

3.4.1. *A preliminary model*

It is of course difficult to establish any general proof of the origins and drivers of superstar subsidiaries on the basis of the two cases that have been presented. In the absence of the study of comparable cases that may display potentially different evolutionary paths, the present cases can only serve as indicative examples and sources of preliminary reflections. It is nevertheless possible to speculate about the importance of the main factors that have been identified, and specifically about the extent to which they may represent necessary and sufficient conditions for the emergence of subsidiaries that make an unusually large contribution to the technological and strategic renewal of the multinational group.

First, sheer market size and the business and technological opportunities it entails seems to be of significant importance. In both subsidiaries, there appear to have been favourable market and environmental conditions for the evolution and the upgrading of technological capabilities at the subsidiary level. At the same time, both SKF and Alfa Laval had a fair number of foreign subsidiaries in other large markets which did not attain superstar status, and therefore market size and munificence alone can only be considered a necessary but not sufficient condition for superstar subsidiaries to emerge.

As for profitability, it is probably the relative size of the contribution to the parent firm that is most important (rather than profitability as such), and in this respect both SKF's German subsidiary and Alfa Laval's US subsidiary were unmatched in their respective multinational groups. Yet, substantial profits would only be possible in relatively large markets, suggesting that large profit contributions are caused by profitable subsidiaries which are active on large markets.[16]

---

[16] In comparison, and although Alfa Laval's sales in Germany would become substantial (by 1912, sales by Bergedorfer Eisenwerk had come close to those of the Swedish units; Wohlert, 1981: 171), the German subsidiary Bergedorfer Eisenwerk from the outset proved financially weak and in relative terms was never as profitable in the early years of operation. The period following the First World War involved significant operational and financial difficulties, and, apart from a few years when modest dividends were paid to the parent company, financial support mostly flowed in the other direction. Five years of consecutive losses were recorded over the period 1929–1933. The UK subsidiary, the De Laval Chadburn Co. Ltd, was established in 1923. Although there were technological ambitions, particularly in the area of industrial separators, four years of initial losses were followed by only marginal profitability in the years 1927–1928, and the main part of the development work was shifted to the Swedish units.

Both of the observed subsidiaries were highly autonomous within their multinational groups. Yet, subsidiary autonomy was common throughout both SKF's and Alfa Laval's international organizations, as was the associated transfer of blueprints, designs, and manufacturing knowledge to various units in the most important markets. In the case of SKF, for antitrust reasons the US subsidiary was kept almost completely independent from the Swedish head-quarters for a large number of years following the Second World War. As such, autonomy does not emerge as a sufficient condition for the development of superstar status, but as indicated above it seems to be a corollary of substantial relative profits and power within the multinational network.

The three factors—market size and munificence, relative profitability, and organizational autonomy—while not sufficient drivers on their own are thus hypothesized to be collectively necessary for initiating the evolution towards superstar status. The conceptual model of Figure 3.3 suggests how the three factors must coincide and interact for a foreign subsidiary to develop superstar status, and that missing out on any of the individual factors will significantly hamper its ability to break out of the frame of the average foreign subsidiary.

It should at the same time be re-emphasized that, partly for methodological reasons, the model remains tentative. It specifically excludes from consideration a number of potentially important factors which could only be partially uncovered by the collected data, especially those connected to unforeseen environmental developments and the strategic intent and

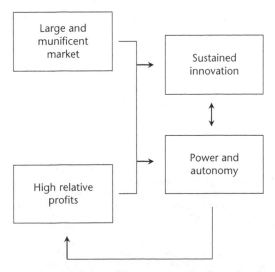

Figure 3.3. Critical drivers of superstar subsidiary development

proactiveness of subsidiary heads and local subsidiary management.[17] Indeed, and given that both SKF and Alfa Laval were established in several markets that would meet the requirements of market size and munificence (and the relative level of technological advantage and baseline degrees of autonomy would be similar across markets), there are reasons to contemplate the existence of precipitating events and developments that may have triggered the evolution towards superstar status. Particularly successful local strategies and skilled local managers, idiosyncratic institutional and political developments in the host country, and moves (or the absence thereof) by local competitors are some potential causes of supra-normal profitability that come to mind.

Another influencing factor may be the more or less fortuitous entry of highly skilled and productive engineers into foreign units, and there are indeed indications that during select periods single individuals have had a disproportionate effect on the technological development of the two foreign subsidiaries. A preliminary search and investigation into the US patents granted to SKF in Germany (including the units SKF GmbH, SKF Kugellagerfabriken GmbH, and SKF Industrial Trading and Development Company) during the peak years of 1971–1990 reveals two individuals out of a total of more than 200 who respectively were registered as inventors in 39 and 33 per cent of all patents (total of 408 patents, median number of registrations across all inventors 2). In terms of new entries recorded over the same period, one or both of the two leading inventors was associated with five out of a total of 16 new entries, or 31 per cent of the total. Comparable figures for Laval Separator Co. over the years 1921–1945 show that one lead inventor—out of a total of just under 50—was involved in 32 per cent of all patents (total of 259 patents, median number of registrations across all inventors 2), almost three times the percentage recorded by the second most prolific inventor. In terms of new entries, the leading inventor was associated with nine out of a total of 19 new entries, or 47 per cent of the total.[18] Yet, the collected information does not allow for a systematic comparison across foreign units of the two parent companies, and the role of individual inventors and other precipitating events remain open to further and more broad-based investigations.

---

[17] For example, the German subsidiary of Alfa Laval did pioneer the plate-heat-exchanger technology in the early 1930s, which (following the separator and milking machines) was to become the third 'big' product category at Alfa Laval. However, within a short time the political uncertainty surrounding the upcoming Second World War would shift technological activity back to the home country, and by 1938 both production and development of plate heat exchangers had been moved to Sweden.

[18] In SKF's German subsidiary, the review of the data further suggests that in many cases patenting activity was associated with groups of three to five inventors. Individual inventors played a much more prominent role in Alfa Laval's US subsidiary, but the observable differences may be explained by patenting policies that differ across countries and units.

3.4.2. *The demise of superstar subsidiaries*

The observed patterns of entry into new technologies by SKF Germany and Alfa Laval's US subsidiary suggest that, once attained, superstar status is not a permanent resting state. The proposed model should be seen as dynamic in the sense that individual factors may be difficult to sustain over extended periods of time and, as such, any aspirations of becoming and remaining a superstar subsidiary should be temporary. The full cycle to and from superstar status would take place over a large number of years and probably decades, as observed in the inverted U-shaped patterns of entry into new technologies indicated by the two observed subsidiaries.

The demise of a superstar subsidiary is particularly visible in the US operations of Alfa Laval, where a reduction of technological activity after the Second World War was accompanied by what appears to have been a systematic withdrawal of technological mandates to headquarters in Sweden (Zander, 1994; Zander and Zander, 1996). The starting point of the process is likely to have been a complex set of events and developments, but prolonged periods of reduced profitability of the US subsidiary seem to have been one important factor. Financial difficulties definitely appear to have caused a loss of organizational autonomy, and in all probability also affected the subsidiary's ability to sustain its historically successful investments in research and development activities. It is also possible that the once unique dynamics of the northeastern parts of the United States lost their significance for the upgrading of technology, thus contributing to the decline in the US subsidiary's technological proficiency.[19]

Overall, these developments suggest that the demise of superstar subsidiaries could be set in motion by changes in any of the three main factors identified by the conceptual model (although shifts in the size and munificence of the local market can be expected to be very long-term), triggering negative cumulative effects across the individual components. It is also possible that factors that are unaccounted for by the preliminary model, such as changes in subsidiary leadership and local subsidiary management can cause or contribute to significant changes in local innovation activity. At the same time, the observed periods of ups and downs in the present two subsidiaries may also be natural occurrences in the long-term evolution of any firm or organization, and further and more broad-based data would be necessary to

---

[19] It could be hypothesized that shifting levels of importance and innovative activity of superstar subsidiaries are interlinked with patterns of technological development in the home country units. Yet, apart from the overall geographical shift of innovative activity that took place in Alfa Laval in the post-war period, the concurrent analysis of the number of new technology entries in the two subsidiaries and their respective home country units did not reveal any clear patterns or tendencies.

fully address and explain the observed developments. It may be speculated that periods of mid-range decline in subsidiary profitability and innovation output create a local sense of urgency that effectively puts the subsidiary back on track as a main player within the multinational network.

3.4.3. *Managerial and policy implications*

From a managerial point of view, the formation of superstar subsidiaries should be perceived as something positive. The two superstar subsidiaries of SKF and Alfa Laval no doubt made a significantly positive financial and technological contribution to their respective parent groups. Despite all the complications that may be associated with the management of capable and powerful foreign subsidiaries, managers at headquarters should acknowledge their positive contribution to the technological and strategic renewal of the multinational group, and to the extent the conceptual model is correct tread carefully in terms of profit remittances and operational control. This is of course easier said than done, as management of the multinational group requires the balancing of exploration and exploitation activities, which includes consideration of the trade-offs between centralization and efficient operations and responsiveness to local conditions and customer needs (Bartlett and Ghoshal, 1989).

Against this backdrop, the opening up of potentially very large markets such as India and China provides a good opportunity to gauge how MNCs perceive the value of having superstar subsidiaries within their international network. It is easy to envision the emergence of technologically and strategically leading units in these particular markets, but that scenario would test whether after years of streamlining and integrating international operations there is still room for the relatively autonomous foreign units that were characteristic of earlier times. To the extent that the proposed model of the evolution towards superstar status is correct, it would also require the subsidiaries in these very large markets to become profitable, and given the level of competitive pressure that can be expected it is not all that certain that supra-normal profits will follow. There are also other complicating factors to be considered, for example that of different approaches to product types and associated research and development logics, but how these particular aspects may influence the emergence of superstar subsidiaries is yet to be seen.

The findings and preliminary conceptual model may also be of interest to policy makers, particularly those concerned with the positive externalities and spillovers generated by foreign subsidiaries of MNCs. One first observation would be that in many cases expectations about significant effects on local business conditions and dynamics should be moderate, as it appears that superstar subsidiaries would only rarely emerge in smaller economies. A second reflection would be that, just as in the case of headquarter managers, taxation and other measures that affect subsidiary performance should be undertaken with some caution. Creating and maintaining a dynamic industrial environment (Porter, 1990; Sölvell, Lindqvist and Ketels, 2003; Lundström and Stevenson, 2005), partly to attract foreign investments in the first place, but also to support foreign-owned subsidiaries in their further development, is also part of the policy agenda. To the extent that the current findings are representative of developments in other superstar subsidiaries, they generally emphasize the careful balance that needs to be maintained between short- and long-term gains from the subsidiary's presence in the local business environment.

3.5. Summary and conclusions

The present study has addressed the lack of attention to long-term, evolutionary developments in advanced foreign subsidiaries of the MNC. It has especially explored the origins and drivers of those foreign subsidiaries which over an extended period of time generate a significantly larger number of entries into new technologies than the average subsidiary of the MNC, and which over the long term will have a correspondingly larger influence on the MNC's technological and strategic development. These superstar subsidiaries appear to be the foreign units that are driving the technological development in the MNC and are also likely to be those that provide local markets with the most significant technological spillovers. Exploring the origins and drivers of the development of this select group of foreign subsidiaries therefore seems to be of both conceptual and practical relevance.

Even though it may be impossible to obtain a complete picture of what makes certain foreign subsidiaries significantly outperform others in the multinational network, the chapter has provided a preliminary conceptual model that outlines the driving forces and factors behind the creation of superstar subsidiaries. We have specifically highlighted the role of large and munificent markets, financially successful and profitable operations, and autonomy within the multinational group. There most likely exist additional variables that the study overlooks and which are too complex to be captured through historical studies alone. In order to confirm the current findings and suggestions, additional studies drawing upon broader and contemporary samples will be needed, controlling for national origin and an additional set of subsidiary characteristics and attributes. Any precipitating events that may set off the evolution towards superstar status would be particularly interesting targets for comparisons across foreign units displaying otherwise similar baseline conditions.

Perhaps, and as indicated by the analysis of patents and inventive activity at the level of subsidiary employees, the sources of superstar subsidiaries are connected to specific individuals whose entry into the corporation and technological contributions are difficult (although not impossible) to predict and influence. The intriguing story that emerges is one where only a small subset of all foreign subsidiaries of the MNC ever reach the advanced stages, only a limited number of these advanced subsidiaries ever manage to make significant and long-lasting contributions to the parent corporation's technological and strategic renewal, and within this limited set of units only a handful of individuals account for and explain outstanding technological and strategic performance. This, however, remains a speculative concluding note which represents but one of a broad set of still unanswered questions about the origins and evolution of advanced foreign subsidiaries of the MNC.

References

Almeida, P. and Phene, A. (2004), 'Subsidiaries and knowledge creation: The influence of the MNC and host country on innovation', *Strategic Management Journal*, 25: 847–864.

Åman, P. (2003), 'Revolution by evolution—Transforming international management in the established MNC'. Doctoral dissertation: Institute of International Business, Stockholm.

Archibugi, D. and Pianta, M. (1992), 'Specialization and size of technological activities in industrial countries: The analysis of patenting data', *Research Policy*, 21(1): 79–93.

Bartlett, C.A. and Ghoshal, S. (1989), *Managing Across Borders: The Transnational Solution*. Boston: Harvard Business School Press.

—— ——(1990), 'The multinational corporation as an interorganizational network', *Academy of Management Review*, 15(4): 603–625.

Birkinshaw, J. and Hood, N. (1998), 'Multinational subsidiary evolution: capability and charter change in foreign-owned subsidiary companies', *Academy of Management Review*, 23(4): 773–795.

——and Morrison, A.J. (1995), 'Configurations of strategy and structure in subsidiaries of multinational corporations', *Journal of International Business Studies*, 26: 729–753.

Blomkvist, K., Kappen, P. and Zander, I. (2010),'Quo vadis? The entry into new technologies in advanced foreign subsidiaries of the multinational corporation', *Journal of International Business Studies*, 41(9): 1525–1549.

Bondeson, G. et al. (1983), *Ett världsföretag växer fram: Alfa Laval 100 år*. Stockholm: Alfa Laval AB.

Cantwell, J. (1989), *Technological Innovation and Multinational Corporations*. Oxford: Basil Blackwell.

—— and Mudambi, R. (2005), 'MNE competence-creating subsidiary mandate', *Strategic Management Journal*, 26: 1109–1128.

Doz, Y. and Prahalad, C.K. (1991), 'Managing MNCs: A search for a new paradigm', *Strategic Management Journal*, 12: 145–164.

Dunning, J.H. (1994), 'Multinational enterprises and the globalization of innovatory capacity', *Research Policy*, 23: 67–88.

Feinberg, S.E. and Gupta, A.K. (2004), 'Knowledge spillovers and the assignment of R&D responsibilities to foreign subsidiaries', *Strategic Management Journal*, 25: 823–845.

Forsgren, M. (2008), *Theories of the Multinational firm: A Multidimensional Creature in the Global Economy*. Cheltenham, UK: Edward Elgar.

Fritz, M. (1983), *Ett världsföretag växer fram—Alfa-Laval 100 år, Del 2, Konsolidering och expansion*. Stockholm: Alfa Laval AB.

—— and Karlsson, B. (2006), *SKF: A Global Economy 1907–2007*. Sundbyberg: Roos Tryckerier AB.

Gårdlund, T. (1983), *Ett världsföretag växer fram—Alfa-Laval 100 år, Del 1, Förhistoria och uppbyggnad*. Stockholm: Alfa Laval AB.

Gittelman, M. (2008), 'A note on the value of patents as indicators of innovation: Implications for management research', *Academy of Management Perspectives*, 22(3): 21–27.

Gupta, A. and Govindarajan, V. (1991), 'Knowledge flows and the structure of control within multinational corporations', *Academy of Management Review*, 16(4): 768–792.

—— ——. (1994), 'Organizing for knowledge flows within MNCs', *International Business Review*, 4: 443–457.

Hagedoorn, J. and Cloodt, M. (2003), 'Measuring innovative performance: Is there an advantage in using multiple indicators?', *Research Policy*, 32: 1365–1379.

Hedlund, G. (1986), 'The hypermodern MNC—A heterarchy?', *Human Resource Management*, 25(1): 9–35.

Holm, U. and Pedersen, T. (eds) (2000), *The Emergence and Impact of MNC Centres of Excellence: A Subsidiary Perspective*. Houndmills: MacMillan Press.

Jaffe, A.B. (1986), 'Technological opportunity and spillovers of R&D: Evidence from firms' patents, profits, and market value', *American Economic Review*, 76: 984–1001.

Jarillo, J.C. and Martinez, J.I. (1990), 'Different roles for subsidiaries: The case of multinational corporations in Spain', *Strategic Management Journal*, 11: 501–512.

Johanson, J. and Vahlne, J.-E. (1977), 'The internationalization process of the firm—A model of knowledge development and increasing foreign market commitments', *Journal of International Business Studies*, 8(1): 23–32.

—— ——(1990), 'The mechanism of internationalization', *International Marketing Review*, 7(4): 11–24.

Kappen, P. (2009), 'Technological evolution in foreign subsidiaries—Among average joes, superstars and the new kids on the block'. Doctoral thesis, Uppsala University.

Kuemmerle, W. (1997), 'Building effective R&D capabilities abroad', *Harvard Business Review*, March–April: 61–70.

Lundström, A. and Stevenson, L. (2005), *Entrepreneurship Policy: Theory and Practice*. New York: Springer.

Maskell, P. and Malmberg, A. (1999), 'Localised learning and industrial competitiveness', *Cambridge Journal of Economics*, 23: 167–185.

Molero, J. and Buesa, M. (1993), 'Multinational companies and technological change: Basic traits and taxonomy of the behaviour of German industrial companies in Spain', *Research Policy*, 22: 265–278.

Mudambi, R. and Navarra, P. (2004), 'Is knowledge power? Knowledge flows, subsidiary power and rent-seeking within MNCs', *Journal of International Business Studies*, 35(5): 385–406.

Nohria, N. and Ghoshal, S. (1997), *The Differentiated Network: Organizing Multinational Corporations for Value Creation*. San Francisco: Jossey-Bass.

Pavitt, K. (1988), Uses and abuses of patent statistics. In van Raan, A.F.J. (ed.), *Handbook of Quantitative Studies of Science and Technology*. North-Holland: Elsevier Science.

Pearce, R. (1989), *The Internationalisation of Research and Development by Multinational Enterprises*. New York: MacMillan.

——and Papanastassiou, M. (1999), 'Overseas R&D and the strategic evolution of MNEs: Evidence from laboratories in the UK', *Research Policy*, 28(1): 23–41.

—— ——(2009), *The Strategic Development of Multinationals: Subsidiaries and Innovation*. New York: Palgrave Macmillan.

Pfeffer, J. and Salancick, G. (1978), *The External Control of Organizations*. New York: Harper and Row.

Porter, M.E. (1990), *The Competitive Advantage of Nations*. New York: The Free Press (2nd edition 1998, New York: MacMillan Business).

Ronstadt, R.C. (1978), 'International R&D: The establishment and evolution of research and development abroad by seven U.S. multinationals', *Journal of International Business Studies*, 9(1): 7–24.

Schmookler, J. (1950), 'The interpretation of patent statistics', *Journal of the Patent Office Society*, 32(2): 123–146.

Sölvell, Ö., Lindqvist, G. and Ketels, C. (2003), *The Cluster Initiative Greenbook*. Stockholm: Ivory Tower AB.

Taggart, J.H. (1997), 'Autonomy and procedural justice: A framework for evaluating subsidiary strategy', *Journal of International Business Studies*, 28: 51–76.

US Department of Commerce (1992), *General Information Concerning Patents*. Washington, DC: US Government Printing Office.

Vernon, R. (1966), 'International investment and international trade in the product cycle', *Quarterly Journal of Economics*, 80(2): 190–207.

Wohlert, K. (1982), *Framväxten av svenska multinationella företag—en fallstudie mot bakgrund av direktinvesteringsteorin Alfa-Laval och separatorindutrin 1876–1914*. Uppsala: Almqvist and Wiksell.

Yamin, M. (2002), Subsidiary entrepreneurship and the advantage of multinationality. In Havila, V., Forsgren, M. and Håkansson, H. (eds), *Critical Perspectives on Internationalization*. Amsterdam: Pergamon.

Zander, I. (1994), 'The tortoise evolution of the multinational corporation—Foreign technological activity in Swedish multinational firms 1890–1990'. Doctoral dissertation: Stockholm School of Economics.

——(2002), 'The formation of international innovation networks in the multinational corporation: An evolutionary perspective', *Industrial and Corporate Change*, 11(2): 327–353.

——and Zander, U. (1996), 'The oscillating multinational firm—Alfa Laval in the period 1890–1990'. In Björkman, I. and Forsgren, M. (eds), *The Nature of the Multinational Firm—Nordic Contributions to International Business Research*. Copenhagen: Copenhagen Business School Press.

4

Knowledge Accession Strategies and the Spatial Organization of R&D

John Cantwell and Feng Zhang

4.1. Introduction

The geographically dispersed organization of multinational corporations (MNCs) has attracted considerable attention over the past a couple of decades. Since Bartlett and Ghoshal (1989) described the organizational structure of MNCs as a 'differentiated network', various strands of literature have suggested significant attitude changes in the relationship between the headquarters and overseas subsidiaries of the equivalent MNC. A variety of terminologies have been used to describe MNCs to incorporate such attitude changes, for instance 'interorganizational network' (Ghoshal and Bartlett, 1990), 'network-based MNC' (Zander, 1998), 'federative MNC' (Andersson, Forsgren and Holm, 2007). In particular, the parent-driven view has been largely abandoned in reference to organizing, especially, locationally dispersed competence-creating activities within the MNC. In addition to the advantages of multinationality that have been extensively discussed in previous literature, such as the flexibility and therefore reduced risks to shifting production and sales across locations as suggested by the real-option theory of MNCs (see Li and Rugman, 2007 for a detailed review), increased economies of scale (Chandler, 1990), or the ability to exchange threats (Graham, 1978), more recently interests in MNCs' ability to integrate related knowledge have emerged (Zander, 1998), the interest in which is specifically associated with MNCs' spatial organization of R&D.

As has been documented, new knowledge generation is generally a process of combining current and acquired knowledge or recombining current knowledge (Kogut and Zander, 1992). In the former case, the ability to create or access new technological knowledge has become vital for the survival and growth of firms, given increasing knowledge complexity. Firms may increasingly have to acquire new knowledge from external sources (Chesbrough, 2003) in order to complement and support their own in-house R&D. As a result, the geographically dispersed organization of MNCs may become a strategic asset by providing channels to acquire competitive capabilities in various host locations. However, this is not to argue that external knowledge sources are only accessed for new knowledge; rather, firms might sometimes draw upon a wider range of existing knowledge that originated from a greater variety of external knowledge sources. It has also been suggested that some duplication of existing knowledge, by facilitating the recombination of existing knowledge in new ways among the geographically dispersed sub-units of an MNC, would generate potential advantages of flexibility and increase the benefits of internal knowledge exchange (Zander, 1998).

As we have argued elsewhere, firms increasingly need and are able to access technologically distant knowledge, namely knowledge in quite different technological areas, given their existing level of technological expertise (Cantwell, Noonan, and Zhang, 2008). While the significance of technological knowledge accumulation for the success of a firm has been emphasized for almost a century (Schumpeter, 1939; Cantwell and Santangelo, 2000), in a world of increasing knowledge complexity the ability of a firm to integrate technologically diversified knowledge through combination and recombination positively affects the performance of the firm. Thus, an MNC's spatial organization of R&D can positively influence the performance of the MNC by increasing the potential for accessing combinable knowledge. However, as yet we have little evidence about whether an MNC's ability to integrate technologically diversified knowledge and its ability to access geographically dispersed knowledge would work complementarily and favorably influence the performance of the MNC.

This study seeks to shed some light on differences of innovative performance at a corporate level among large industrial MNCs by simultaneously investigating the technological content and the geographical pattern of their technological knowledge accumulation. In particular, we will look at their knowledge accumulation from geographically dispersed sources, as well as their knowledge accumulation across technological fields. It is worth stressing that we do not intend to take a parent-driven view of MNCs by focusing on corporate-level innovative performance considered as a unitary entity. Rather, since competence-creating activities have been increasingly geographically dispersed as a result of subsidiary-level initiatives or independent entrepreneurship within at least some of today's MNCs, the spatial organization and reach of the individual sub-units of MNCs becomes an important, yet understudied, factor in explaining firm heterogeneity in the same industry.

The design of current study seeks to address this issue. Moreover, we aware that there are other types of knowledge and performance indicators, although this study focuses on technological knowledge and thereby the innovative performance of firms as such.

The empirical analysis employs patents granted to the world's largest firms in the electrical equipment (EE) industry by the US Patent and Trademark Office (USPTO) from 2001 to 2003. We chose this industry, because firms in the EE industry are among those which have the highest propensity to patent, and patent-citation data allow us to operationalize the concept of knowledge accumulation across technological and geographical boundaries that are our focus of attention here. To measure the innovative performance of each MNC relative to other such firms, we used the accumulated number of patents normalized by the MNC's annual revenue. The revenue data is from *Fortune* magazine and the accounting statements of each MNC. We have found that beyond a certain threshold, the higher a firm's ability to integrate technologically diversified knowledge, the better the firm's innovative performance. Meanwhile, a firm's ability to access geographically dispersed knowledge might initially enhance the firm's performance, but a positive effect may be replaced by a negative effect if the firm pushes too hard to access too wide a geographical dispersion of knowledge, namely to access knowledge across many different geographical locations. Moreover, this negative effect is reinforced if a firm tries to access geographically dispersed sources for technologically diversified knowledge. This result may suggest a potential tradeoff between these two types of capabilities of firms. Moreover, we found that EE firms with broader technological knowledge portfolios, which we have termed 'generalists', have on average enjoyed a better performance than firms with a narrower technological knowledge base, namely 'specialists'. This result suggests that the scope of firms' current knowledge bases might influence their future innovative performance, which is consistent with our expectation regarding firms' performance in the current knowledge economy. The findings of this study generate important insights on how the accession and utilization of geographically dispersed technological knowledge affect the innovative performance at corporate level. Also, this study contributes to the better understanding of firm heterogeneity in the structures of international knowledge accumulation within the same industry.

The next section reviews the previous literature and develops hypotheses. Data and methods are described in the third section, followed by the empirical results. The last section discusses findings and implications.

4.2. Theoretical development

Hymer emphasized the desire of firms to strengthen their market power in explaining the international expansion of firms (Dunning, 2001). In conventional MNCs, market power was supposed to be generated initially in the home market of an MNC and then be transferred to foreign markets through foreign direction investment (FDI). Internalization theory explains FDI by comparing the cross-border transaction costs within firms in general and that in arm-length markets (Buckley and Casson, 2002). Evolutionary theorists agree that firms may have higher efficiency than markets, but such efficiency may be derived more from the fact that firms provide a social community of voluntaristic action, instead of high transaction costs in markets as suggested by internalization theory (Kogut and Zander, 1992). One of the key characteristics of the MNC is the cross-border transaction of tangible and intangible assets within the same organization, on the advantages of which the discussion about the potential benefits of being an MNC has been focused. For instance, real-option theory argues that MNCs might enjoy the flexibility to shift production across locations, and reduce risks through sales in different markets (Zander, 1998; Li and Rugman, 2007); moreover, participating in global markets allows MNCs to enjoy increased economies of scale (Chandler, 1990), as well as the ability to exchange threats with major global competitors and so enhance their strategic security (Graham, 1978). However, given the parent-driven attitude adopted in the conventional analysis, the literature was largely limited to the advantages of internationalizing production or sales function of MNCs (motivated market-seeking, resource-seeking, or efficiency-seeking FDI), while some strategically important functions, such as R&D, were often supposed to be highly centralized within the headquarters of MNCs.

The 1980s witnessed the start of a co-evolution of many MNCs and host locations (Nelson and Winter, 1982; Nelson, 1995), a process which is still going on today. One important consequence is that some overseas subsidiaries have increasingly evolved to take on a more strategic role and participate in locally competence-creating innovative activities that extend the profile of competencies of their respective MNC groups (Birkinshaw, Hood, and Jonsson, 1998; Zander, 1999; Frost, 2001; Zander, 2002). In particular, overseas subsidiaries may generate new knowledge for their individual parent through integrating their current knowledge and the acquired knowledge from host environment (Birkinshaw et al., 1998; Andersson, Forsgren, and Holm, 2002; Frost, Birkinshaw, and Ensign, 2002). Their geographically dispersed sub-units thereby become one of the advantages of MNCs by providing channels to access idiosyncratic knowledge in many host locations. Moreover, the duplication of existing knowledge among the geographically dispersed sub-units of an MNC may also generate potential advantages of flexibility and the benefits of internal knowledge exchange for the MNC (Zander, 1998). In other words, their geographically dispersed organization allows MNCs to capture more benefits from their combinative capabilities than domestic firms through synthesizing and applying current and acquired knowledge (Kogut and Zander, 1992).

Consequently, greater interest has emerged in the advantages of MNCs to integrate knowledge, which may incorporate two interrelated aspects, namely the capability to integrate technologically distant knowledge (Patel and Pavitt, 1997; Caminati, 2006), and the capability to integrate geographically dispersed knowledge (Dunning and Lundan, 1998; Tallman and Phene, 2007). The former might be a more generic pressure for firms, given that the complexity of technological innovation in general is increasing. In particular, the number of technologies required per product is increasing in many industries, as a result, for example, of the shift from mechanical to electro-mechanical to electronic systems in the automobile industry (Miller, 1994; Granstrand, Patel, and Pavitt, 1997). In the pharmaceutical industry the rise of biotechnology and ICT applications have been critical, as well as the role of optics and laser technologies for medical instruments (Nightingale, 2000). Therefore, firms increasingly have to deal with much more difficult and multidisciplinary technological problems. It has been argued that the technological complexity is one of the major reasons for firms to access external knowledge (Cantwell et al., 2008). Although knowledge accumulation across organizational boundaries (or the extent of embeddedness of firms in a supporting environment) is not our focus in this current study, it is reasonable to argue that firms may enjoy a better performance if they can incorporate an increasing technological complexity in their competence creation. The geographically dispersed organization of MNCs may increase their opportunity to access technologically diversified knowledge in various host locations. However, previous literature has mainly focused on subsidiary-level knowledge accumulation, especially the combination of technologically distant knowledge, for instance, the sourcing of information and communication technologies by the subsidiaries of pharmaceutical firms. To what extent the performance of geographically dispersed competence creation affects the performance of the MNC as a whole has not yet been investigated. Consequently, we expect that the higher the overall ability of an MNC to integrate technologically diversified knowledge the better the corporate-level innovative performance of the MNC.

Hypothesis 1: The ability to draw upon technologically diversified knowledge on average is positively associated with a better innovative performance at corporate-level.

The ability to access geographically dispersed knowledge is more specific to MNCs than other firms. The significance of locational advantages for MNCs has been argued for decades, for instance in the typologies of FDI (Dunning, 1993; Kuemmerle, 1999). Meanwhile, many host countries have also evolved. In other words, at least some MNCs today not only search for strategically important long-established assets from host locations, but they also enjoy broader options to contribute to a process of change within locations, as many host countries, even some developing economies, have been upgrading their capabilities. While knowledge spillovers are often largely localized (Jaffe, Trajtenberg, and Henderson, 1993), the organization of firms may help to overcome some of the difficulties in geographically distant knowledge transfer by providing a common social community (Kogut and Zander, 1992). Therefore, MNCs have a greater chance of accessing and integrating knowledge across geographically distant locations where they have sub-units in those locations. In the current knowledge economy with ever increasing knowledge interconnectedness, the ability to access technologically diversified knowledge in different host locations through geographically dispersed organization has become a potential advantage of MNCs, and therefore may improve their innovative performance.

Hypothesis 2: The ability to access geographically dispersed technological knowledge on average is positively associated with a better innovative performance at corporate-level.

We still have little evidence about whether an MNC's ability to integrate technologically diversified knowledge and its ability to access geographically dispersed knowledge tend to work together complementarily and so favorably influence the overall technological performance of the MNC. On the one hand, given our reasoning above, one might argue that the need for firms to integrate more technologically diversified knowledge may encourage them to search across more geographically dispersed knowledge sources, given that the focus of specialization in knowledge creation varies considerably across different locations. On the other hand, it has been argued that the headquarters of a federative MNC might face a potential dilemma, namely that 'externally embedded subsidiaries can provide access to a variety of competencies, but they may also reduce the subsidiaries' interest in contributing to the overall performance of the MNC' (Andersson et al., 2007). The rent-seeking behaviour of subsidiaries (Mudambi and Navarra, 2004) implies a similar idea. This constraint upon the capacity of the MNC group as a whole to capitalize upon both technological and geographic diversity simultaneously may be reinforced by the greater difficulty inherent in combining knowledge sources across both geographic and technological space at the same time. In other words, the improved capabilities within the spatial organization of R&D may still have its limitations in terms of enhancing overall corporate-level performance at an international level. This study seeks to shed some light on this issue by testing the effects of the interaction between a firm's ability to integrate technologically diversified knowledge and its ability to access geographically dispersed knowledge on corporate-level innovative performance. Given the possibility of either argument above, for the time being our third hypothesis is as follows:

> *Hypothesis 3: The ability to access geographically dispersed technological knowledge, which is also technologically diversified, on average is positively associated with a better innovative performance at corporate level.*

4.3. Data and methods

Since firms in the electrical equipment industry are among those which have the highest propensity to patent, we use patents granted to the world's largest firms in the EE industry by the US Patent and Trademark Office (USPTO) from 2001 to 2003. We extracted 82,435 patents, invented by 66 EE firms from 12 countries and areas. In addition, *Fortune* and the accounting statements of firms were used to collect their annual revenue for the year 2002. With citing patents as the reference category, we examined the pattern of the patents they cite, as an indicator of the technological knowledge sources on which they have drawn. The citation records of patents to earlier patents allow us to measure whether, and if so to what extent, firms have drawn upon knowledge across technological and geographical boundaries. A total of 513,017 pairs of citing and cited patents were extracted for regression analysis.[1]

There has been a historical discussion about the advantages and disadvantages of using patent and patent-citation data (see Cantwell, 2006, for a detailed review). One concern that may be relevant to the current study is whether patent citations could represent real technological knowledge flows (Griliches, 1990; Alcacer and Gittelman, 2006). Several studies have showed that patent citations are a reasonable although 'noisy' proxy measure for knowledge flows (Jaffe, Trajtenberg, and Fogarty, 2000; Duguet and Macgarvie, 2005). More importantly, in this chapter we are interested in the change in the structure of the patterns of knowledge accumulation over time. By the term 'knowledge accumulation' in this chapter, we mean the use or incorporation of some specific prior technological knowledge within some subsequent novel contribution to knowledge. In other words, in general new knowledge combines and builds upon certain received wisdoms or prior states of the art. Note that this conceptualization of how knowledge is

---

[1] Only cited patents from 1963 onwards are included in the current analysis.

gradually combined and developed into new forms takes an objective rather than a subjective perspective on the received patterns of knowledge-sourcing or knowledge-accumulation, in which inventors need not themselves be aware of the ultimate point of origin of the sources on which they build.

4.4. Descriptive statistics

We employed records of patent data over a ten-year period to illustrate the change in the structure of knowledge accumulation of *EE* firms over time. We divided all the pairwise citations into four categories, namely those that were intra-technology-field and intra-class, intra-technology-field but inter-class, inter-technological-field and intra-CEMT, and inter-CEMT. The 56 technological fields considered are derived from an appropriate combination of the classes and sub-classes of the US patent class system. In addition, a more aggregate-level classification of a broad range of Chemical, Electrical, Mechanical, and Transport technologies (CEMT) is constructed based on a further grouping of technology fields. Table 4.1 illustrates the importance of each category in firms' knowledge accumulation over time. Each line in Table 4.1 adds up to 100 per cent. Whereas the first two columns, namely intra-class and intra-technological-field citations, still dominate the overall citation pattern as they did historically, the inter-technological-field and inter-CEMT knowledge accumulation (the last two columns) increased over the ten-year period. In other words, increasingly *EE* firms source knowledge from more distant technological areas. We further identified three geographical sources of technological knowledge, namely home country, host country, or a third country, by comparing the geographical locations of the inventors of pairwise citing and cited patents. Table 4.2 shows that the home countries of firms continued to play a dominant but slightly decreasing role in the knowledge

Table 4.1. Cross-technological-category citations over time (all patents)

Year	Intra-tech & intra-class (%)	Intra-tech & inter-class (%)	Inter-tech & intra-CEMT (%)	Inter-CEMT (%)
1996	38.83	27.68	19.55	13.94
1997	36.98	28.71	19.74	14.57
1998	36.13	28.81	20.72	14.34
1999	37.30	27.92	20.76	14.02
2000	37.61	25.10	21.93	15.36
2001	37.68	24.48	21.76	16.08
2002	37.42	22.87	22.25	17.46
2003	37.60	21.02	22.42	18.96
2004	37.91	20.48	23.18	18.43
2005	37.25	19.06	24.96	18.73
Change	−1.58	−8.62	5.41	4.79

Table 4.2. Cross-geographical-boundary citations over time (all patents)

Year	Home country (%)	Host country (%)	Third countries (%)
1996	49.20	5.76	45.04
1997	48.97	6.83	44.20
1998	45.74	7.48	46.78
1999	43.50	9.49	47.01
2000	43.54	9.45	47.01
2001	44.08	7.95	47.97
2002	43.80	7.64	48.56
2003	44.62	7.67	47.71
2004	44.19	8.20	47.61
2005	45.50	7.15	47.35
Change	−3.70	1.39	2.31

accumulation of *EE* firms. Correspondingly, international knowledge sources, namely host and third-country knowledge, have slightly increased their contribution over time. *EE* firms in this study have continued to draw most heavily upon knowledge from their home country of origin, although this of course reflects the fact that most of the (citing) patents of an MNC group are still generated by the parent company. Although host countries contribute less than 10 per cent of the total knowledge accumulation of *EE* firms, this category has been increasing over time, which is consistent with the emergence of competence-creating subsidiaries in many large MNCs since 1980s.

We included both parent-invented and subsidiary-invented patents in the calculation above. A dominant share of parent-invented patents in the overall patenting portfolio of *EE* firms will create a tendency for technological knowledge to be sourced from their home country, given the localization of knowledge flows. Therefore, we divided citing patents into two categories, namely parent-invented and subsidiary-invented patents. It has been shown elsewhere that, at least for most technology leaders, the home-country headquarters has been and remains the single most important source and centre of knowledge generation (Cantwell, 2006). Table 4.3 shows that although the share of parent-invented patents has been decreasing over time, they still continue to dominate the technological profile of *EE* firms, accounting for over 80 per cent of patent invention. On the other hand, the contribution of overseas subsidiaries in terms of patent generation increased over the ten-year period, which is consistent with the view that the overseas subsidiaries of MNCs are increasingly taking responsibility for competence-creating activities (Bartlett and Ghoshal, 1986).

Given the differences between parent-invented and subsidiary-invented patents identified above, Tables 4.4 and 4.5 further investigate their knowledge-accumulation pattern across technological and geographical boundaries (those illustrated in Tables 4.1 and 4.2 for all patents). Table 4.4 shows that both parent-invented and subsidiary-invented patents have increasingly

Table 4.3. Shares of parent-/subsidiary-invented patents (patent-level)

Year	Parent-invented	Subsidiary-invented
1996	86.28	13.72
1997	84.07	15.93
1998	82.57	17.43
1999	80.05	19.95
2000	79.94	20.06
2001	81.57	18.43
2002	80.18	19.82
2003	80.85	19.15
2004	80.19	19.81
2005	80.76	19.24
Change	−5.52	5.52

Table 4.4a. Cross-technological-category citations of parent-invented patents

Year	Intra-tech & intra-class (%)	Intra-tech & inter-class (%)	Inter-tech & intra-CEMT (%)	Inter-CEMT (%)
1996	38.58	27.67	19.53	14.22
1997	37.09	28.43	19.55	14.93
1998	36.78	27.88	21.02	14.32
1999	37.33	26.91	21.21	14.55
2000	37.72	24.51	21.86	15.91
2001	37.64	23.87	22.13	16.36
2002	37.22	22.49	22.69	17.60
2003	36.81	20.94	22.66	19.59
2004	36.55	20.89	23.51	19.05
2005	36.69	19.17	25.06	19.08
Change	−1.89	−8.50	5.53	4.86

tended to cite knowledge from technologically distant areas, which is consistent with the results in Table 4.1. The comparison of Tables 4.4a and 4.4b shows that the knowledge structure of parent-invented and that of subsidiary-invented patents are similar in terms of utilizing cross-technological category knowledge. While the intra-class category has the highest single share among all categories for both parent-invented and subsidiary-invented patents, knowledge sourcing within individual technological fields dominates the overall structure of knowledge accumulation. In particular, the first two columns, namely 'intra-tech and intra-class' and 'intra-tech and inter-class', together could be defined as intra-technological-field knowledge accumulation, which counts for over 50 per cent of annual knowledge sourcing of the parent or subsidiaries of *EE* firms. This finding confirms that innovation is typically an incremental or technologically localized process, which relies on the use or incorporation of previous knowledge within the same domain as the field in which new contribution is being created.

Table 4.4b. Cross-technological-category citations of subsidiary-invented patents

Year	Intra-tech & intra-class (%)	Intra-tech & inter-class (%)	Inter-tech & intra-CEMT (%)	Inter-CEMT (%)
1996	40.37	27.77	19.70	12.16
1997	36.40	30.18	20.71	12.71
1998	33.03	33.23	19.29	14.45
1999	37.20	31.98	18.95	11.87
2000	37.18	27.47	22.20	13.15
2001	37.85	27.17	20.10	14.88
2002	38.22	24.41	20.50	16.87
2003	40.93	21.34	21.40	16.33
2004	43.46	18.84	21.86	15.84
2005	39.62	18.59	24.55	17.24
Change	−0.75	−9.18	4.85	5.08

Table 4.5a. Cross-geographical-boundary citations of parent-invented patents

Year	Home country (%)	Third countries (%)
1996	53.97	46.03
1997	54.56	45.44
1998	51.80	48.20
1999	50.75	49.25
2000	50.91	49.09
2001	50.88	49.12
2002	51.07	48.93
2003	51.57	48.43
2004	51.30	48.70
2005	52.57	47.43
Change	−1.40	1.40

Table 4.5 reports the cross-geographical-boundary citation patterns of patent-invented and subsidiary-invented patents. Since the home and host countries of parent company are the same, the citations of parent-invented patents only have two geographical sources, namely home country, or third countries (namely all foreign countries) (see Table 4.5a). It seems that parent-invented patents have been evenly utilizing technological knowledge from local (namely home-country) and international (namely third-country) sources. Table 4.5b shows that subsidiary-invented patents tend to mainly cite knowledge sources in the host location of the subsidiary (over 37 per cent) and third countries (over 37 per cent). Since the headquarters remains the most important knowledge generation centre within an MNC (Cantwell, 2006), we expected that the home country of a subsidiary would be one of the major knowledge sources for the subsidiary. Although we did not distinguish the internal and external knowledge accumulation of firms in this study, the

Table 4.5b. Cross-geographical-boundary citations of subsidiary-invented patents

Year	Home country (%)	Host country (%)	Third countries (%)
1996	19.14	42.00	38.86
1997	19.48	42.84	37.68
1998	17.04	42.91	40.05
1999	14.39	47.59	38.02
2000	14.14	47.12	38.74
2001	13.97	43.11	42.92
2002	14.37	38.55	47.08
2003	15.25	40.05	44.70
2004	15.42	41.40	43.18
2005	15.80	37.17	47.03
Change	−3.34	−4.83	8.17

column 'home country' in Table 4.5b seems to suggest that home-country knowledge sources are less important than other sources in the overall knowledge accumulation of most subsidiaries, and that the importance of home-country knowledge sources has been decreasing over time. Moreover, while we expected that overseas subsidiaries would increasingly use local knowledge sources in their individual host location, as suggested by previous literature (Birkinshaw and Hood, 1998), interestingly the 'host country' category in Table 4.5b, which represents the local knowledge sourcing of overseas subsidiaries, has been decreasing. In other words, the results suggest that overseas subsidiaries of *EE* firms increasingly access knowledge sources in international locations (namely the 'third countries' of a subsidiary represent international locations for the subsidiary). The advances in communication technologies and the catching-up of many developing countries in electronics fields might partly explain such a trend.

To achieve a better understanding of the heterogeneity of firms within the same industry, we divided *EE* firms in the current study into two categories, namely generalists and specialists. We calculated the dispersion of each firm's technological knowledge creation across 56 technological fields. In particular, we employed an RTA index to measure a firm's technological expertise in each technological field.

$$RTA_{ij} = \left(P_{ij} / \sum_i P_{ij} \right) / \left(\sum_j P_{ij} / \sum_{ij} P_{ij} \right) \tag{1}$$

where P_{ij} is the number of patents of firm i in field j. We then calculated the diversification of each firm's RTA distribution of activity across 56 technological fields:

$$D_i = \mu_i / \sigma_i \tag{2}$$

Table 4.6a. Cross-technological-category citations of generalist-invented patents

Year	Intra-tech & intra-class (%)	Intra-tech & inter-class (%)	Inter-tech & intra-CEMT (%)	Inter-CEMT (%)
1996	41.08	25.50	18.61	14.81
1997	38.96	26.12	19.34	15.58
1998	37.20	27.84	19.67	15.29
1999	40.01	25.25	20.15	14.59
2000	40.47	22.97	21.43	15.13
2001	41.34	22.57	20.07	16.02
2002	39.93	22.61	19.89	17.57
2003	39.09	20.33	20.42	20.16
2004	40.29	19.83	20.64	19.24
2005	39.46	18.99	22.28	19.27
Change	−1.62	−6.51	3.67	4.46

Table 4.6b. Cross-technological-category citations of specialist-invented patents

Year	Intra-tech & intra-class (%)	Intra-tech & inter-class (%)	Inter-tech & intra-CEMT (%)	Inter-CEMT (%)
1996	36.03	30.40	20.73	12.84
1997	34.83	31.52	20.17	13.48
1998	35.01	29.82	21.82	13.35
1999	34.93	30.26	21.30	13.51
2000	35.25	26.86	22.34	15.55
2001	34.55	26.12	23.21	16.12
2002	34.99	23.12	24.54	17.35
2003	36.19	21.67	24.32	17.82
2004	35.93	21.03	25.32	17.72
2005	35.52	19.11	27.06	18.31
Change	−0.51	−11.29	6.33	5.47

where μ^i denotes the mean of each firm's RTAs across 56 technology fields, and σ^i represents the standard deviation of the firm's RTAs across 56 technology fields. A high D index of a firm indicates that the firm has distributed its knowledge accumulation efforts over many different technological fields. Consequently, a firm is defined as a generalist if the firm's D is larger than the mean of all firms' D index; otherwise, a firm is defined as a specialist.

Tables 4.6a and 4.6b reproduce the breakdown of Table 4.1 for generalists and specialists, respectively. The first category, namely 'intra-tech and intra-class' knowledge, dominates the knowledge accumulation of both generalists and specialists. However, the rising share of the last two columns in the table, namely 'inter-tech' and 'inter-CEMT', suggest that both generalists and specialists increasingly tend to integrate technologically complex knowledge in their innovations.

Tables 4.7a and 4.7b show the knowledge-accumulation pattern across geographical boundaries for generalists and specialists. The results show that at a group level both generalists and specialists tend to use mainly knowledge

Table 4.7a. Cross-geographical-boundary citations generalist-invented patents

Year	Home country (%)	Host country (%)	Third countries (%)
1996	50.49	4.06	45.45
1997	50.52	4.68	44.80
1998	47.25	5.43	47.32
1999	44.77	6.42	48.81
2000	43.19	7.59	49.22
2001	41.51	7.34	51.15
2002	41.65	6.74	51.61
2003	42.60	7.28	50.12
2004	39.76	8.78	51.46
2005	40.30	7.98	51.72
Change	−10.19	3.92	6.27

Table 4.7b. Cross-geographical-boundary citations of specialist-invented patents

Year	Home country (%)	Host country (%)	Third countries (%)
1996	47.59	7.87	44.54
1997	47.29	9.16	43.55
1998	44.17	9.62	46.21
1999	42.38	12.18	45.44
2000	43.82	10.99	45.19
2001	46.28	8.46	45.26
2002	45.88	8.52	45.60
2003	46.53	8.04	45.43
2004	47.90	7.72	44.38
2005	49.58	6.50	43.92
Change	1.99	−1.37	−0.62

sources from their home country and third countries, which echoes the findings in Table 4.2. While specialists have slightly increased their reliance on knowledge sources in their respective home countries, generalists have reduced their reliance by about 10 per cent over the ten-year period. This finding suggests that the technological portfolio of home countries may not be able to support the increasingly broadened technological scope of *EE* firms with expertise across a full range of diversified technological fields. In other words, generalists might face higher pressure than specialists to explore knowledge sources in diversified international locations to maintain their technological competitiveness. On the other hand, since this study focuses on the world's largest *EE* firms, which mainly originate from the global 'centres of excellence' of the *EE* industry, such as the USA, Japan, Germany, and Taiwan, these centres also attracted considerable foreign investment in the *EE* and related industries. In other words, the home countries of the leading *EE* firms normally have high levels of technological expertise in *EE*-related areas, so that specialists with their more focused technological knowledge accumulation seem to be able to continue to draw upon this

Table 4.8. Share of parent-/subsidiary-invented patents for generalists and specialists

Types of firm	Origin of inventions	Percent
Specialists	Parent	40.58
	Subsidiary	8.39
Generalists	Parent	41.45
	Subsidiary	9.58
Total		100

kind of specialized knowledge pool in their individual home countries over time.

Table 4.8 further breaks down parent-/subsidiary-invented patents for generalists and specialists. There is no significant difference between generalists and specialists in terms of the number of parent-/subsidiary-invented patents. Tables 4.7 and 4.8 together suggest that over time the knowledge structure of generalists in the *EE* industry may become more distinctive in contrast to that of specialists, and vice versa. The distinction is not attributable to internal organizational restructuring as such, since Table 4.8 shows that generalists and specialists are not significantly different in terms of the overall degree to which they decentralize competence-creating activities to their subsidiaries; rather, the distinction may arise more from the different geographical pattern of knowledge accumulation (the range of sources upon which new knowledge is built) in generalists and specialists, as suggested in Tables 4.7a and 4.7b.

4.5. Econometrical models

Given the nature of the patent data that we are using in the current study, we constructed variables to test our hypotheses using regression models. The dependent variable of this study is the innovative performance of a firm. It is measured in the following way:

$$\text{Performance}_i = \text{Number of Patents}_i/\text{Sales}_i \tag{3}$$

where 'Performance$_i$' is the innovative performance of firm i, 'Number of Patents$_i$' is the total number of patents invented by firm i from 2001 to 2003, and 'Sales$_i$' is the annual revenue of firm i in 2002. It is worth emphasizing that although we limited our analysis only to the world's largest *EE* firms, they still differ significantly in terms of firm size. Since we used those patents invented between 2001 and 2003 by the *EE* firms in our econometrical models to avoid issues associated with significant fluctuations in the annual number of patents granted to a firm, we employed each firm's sales revenue in 2002, the mid-year, to normalize for firm size. In other words, the denominator in equation (3) above is simply a control for firm size. Since the dependent variable used in this study is continuous, we employed an OLS regression technique.

To measure the knowledge sourcing across technological boundaries, we utilized a diversification index:

$$DIV_i = \mu_i/\sigma_i \tag{4}$$

where DIV_i is the diversification index of the knowledge sources cited by each citing patent i, μ_i denotes the mean of the shares of cited patents across 56 technology fields for each citing patent i, and σ_i represents the standard deviation of the shares of cited patents across 56 technology fields for each citing patent i. We then calculated the average DIV of each firm over the studied period. Because the DIV index is the reciprocal of coefficient of variation (CV), distributions with larger DIV values have higher-variance across fields than distributions with lower DIV, which is to say that the more complex the pattern of knowledge accumulation on which a technology draws, the higher is its DIV index. We also calculated a squared DIV to measure the potential non-linear relationship between a firm's ability to integrate technologically diversified knowledge and its innovative performance.

We also employed an equivalent dispersion index to measure the geographical dispersion of technological knowledge sourcing. Instead of measuring the dispersion of knowledge sources across technological fields, in this case we measure the dispersion of knowledge sources across geographical locations:

$$DIS_i = \mu_i/\sigma_i \tag{5}$$

where DIS_i is the geographical dispersion index of the knowledge sources cited by the citing patent i, μ_i denotes the mean of the shares of cited patents across 62 geographical locations for each citing patent i, and σ_i represents the standard deviation of the shares of cited patents across 62 geographical locations for citing patent i. We then calculated the average DIS of each firm. We further include a squared DIS to measure a potential non-linear relationship.

To test H3, we included an interaction between the DIV and DIS indices in our models. Moreover, following the approach to firm heterogeneity taken above, we divided *EE* firms into two categories, namely generalists and specialists. A dummy variable is included in statistical models to control for firm heterogeneity of this kind within the *EE* industry. The variable (*G*) equals one if a firm is classified as a generalist; and zero, otherwise. Finally, we controlled for the average technological advantages of the home and host countries of citing patents in their patenting fields. The technological advantage of a country is measured by the patenting share of the country in each technological field using USPTO patent data of the world's largest firms from 1996 to 2005. We then calculated the mean share for the home country and relevant host countries of each firm across its patenting fields. While the technological advantages of a country may affect the likelihood of firms sourcing knowledge from that country, the overall worldwide geographical distribution of knowledge in a technological field might also affect the pattern of knowledge sourcing. Therefore, we further controlled for the geographic dispersion of patent shares across all countries for each technological field using the same data, and for each firm created a weighted average dispersion across the fields in which it was active.

4.6. Statistical results

Table 4.9 reports the two-tailed Pearson correlation matrix for all the variables. Although this study focuses on the world's largest EE firms, examining the distribution of our dependent variable shows that there are significant variations among firms in terms of their innovative performance. Control variables measuring the technological advantages of home and host countries are significantly correlated. This may be due to the fact that the home and host countries of parent-invented patents are the same country, so we only include one of these two controls in a regression model at a time. Moreover, the control variable measuring the relevant host country's technological advantages is highly but negatively correlated with the independent variable measuring the geographical dispersion of knowledge sources (namely DIS). This result seems to suggest that firms tend to limit the locations of their knowledge searching if the host locations of the firm have strong technological advantages.

Table 4.10 reports the statistical results of regression models with independent variables constructed by employing all the 82,435 patents. All the models are statistically significant. Model 1 includes only the simplest measures of independent variables. The positively significant coefficient on DIV suggests that a firm's ability to integrate technologically diversified knowledge is positively associated with the firm's innovative performance. Although the variable DIS is not significantly different from zero, the negative coefficient of the variable suggests that the integration of geographically dispersed knowledge may adversely affect the firm's innovative performance. Models 2 to 5 further support this argument. Model 2 adds the squared terms of the independent variables, namely DIV and DIS. The results show that a firm's ability to integrate technologically diversified knowledge has a curvilinear relationship with the firm's innovative performance, in particular, a U-shape relationship. Therefore, our H1 is supported by the positively significant coefficients on DIV in Model 1 and on the squared term of DIV in Model 2, suggesting that firms tend to be able to capture benefits reflected in better innovative performance if

Table 4.9. Two-tailed Pearson correlation matrix (all patents)

	N	Mean	Median	Std dev	1	2	3	4	5	6	7
1 Innovative performance	66	0.1285	0.0721	0.1884	1						
2 Tech diversification (DIV)	66	16.6125	16.5825	1.0302	0.2705	1					
					0.0280						
3 Geographical dispersion (DIS)	66	16.3770	16.3141	0.8896	−0.0592	0.3274	1				
					0.6369	0.0073					
4 Generalists (G)	66	0.4394	0.0000	0.5001	0.2251	−0.3542	−0.2295	1			
					0.0692	0.0035	0.0638				
5 Within tech-field geographical dispersion	66	2.7778	2.6321	0.6161	−0.1857	0.4389	0.2511	−0.2981	1		
					0.1355	0.0002	0.0420	0.0151			
6 Home country tech share	66	30.9507	37.0673	19.2584	0.2288	0.2632	−0.3726	−0.0340	0.0520	1	
					0.0646	0.0327	0.0021	0.7863	0.6784		
7 Host country tech share	66	36.2427	36.3980	3.5089	0.0835	−0.0256	**−0.7879**	0.0774	−0.0631	**0.5984**	1
					0.5049	0.8381	<.0001	0.5366	0.6149	<.0001	

they have the higher level of capabilities that may be needed to absorb and integrate technologically diversified knowledge effectively. We employed Model 2 as a baseline model, and calculated the threshold value at which a firm's DIV would begin to positively affect the firm's innovative performance. Since the minimum value of DIV is 14.16 and its maximum value is 20.16, we tested the integers between 14 and 20 and found that when the value of a firm's DIV is larger than 16, the effect of DIV on innovative performance becomes positive. This result is consistent with the discussion about how increasing technological complexity is a challenge that many industrial firms are facing (Cantwell et al., 2008). Firms that are able to incorporate such technological complexity into their knowledge accumulation are more likely to sustain a better performance.

While the coefficient on DIS becomes positively significant in Model 2, the squared term on DIS is negatively significant. In other words, a firm's ability to access geographically dispersed knowledge sources may initially improve the firm's innovative performance, but this positive effect may be replaced by a negative effect if the firm pushes too hard to integrate highly geographically dispersed knowledge, leading to an inverted-U-shape relationship. We also calculated the threshold value of DIS using the same settings as we had for DIV above. Since the minimum value of DIS is 12.80 and its maximum value is 18.72, we tested the integers between 12 and 18. We find that when the value of a firm's DIS reached 17, the positive effect of DIS on innovative performance became negative. Models 3 to 5 further add the interaction between independent variables, as well as controls. The interaction between DIV and DIS never reaches significance, and it drives out the significance of DIS. This result suggests that the positive effect of a firm's ability to access geographically dispersed knowledge sources on the firm's performance is conditional on the fact that the firm is not trying to access geographically dispersed knowledge sources for technologically diversified knowledge. The limited managerial time and the difficulties of coordination across greater geographical distances might partly explain this result. In other words, there may be a tradeoff between these two types of capabilities. Therefore, H3 is not supported, and nor is our H2 in general, given that the coefficient of DIS is not significant in most of the models, and that the coefficients on the squared DIS are negatively significant across all models.

The dummy variable G shows that generalists have better performance than do specialists in the EE industry. This result is consistent with that of Cantwell et al. (2008). In a study of foreign-owned subsidiaries in the German pharmaceutical industry, we found that chemical firms (as generalists) are more open than are pure pharmaceutical firms (as specialists) in their innovation systems, in the sense of having a greater capacity to access external knowledge in distant technological fields (Cantwell et al., 2008). In the current knowledge-

Table 4.10. OLS regression predicting innovative performance of MNCs (all patents)

Variables	All technologies				
	1	2	3	4	5
Intercept	−0.2839	2.7487	6.8948	6.0145	7.0176
Tech diversification (DIV)	**0.0594****	**−1.0078*****	**−1.4511****	**−1.2674****	**−1.3285****
	(0.0232)	(0.3771)	(0.5468)	(0.5122)	(0.5189)
DIV*DIV		**0.0315*****	**0.0263****	**0.0243****	**0.0257****
		(0.0111)	(0.0120)	(0.0115)	(0.0116)
Geographical dispersion (DIS)	−0.0350	**0.6965***	0.6372	0.5280	0.5329
	(0.0268)	(0.4028)	(0.4055)	(0.3771)	(0.3746)
DIS*DIS		**−0.0223***	**−0.0393****	**−0.0327***	**−0.0348***
		(0.0124)	(0.0196)	(0.0181)	(0.0180)
DIV*DIS			0.0374	0.0324	0.0340
			(0.0334)	(0.0307)	(0.0308)
Controls					
Generalists (G)				**0.0828***	**0.0793***
				(0.0442)	(0.0443)
Within tech-field geographical dispersion				**−0.1023*****	**−0.1006*****
				(0.0363)	(0.0363)
Home country tech share				0.0009	
				(0.0012)	
Host country tech share					−0.0083
					(0.0101)
p-value	**0.0393**	**0.0036**	**0.0051**	**0.0002**	**0.0002**
R-square	9.76	22.23	23.81	39.13	39.31
Adj R-square	6.90	17.13	17.47	30.59	30.80

Note: ***, $p < 0.01$; **, $p < 0.05$; *, $p < 0.10$; standard errors in parentheses.

driven economy, this result may be attributable to the fact that generalists have a broader knowledge base, which increases their potential for generating new knowledge through combination and recombination. In general, adding control variables to Models 4 and 5 does not change the main results discussed above. Finally, we used a logarithmic functional form for both our dependent variable 'Innovative Performance' and independent variables 'DIV' and 'DIS', and re-ran the regression models in Table 4.9 as a robustness test. However, the model fits were significantly decreased, so we confine the presentation of our empirical results to those reported in Table 4.9.

4.7. Discussion and conclusion

This study investigates the knowledge-accumulation pattern of the world's largest firms in the EE industry, and focuses on its effects on corporate-level innovative performance. We have found that an MNC's ability to integrate technologically diversified knowledge and its ability to access geographically dispersed knowledge sources can positively affect the innovative performance of the MNC as a whole, but to different extents. A U-shape relationship is observed in the former case, such that beyond a certain threshold level of technological diversification, the greater the scope that the firm has to integrate technologically diversified knowledge the better the its performance. However, an inverted-U-shape relationship is observed in the latter context; in particular, although a firm's capacity to access geographically dispersed knowledge might initially enhance its performance, a positive effect may be replaced by a negative effect if the firm pushes too hard to integrate highly geographically dispersed knowledge. The interaction between the scope for integrating technologically diversified knowledge (DIV) and the scope for accessing geographically dispersed knowledge (DIS) is not significant at all. The individual results for DIV and DIS seem to suggest that mixing together these two routes towards knowledge combination might lead to an unfavorable outcome for firms' innovative performance. In particular, an MNC may benefit from the integration of technologically diversified knowledge, but when doing so such component knowledge inputs may have to be accessed from a limited number of geographical locations to reduce the costs of geographically distant knowledge sourcing. This result is consistent with our findings elsewhere, namely Cantwell et al. (2008) in a study of foreign-owned pharmaceutical firms in Germany, in which we found that MNCs tend to use geographically local inter-firm networks for technologically distant knowledge, but to rely mainly on international intra-firm networks for less complex or technologically closer types of knowledge.

The findings of this study generate important insights into how the accession and utilization of geographically dispersed technological knowledge affect the innovative performance of MNC groups at a corporate level. While the literature on 'federative MNCs' or 'network-based MNCs' and some evolutionary approaches have emphasized the benefits of the geographically dispersed organization of MNCs in exposing the firm to diversified technological knowledge (Ghoshal and Bartlett, 1990; Kogut and Zander, 1992; Andersson et al., 2007), the results of this study suggest that the potential advantages from multinationality for knowledge combinations are not to be taken for granted. The accession of geographically dispersed knowledge that is technologically diversified may raise the costs of recontextualizing knowledge in a new setting, and so fail to increase the flexibility of the competence creation of the MNC group; instead it may increase the managerial burdens of the firm, and therefore become a disadvantage.

Moreover, we found that generalists on average have better innovative performance than specialists. This finding supports our first hypothesis in the sense that the scope of a firm to integrate technologically diversified knowledge should positively affect the firm's innovative performance, given that generalists by definition have more diversified knowledge portfolios. This finding may also contribute to a better understanding of firm heterogeneity in the structures of international knowledge accumulation observed within the same industry.

The measures of our independent variables in this study were aggregated at a firm level; this increase in the generality of our approach may lose some important information that might be gathered at the more detailed level of an analysis of individual patents and patent citations. Therefore, in future research we may consider using some other approaches to investigate the structures of technological knowledge accumulation in greater depth. Moreover, in this chapter we have not distinguished between the roles of the internal and external knowledge accumulation of firms, which raises a further set of issues that also warrant consideration. Finally, we have investigated the innovative performance of firms only within a limited time frame. In further research it would be useful to examine similar questions using panel data over a longer period and incorporating the distinction between the internal and external elements of the sources of knowledge accumulation in MNCs.

References

Alcacer, J. and Gittelman, M. (2006), 'Patent citations as a measure of knowledge flows: The influence of examiner citations', *Review of Economics and Statistics*, 88: 774–779.

Andersson, U., Forsgren, M. and Holm, U. (2002), 'The strategic impact of external networks: Subsidiary performance and competence development in the multinational corporation', *Strategic Management Journal*, 23: 155–165.

—— —— —— (2007), 'Balancing subsidiary influence in the federative MNC: A business network view', *Journal of International Business Studies*, 38: 802–818.

Bartlett, C.A. and Ghoshal, S. (1986), 'Tap your subsidiaries for global reach', *Harvard Business Review*, 64: 87–94.

—— —— (1989), *Managing Across Borders: The Transnational Solution*. Boston: Harvard Business School Press.

Birkinshaw, J. and Hood, N. (1998), 'Multinational subsidiary evolution: Capability evolution and charter change in foreign-owned subsidiary companies', *Academy of Management Review*, 23: 773–795.

—— and Jonsson, S. (1998), 'Building firm-specific advantages in multinational corporations: The role of subsidiary initiative', *Strategic Management Journal*, 19: 221–241.

Buckley, P.J. and Casson, M.C. (2002), 'A long-run theory of the multinational enterprise', in Buckley, P.J. and Casson, M.C. (eds), *The Future of the Multinational Enterprise*. New York: Palgrave Macmillan.

Caminati, M. (2006), 'Knowledge growth, complexity, and the returns to R&D', *Journal of Evolutionary Economics*, 16: 207–229.

Cantwell, J.A. (2006), *The Economics of Patents*. Northampton: Edward Elgar.

Cantwell, J.A. and Santangelo, G.D. (2000), 'Capitalism, profits and innovation in the new techno-economic paradigm', *Journal of Evolutionary Economics*, 10: 131–157.

—— Noonan, C. and Zhang, F. (2008), 'Technological complexity and the restructuring of subsidiary knowledge sourcing iniIntra-multinational and inter-firm networks', *Annual Conference of Academy of International Business*. Milan: Birkinsh.

Chandler, A.D. (1990), *Scale and Scope. The Dynamics of Industrial Capitalism*. Cambridge, MA: Belknap Press.

Chesbrough, H.W. (2003), 'The era of open innovation', *MIT Sloan Management Review*, 44: 35–41.

Duguet, E. and Macgarvie, M. (2005), 'How well do patent citations measure flows of technology? Evidence from French innovation surveys', *Economic Innovation and New Technology*, 14: 375–393.

Dunning, J.H. (1993), The emergence and maturing of international production: An historical excursion. In Dunning, J.H. (ed.), *Multinational Enterprises and the Global Economy*. Reading, MA: Addison-Wesley.

—— (2001), The key literature on IB activities: 1960–2000. In Rugman, A.M. and Brewer, T.L. (eds), *The Oxford Handbook of International Business*. New York: Oxford University Press.

—— and Lundan, S.M. (1998), 'The geographical sources of competitiveness of multinational enterprises: An econometric analysis', *International Business Review*, 7: 115–133.

Frost, T.S. (2001), 'The geographic sources of foreign subsidiaries' innovations', *Strategic Management Journal*, 22: 101–123.

——, Birkinshaw, J.M. and Ensign, P.C. (2002), 'Centers of excellence in multinational corporations', *Strategic Management Journal*, 23: 997–1018.

Ghoshal, S. and Bartlett, C.A. (1990), 'The multinational corporation as an interorganizational network', *Academy of Management Review*, 15: 603–625.

Graham, E.M. (1978), 'Transatlantic investment by multinational firms: A rivalistic phenomenon?' *Journal of Post Keynesian Economics*, 1: 82–99.

Granstrand, O., Patel, P. and Pavitt, K. (1997), 'Multitechnology corporations: Why they have distributed rather than distinctive core competencies', *California Management Review*, 39: 8–25.

Griliches, Z. (1990), 'Patent statistics as economic indicators: A survey', *Journal of Economic Literature*, 28: 1661–1707.

Jaffe, A.B. Trajtenberg, M. and Henderson, R. (1993), 'Geographic localization of knowledge spillovers as evidenced by patent citations', *The Quarterly Journal of Economics*, 108: 577–598.

—— —— and Fogarty, M.S. (2000), 'Knowledge spillovers and patent citations: Evidence from a survey of inventors', *The American Economic Review*, 90: 215-218.

Kogut, B. and Zander, U. (1992), 'Knowledge of the firm, combinative capabilities, and the replication of technology', *Organization Science*, 3: 383–397.

Kuemmerle, W. (1999), 'The drivers of foreign direct investment into research and development: An empirical investigation', *Journal of International Business Studies*, 30: 1–24.

Li, J. and Rugman, A.M. (2007), 'Real options and the theory of foreign direct investment', *International Business Review*, 16: 687–712.

Miller, R. (1994), 'Global R and D networks and large-scale innovations: The case of the automobile industry', *Research Policy*, 23: 27–46.

Mudambi, R. and Navarra, P. (2004), 'Is knowledge power? Knowledge flows, subsidiary power and rent-seeking within MNCs', *Journal of International Business Studies*, 35: 385–406.

Nelson, R. (1995), 'Co-evolution of industry structure, technology and supporting institutions, and the making of comparative advantage', *International Journal of the Economics of Business*, 2: 14.

—— and Winter, S. (1982), *An Evolutionary Theory of Economic Change*. Cambridge, MA: Harvard University Press.

Nightingale, P. (2000), 'Economies of scale in experimentation: Knowledge and technology in pharmaceutical R&D', *Industrial and Corporate Change*, 9: 315–359.

Patel, P. and Pavitt, K. (1997), 'The technological competencies of the world's largest firms: Complex and path-dependent, but not much variety', *Research Policy*, 26: 141–156.

Schumpeter, J.A. (1939), *Business Cycles: A Theoretical Historical and Statistical Analysis of the Capitalist Process*. New York and London: McGraw Hill.

Tallman, S. and Phene, A. (2007), 'Leveraging knowledge across geographic boundaries', *Organization Science*, 18: 252–260.

Zander, I. (1998), 'The evolution of technological capabilities in the multinational corporation—Dispersion, duplication and potential advantages from multinationality', *Research Policy*, 27: 17–35.

—— (1999), 'Whereto the multinational? The evolution of technological capabilities in the multinational network', *International Business Review*, 8: 261–291.

—— (2002), 'The formation of international innovation networks in the multinational corporation: An evolutionary perspective', *Industrial and Corporate Change*, 11: 327–353.

Part II
Firm-Level Return to R&D Strategies

5

How Good Are Patents as Innovation Indicators? Evidence from German CIS Data

Alfred Kleinknecht and Henk Jan Reinders

5.1. Introduction

In the absence of better innovation data, patents have frequently been used as indicators of industrial innovation. Advantages are that patent data are available over long time periods, are classified by technical fields, their novelty is checked by patent examiners, there is no confidentiality problem restricting research, and databases are increasingly accessible online. The availability of patent records over long periods allows addressing a number of intriguing questions as outlined by Griliches (1990). For example:

- Are there diminishing returns to R&D in certain historical periods (e.g. 1930 and 1940s, 1970s) and can lower patenting activities in such periods be related to indicators of economic performance such as productivity growth, profits, or stock market performance? And, if so, what is the cause and effect?
- Are smaller firms indeed more efficient innovators, as they produce significantly higher numbers of patents per unit of R&D input? Or is this simply due to substantial amounts of small-scale and informal R&D in smaller firms that tend to be quite poorly measured in the official R&D surveys (Kleinknecht, 1987)?
- Is there a long-run exhaustion of inventive and technological opportunities as patent applications and patents granted grow slower than R&D and GDP?
- Do the higher rates of patenting per unit of R&D in industrial clusters indeed indicate that firms in those clusters benefit from agglomeration externalities?
- Does the relationship between demand and patenting indeed show that innovations essentially depend on the growth of effective demand?

- Does the high rate of patenting in university–industry collaborations indeed prove that there is a 'positive contribution of basic research in universities to the overall level of domestic inventive activity as measured by the total number of domestic patent applications'? (Griliches, 1990: 327).

Addressing such questions, however, meets a number of difficulties which many authors acknowledge. Such acknowledgments are usually followed by the standard caveat that the 'results should be interpreted with caution'. This caveat seems to give absolution for sins and permits the continuing use of patent data.

In his thorough survey on patent data as innovation indicators, Griliches (1990) gives an impressive account of technical difficulties that arise when using patent records. Some of these problems can be tackled, others not. Problems relate to the adequate classification of patents by their sector of origin (the patent 'producer') versus the industries of their final use in which they may raise productivity. There are some problems of correct classification by technical fields and much bigger problems in transferring data from the technical classification by patent offices to industry classifications. Even with firm-level data, there can be severe allocation problems in the case of multi-divisional conglomerates with multiple lines of business. And, of course, patents can vary widely in their commercial importance. Another handicap in numerous analyses is that one arrives at '...very high estimates of both the variance and skewness in the distribution of patent values.' (Griliches, 1990: 336). A number of these problems can be tackled in a satisfactory way. For example, in dealing with the widely differing commercial importance of patents we can trust in the law of large numbers. Or inter-industry differences in innovations that are not patented (or in patents that are not used for commercial purposes) could be handled by the use of sector dummies.

There remains, nonetheless, the problem of what Mike Scherer (1983) termed an innovator's 'propensity to patent'. Most researchers using patents as an indicator of innovation hope that 'real' innovations are somehow correlated to patents. Some studies suggest they are (e.g. Acs and Audretsch 1989; Hagedoorn and Cloodt 2003). Doubts about neat correlations were raised by Scherer (1983) who found a substantial variation across industries in numbers of patents per unit of R&D. Moreover, Levin et al. (1987) reported the surprising result that patents are not the most important means for protection of innovative knowledge, other means such as lead times or secrecy being more important. These outcomes were confirmed by Brouwer and Kleinknecht (1999), showing that, on average, besides lead times and secrecy, 'keeping qualified people in the firm' (a proxy for tacit knowledge) was still ranking higher than patenting. Besides that, Brouwer and Kleinknecht confirmed evidence reported by Arundel and Kabla (1998) that the propensity to patent an innovation differs substantially across industries.

The main problem signalled by Griliches (1990) and other contributors (Kuznets, 1962; Mansfield, 1986) is that for our judgment about patents as an innovation indicator, and for many analyses using patents, we do not have information about one key issue: percentages of non-patented innovations. At the time when Griliches wrote his survey (1990), there was simply little systematic statistical information available about what we really want to measure: i.e. 'innovation', which is usually defined as the market introduction of a technologically new (or renewed) product, service, or process. At the time, researchers could only compare patent data to other (indirect) indicators of innovation such as the R&D input into the innovation process or productivity growth. This leaves the problem unsolved that deviations between R&D and patents can be influenced either by differences in R&D productivity, or by differing propensities to patent outcomes of the R&D process. As a consequence, Griliches (1990) had to conclude that he had some tentative answers to the above-sketched questions, but he could not be sure about their validity. Fortunately, the European Community Innovation Survey (CIS) has developed direct measures of innovation, asking firms about which part of their presently sold products fell into the following categories over the past three years:

- Remained essentially unchanged (neglecting trivial product changes)
- Have been technologically improved
- Were introduced entirely new.

Subsequently, firms are asked to report shares in their total sales taken by these three categories. Moreover, firms are asked to report which of their innovative products were 'first in the market' or only 'new to the firm'. The former can be considered as innovations, while the latter stand for imitative renewal. These indicators have been extensively tested (e.g. Kleinknecht, 1993) and gradually refined in expert meetings organized by the OECD and the European Commission (see also the various editions of the OECD Oslo Manual (OECD, 2004a, 2004b, 2004c)). The CIS shares-in-sales data on 'innovation output' have meanwhile been generally accepted and are widely used in research. Besides product innovators, the CIS identifies process innovators. Moreover, product innovators are split into firms that have physical goods innovations and/or service innovations.

A severe limitation on the research in this chapter relates to patenting. The CIS simply asks whether a firm applied for (any type of) patent protection, without giving information about numbers of applications, country coverage, type of patent office (national, EU, US, etc.), nor can we assess the importance of a patent application through citation analyses. On the other hand, we do have firm-level data in which we compare a reliable direct measure of innovation to the zero/one information about whether a firm did or did not apply for patent protection. This allows for a much sharper analysis than was possible before we could use CIS data.

This chapter is structured as follows. In section 5.2, we present descriptive data about percentages of innovators that apply for patents. Relating patent applications to the measures of innovation in the German CIS, we conclude that patent applications are mainly submitted by innovators who develop new (physical) goods innovations. Service and process innovators show substantially lower patenting rates.

Section 5.3 reports on a multivariate analysis of factors that influence an innovating firm's probability of seeking patent protection, finding that collaboration with universities increases the propensity to patent, while collaboration with other partners does not. An innovator's orientation to local and national markets reduces, while international market orientation increases, the probability of applying for patents. Our estimates suggest dividing industries into two classes: high- versus low-patent-propensity industries. Low-patent-propensity industries include all service industries as well as most traditional manufacturing industries. The probabilities estimated might give a clue to users of patent databases about the extent of their measurement bias when using patents as an innovation indicator. Section 5.4 rounds up with discussions and conclusions.

5.2. Descriptive observations

Figure 5.1 shows numbers of firms in the German CIS that have applied for patents, divided by types of innovators. Product innovators show fairly high percentages of patent applicants. Only firms that report having joint product- and process-innovation efforts have even higher probabilities of applying for patents. Pure service innovators and pure process innovators show only small percentages of patent applicants.

The early work by Scherer (1983) has already suggested that the propensity to patent might differ substantially across industries. This is confirmed by Figure 5.2. Numbers behind Figure 5.2 can be found in the appendix (Table A5.1). It should be noted that the data in Figure 5.2 stem from three quite different sources, and are measured at different times and with different concepts:

- The data by Arundel and Kabla (1998) relate to a firm's probability of patenting a major product or process innovation and are taken from the so-called PACE survey that was confined to Europe's largest firms during the early 1990s. This multi-country survey does not claim to be representative for individual countries.

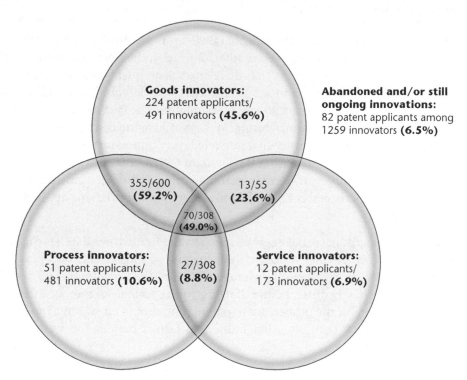

Figure 5.1. Percentages of innovators that apply for patents

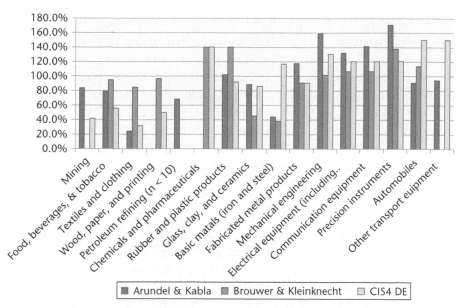

Figure 5.2. Average propensities to patent product innovations across industries: three independent sources compared (for each source, the mean is set equal to 100)

- The data by Brouwer and Kleinknecht (1999) are from the pilot round of the CIS survey (1992) that is representative for firms in the Netherlands with ten employees or more. Note that these are data on qualitative judgments on a Likert scale from 0 (= insignificant) to 5 (= crucial) of the value of patents as a means of protection against imitators. The data are confined to innovators in Dutch manufacturing. We report here the percentages of innovating firms by industry that answered 'very important' and 'crucial'.
- 'CIS 4 DE' stands for data from the German CIS in year 2004. This is a representative survey in German manufacturing and service industries. The figure reports percentages of innovators that report having applied for patents.

For ease of comparison, we have set the mean values in the three datasets each equal to 100. It is remarkable to see that, in spite of substantial conceptual differences, differences in sample coverage and years, the three sources do not deviate too much. Of course, before drawing strong conclusions about inter-industry variations of the propensity to patent, one should engage in a multi-variate analysis that controls other influential factors besides the sector of principal activity.

5.3. The empirical model

Given the fairly low patent-application percentages in Figure 5.1 for process and service innovators, we confine our multivariate analysis to product innovators (and innovators doing joint product and process innovations). Figure 5.1 clearly indicates that, using patents as an indicator of innovation, we would substantially undercount service and process innovators compared to goods innovators. As noted before, we have fairly limited information on patenting: we know only whether an innovator has applied for any patent, without distinction by country coverage, type of patent, or patent numbers. The suitable model is then logistic regression which distinguishes two states:

1. The innovator has applied for patents.
2. The innovator has not applied for patents.

The logit model informs us about factors that influence the probabilities of a firm being in either of these two states. In our logit model, we consider the following factors relevant to a firm's patenting propensity.

First, the literature suggests that differences in patenting propensities across industries are of interest. We test this by using fairly detailed sector dummies.

Second, it is likely that firms that have strong R&D competencies are more likely to have patentable knowledge. We control for this by including a firm's R&D budget as a percentage of sales.

Third, it is likely that internationally operating firms will patent more fre-quently as they meet more competitors that have the competences for success-ful imitation of innovations that are not patented. We therefore include qualitative information about the markets served by a firm (distinguishing local/regional, national, and European markets, besides markets outside Europe).

Fourth, Brouwer and Kleinknecht (1999) found that firms collaborating on R&D with other organizations also have significantly higher patenting prob-abilities. The rationale could be that firms do not fully trust their partners and therefore protect their most precious knowledge before engaging into R&D collaboration. Moreover, it could be argued that codification of knowledge in patents facilitates the use of knowledge assets in contract negotiations. The CIS covers fairly detailed questions about types of collaboration partners (e.g. clients, suppliers, competitors, public and private R&D institutions) detailed by location (regional and national partners, EU and outside-EU partners).

Fifth, besides controlling for the influence of formal R&D collaboration, we also control for knowledge transfer through (informal) contacts, making use of the type of information sources a firm reported having used during the innovation process.

Sixth, the German CIS asks firms to subdivide their product innovations into goods versus service innovations. Figure 5.1 suggests that patent applica-tions occur much more frequently for goods innovations compared to service innovations. We take this into account through the inclusion of a dummy for goods versus services.

Seventh, the CIS distinguishes new products by degree of novelty. Are they 'new to the firm' (i.e. already known in the market)? Or are they 'first in the market'? We tend to consider the former as imitative innovations and the latter as 'true' innovations, and expect the latter to be accompanied by sub-stantially higher numbers of patent applications. This will be captured by a dummy for 'new to the firm' versus 'first in the market' innovations. More-over, we estimate two versions of our model. Model 1 includes firms that have products 'new to the firm' and/or 'first in the market'. Model 2 covers firms that only have products 'first in the market'.

Eighth, the CIS also asks by whom an innovation was developed, giving three answering options: (1) Mainly by your own enterprise; (2) By your enterprise in collaboration with others; and (3) Mainly by other organizations. In the third case, one would expect that a firm is less likely to apply for patent protection. We therefore use a dummy that has the value of 1 for the first two options and zero for the third option.

Last but not least we include firm size (log of turnover) as a control variable. As patenting is given as a zero/one variable, it is obvious that large, multiproduct companies have substantially higher probabilities of answering 'yes' than do smaller firms.

5.4. Results and conclusions

Table 5.1 summarizes our logit estimates. It should be noted that our estimates are robust to numerous alternative specifications. For example, for many coefficients, it makes little difference whether we do or do not include industry dummies. Moreover, we tentatively replaced R&D intensity by two other indicators: (1) a firm's R&D intensity minus the average of its sector of

Table 5.1. Factors that influence a product innovator's probability of applying for a patent. Summary of logit estimates on German CIS 4 (2004) data

	Model 1: Innovators having 'new to the firm' and/or 'first on the market' products		Model 2: Only innovators having 'first on the market' products	
Independent variables of interest:	**Odds ratios:**	**z-values:**	**Odds ratios:**	**z-values:**
R&D intensity (R&D budgets on sales)	1.658	3.32***	1.685	2.48***
Cooperation with universities	2.575	5.09***	3.139	4.25***
Clients are a source of information for innovation	2.893	2.27***	3.100	1.45
Innovation is 'first in the market' (other than 'new to the firm')	2.221	5.42***	omitted	omitted
The firm serves local or regional markets	0.735	−1.93*	0.528	−2.87**
The firm serves European markets	1.148	0.72	1.249	0.81
The firm serves markets outside Europe	1.622	2.90***	1.603	2.05***
Control variables:				
Firm size (log of turnover)	1.641	10.27***	1.625	7.39***
Goods (other than service) innovator	3.073	3.21***	4.071	2.44**
Innovation was mainly developed by other parties	0.046	−2.97***	0.317	−0.97
Industry dummies[##] (reference group: textiles & clothing)				
Mining	0.715	0.37	2.310	0.74
Food, beverages & tobacco	0.358	−1.73*	0.570	−0.62
Wood, paper, printing	1.515	0.79	4.213	1.87*
Publishing	0.544	−0.96	1.386	0.38
Petroleum refining, chemicals, pharmaceuticals	3.914	2.87***	9.763	3.18***
Rubber & plastics	3.816	2.69***	7.705	2.76***
Glass, clay & ceramics	1.811	1.01	3.730	1.62
Basic metals	1.012	0.02	1.762	0.65
Metal products	4.333	3.13***	8.712	3.03***
Mechanical engineering	4.536	3.34***	10.877	3.43***
Computers, electrical machinery, communication equipment, precision engineering	4.851	3.58***	10.329	3.44***
Automobiles & other transport equipment	6.699	3.41***	23.234	3.42***
Furniture, recycling	4.852	2.98***	14.409	3.29***
Electricity, gas & water	0.317	−1.27	3.175	0.82
Other wholesale trade	0.878	−0.18	1.812	0.56
Land, water & air transport	1.052	0.07	2.500	0.80

Travel agencies	0.137	−1.60	0.612	−0.34
Post & telecom	0.474	−0.65	1.695	0.40
Financial intermediation, real estate, renting	0.057	−3.15***	0.199	−1.17

##The following sectors dropped out due to low numbers of observations: Leather & leather goods; Construction; Sales, maintenance & repair of motor vehicles; Retail trade; Hotels & restaurants.

Number of observations:	1,461	713
Pseudo R-squared:	0.41	0.36
Prob. chi-squared:	0.0000	0.000
LR chi-squared (29)	825.9	345.2
Log likelihood	−589.5	−305.1

Notes: *Significant at 90% level; **Significant at 95% level; ***Significant at 99% level

principal activity; and (2) qualitative information about whether the firm considered R&D as an occasional or as a permanent activity. From all three versions we can conclude that patent applications are mainly filed by firms that, in one way or another, have R&D as a strong core function. Unfortunately, as we have no information on numbers of patents, we cannot derive conclusions about patents growing more or less than proportionately with R&D input.

We can also conclude that firms that serve international markets (notably outside the European Union) have substantially higher probabilities of applying for patents compared to firms oriented to national or local markets. Only in a single specification of the model we found that firms exporting within the European Union also have higher patenting propensities. In most versions, the coefficient was positive but not significant.

R&D collaboration with universities is, in all versions, highly significant and positive. A possible interpretation is that such collaborative projects may be closer to basic research that offers more possibilities for developing patentable knowledge, but other interpretations are possible. For example, some universities (e.g. Delft University of Technology) remunerate scientists for acquiring patents in their internal allocation of research money. Obviously, such practices inflate numbers of patents. Whatever our interpretation may be, this finding has an impact on the above-quoted observation by Griliches (1990): the fact that we find relatively more patents coming from university–industry projects does not necessarily prove that strong university spillovers enhance innovation (if measured by patents).

In a single specification only, we also found that R&D collaboration with competitors was (just) significant. Contrary to Brouwer and Kleinknecht (1999), we find that R&D collaboration with other types of partners (e.g. clients, suppliers, private R&D labs, etc.) does not increase the propensity to patent. It should be noted, however, that Brouwer and Kleinknecht were able to judge from numbers of patents while we have only zero/one information on patents. Among the sources of information that were important during the innovation process, only the use of clients and universities as an information source was significant. Using universities as R&D collaboration partners and as information sources, however, often coincides and therefore the latter often appeared as insignificant (due to multicollinearity). Clients as an information source turned out to be significant only when we included R&D collaboration irrespective of the type of partners.

The control variables behave as expected. First, firms having products that are 'first in the market' have significantly higher probabilities of applying for patent protection compared to firms whose products are 'new to the firm'. One might find it surprising that firms that have imitative innovations ('new to the firm') still apply for patents. One possible explanation might be that the division by degree of 'newness' is not as clean as the developers of the CIS might have hoped. Another possible explanation might be that many imitative efforts are accompanied by developing some original new knowledge that the firm considers worth patenting. Second, innovations that are based on physical goods are much more frequently patented than service innovations. And third, if an innovation was developed by some other organization (i.e. not by the firm itself or by the firm in collaboration with others), the probability of applying for a patent tends to be lower in most specifications. At least, this holds for imitative innovations (but, in almost all specifications, not for 'true' innovations).

The descriptive table in the appendix gives the impression that one can subdivide industries roughly into three categories:

1. Service industries (NACE 40–74) that have quite low propensities to patent
2. Traditional manufacturing industries (NACE 10–22; i.e. mining; food, beverages & tobacco; textiles & clothing; wood, paper & printing) having a medium propensity to patent
3. High-patenting-propensity sectors such as chemical & pharmaceuticals; rubber & plastic products; glass, clay & ceramics; basic metals and metal products; mechanical engineering; electrical equipment, communication equipment, precision instruments; automobiles and other transportation equipment; furniture and recycling.

By controlling other influential factors, our logit estimate gives a slightly different picture. Taking textiles & clothing as the reference sector, we find only a few industries that have a significantly lower propensity to patent. In fact, the coefficients of the industry dummies in Table 5.1 suggest we might divide industries roughly into two classes:

1. Low-patent-propensity industries, including mining; food, beverages & tobacco; wood, paper & printing; publishing; glass, clay & ceramics; basic metals; electricity, gas & water supplies; wholesale trade; land, water & air transport; travel agencies; post & telecom; financial intermediation, real estate & renting.

2. <u>High</u>-patent-propensity industries, including petroleum refining, chemicals & pharmaceuticals; rubber & plastics; metal products; mechanical engineering; computers, electrical machinery, communication equipment, precision engineering; automobiles & other transport equipment; furniture & recycling.

Incidentally, the latter finding explains why Hagedoorn and Cloodt (2003) concluded that the propensity to patent an innovation is roughly the same over the four (high-tech) industries they studied (i.e. aerospace & defence, computers & office machinery, pharmaceuticals, and electronics & communications).

If we accept the CIS concept that a firm is an 'innovator' if it has sales from products that are 'first in the market' (introduced during the past three years), we can conclude that those who use(d) patents as an innovation indicator clearly overestimate numbers of innovators in the second group compared to the first group. Underestimation of rates of innovating firms will be notably severe with respect to services (compared to physical-goods innovations). Moreover, as could be seen from the descriptive statistics, patent statistics underestimate process innovators.

The outcomes give the impression that patent data are biased by the history of the patent system. This system was originally developed in order to protect (physical) product innovations in 'hard' manufacturing industries that have substantial product-development efforts. At those times, there was seemingly much less need to protect process innovations or 'soft' service innovations. Today, we realize that service innovations may be quite relevant to modern economies, but the old patent system is seemingly less suited to protect service innovations.

Appendix

Table A5.1. Propensities to patent a product innovation across industries: three sources compared

Propensity to patent across industries		According to Arundel and Kabla	According to Brouwer and Kleinknecht	All product innovations CIS4 (Germany)
NACE				
10–14	Mining	27.7%		22.2%
15–16	Food, beverages and tobacco	26.1%	24.6%	29.8%
17–19	Textiles and clothing	8.1%	22.1%	16.9%
20–22	Wood, paper and printing		25.1%	26.6%
23	Petroleum refining	22.6%		
24	Chemicals and pharmaceuticals		36.3%	74.4%
25	Rubber and plastic products	33.7%	36.4%	48.9%

Continued

Table A5.1 *Continued*

Propensity to patent across industries		*According to Arundel and Kabla*	*According to Brouwer and Kleinknecht*	All product innovations CIS4 (Germany)
26	Glass, clay and ceramics	**29.3%**	**11.8%**	**45.8%**
27	Basic metals (iron and steel)	**14.6%**	**9.9%**	**62.0%**
28	Fabricated metal products	**38.8%**	**23.6%**	**48.2%**
29	Mechanical engineering	**52.4%**	**26.4%**	**69.3%**
30–31	Electrical equipment (including computers)	**43.6%**	**27.7%**	**64.0%**
32	Communication equipment	**46.6%**	**27.7%**	**64.0%**
33	Precision instruments	**56.4%**	**35.8%**	**64.0%**
34	Automobiles	**30.0%**	**29.6%**	**79.6%**
35	Other transport equipment	**31.2%**		**79.6%**
36	Manufacture of furniture			**51.7%**
37	Recycling			**51.7%**
40–41	Electricity, gas, steam and (hot) water supply			**7.3%**
51	Wholesale trade and commission trade (except motor vehicles)			**7.6%**
60–62	Land, water and air transport			**9.7%**
63	Auxiliary transport activities; travel agencies			**2.1%**
64	Post and telecommunication			**8.3%**
65–67	Financial intermediation			**1.4%**
72–74	Business activities (e.g. consultancy; R&D)			**14.9%**

Notes: (1) Arundel and Kabla (1998) report percentages of innovations that are patented. (2) Brouwer and Kleinknecht (1999) use a qualitative measure; here the percentage is given of Dutch manufacturing firms that appreciate the value of patent protection for product and process innovation as 'very important' or 'crucial'. (3) The coloured cells for CIS4 are combined groups and the average propensity to patent is taken for these industries together, since no distinction is made within CIS4 for these industries.

Table A5.2. Descriptive data

Variables	Mean	Median	SD	Min	Max
Independent variables of interest					
R&D intensity (R&D budgets on sales)	0.029	0.008	0.058	0	0.482
Cooperation with universities	0.218	0	0.413	0	1
Clients are an important source of information	0.949	1	0.221	0	1
Innovation is 'first in the market' (other than 'new to the firm')	0.488		0.500	0	1
The firm serves local/regional/national markets	0.380	0	0.486	0	1
The firm serves European markets	0.630	1	0.483	0	1
The firm serves markets outside Europe	0.448	0	0.497	0	1
Control variables					
Firm size (log of turnover)	16.827	16.706	2.112	10.806	24.293
Goods (other than service) innovator	0.786	1	0.410	0	1
Innovation was mainly developed by other parties	0.055	0	0.229	0	1
Patent application	0.436	0	0.496	0	1

References

Acs, Z.J. and Audretsch, D.B. (1989), Patents as a measure of innovative activity, *Kyklos*, 42: 171.

Arundel, A. and Kabla, I. (1998), 'What percentage of innovations are patented? Empirical estimates for European firms', *Research Policy*, 27: 127–141.

Brouwer, E. and Kleinknecht, A. (1999), 'Innovative output, and a firm's propensity to patent: An exploration of CIS micro data', *Research Policy*, 28: 615–624.

Griliches, Z. (1990), 'Patent statistics as economic indicators—a survey', *Journal of Economic Literature*, 28: 1661–1707.

Hagedoorn, J. and Cloodt, M. (2003), 'Measuring innovative performance: Is there an advantage in using multiple indicators?', *Research Policy*, 32: 1365–1379.

Kleinknecht, A. (1987), 'Measuring R&D in small firms: How much are we missing?' *Journal of Industrial Economics*, 36: 253–256.

—— (1993), Testing innovation indicators for postal surveys: Results from a five-country project. In: Kleinknecht, A. and Bain, D. (eds), *New Concepts in Innovation Output Measurement*. London: Macmillan and New York: St. Martin's Press.

Kuznets, S. (1962), Inventive activity: Problems of definitions and measurement. In Universities-National Bureau (ed.), *The Rate and Direction of Inventive Activity: Economic and Social Factors*. Princeton: Princeton University Press.

Levin, R.C., Klevorick, A.K., Nelson, R.R., Winter, S.G., Gilbert, R. and Griliches, Z. (1987), 'Appropriating the returns from industrial research and development', *Brookings Papers on Economic Activity*, 783–831.

Mansfield, E. (1986), 'Patents and innovation: An empirical study', *Management Science*, 32: 173–181.

OECD (2004a), 'The fourth community innovation survey'. http://www.oecd.org/dataoecd/52/35/40140021.pdf

—— (2004b), 'The fourth community innovation survey (CIS 4): Methodological recommendations'. http://www.oecd.org/dataoecd/53/11/40140079.pdf

—— (2004c), 'Oslo manual: Proposed guidelines for measuring and interpreting technological innovation data'. http://www.oecd.org/dataoecd/35/61/2367580.pdf

Scherer, F.M. (1983), 'The propensity to patent', *International Journal of Industrial Organization*, 1: 107–128.

6

The Importance of Process and Product Innovation for Productivity in French Manufacturing and Service Industries

Jacques Mairesse and Stephane Robin

6.1. Introduction

This chapter investigates the effect of innovation on the productivity of firms when two technological paths are available: product innovation on the one hand, and process innovation on the other. This is done by estimating a nonlinear multiple-equation econometric model, which allows us to control for both selection and endogeneity. This model encompasses three stages. The first stage deals with R&D activities, in terms of both propensity and intensity. The second stage represents the 'knowledge production function', distinguishing between product and process innovation. The third and final stage identifies the impact of both types of innovation on labour productivity.

This model is estimated on two waves of the French component of the Community Innovation Survey (CIS): CIS3, which covers the years 1998–2002, and CIS4, which covers the years 2002–2004. Using both waves of the survey, we conduct an inter-temporal comparison on the manufacturing industry. Using the fourth wave, we also compare the innovation–productivity relationship in the manufacturing industry and in the services. Process innovation appears as the main driver of labour productivity in the manufacturing industry in both periods, but further analyses reveal that it is actually difficult to disentangle the respective effects of product and process innovation. Both types of innovation actually seem to capture 'overall' innovation, and when a single indicator of innovation is used, it always has a significantly positive impact on labour productivity, both in the manufacturing industry and in the services.

The remainder of this study is organized as follows. In Section 6.2, after discussing issues pertaining to product and process innovation in our general framework of the R&D–innovation–productivity relationship, we detail the specification of the econometric model, and present the estimation procedures. In Section 6.3, we describe the data and define the explanatory variables used in the various equations of the model. Section 6.4 is dedicated to the presentation and interpretation of the results, and to some sensitivity analyses. We conclude in a final section.

6.2. Motivation and econometric modelling

6.2.1. *Accounting for product and process innovation in the CDM model*

Our contribution brings together two strands of literature: (1) empirical studies of the relationship between R&D and the output of innovation, and (2) studies dealing with the impact of innovation on productivity. To do so, we follow the approach initially proposed by Crépon et al. (1998), who developed a 'structural' model linking R&D, innovation and productivity. This model—usually referred to as the 'CDM' model—has enjoyed significant success in the literature over the recent years. CDM-type models are generally built as three-stage econometric models that relate productivity to new knowledge that depends on firms' R&D effort, which is in turn determined by a number of firm- and environment-specific factors.

Recent applications of this framework include Griffith et al. (2006), who attempt to extend this framework by taking into account process as well as product innovation. They estimate their variant of the CDM model in four EU countries (France, Germany, Spain, and the United Kingdom). Chudnosky et al. (2006) estimate a similar model on Argentine firm-level data. In addition, they propose a short summary of CDM-type studies implemented between 1998 and 2006. For an overall survey, see also Mairesse and Mohnen (2010). Other recent studies based on a CDM approach include Mairesse et al. (2005), Raffo et al. (2008), and Hall et al. (2009).

Our variant of the CDM model follows in the footsteps of Griffith et al. (2006), and tries for a number of improvements in both the specification and the estimation methods. Before detailing those, it may be useful to discuss the importance of adequately taking into account both product and process innovation in a CDM-type model.

129

While economic theory offers little guidance regarding the respective (and potentially different) impacts of product and process innovation on firms' productivity, empirical applications such as ours face a recurrent measurement problem. When a productivity measure is computed using firm-level data, this measure is generally based on a value expressed in monetary units (such as total sales or value added). Information on individual prices is generally not available in microeconomic data (especially in survey data), making it impossible to measure firms' output in real terms of say 'quantity' or 'volume', of goods produced (see Griliches, 1979; Mairesse and Jaumandreu, 2005). The distinction between volume and value-based measures of productivity has important implications for empirical studies of the impact of innovation, all the more so in studies which distinguish between product and process innovation.

Indeed, while both types of innovation could, in theory, lead to productivity gains that are difficult to assess in empirical studies relying on value-based measures of productivity. First of all, a process innovation reduces the costs of production, which can lead a firm to lower its output price. Since we do not measure the firm's output in real terms, but only its global sales or value added, we may observe a negative impact of process innovation on productivity simply because the firm is now selling the same output at a lower price. This negative impact is, however, artificial, and only arises because we are not able to disentangle firm sales into an output level and a price. In this situation, process innovation would actually have improved the firm's competitiveness, even though we would observe a negative impact of process innovation on our (imperfect) measure of productivity.

The same measurement issue can lead to the reverse problem as far as product innovation is concerned. By definition, a product innovation leads to a 'new' or 'improved' product, which is considered as 'better' either because it presents a new feature and its quality has actually been improved, or because it simply looks different. A firm may decide to sell this product at a higher price to reflect the fact that it is a new, a better quality or simply a different product. In this case, we may observe an artificially high effect of product innovation on productivity, again because we are not able to disentangle prices and output levels in our value-based measure of productivity. This phenomenon may be even more important in the services industry, where prices are often supposed to signal the quality of the services that are delivered.

The aforementioned difficulties can be aggravated by the fact that product and process innovations are often concurrent, because the introduction of a new product often requires some significant change in the process of production. This can lead to a correlation between indicators of product and process innovation, which may explain why empirical studies often diverge in their conclusions regarding their respective impacts on productivity. A similar analysis can even lead to different conclusions across different samples. For instance, in their version of the CDM model, Griffith et al. (2006) find a positive impact of process innovation on labour productivity in France, but no impact whatsoever in Germany, Spain, or the UK. Raffo et al. (2008), who estimate a similar CDM-type model, find a positive impact of process innovation in France, Spain, Brazil, and Mexico, but no impact in Switzerland or Argentina. Although we are not able in the present study to avoid the above-mentioned difficulties, we must be aware of them in the interpretation of our results.

6.2.2. Econometric specification

Our aim is to estimate a variant of the CDM model accounting for both product and process innovation, in the line of Griffith et al. (2006). Our model can be written as a recursive system of five econometric equations,[1] three of which are non-linear:

$$\begin{cases} r_i = 1(x_{1i}\beta_1 + u_{i1} > 0) \\ \ln rd_i = x_{2i}\beta_2 + u_{i2} \\ prod_i = 1(\alpha_3 \ln rd_i + x_{3i}\beta_3 + u_{i3} > 0) \\ proc_i = 1(\alpha_4 \ln rd_i + x_{4i}\beta_4 + u_{i4} > 0) \\ \ln LP_i = \delta.prod_i + \gamma.proc_i + x_{5i}\beta_5 + u_{i5} \end{cases} \quad (1)$$

where $1(.)$ denotes the indicator function, which is equal to 1 if its argument is true, and to 0 otherwise. The x_{ki}'s (with $k = 1, \ldots, 5$) are vectors of explanatory variables, and the u_{ik}'s (with $k = 1, \ldots, 5$) are random-error terms. Finally, β_k (with $k = 1, \ldots, 5$) denotes a vector of parameters to be estimated, while α_3, α_4, γ, and δ are single parameters to be estimated. We relied on different procedures to estimate System (1). Before detailing these estimation procedures, let us examine what each of the five equations represents.

The first equation in System (1) accounts for selection into R&D. It explains the probability that firm i does R&D on a continuous basis, and is specified as a probit model, i.e. $P(r_i = 1) = \Phi(x_{1i}\beta_1)$, where $r_i = 1$ if firm i reports R&D expenditures, and $r_i = 0$ otherwise. The second equation describes the R&D effort of firm i, conditional on doing R&D. It is specified as a linear equation, which relates the log of R&D intensity (defined as the ratio of R&D expenditures to the number of employees) to a number of potential determinants x_{2i}. Taken together, and assuming that u_1 and u_2 are bivariate normal with

---

[1] The system is recursive in the sense that the five equations are nested in three clearly defined stages, each stage being modelled as the determinant of the next one. Thus, the first two equations model firms' R&D effort (first stage), which is a determinant of the 'knowledge production function' (second stage), represented by the next two equations. Innovation (the knowledge output of the second stage) is a determinant of firms' labour productivity, modelled in the fifth equation using a standard production function framework (third stage).

correlation coefficient ρ_{12}, these two equations define a generalized (or type II) tobit model.

The third equation in System (1) models the probability that a firm introduces a product innovation over a period of time (equal to three years in the CIS). The fourth does the same with regard to process innovation. Each one of these two equations is specified as a probit model which includes an endogenous regressor and several exogenous regressors. The endogenous regressor is $\ln rd_i$, the log of R&D intensity. The exogenous regressors are control variables included in the x_{3i} and x_{4i} vectors respectively. Taken together, and assuming that u_3 and u_4 are correlated with correlation coefficient ρ_{34}, these two equations define a bivariate probit model. This specification takes into account the fact that product and process innovation can be jointly determined.

Economically, this bivariate probit model represents what is known in the literature as the 'knowledge production function'. The knowledge production function relates measures of new knowledge (innovations) to innovation inputs (such as R&D expenditures). In our representation of the knowledge production function, $\ln rd_i$ is potentially endogenous. Indeed, unobservable characteristics could increase both a firm's R&D effort and its 'innovativeness' or 'innovativity' (i.e. its 'productivity' in producing innovations, as defined in Mairesse and Mohnen, 2002; and Mohnen et al., 2006). We explain below how each estimation procedure deals with this potential endogeneity.

The fifth and final equation in System (1) models the log of labour productivity LP_i (defined as the ratio of value added to the number of employees) as a function of product innovation, process innovation and a number of control variables (including a proxy for physical capital). Again, product (and process) innovation is potentially endogenous as unobserved factors could influence both the innovation process and the production process. We explain below how each estimation procedure deals with this potential endogeneity. Economically, the fifth equation in System (1) derives from a Cobb-Douglas type production function where the main inputs are labour, capital, and knowledge (represented by the two indicator variables $prod_i$ and $proc_i$). The role of materials as an input is implicitly taken into account through the use of value added (rather than turnover) to define labour productivity.

6.2.3. Estimation procedures

The original CDM model was estimated simultaneously using asymptotic least squares (ALS). Although system estimators provide a gain in efficiency, most subsequent applications of the CDM framework (such as the ones mentioned in Section 6.2.1) usually estimate the three stages sequentially, with the predicted output of a given stage being used as an explanatory variable in the next one. In the present research, we adopt two distinct procedures to estimate this model: (1) a three-step sequential estimation procedure similar to that used by Griffith et al. (2006), and (2) a two-step sequential estimation procedure in which the innovation production function and the productivity equation are jointly estimated. The former is supposedly more robust but less efficient, whereas the latter is potentially more efficient but less robust. In our empirical application, we will be able to check whether these two procedures lead to consistent results.

The three-step sequential estimation procedure is the most commonly used in the literature. In the first step, we estimate the generalized tobit model which describes both selection into R&D and R&D intensity. In the second step, we estimate the bivariate probit model which depicts the knowledge production function, using the predicted (rather than actual) value of R&D intensity as a regressor.[2] The third and final step consists of estimating the labour productivity equation, using the predicted values of the probabilities to innovate as regressors (rather than the indicators). We use maximum-likelihood estimation in the first two steps, and ordinary least squares (OLS) in the third one. In this estimation procedure, we address the above-mentioned endogeneity issues in the second and third steps by replacing the potentially endogenous regressors with their predicted values (obtained from the previous step). Standard errors are bootstrapped to correct for the bias induced by the inclusion of predicted regressors. For identification, we rely on 'instruments' included in the previous step and excluded from the current step (the list of instruments for each step will be detailed in Section 6.3.2).

The two-step sequential estimation procedure is a potentially more efficient variant of the three-step procedure described above. The first step is actually identical in both procedures: we estimate a generalized tobit model to describe both selection into R&D and R&D intensity. In the two-step procedure, however, the knowledge production function and the productivity equation are jointly estimated by maximum likelihood, using the predicted value of R&D intensity in the product- and process-innovation equations. In other words, the second step of this procedure consists in estimating by maximum likelihood the following three-equation model, which combines two nonlinear (probit) equations and a linear equation:

---

[2] Using a bivariate probit rather than two separate probits (as in Griffith et al., 2006; and Raffo et al., 2008) has two advantages. First, by allowing unobserved factors to jointly affect product and process innovation, the bivariate probit may do a better job of accounting for the potential correlation between both types of innovation. Second, the estimation of a bivariate probit may yield a gain in efficiency in the estimation of the CDM model.

$$
\begin{cases}
prod_i = 1(\alpha_3 \ln \hat{r}_i + x_{3i}\beta_3 + u_{i3} > 0) \\
proc_i = 1(\alpha_4 \ln \hat{r}_i + x_{4i}\beta_4 + u_{i4} > 0) \\
\ln LP_i = \delta.prod_i + \gamma.proc_i + x_{5i}\beta_5 + u_{i5}
\end{cases}
\tag{2}
$$

where $\ln \hat{r}_i$ denotes the predicted value of $\ln rd_i$ (obtained from the first step of the procedure). In Model (2), u_{i3}, u_{i4}, and u_{i5}, the error terms, are assumed to be trivariate normal. This implies that the contributions to the likelihood will be connected by the correlation coefficients of the error terms. There are three components to the likelihood, two of which correspond to the likelihood of a probit and one to the likelihood of a linear model. Thus, the likelihood of Model (2) can be written as:

$$
\begin{aligned}
L = {} & \prod_i [\Phi(\alpha_3 \ln \hat{r}_j + x_{3i}\beta_3 | \rho_{34}, \rho_{35})]^{prod_i} [1 - \Phi(\alpha_3 \ln \hat{r}_i + x_{3i}\beta_3 | \rho_{34}, \rho_{35})]^{1-prod_i} \\
& \times [\Phi(\alpha_3 \ln \hat{r}_i + x_{i4}\beta_4 | \rho_{34}, \rho_{45})]^{prod_i} [\Phi(\alpha_4 \ln \hat{r}_i + x_{i4}\beta_4 | \rho_{34}, \rho_{45})]^{1-prod_i} \\
& \times \frac{1}{\sigma_5} \emptyset \left[\frac{\ln LP_i - x_{i5}\beta_5 - \delta.prod_i - \gamma.proc_i}{\sigma_5} | \rho_{35}, \rho_{45} \right]
\end{aligned}
\tag{3}
$$

where ρ_{jk} denotes the correlation coefficient between errors u_j and u_k (with $j = 3, 4, 5$; and $k = 3, 4, 5$), and σ_5 the standard deviation of random error u_5. By convention, φ and Φ respectively denote the density and c.d.f. of the normal distribution.

In practice, Model (2) is simultaneously estimated by full-information maximum likelihood, using the conditional mixed process application (CMP) developed by Roodman (2009). Maximizing the log-likelihood of this model requires solving a multiple integral of dimension 3, which cannot be done analytically. To solve this problem, the CMP program relies on a GHK-type numerical simulation algorithm.

In theory, we could expect the two-step procedure to be somewhat more efficient, but potentially less robust, than the three-step procedure. From an empirical perspective, we are interested in checking whether the two procedures give similar results (in terms of both the signs and magnitudes of the estimated parameters of interests). The empirical application is conducted on the third and fourth waves of the French component of the CIS, in both the manufacturing (for CIS3 and CIS4) and services (for CIS4 only) industries. This will allow us to observe the evolution of the innovation–productivity relationship in the French manufacturing industry over two periods of time (1998–2000 and 2002–2004). We will also be able to compare this relationship in the manufacturing and services industries in the most recent observation period (2002–2004).

6.3. Data and variables

6.3.1. *The French CIS3 and CIS4 databases*

The present study uses firm-level data from the third and fourth waves (CIS3 and CIS4) of the French component of the CIS. The CIS is a harmonized survey that is carried out by national statistical agencies in all EU member states under the co-ordination of Eurostat. CIS3 and CIS4 were conducted in 2001 and 2005 respectively and provide information for the periods 1998–2000 and 2002–2004. Both waves of the survey provide information on firms' R&D activities, sources of knowledge, intellectual-property protection, product and process innovations, other forms of innovation (e.g. organizational changes) and abandoned innovations.

However, the two waves present some key differences. The French CIS3 gives some information about firms' investment in physical capital. It also allows researchers to distinguish between different types of human capital (i.e. low-skill and high-skilled, the latter being measured by the proportion of employees with higher education in the workforce). The information about physical and human capital has disappeared in CIS4, which has been extended into two other directions: firstly, CIS4 samples firms with 10 employees or more, whereas CIS3 only included firms with 20 employees or more; secondly, CIS3 was focused mostly on manufacturing firms, whereas CIS4 covers the services industry quite extensively.

This structure of the data will lead us to use CIS3 and CIS4 to draw two different comparisons. First, we will examine how the relationship between R&D activities, innovation, and productivity in the French manufacturing industry has evolved across time, i.e. from the years 1998–2000 to the years 2002–2004. To do so, we will compare the results obtained with the sample of CIS3 manufacturing firms, to those obtained with the sample of CIS4 manufacturing firms. Second, we will use CIS4 to examine whether this relationship differs between the manufacturing and services industries in the recent period.

In order to be able to draw relevant conclusions from these comparisons, we selected three samples of firms with 20 employees of more from both CIS3 and CIS4: two manufacturing samples (a sample of 3524 firms from CIS3 and a sample of 4955 firms from CIS4) and a services sample (3599 firms from CIS4). Table 6.1 gives a breakdown of these three samples by category of industry. These industry categories are based on the two-digit NACE classification, aggregated in a fashion similar to that of Griffith et al. (2006). We cleaned all three samples in the usual way: we deleted a few observations with extreme values of turnover, observations where the absolute value of the rate of growth

135

Table 6.1. Number and proportion of firms by industry in manufacturing and services for CIS3 and CIS4

| Industry | Nace | CIS3 | | | | CIS4 | | | |
| | | Before matching | | After matching | | Before matching | | After matching | |
		N	%	N	%	N	%	N	%
Textile	17–19	475	13.5	475	13.5	648	13.1	636	13.2
Wood/Paper	20–22	386	11.0	386	11.0	706	14.2	654	13.5
Chemicals	23–24	374	10.6	374	10.6	451	9.1	445	9.2
Plastic/Rubber	25	276	7.8	276	7.8	313	6.3	311	6.4
Non-metallic min.	26	168	4.8	168	4.8	273	5.5	265	5.5
Basic metals	27–28	607	17.2	607	17.3	699	14.1	684	14.2
Machinery	29	418	11.9	413	11.7	439	8.9	433	9.0
Electrical	30–33	452	12.8	452	12.9	657	13.3	644	13.3
Vehicles	34–35	192	5.4	191	5.4	483	9.7	475	9.8
Miscellaneous	36–37	176	5.0	176	5.0	286	5.8	284	5.9
All Manufacturing		**3,524**	**100**	**3,518**	**100**	**4,955**	**100**	**4,831**	**100**
Hotels/Restaurants	55					505	14.0	482	13.9
Communication	64					78	2.2	72	2.1
Housing/Real Estate	70					269	7.5	258	7.4
Rental	71					179	5.0	171	4.9
ICT services	72					406	11.3	397	11.5
Services to firms	74					2,162	60.1	2,087	60.2
All Services						**3,599**	**100**	**3,467**	**100**

Notes: The industry definition is based on the classification system NACE (*Nomenclature générale des activités économiques dans les Communautés Européénnes*) as published by Eurostat, using two-digit levels. 'Matching' refers here to the matching of our survey data with administrative data on firms (which provided information on physical capital and value added).

of turnover is larger than 100 per cent, and observations where R&D expenditures represent more than 50 per cent of turnover.

Besides clean samples, our analysis also requires information on physical capital that is not available in CIS4. We obtained this information by matching CIS4 with administrative data from the French yearly firm census (EAE).[3] In order to have similar variables in all samples, we also matched CIS3 with the same administrative data (over a different period). This provided us, for each wave of the CIS, with two possible proxies for physical capital, observed in t, t-1, and t-2 (t being the year the CIS was conducted). The first proxy is investment, and the second one is the book value of fixed assets. Matching CIS3 and CIS4 with the relevant yearly firm survey also provided us with value added, which we use to compute labour productivity. Using value added rather than turnover allows us to control implicitly for the effect of materials in the labour productivity equation of the model.

As can be seen in Table 6.1, matching the CIS data with administrative data did not cause a greater loss of observations that the loss which would have resulted from a simple cleaning of the data. In any sample, we lose very few firms from matching and the distribution of firms across industry categories remains the same after matching the data.[4] This suggests that we do not have to fear selection biases arising from either cleaning or matching. This first impression was confirmed by a thorough examination of the distribution of key variables in the initial and final (matched) samples.

6.3.2. Choice of explanatory variables

We now detail the choice of explanatory variables used in the empirical specification of our econometric model. This choice of variable has been made in accordance with the original theoretical framework proposed in Crépon et al. (1998), taking into account some of the changes introduced to this initial CDM framework by Griffith et al. (2006), and trying to circumvent some limitations of the latter.

The x_1 vector of regressors used in the first—'selection into R&D'—equation of System (1) includes proxy variables for a firm's ability to rip profit from innovation (appropriability conditions), and for market conditions and other Schumpeterian determinants of innovation. Appropriability conditions are represented by two dummy variables which describe how firms protected

---

[3] For manufacturing, we had to leave aside the agro-food industry, which is surveyed in the CIS but not covered in the administrative data. For services, we had to leave aside three sectors that are surveyed in CIS4 but not covered in the administrative data: 'Transport services', 'Trade', and 'R&D services'. The latter is so specific anyway that it deserves a separate study.

[4] Note also that the distribution of manufacturing firms across industries does not change much from CIS3 to CIS4.

their inventions during the observation period. The first (*formal protection*) is equal to 1 if a firm used patents, design patterns, trademarks, or copyrights, and to 0 otherwise. The second variable (*strategic protection*) is equal to 1 if a firm relied on complexity of design, secrecy, or lead-time advantage on competitors, and to 0 otherwise. Market conditions are partly captured by a binary indicator of *international competition* (equal to 1 if a firm's most significant market is international, and to 0 otherwise). This variable may also be a proxy for the degree of openness of a firm to the international market. Therefore, market conditions in a more Schumpeterian sense are more aptly captured, in each application of the model, by the sets of *industry dummy variables* presented in Table 6.1 (and based on the two-digit NACE codes). These industry dummies give an indication of a firm's main market during the observation period, and may thus control for market characteristics such as concentration.

The other usual Schumpeterian determinant of innovation included in the x_1 vector is *firm size*. It is measured by the number of employees *two years before* the year of the survey, and represented by a five-category variable: (1) less than 50 employees, (2) 50 to 99 employees, (3) 100 to 249 employees, (4) 250 to 999 employees, and (5) 1000 or more employees. In order to make identification of the model easier, we chose to exclude firm size from the second equation of System (1), i.e. the 'R&D intensity equation'. The choice of size as an exclusion variable was dictated by the results of previous studies. For instance, Griffith et al. (2006) have shown that, in several European countries (and particularly in France), firm size influences the probability to do R&D, but not the amount of investment in R&D.

Finally, in accordance with the original framework of Crépon et al. (1998), the x_1 vector also includes variables indicating to which extent innovation was *demand pulled* or *technology pushed* in the three-digit industry where a firm operated during the observation period. These variables are built using a question that is specific to French CIS surveys. In each case, three variables give the share of firms where innovation was weakly/mildly/strongly influenced by market (or technological) conditions, while a fourth variable indicating no influence at all is taken as the reference. By measuring these variables at the three-digit industry level rather than at the firm level, we get around a difficulty raised by most innovation surveys: the fact that only innovating firms answer questions pertaining to the nature of innovation.

The x_2 vector used in the second—'R&D intensity'—equation of System (1) includes the same variables as the x_1 vector, except firm size. However, the x_2 vector includes three variables which are only observed when firms report R&D expenditures, and which may be useful to further characterize the R&D process. These three additional variables are: (1) *cooperation* in innovation activities, (2) *public funding*, and (3) *sources of information* used in the innovation process. *Cooperation* is a dummy variable equal to 1 if a firm had some cooperative agreements on innovation activities during the observation period, and equal to 0 otherwise. *Public funding* is captured by a set of three non-mutually exclusive binary variables: (1) *local funding*, which indicates funding from local or regional authorities, (2) *national funding*, which indicates funding from the national government, and (3) *EU funding*, which indicates funding from the EU, including that received through participation in a Framework Programme. Similarly, *sources of information* are represented by a set of dummy variables which includes internal sources (within the firm), internal sources within the group (if the firm belongs to a group), suppliers, customers, competitors, and public research (i.e. universities or government labs).

The x_3 vector of regressors used in the third equation of System (1)—the 'product innovation equation'—includes an endogenous variable and three exogenous variables. The endogenous variable is the log of R&D intensity (predicted from the previous stage of the model). The exogenous variables are appropriability conditions (captured by the same indicators of invention protection as above),[5] firm size (defined in exactly the same way as above), and the set of industry-specific dummies already described above and presented in Table 6.1. The x_4 vector of regressors used in the fourth equation of System (1)—the 'process innovation equation'—includes exactly the same variables as x_3, plus an additional variable. This additional variable is the amount of investment in *physical capital*, measured by the log of investment intensity in t-2 (t being the year the survey was conducted).[6] The rationale for including this variable is that, by definition, process innovation involves changes in the production line, which may require the acquisition of new machinery and equipment. The variable is lagged by two years in order to reduce potential simultaneity problems, which may arise since innovation is reported over the last three years (i.e. innovation can occur in t-2, t-1, or t).

The x_5 vector of regressors used in the fifth and final equation of System (1)—the 'labour productivity equation'—includes two endogenous variables and three exogenous variables. The two endogenous variables are the indicators of product and process innovation used as dependent variables in the innovation equations. In the three-step estimation procedure, these variables are the predicted marginal probabilities from the previously estimated bivariate probit. In the two-step sequential procedure, we use the actual (observed) binary indicators. The exogenous variables are firm size (defined in the same way as above), our set of industry-specific dummy variables and a proxy for

---

[5] Our indicators of invention protection are used as instruments, in the sense that they are included in both x_3 and x_4, but not in the labour productivity equation, where product and process innovation are endogenous regressors.

[6] Investment intensity is defined here as the ratio of investment to the number of employees.

physical capital. In order to leave less scope for potential endogeneity problems, this proxy for physical capital is different from the one included in x_4. In the labour productivity equation, we measure physical capital using (the log of) the book value of fixed assets per employee at t-1 (t being the year the survey was conducted). The variable is lagged by one year in order to account for the stock of physical capital at the end of the (previous) year.

6.3.3. Comparison of the samples

We have now presented our data sources and explained which variables will be used in the econometric model. Before moving to the results of the analysis, we briefly compare the three matched samples. Table 6.2 gives summary statistics for all of our dependent and explanatory variables in all three matched samples. Although differences in mean are often significant, the CIS3 and CIS4 manufacturing samples look very similar on average. In particular, the value of our measure of labour productivity (computed using value added) is quite similar, even without the use of a deflator, and the difference is not statistically significant. The main differences between the two manufacturing samples concern innovation: there are more process innovators in CIS4 (45 per cent versus only 32 per cent in CIS3), and innovation seems to have become more demand-pulled. The importance of invention protection (and more specifically strategic protection) has also grown from CIS3 to CIS4. Finally, international competition has intensified in CIS4.

Focusing only on CIS4 emphasizes the differences between manufacturing and services in the recent period. Differences in means are more systematically significant across manufacturing and services than they were across the two manufacturing samples. Computed as the ratio of turnover to employees, labour productivity appears to be much lower in the services (130 euros per worker versus roughly 200 euros in the CIS3 and CIS4 manufacturing samples). When it is computed using value added instead of turnover, labour productivity is actually a little higher in the services (62 euros per worker versus roughly 55 euros in the manufacturing samples), and the difference is statistically significant. The reason is naturally that turnover-based labour productivity measures take into account the costs of materials which correspond to much higher shares in manufacturing than in the services. The value-added-based measures abstracting from such differences may be preferred and viewed as more consistent with the fact that France (like most Western European countries) is gradually becoming a services-driven economy.

A major difference between manufacturing and services is that the proportion of firms doing R&D continuously is much lower in the latter (14 per cent versus 33 per cent in the manufacturing industry). The proportion of firms receiving public support to innovate is also much lower in the services: for

Table 6.2. Summary statistics for the final samples

	CIS3	CIS4	
	Manufacturing	Manufacturing	Services
Knowledge/Innovation:			
Continuous R&D engagement	0.38***	0.33	0.14***
R&D per employee	7.41	7.66	7.50
(for firms w/continuous R&D)			
Innovation (product and/or process)	0.52***	0.57	0.36***
Process innovation	0.32***	0.45	0.31***
Product innovation	0.47***	0.43	0.23***
Share of sales with new products	0.24*	0.23	0.19***
(for firms with product innovation)			
Labour productivity (Turnover)	182.64**	209.75	130.05***
Labour productivity (Value added)	54.01	55.05	62.4***
Public Support:			
Local funding (1 if yes, 0 if no)	0.06**	0.05	0.01***
National funding (1 if yes, 0 if no)	0.16***	0.12	0.04***
EU funding (1 if yes, 0 if no)	0.05**	0.04	0.02***
Innovation was:			
Not demand pulled	0.03***	0.05	0.11***
Weakly demand pulled	0.07***	0.04	0.06***
Mildly demand pulled	0.28***	0.21	0.22***
Strongly demand pulled	0.61***	0.70	0.62***
Not technology pushed	0.12***	0.15	0.23***
Weakly technology pushed	0.23***	0.19	0.15***
Mildly technology pushed	0.43***	0.37	0.32***
Strongly technology pushed	0.22***	0.29	0.30***
Sources of information			
(for firms doing R&D or innovating):			
Internal sources (w/in the firm)	0.47**	0.50	0.30***
Internal sources (w/in the group)	0.22***	0.28	0.17***
Suppliers	0.28***	0.32	0.19***
Customers	0.42***	0.37	0.20***
Competitors	0.33***	0.23	0.13***
Universities/Government labs	0.11	0.12	0.05***
Appropriability conditions:			
Formal protection dummy variable	0.45***	0.51	0.29***
Strategic protection dummy variable	0.28***	0.39	0.17***
Cooperation dummy variable	0.27**	0.29	0.16***
Other:			
International competition	0.41***	0.54	0.19***
Size: <50 employees	0.29***	0.34	0.39***
Size: 50–99 employees	0.18	0.20	0.20
Size: 100–250 employees	0.20***	0.18	0.16
Size: 250–999 employees	0.24	0.23	0.20***
Size: ≥1,000 employees	0.08***	0.06	0.05
Observations	3518	4831	3467

Notes: The table displays average values. All monetary values are in thousands of euros. CIS3 (CIS4) variables are observed over 1998–2000 (2002–2004), except R&D per employee, labour productivity and investment per employee, which are observed in 2000 (2002), and firm size (number of employees), which is measured in 1998 (2002).
***, **, and * indicate differences in means (with respect to CIS4 Manufacturing) significant at the 1%, 5%, and 10% levels, respectively.

instance, only 4 per cent of service firms receive government funding, versus 12 per cent in the manufacturing industry. Service firms seem less involved in knowledge sourcing, as the proportion of firms relying on the various sources of information covered by CIS4 is systematically lower than in the manufacturing industry. Service firms are also less concerned with appropriability conditions. This is consistent with their lower investment in R&D, but also with the fact that patenting is virtually nonexistent in services industries. Finally, service firms seem more oriented towards local or national markets, as they are facing less pressure from international competition.

To put it in a nutshell, although there are contrasts between the two French manufacturing samples observed at different periods, these contrasts are less important than the differences between the services and manufacturing industries in the same period. These differences should be kept in mind when studying innovation, as they highlight the specificity of the services.

6.4. Results

In this section, the results obtained with the three-step sequential procedure model are presented as a benchmark. Table 6.3 and Table 6.4 give these results for the French manufacturing industry observed in CIS3 and CIS 4 respectively, while Table 6.5 presents them for the French services industry observed in CIS4. Table 6.6 presents the correlation coefficients of the generalized residuals of the model for each one of these three samples. In the following two subsections, we comment on these results and compare them to those obtained with the potentially more efficient two-step estimation procedure (the full tables of results for this procedure are presented in the appendix).

6.4.1. Manufacturing in CIS3 and in CIS4

The first comparison that can be conducted on the basis of our estimations concerns the manufacturing industry, which is observed for both CIS3 (1998–2000) and CIS4 (2002–2004). We achieve this comparison by comparing the results presented in Table 6.3 with those presented in Table 6.4. We also compare both series of results with those obtained with the two-step estimation procedure and presented in Tables A6.1 and A6.2 in the appendix, respectively.

We first discuss the estimates of the selection and R&D-intensity equations. In the selection equation, firm size appears as a major determinant of the propensity to do R&D, which is consistent with both the Schumpeterian tradition and the empirical literature. Calculation of the marginal effects

Table 6.3. Estimates of the three-step sequential model (CIS3, manufacturing)

	R&D equations		Innovation production function		Productivity
	Selection	Intensity	Product	Process	
Log(R&D intensity)	—	—	1.18***	0.73***	—
			(0.08)	(0.07)	
Product innovation	—	—	—	—	0.05
					(0.09)
Process innovation	—	—	—	—	0.41***
					(0.12)
Log(Physical capital intensity)	—	—	—	0.11***	0.13***
				(0.02)	(0.01)
International competition	0.40***	0.44***	—	—	—
	(0.06)	(0.08)			
Cooperation	—	0.25***	—	—	—
		(0.07)			
Appropriability conditions					
Formal protection	0.96***	0.30***	0.53***	0.16**	—
	(0.06)	(0.09)	(0.06)	(0.06)	
Strategic protection	0.73***	0.30***	0.39***	0.32***	—
	(0.06)	(0.08)	(0.08)	(0.07)	
Funding					
Local funding	—	0.03	—	—	—
		(0.12)			
National funding	—	−0.14	—	—	—
		(0.08)			
EU funding	—	0.46***	—	—	—
		(0.13)			
Firm size (*ref.: < 50 employees*)					
50 to 99 employees	0.28***	—	0.22***	0.13	−0.09***
	(0.08)		(0.08)	(0.08)	(0.02)
100 to 249 employees	0.39***	—	0.09	0.23***	−0.15***
	(0.08)		(0.08)	(0.08)	(0.03)
250 to 999 employees	0.78***	—	0.36***	0.27***	−0.13***
	(0.08)		(0.09)	(0.08)	(0.02)
≥ 1,000 employees	0.92***	—	0.25**	0.38***	−0.04
	(0.11)		(0.12)	(0.12)	(0.05)
Two-digit industry	0.000	0.000	0.000	0.000	0.000
Demand pulled/Techn. pushed	0.833	0.000	—	—	—
Sources of information	—	0.072	—	—	—
Sigma		1.29***	—	—	—
		(0.04)			
Rho	0.35***		0.47***		—
	(0.05)		(0.03)		
Goodness-of-Fit	Log-likelihood: -3667.18		Log-likelihood: -2760.66		Adj. R^2 = 0.27
	Test of 'β = 0': 523.60***		Test of 'β = 0': 1644.92***		

Notes: * Significant at the 10% level, ** Significant at the 5% level, *** Significant at the 1% levelRobust standard errors in parentheses. For the sake of concision, we report only the p-values of a test of the joint significance of the two-digit industry dummy variables, 'demand pulled/technology pushed' indicators, and 'sources of information' indicators. Physical capital is measured by the log of investment intensity at time t-2 in the process equation, and by the log of book value at t-1 in the productivity equation.

Table 6.4. Estimates of the three-step sequential model (CIS4, manufacturing)

	R&D equations		Innovation production function		Productivity
	Selection	Intensity	Product	Process	
Log(R&D intensity)	—	—	1.27***	0.90***	—
			(0.07)	(0.06)	
Product innovation	—	—	—	—	−0.08
					(0.13)
Process innovation	—	—	—	—	0.45***
					(0.16)
Log(Physical capital intensity)	—	—	—	0.08***	0.10***
				(0.02)	(0.01)
International competition	0.51***	0.51***	—	—	—
	(0.05)	(0.10)			
Cooperation	—	0.36***	—	—	—
		(0.08)			
Appropriability conditions					
Formal protection	0.59***	0.43***	0.09	−0.16***	—
	(0.05)	(0.10)	(0.05)	(0.06)	
Strategic protection	0.67***	0.61***	−0.17**	−0.01	—
	(0.05)	(0.09)	(0.06)	(0.06)	
Funding					
Local funding	—	−0.03	—	—	—
		(0.14)			
National funding	—	0.07	—	—	—
		(0.09)			
EU funding	—	0.40***	—	—	—
		(0.14)			
Firm size (ref.: < 50 employees)					
50 to 99 employees	0.18***	—	0.05	0.01	−0.05**
	(0.07)		(0.06)	(0.06)	(0.02)
100 to 249 employees	0.39***	—	0.07	0.05	−0.10***
	(0.07)		(0.07)	(0.06)	(0.02)
250 to 999 employees	0.63***	—	0.21***	0.05	−0.06**
	(0.06)		(0.07)	(0.06)	(0.02)
≥ 1,000 employees	1.07***	—	0.35***	0.34***	0.02
	(0.10)		(0.12)	(0.11)	(0.04)
Two-digit industry	0.000	0.000	0.000	0.000	0.000
Demand pulled/Techn. pushed	0.014	0.000	—	—	—
Sources of information	—	0.053	—	—	—
Sigma	—	1.46***	—	—	—
		(0.04)			
Rho	0.28***		0.44***		—
	(0.06)		(0.03)		
Goodness-of-fit	Log-likelihood: -5061.75		Log-likelihood: -4318.03		Adj. R^2 = 0.21
	Test of 'β = 0': 444.41***		Test of 'β = 0': 2205.76***		

Notes: * Significant at the 10% level, ** Significant at the 5% level, *** Significant at the 1% level. Robust standard errors in parentheses. For the sake of concision, we report only the p-values of a test of the joint significance of the two-digit industry dummy variables, 'demand pulled/technology pushed' indicators, and 'sources of information' indicators. Physical capital is measured by the log of investment intensity at time t-2 in the process equation, and by the log of book value at t-1 in the productivity equation.

Table 6.5. Estimates of the three-step sequential model (CIS4, services)

	R&D equations		Innovation production function		Productivity
	Selection	Intensity	Product	Process	
Log (R&D intensity)	—	—	0.32***	0.20***	—
			(0.04)	(0.03)	—
Product innovation	—	—	—	—	0.27
					(0.45)
Process innovation	—	—	—	—	0.27
					(0.52)
Log (Physical capital intensity)	—	—	—	−0.01	0.18***
				(0.02)	(0.01)
International competition	0.44***	0.90***	—	—	—
	(0.07)	(0.20)			
Cooperation	—	0.07	—	—	—
		(0.17)			
Appropriability conditions					
Formal protection	0.71***	0.94***	0.28***	0.26***	—
	(0.07)	(0.23)	(0.08)	(0.07)	
Strategic protection	0.89***	1.11***	0.49***	0.50***	—
	(0.07)	(0.22)	(0.09)	(0.09)	
Funding					
Local funding	—	−0.40	—	—	—
		(0.34)			
National funding	—	0.77***	—	—	—
		(0.21)			
EU funding	—	−0.27	—	—	—
		(0.31)			
Firm size (ref.: < 50 employees)					
50 to 99 employees	0.23***	—	0.16*	0.17**	−0.07*
	(0.08)		(0.09)	(0.08)	(0.04)
100 to 249 employees	0.25***	—	0.17*	0.23***	−0.08**
	(0.09)		(0.09)	(0.08)	(0.04)
250 to 999 employees	0.39***	—	0.35***	0.40***	−0.15***
	(0.09)		(0.09)	(0.08)	(0.04)
≥ 1,000 employees	0.83***	—	0.77***	0.69***	−0.29***
	(0.14)		(0.13)	(0.12)	(0.05)
Two-digit industry	0.069	0.050	0.148	0.141	0.000
Demand pulled/Techn. pushed	0.005	0.000	—	—	—
Sources of information	—	0.503	—	—	—
Sigma	—	2.05** (0.14)	—	—	—
Rho	0.62***		0.65***		—
	(0.07)		(0.03)		
Goodness-of-fit	Log-likelihood: -1987.65		Log-likelihood: -2177.52		Adj. R^2 = 0.42
	Test of 'β = 0': 233.42***		Test of 'β = 0': 747.34***		

Notes: * Significant at the 10% level, ** Significant at the 5% level, *** Significant at the 1% level. Robust standard errors in parentheses. For the sake of concision, we report only the p-values of a test of the joint significance of the 2-digit industry dummy variables, 'demand pulled/technology pushed' indicators, and 'sources of information' indicators. Physical capital is measured by the log of investment intensity at time t-2 in the process equation, and by the log of book value at t-1 in the productivity equation.

Table 6.6. Correlation coefficients of generalized residuals for each sample

	CIS3					CIS4, Manufacturing					CIS4, Services				
	(1)	(2)	(3)	(4)	(5)	(1)	(2)	(3)	(4)	(5)	(1)	(2)	(3)	(4)	(5)
(1)	1					1					1				
(2)	0.18***	1				0.23***	1				0.23***	1			
(3)	0.13***	0.34***	1			0.34***	0.11***	1			0.22***	0.33***	1		
(4)	0.06**	0.19***	0.26***	1		0.20***	0.02	0.25***	1		0.14***	0.34***	0.39***	1	
(5)	0.19***	−0.01	−0.02	−0.03*	1	0.01	0.17***	0.01	−0.05***	1	0.17***	0.01	−0.03	−0.02	1

Notes: (1) R&D propensity, (2) R&D intensity, (3) Product innovation, (4) Process innovation, (5) Labour productivity. * Significant at the 10% level;
** Significant at the 5% level; *** Significant at the 1% level.

shows that, in both CIS3 and CIS4, the probability of doing R&D is increasing with firm size (firms with less than 50 employees being the category of reference). In CIS3, as the size class increases, marginal effects rise from 0.11 (with a standard deviation of 0.03) to 0.14 (0.03), 0.30 (0.02) and finally 0.35 (0.03). In CIS4, they rise from 0.06 (with a standard deviation of 0.02) to 0.14 (0.02), 0.22 (0.02), and 0.41 (0.03).

Moreover, manufacturing firms that are better able to protect their inventions or innovations are also more likely (1) to do R&D continuously and (2) to invest more in R&D. In CIS3 and CIS4, both formal and strategic means of protection are associated with a higher propensity to do R&D and with a higher R&D intensity. These results are consistent with the theoretical literature, which suggests that firms will not start innovating (and will not invest in R&D) if they cannot protect the output of their innovation in a way that guarantees a higher profit. Finally, international competition and cooperation are positively associated with a higher R&D intensity in both samples, but the magnitudes of the effects are stronger in CIS4 than in CIS3. International competition can be seen here as a proxy for openness to the international market rather than a proxy for competition in the strict sense. Our results suggest that French firms that have a higher international exposure may also invest more in R&D (and our summary statistics suggest that this exposure has increased between CIS3 and CIS4).

. We now discuss the estimates of the 'knowledge production function' equations. The most important result concerns the effect of the endogenous explanatory variable 'log of R&D intensity'. This variable is significant in the product and process innovation equations, in both CIS3 and CIS4 manufacturing samples. Calculation of the marginal effects shows that, in CIS3, a one-unit increase in the log-R&D intensity results in a 47 per cent (25 per cent) increase in the probability of doing product (process) innovation, with a standard deviation of 3 per cent (2 per cent). Similarly, in CIS4, a one-unit increase in the log-R&D intensity results in a 50 per cent (36 per cent) increase in the probability of doing product (process) innovation, with a standard deviation of 2 per cent (2 per cent). Thus, in both manufacturing samples, the magnitude of the effect of R&D is stronger on product than on process innovation.[7]

The two-step estimation procedure confirms the above results on the knowledge production function. In both manufacturing samples (see Tables A6.1

---

[7] This difference could simply mean that product innovation requires more R&D than process innovation. However, process innovation generally implies the purchase of new machines and equipment. We controlled for this by including a proxy for physical capital in the 'process innovation' equation. This proxy is significant (with a positive effect) in both manufacturing samples, which can also explain why the effect of R&D appears to be weaker in the 'process innovation' equation.

and A6.2 in the appendix), we find a significantly positive effect of R&D on product and process innovation. The magnitude of this effect is always stronger on product than on process innovation.[8] With the two-step estimation procedure, the marginal effect of the log-R&D intensity on product (process) innovation is equal to 49 per cent (25 per cent) in the CIS3 sample and to 50 per cent (34 per cent) in the CIS4 manufacturing sample. These values are very close to those obtained with our benchmark estimates.[9]

Finally, we turn to our most important result: the effect of each type of innovation on labour productivity. According to our benchmark three-step sequential estimates, process innovation appears as the main driver of labour productivity in both manufacturing samples, whereas the impact of product innovation is never significant. In the CIS3 (CIS4) manufacturing sample, being a process innovator results in a 41 per cent (45 per cent) increase in the log of labour productivity, with a standard deviation of 12 per cent (15 per cent). The two-step estimation procedure confirms these results, showing that product innovation has no significant impact on labour productivity, and that only process innovation matters. The estimates obtained with this procedure are however slightly weaker than those obtained with the three-step procedure: in the CIS3 (CIS4) manufacturing sample, being a process innovator results in a 35 per cent (38 per cent) increase in the log of labour productivity, with a standard deviation of 10 per cent (10 per cent).

The dominance of process innovation as a driver of productivity in both manufacturing samples is in line with the findings of previous studies (Griffith et al., 2006; Raffo et al., 2008). However, given the difficulties mentioned in Section 6.2.1 (especially the potentially strong correlation between product and process innovation), this result deserves to be examined more closely. A look at Table 6.6 suggests that such a correlation might be at work here, because unobserved factors may affect both types of innovation in the same direction. Indeed, the correlation coefficient between the generalized residuals of the product and process equations is significantly positive in both manufacturing samples. This can also be seen in the fact that the correlation coefficient of the errors of the bivariate probit, estimated as part of the likelihood function in both procedures, is also significantly positive.[10] We therefore conduct a more thorough examination of the respective impact of product and process innovation in Section 6.4.3.

---

[8] Again, the proxy for physical capital included in the 'process innovation' equation is always significant, with a positive effect.

[9] And so are their standard errors which, for the sake of clarity, we do not display here.

[10] This correlation coefficient is equal to 0.47 in the CIS3 manufacturing sample according to both estimation procedures. It is equal to 0.43 or 0.44 in the CIS4 manufacturing sample, depending on which procedure is used.

6.4.2. *Manufacturing and services in CIS4*

We now turn to the comparison between the CIS4 manufacturing and services samples. To achieve this comparison, we compare the results presented in Table 6.5 with those already presented in Table 6.4. As in Section 6.4.1, we also compare both series of results with those obtained with the two-step estimation procedure, which are presented in Tables A6.2 and A6.3 in the appendix.

We first discuss the estimates of the selection and R&D-intensity equations. This discussion will be brief, as these results are essentially the same as those observed when comparing both manufacturing samples across time. First of all, we find that size is as important a determinant of the propensity to do R&D in the services as it was in the manufacturing industry. However, while the probability of doing R&D continuously still increases with firm size, the marginal effects are much smaller in the services industry. From the smallest to the largest size, marginal effects rise from 0.04 (with a standard deviation of 0.02) in the first two size classes, to 0.07 (0.02) and ultimately 0.20 (0.04) for the largest firms. Moreover, as in the manufacturing industry, service firms that are better able to protect their inventions or innovations are also more likely (1) to do R&D continuously and (2) to invest more in R&D. The estimated effects of both formal and strategic means of protection are significantly positive in both R&D equations. Finally, as in the manufacturing industry, international competition and cooperation are both positively associated with a higher R&D intensity.

An interesting contrast appears between manufacturing and service firms: whether in CIS3 or in CIS4, manufacturing firms are likely to invest more in R&D when they receive funding from the EU. Other types of public support do not seem to matter for these firms. By contrast, service firms are likely to invest more in R&D when they receive funding from their national government, whereas other types of public support do not seem to matter. It may be that, because the main markets of service firms are national rather than international, these firms seek support, when doing R&D, from national rather than supranational authorities that are less likely to be interested in their performances. It must also be noted from Table 6.2 that local and EU-level funding are far from widespread in the services industry, which may be what drives this result.

We now discuss the estimates of the 'knowledge production function' equations. In the service industries as in the manufacturing industries, the effect of the log-R&D intensity is significant in both innovation equations, but stronger in the product innovation equation than in the process innovation equation. In the former (latter), the marginal effect of the log-R&D intensity is equal to 9 per cent (7 per cent), with a standard deviation of 1 per cent

(1 per cent). Both figures are considerably smaller than those computed in the CIS4 manufacturing sample. The estimates obtained with the two-step procedure (see Table A6.3 in the appendix) lead to the same marginal effects. These results incidentally raise the nagging question of exactly what is product/process innovation in the services industry. Our findings suggest that in both cases, R&D does matter for innovation in the services, but is certainly not the only key resource.

We finally turn to the discussion of the effect of each type of innovation in the labour productivity equation. Here, a striking contrast appears between the estimates obtained in the manufacturing industry (where productivity appeared to be driven by process innovation) and those obtained in the services industry. In the latter, neither product nor process innovation appears to have a significant impact on labour productivity. A possible explanation for the non-significance of process innovation could be found in the measurement issue highlighted in Section 6.2.1.

However, a comparison with the two-step estimation procedure points towards a more precise interpretation. According to the two-step procedure, productivity in the services would actually be driven by product (rather than process) innovation: as can be seen in Table A6.3 in the appendix, being a product innovator is associated with a significant 39 per cent increase in labour productivity. These diverging conclusions may come from the fact that the three-step estimation procedure relies on the predicted values of the innovation indicators, whereas the two-step procedure relies on the actual, observed indicators. What they suggest, however, is that, in the services industry, both types of innovation are likely to be concurrent, up to the point that they both measure 'overall' innovation, as explained in Section 6.2.1. Depending on the estimation procedure, the positive effect of product innovation dominates or absorbs the effect of process innovation.

This interpretation is reinforced by the fact that unobserved factors may affect product and process in the same direction, as can be seen in Table 6.6. The correlation coefficient between the generalized residuals of the product and process equations is significantly positive and much higher (0.39) in the services sample than in the manufacturing samples (0.26 in CIS3 and 0.25 in CIS4). Similarly, the correlation coefficient of the errors of the bivariate probit model is higher in the services sample (around 0.64 or 0.65, depending on which estimation procedure is used) than it was in the manufacturing samples. The above-mentioned interpretation therefore deserves a closer examination, which is conducted in Section 6.4.3 through sensitivity analyses.

6.4.3. Sensitivity analyses

The main result of our analysis can be summarized as follows: in the manufacturing industries and across both periods, labour productivity appears primarily driven by process innovation, while in the services industry, if anything, it would be by product innovation. In view of the difficulties in disentangling the productivity impact of both types of innovation indicators, it could in fact be that they both approximately proxy for 'overall' innovation. This would explain why productivity appears to be sometimes correlated with product innovation or with process innovation, and even sometimes uncorrelated with both. In this section, we examine the robustness of these results by estimating variants of our model where we either (1) neglect one type of innovation, or (2) simply rely on an indicator of overall innovation.

In a first variant, the knowledge production function is simply the product innovation equation, specified as a probit model. We neglect process innovation, as if all innovation were actually product innovation. (This model is therefore an alternative specification of the original CDM model by Crépon et al. 1998.) In a second variant of the model, the knowledge production function is simply the process innovation equation, again specified as a probit model. This time, product innovation is neglected, as if all innovation were actually process innovation. In a third and final variant of the model, the knowledge production is specified as a probit model where the dependent variable is an indicator which equals 1 if a firm innovates in product and/or process, and 0 otherwise. Each variant encompasses only one knowledge production equation, which means that System (1) collapses to four equations instead of five.

Table 6.7 presents the key estimates, obtained with the three-step procedure, for: (1) our original model (i.e. the full model with both process and product innovation), (2) the model with only product innovation, (3) the model with only process innovation, and (4) the model with a single indicator of overall innovation. The key estimates for each model are (1) the effect of log-R&D intensity on innovation and (2) the effect of innovation on labour productivity. We discuss these key estimates and compare them to those obtained with the two-step estimation procedure (presented in Table A6.4 in the appendix).

Table 6.7 provides strong support for the assumption that our indicators of product and process innovation are actually both measuring 'overall' innovation. First of all, in the model that only considers product innovation, its predicted probability always has a positive effect on labour productivity. According to the three-step procedure estimates, being a product innovator is associated with an increase in labour productivity of about 30 per cent, 27 per cent, and 60 per cent in the CIS3 manufacturing sample, CIS4 manufacturing sample, and CIS4 services sample respectively. Estimating the same model with the two-step procedures yields estimates equal to 29 per cent, 26

Table 6.7. Key estimates of the CDM model with alternative versions of the knowledge production function

Knowledge production function = product innovation, process innovation (bivariate probit)

	CIS3			CIS4, Manufacturing			CIS4, Services		
	Prod.	Proc.	LP	Prod.	Proc.	LP	Prod.	Proc.	LP
Log (R&D intensity)	1.18*** (0.08)	0.73*** (0.07)	—	1.27*** (0.07)	0.90*** (0.06)	—	0.32*** (0.04)	0.20*** (0.03)	—
Product innovation	—	—	0.05 (0.09)	—	—	−0.08 (0.13)	—	—	0.27 (0.45)
Process innovation	—	—	0.41*** (0.12)	—	—	0.45*** (0.16)	—	—	0.27 (0.52)

Knowledge-production function = product innovation (simple probit)

	CIS3		CIS4, Manufacturing		CIS4, Services	
	Prod.	LP	Prod.	LP	Prod.	LP
Log (R&D intensity)	1.27*** (0.07)	—	1.31*** (0.06)	—	0.32*** (0.03)	—
Product innovation	—	0.30*** (0.04)	—	0.27*** (0.03)	—	0.60*** (0.06)

Knowledge-production function = process innovation (simple probit)

	CIS3		CIS4, Manufacturing		CIS4, Services	
	Proc.	LP	Proc.	LP	Proc.	LP
Log (R&D intensity)	0.71*** (0.06)	—	0.90*** (0.06)	—	0.18*** (0.03)	—
Process innovation	—	0.49*** (0.06)	—	0.35*** (0.04)	—	0.59*** (0.06)

Knowledge-production function = 'overall' innovation (simple probit)

	CIS3		CIS4, Manufacturing		CIS4, Services	
	Inno.	LP	Inno.	LP	Inno.	LP
Log (R&D intensity)	1.45*** (0.08)	—	1.48*** (0.08)	—	0.24*** (0.03)	—
'Overall' innovation	—	0.31*** (0.04)	—	0.28*** (0.03)	—	0.53*** (0.06)

Notes: * Significant at the 10% level, ** Significant at the 5% level, *** Significant at the 1% level Robust standard errors in parentheses.
Prod. = Product innovation, *Proc.* = Process innovation, *Inno.* = 'overall' innovation, *LP* = Labour productivity.

per cent, and 48 per cent respectively (see Table A6.4 in the appendix), i.e. elasticities that remain stable in the manufacturing samples, but become somewhat lower in the services sample.

Similarly, in the model that only considers process innovation, its predicted probability has a positive effect on labour productivity in all three samples. According to the three-step procedure estimates, being a process innovator increases labour productivity by 49 per cent, 35 per cent, and 59 per cent in the CIS3 manufacturing, CIS4 manufacturing, and CIS4 services samples respectively. Again, the two-step procedures yield estimates that are roughly stable in the manufacturing samples (41 per cent and 37 per cent for CIS4 and CIS3 respectively), but definitely lower in the services sample (40 per cent).

Last but not least, the model where the knowledge production function models 'overall' innovation (without distinguishing between product and process) shows that the predicted innovation probability always has a positive effect on labour productivity. The estimated elasticities effects obtained with the benchmark three-step procedure are equal to 31 per cent, 28 per cent, and 53 per cent in the CIS3 manufacturing, CIS4 manufacturing, and CIS4 services samples respectively. The estimates obtained when estimating the model with the two-step procedure are very similar in the manufacturing samples (29 per cent and 25 per cent for CIS3 and CIS4 respectively) and somewhat lower in the services samples (40 per cent).

In a nutshell, our sensitivity analysis suggests that our indicators of product and process innovation tend to capture the overall effect of innovation. This seems to be especially the case in the services industry, where the high estimates effect points at a stronger divide between innovating firms and non-innovators. In the end, disentangling the respective effects of product and process innovation could well prove to be a harder task than most studies consider. Experiments with an interaction term in the three-step procedure showed that the problem was actually pervasive, and that it might be preferable to consider only overall innovation.[11]

6.5. Conclusion

In this chapter, we examined the effect of innovation on labour productivity in France, using a CDM-type framework that accounts for research activities and for both product and process innovation. We estimated a multiple-equation

---

[11] We did not conduct similar experiments with the two-step procedure, because there are no clear rules on how to introduce (let alone instrument) an interaction term between two non-predicted endogenous regressors in a FIML simultaneous-equation model such as Model (2). We keep this issue for future research.

econometric model using three-step and two-step estimation procedures based on maximum likelihood. The model was specified as a system of five equations. The first two accounted for the propensity to do R&D and for the amount of investment in R&D. The next two equations modelled the knowledge production function, distinguishing between product and process innovation. The final equation measured the impact of each type of innovation on labour productivity.

We estimated this model on the third and fourth waves of the French component of the Community Innovation Survey (CIS3 and CIS4). Our main results point to process innovation as the main driver of labour productivity in the manufacturing industry in both waves. However, a more careful examination, through sensitivity analyses, suggests that our indicators of product and process innovation both account for 'overall' innovation, especially in the services industry. When a given type of innovation is singled out, it has a positive effect on labour productivity in all periods and in all samples. Similarly, when an indicator of overall innovation is built, its effect on labour productivity is always positive, in all industries. Thus, disentangling the effects of product and process innovation may sometimes be more difficult than is usually thought. In such a situation, relying on a single general indicator of innovation might be preferable.

Appendix

Table A6.1. Estimates of the two-step sequential model (CIS3, manufacturing)

	R&D equations		Innovation production function		Productivity
	Selection	Intensity	Product	Process	
Log(R&D intensity)	—	—	1.24***	0.74***	—
			(0.07)	(0.06)	
Product innovation	—	—	—	—	0.08
					(0.08)
Process innovation	—	—	—	—	0.35***
					(0.10)
Log(Physical capital intensity)	—	—	—	0.14***	0.08***
				(0.02)	(0.01)
International competition	0.40***	0.44***	—	—	—
	(0.06)	(0.08)			
Cooperation	—	0.25***	—	—	—
		(0.07)			
Appropriability conditions					
Formal protection	0.96***	0.30***	0.54***	0.16**	—
	(0.06)	(0.09)	(0.06)	(0.06)	
Strategic protection	0.73***	0.30***	0.32***	0.24***	—
	(0.06)	(0.08)	(0.07)	(0.06)	
Funding					
Local funding	—	0.03	—	—	—
		(0.12)			
National funding	—	−0.14	—	—	—
		(0.08)			
EU funding	—	0.46***	—	—	—
		(0.13)			
Firm size (*ref.: < 50 employees*)					
50 to 99 employees	0.28***	—	0.23***	0.16**	−0.10***
	(0.08)		(0.07)	(0.08)	(0.02)
100 to 249 employees	0.39***	—	0.09	0.21***	−0.12***
	(0.08)		(0.07)	(0.08)	(0.03)
250 to 999 employees	0.78***	—	0.37***	0.23***	−0.07**
	(0.08)		(0.07)	(0.08)	(0.03)
≥ 1,000 employees	0.92***	—	0.26**	0.33***	0.01
	(0.11)		(0.12)	(0.11)	(0.04)
Two-digit industry	0.000	0.000	0.000	0.000	0.000
Demand pulled/Techn. pushed	0.833	0.000	—	—	—
Sources of Information	—	0.072	—	—	—
Sigma	—	1.29***	—	—	0.49***
		(0.04)			(0.02)

Rho	0.35***	Rho (Product, Process) = 0.47*** (0.03)
	(0.05)	Rho (Product, Productivity) = −0.23*** (0.08)
		Rho (Process, Productivity) = −0.49*** (0.10)
Goodness-of-fit	Log-likelihood: −3667.18	Log-likelihood: −4984.86
	Test of 'β = 0': 523.60***	Test of 'β = 0': 1241.70***

Notes: * Significant at the 10% level; ** Significant at the 5% level; *** Significant at the 1% level. Robust standard errors in parentheses. For the sake of concision, we report only the *p*-values of a test of the joint significance of the two-digit industry dummy variables, 'demand pulled/technology pushed' indicators, and 'sources of information' indicators. Physical capital is measured by the log of investment intensity at time t-2 in the process equation, and by the log of book value at t-1 in the productivity equation.

Table A6.2. Estimates of the two-step sequential model (CIS4, manufacturing)

	R&D equations		Innovation production function		Productivity
	Selection	Intensity	Product	Process	
Log(R&D intensity)	—	—	1.29***	0.85***	—
			(0.06)	(0.06)	
Product innovation	—	—	—	—	−0.04
					(0.08)
Process innovation	—	—	—	—	0.38***
					(0.10)
Log(Physical capital intensity)	—	—	—	0.13***	0.07***
				(0.02)	(0.01)
International competition	0.51***	0.51***	—	—	—
	(0.05)	(0.10)			
Cooperation	—	0.36***	—	—	—
		(0.08)			
Appropriability conditions					
Formal protection	0.59***	0.43***	0.08	−0.09*	—
	(0.05)	(0.10)	(0.05)	(0.06)	
Strategic protection	0.67***	0.61***	−0.19***	−0.04	—
	(0.05)	(0.09)	(0.06)	(0.06)	
Funding					
Local funding	—	−0.03	—	—	—
		(0.14)			
National funding	—	0.07	—	—	—
		(0.09)			
EU funding	—	0.40***	—	—	—
		(0.14)			
Firm size (ref.: < 50 employees)					
50 to 99 employees	0.18***	—	0.06	−0.0004	−0.04*
	(0.07)		(0.06)	(0.06)	(0.02)
100 to 249 employees	0.39***	—	0.06	0.02	−0.08***
	(0.07)		(0.06)	(0.06)	(0.02)
250 to 999 employees	0.63***	—	0.21***	0.01	−0.02
	(0.06)		(0.06)	(0.06)	(0.02)
≥ 1,000 employees	1.07***	—	0.36***	0.28**	0.07*
	(0.10)		(0.12)	(0.11)	(0.04)
Two-digit industry	0.000	0.000	0.000	0.000	0.000
Demand pulled/Techn. pushed	0.014	0.000	—	—	—
Sources of information	—	0.053	—	—	—
Sigma	—	1.46***	—	—	0.50***
		(0.04)			(0.02)

Rho	0.28***	Rho (Product, Process) = 0.43*** (0.03)
	(0.06)	Rho (Product, Productivity) = -0.08 (0.06)
		Rho (Process, Productivity) = -0.52*** (0.10)
Goodness-of-fit	Log-likelihood: -5061.75	Log-likelihood: -7509.18
	Test of '$\beta = 0$': 444.41***	Test of '$\beta = 0$': 1662.29***

Notes: * Significant at the 10% level; ** Significant at the 5% level; *** Significant at the 1% level. Robust standard errors in parentheses. For the sake of concision, we report only the *p*-values of a test of the joint significance of the 2-digit industry dummy variables, 'demand pulled/technology pushed' indicators, and 'sources of information' indicators. Physical capital is measured by the log of investment intensity at time *t*-2 in the process equation, and by the log of book value at *t*-1 in the productivity equation.

Table A6.3. Estimates of the two-step sequential model (CIS4, services)

	R&D equations		Innovation production function		Productivity
	Selection	Intensity	Product	Process	
Log(R&D intensity)	—	—	0.34***	0.22***	—
			(0.03)	(0.03)	—
Product innovation	—	—	—	—	0.39***
					(0.08)
Process innovation	—	—	—	—	0.09
					(0.09)
Log(Physical capital intensity)	—	—	—	−0.005	0.15***
				(0.02)	(0.01)
International competition	0.44***	0.90***	—	—	—
	(0.07)	(0.20)			
Cooperation	—	0.07	—	—	—
		(0.17)			
Appropriability conditions					
Formal protection	0.71***	0.94***	0.29***	0.26***	—
	(0.07)	(0.23)	(0.06)	(0.07)	
Strategic protection	0.89***	1.11***	0.43***	0.44***	—
	(0.07)	(0.22)	(0.07)	(0.10)	
Funding					
Local funding	—	−0.40	—	—	—
		(0.34)			
National funding	—	0.77***	—	—	—
		(0.21)			
EU funding	—	−0.27	—	—	—
		(0.31)			
Firm size (ref.: < 50 employees)					
50 to 99 employees	0.23***	—	0.15**	0.16**	−0.07**
	(0.08)		(0.06)	(0.08)	(0.03)
100 to 249 employees	0.25***	—	0.19***	0.24***	−0.08***
	(0.09)		(0.07)	(0.08)	(0.03)
250 to 999 employees	0.39***	—	0.38***	0.41***	−0.15***
	(0.09)		(0.06)	(0.08)	(0.03)
≥ 1,000 employees	0.83***	—	0.74***	0.68***	−0.28***
	(0.14)		(0.10)	(0.12)	(0.04)
Two-digit industry	0.069	0.050	0.000	0.007	0.000
Demand pulled/Techn. pushed	0.005	0.000	—	—	—
Sources of information	—	0.503	—	—	—
Sigma	—	2.05**	—	—	0.57***
		(0.14)			(0.01)

Rho	0.62***	Rho (Product, Process) = 0.64*** (0.03)
	(0.07)	Rho (Product, Productivity) = −0.45*** (0.06)
		Rho (Process, Productivity) = −0.27** (0.10)
Goodness-of-fit	Log-likelihood: −1987.65	Log-likelihood: −4775.80
	Test of '$\beta = 0$': 233.42***	Test of '$\beta = 0$': 1016.62***

Notes: * Significant at the 10% leve; ** Significant at the 5% level; *** Significant at the 1% level. Robust standard errors in parentheses. For the sake of concision, we report only the *p*-values of a test of the joint significance of the 2-digit industry dummy variables, 'demand pulled/technology pushed' indicators, and 'sources of information' indicators. Physical capital is measured by the log of investment intensity at time *t*-2 in the process equation, and by the log of book value at *t*-1 in the productivity equation.

Table A6.4. Key two-step estimates of the CDM model with alternative knowledge production functions

Knowledge production function = product innovation, process innovation (bivariate probit)

	CIS3			CIS4, Manufacturing			CIS4, Services		
	Prod.	*Proc.*	*LP*	*Prod.*	*Proc.*	*LP*	*Prod.*	*Proc.*	*LP*
Log(R&D intensity)	1.24*** (0.07)	0.74*** (0.06)	—	1.29*** (0.06)	0.85*** (0.06)	—	0.34*** (0.03)	0.22*** (0.03)	—
Product innovation			0.08 (0.08)			−0.04 (0.10)			0.39*** (0.08)
Process innovation			0.35*** (0.10)			0.38*** (0.10)			0.09 (0.09)

	CIS3		CIS4, Manufacturing		CIS4, Services	
	Prod.	*LP*	*Prod.*	*LP*	*Prod.*	*LP*
Log(R&D intensity)	1.29*** (0.07)	—	1.29*** (0.06)	—	0.34*** (0.03)	—
Product innovation		0.29*** (0.03)		0.26*** (0.03)		0.48*** (0.05)

	CIS3		CIS4, Manufacturing		CIS4, Services	
	Proc.	*LP*	*Proc.*	*LP*	*Proc.*	*LP*
Log(R&D intensity)	0.72*** (0.06)	—	0.84*** (0.06)	—	0.22*** (0.03)	—
Process innovation		0.41*** (0.04)		0.37*** (0.05)		0.40*** (0.06)

	CIS3		CIS4, Manufacturing		CIS4, Services	
	Inno.	*LP*	*Inno.*	*LP*	*Inno.*	*LP*
Log(R&D intensity)	1.47*** (0.08)	—	1.44*** (0.08)	—	0.28*** (0.03)	—
'Overall' innovation		0.29*** (0.02)		0.25*** (0.02)		0.40*** (0.05)

Notes: * Significant at the 10% level; ** Significant at the 5% level; *** Significant at the 1% level. Robust standard errors in parentheses.
Prod. = Product innovation, Proc. = Process innovation, Inno. = 'overall' innovation, LP = Labour productivity.

References

Chudnosky, D., Lopez, A. and Pupato, G. (2006), 'Innovation and productivity in developing countries: A study of Argentine manufacturing firms' behavior (1992–2001)', *Research Policy*, 35: 266–288.

Crépon, B., Duguet, E. and Mairesse, J. (1998), 'Research, innovation and productivity: An econometric analysis at the firm level', *Economics of Innovation and New Technology*, 7: 115–158.

Griffith, R., Huergo, E., Mairesse, J. and Peters, B. (2006), 'Innovation and productivity across four European countries', *Oxford Review of Economic Policy*, 22(4): 483–498.

Griliches, Z. (1979), 'Issues in assessing the contribution of research and development to productivity growth', *Bell Journal of Economics*, 87(5): 537–64.

Hall, B.H., Lotti, F. and Mairesse, J. (2009), 'Innovation and productivity in SMEs: Empirical evidence for Italy', *Small Business Economics*, 33: 13–33.

Mairesse, J. and Jaumandreu, J. (2005), 'Panel-data estimates of the production function and the revenue function: What difference does it make?', *The Scandinavian Journal of Economics*, 107(4): 651–72.

Mairesse, J. and Mohnen, P. (2010), 'Using innovation surveys for econometric analysis', in B.H. Hall and N. Rosenberg (eds), *Handbook of the Economics of Innovation*, Vol. II. London: Burlington Academic Press, pp. 1129–1155.

Mairesse, J. and Mohnen, P. (2002), 'Accounting for innovation and measuring innovativeness: An illustrative framework and an application', *American Economic Review*, 92(2): 226–230.

Mairesse, J., Mohnen, P. and Kremp, E. (2005), 'The importance of R&D and innovation for productivity: A reexamination in light of the 2000 French Innovation Survey', Annales d'economie et de statistique (Contributions in memory of Zri Griliches, ed. Jacques Mairesse and Manuel Trajtenberg 79/80: 487–527.

Mohnen, P., Mairesse, J. and Dagenais, M. (2006), 'Innovativity: A comparison across seven European countries', *Economics of Innovation and New Technology*, 15(4/5): 391–413.

Raffo, J., Lhuillery, S. and Miotti, L. (2008), 'Northern and southern innovativity: A comparison across European and Latin American countries', *European Journal of Development Research*, 20(2): 219–239.

Roodman, D. (2009), 'Estimating fully observed recursive mixed-process models with cmp', CDG Working Paper 168, Washington, DC: Center for Global Development.

7

R&D Collaboration and Innovative Performance

René Belderbos, Geert Duysters, and Anna Sabidussi

7.1. Introduction

In the last decades, innovation has become progressively more complex due to the increased speed, pace, and costs of technology development. In response to this trend, we have witnessed an unprecedented diffusion of inter-firm relationships in technology development and innovation, such as joint R&D activities, licensing and cross-licensing, and corporate venture activities. The phenomenon has been labelled 'open innovation' (Chesbrough, 2003), and this term has been used as an umbrella concept referring to the wide-spread use of the various forms of inter-firm relationships in innovation. Among these external relationships in innovation, technology alliances in particular have become ubiquitous in corporate life. In parallel, an increasing body of academic literature has studied the antecedents and performance consequences of R&D collaboration. However, despite the abundant research on the topic, surprisingly limited attention has been paid to clearly defining the state-of-the-art of our current knowledge about the relationship between R&D collaboration and innovative performance.[1] The need for a systematic literature review is obvious given the burgeoning literature and variety of theoretical angles, methods, and data adopted by the various studies, which precludes an unequivocal interpretation of findings. It is therefore unclear which research questions have been addressed and which ones have remained unsolved, and which contingencies shape the relationship between R&D collaboration and performance. A critical and systematic overview of the

---

[1] One of the few exceptions is the review of de Man and Duysters (2005).

findings obtained by previous studies can pave the way for future research in unexplored areas. For managerial practice, shedding light on what can be achieved and what cannot be obtained through cooperation may support the strategic decisions about external partnerships.

The present chapter provides such a systematic overview of the results of prior academic studies of the relationship between R&D collaboration and innovative performance, focusing on 66 paper contributions in the last decade. We will distinguish the contributions with respect to the level of analysis (the dyadic level, the level of alliance portfolios, and the level of broader alliance networks) and the type of performance measure (patents, product and process innovations, and economic performance of the firm). The chapter is structured as follows. In the next section we describe the trends in the development of R&D cooperation. Next, we illustrate the theoretical framework of the relationship between R&D cooperation and innovative performance. In the methods section, we explain the selection criteria and method of processing the literature. Finally, we present the results of the literature review and discuss the relevance of our findings for both managerial practice and academic research.

7.2. Trends in R&D collaboration

R&D cooperation refers to the relationship between two entities that remain autonomous while cooperating in R&D activities. The above relationship is often referred to as strategic partnership and it may take a variety of organizational modalities including (R&D) joint ventures, minority equity stakes, and contractual joint research or development alliances. In this chapter, the terms 'alliance', 'partnership', and 'cooperation/collaboration' will be used interchangeably to refer to the above cooperation forms.

Although cooperative initiatives among companies are not in themselves a new phenomenon, what has been remarkable in the last decades is their diffusion. As confirmed by Hagedoorn (2002), until the 1960s R&D collaborations were relatively scarce. The number of new technology alliances began to rise slowly in the 1970s and the upward trend was more pronounced at the end of the decade. Yet it is in the 1980s that the acceleration in the trend becomes more striking (Hagedoorn, 2002). Despite the general observation that high-technology sectors such as pharmaceuticals, information technology, aerospace, and defence are more likely to display high levels of technology partnerships, Hagedoorn (2002) reports that R&D alliance activity only became strongly concentrated in the above sectors from the 1980s and onwards. In reporting the evolution of more recent technology alliances, de Man and Duysters (2005) note that at the end of the 1980s the number of newly established partnerships tends to slow down. An explanation is that companies, after the initial enthusiasm, started to realize that cooperation represents not only an opportunity but also a managerial challenge. Firms became aware that alliances are not 'a panacea to all their problems', and this is reflected in the increased number of alliance failures reported in those years (de Man and Duysters, 2005: 1377). Narula (1999) offers insights into the international pattern of technology alliances by examining the trends in R&D partnerships among the Triad (North America, Europe, and Asia). Triad companies engaged in 94.6 per cent of the total alliances (Narula and Hagedoorn, 1999). Firms from the US, Japan, and Germany contributed respectively to 64.1 per cent, 25.6 per cent, and 11.3 per cent of the alliances established (Narula and Hagedoorn, 1999). From a European point of view, in the mid-1980s R&D cooperation among firms was encouraged by the European Commission by the establishment of a 'Big 12 round table' to foster joint R&D initiatives (Narula, 1999). The same period corresponds to the rise of both subsidized and non-subsidized alliances among EU companies. In the 1990s, the above trend abated notably and EU companies preferred to engage in relationships with US partners that were more advanced in key technological areas (Narula, 1999).

After the decline in alliance activity at the end of the 1980s, the tendency to enter in new partnerships accelerated again. Figure 7.1 gives an overview of the trends in R&D partnerships since the 1990s.

The new rise in technology alliances is due to several factors. Among others, an important role was played by the high technological and environmental turbulence to which companies were exposed. Technology life cycles became progressively shorter, requiring companies to constantly invest in new technology development. In this context, the constant rise of the costs and risks associated with R&D activities induced companies to share the burden of innovative endeavours with partners. The increased convergence of technologies and the need to offer clients complete solutions made it even more

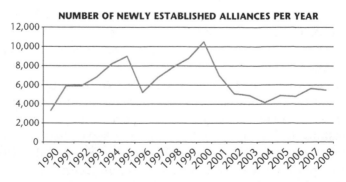

Figure 7.1. Trends in R&D alliances

complex for a single company to compete without cooperating with external parties. As it emerges from Figure 7.1, a new peak in alliance activity occurred at the end of the 1990s. In particular, between 1995 and 2000 the growth of the Internet sector spurred the rise in the number of newly established alliances. Established companies were trying to get involved in Internet-related activities and alliances seemed to offer the vehicle to participate in the equity-value rise associated with the 'dot-com' phenomenon. The burst of the speculative Internet bubble may partially explain the subsequent reduction in the number of newly established alliances. Finally, recent years are characterized by a more stable pattern.

Overall, the trends in technology-alliance activity confirm that R&D cooperation represents a relevant and widespread strategy adopted by companies. The popularity of alliances has puzzled the academic community, especially when considering their high failure rate. A recent study of the Network of Social Innovation (NSI, 2009) reports that alliances fail to deliver the promised results in, on average, 47 per cent of the cases. Although the failure rate has been decreasing in recent years, alliance success is far from being easily achieved. When international alliances are considered, the failure rate is slightly higher (around 51 per cent), as they are likely to be more challenging than domestic relationships due to cross-cultural differences. Despite the difficulties associated with alliances, the same study (NSI, 2009) reported that 61 per cent of the respondents expect that the alliances will contribute to more than 40 per cent of the company market value in 2013. Cooperation seems to be perceived by managerial practice as challenging but potentially highly rewarding. In the next section, we discuss the potential effects of R&D collaboration on innovative performance.

7.3. The impact of R&D cooperation on innovative performance

The extant literature suggests that there are both enhancing and inhibiting factors at work in the relationship between cooperation and innovative performance. Figure 7.2 summarizes the main aspects of relevance for the purpose of our study.

R&D cooperation may foster innovation for three reasons. The first refers to accessing new knowledge and learning (Hagedoorn, 1993; Baum et al., 2000; George et al., 2001; Tsai, 2009). Technological advancements often result from combining different technologies from diverse technological or scientific areas. In such a situation, it is unlikely that one single company may have access to all the competences required to deliver innovations. Partnering allows companies to access new knowledge that is not internally available. Being exposed to new knowledge may also stimulate new ideas and creativity

Innovation enhancing	Innovation inhibiting
• Lower risk of innovation • Combination of competences • Exchange of ideas to stimulate creativity • Radar function • Speed of innovation	• Transfer of knolwedge accross organizational boundaries is difficult • Competition between partners • High rates of alliance failure in general • Portfolio complexity

Figure 7.2. Performance drivers of R&D cooperation

within the organization. Additionally, companies may enhance innovative endeavours by combining their competences and resources with their partners. In this sense, the role of resource complementarity has been acknowledged by the literature as a prerequisite for fostering the value potential of alliances and generating synergies (Harrison et al., 2001). In a related but still different view taken in the economics literature, the main rationale for R&D cooperation is to internalize knowledge spillovers to other (competing) firms (Cassiman and Veugelers, 2002; Belderbos, Carree and Lokshin). In case spillovers and the associated limitations to the appropriation of the fruits of R&D limit the incentives to invest, collaboration in R&D that is complemented by efforts to encourage knowledge flows between the collaborating partners is a more effective manner to organize R&D (Cassiman et al., 2002).

The second important class of benefits expected by R&D cooperation refers to the possibility of cost and risk sharing in the R&D process (Hagedoorn, 1993; Cincera et al., 2003; Faems et al., 2005). The R&D process is characterized by high levels of uncertainty as the outcome of technology search is by its nature unpredictable. Moreover, in many sectors, development of new products entails considerable expense. For instance, it has been estimated that the R&D cost per new drug was more than 800 million dollars in 2000, up from 231 million in 1987 (Di Masi et al., 2003). By sharing those costs and uncertainties with external partners, companies are better positioned to pursue multiple research activities. Beside cost and risk sharing, inter-firm cooperation may provide lead-time advantages in innovation races (Chang, 2003). In dynamic environments, competition is based on shortening the time to market. In this respect, companies may cooperate to shorten the time needed to develop a technology and embed it into a new product. Being the first to introduce products of a new technological generation into the market allows companies to appropriate first-mover advantages such as brand loyalty, earlier returns on investment, and longer time-span before the technology life cycle declines (Shilling and Hill, 1998). Third, R&D cooperation serves a radar function by allowing companies 'to get a sneak preview of a variety of techno-logical opportunities without committing to them' (de Man and Duysters, 2005: 1379).

On the other hand, R&D cooperation may also fail to contribute to innova-tion and its cost may outweigh the benefits. In their critical discussion, Das and Teng (2000) argue that internal tensions can offer an explanation for inter-firm relationships' failure. In particular, there is a certain degree of tension between cooperation and the competition implicit in any cooperation (Das and Teng, 2000). As pursuing self-interest may not always be compatible with pursuing mutual interest, the resulting conflicts undermine the succes of an alliance. Partner firms may behave opportunistically and utilize knowledge in separate innovation activities, reducing the opportunities for the firm to appropriate the fruits of its technology-development activities. Even in situa-tions of limited conflict, the difficulty of coordinating joint activities is accen-tuated by differences (e.g. of a cultural nature) among partners (Park and Ungson, 2001). Additionally, due to the tacit nature of knowledge, exchang-ing it across firms' boundaries is in itself challenging. Developing relational capabilities easing the knowledge transfer may be required in order to leverage the alliance potential (Collins and Hitt, 2006), but the difficulties associated with this process may limit the effectiveness of cooperation. Finally, firms are rarely engaged in a single alliance. More typically, companies are involved in multiple and simultaneous relationships. The challenges associated with man-aging several alliances at the same time differ from those associated with a single partnership. The complexities deriving from a high number of links and diversity of the partners may represent more a managerial burden than an opportunity, and may ultimately undermine performance (Duysters and Lokshin, 2011).

Although our overview is not exhaustive and other motives to expect positive and negative effects of R&D cooperation on innovation may exist, overall it suggests that there are no valid arguments to predict a priori that one effect should prevail over the other. Mapping and classifying the findings of the empirical literature can therefore increase our understanding of the phe-nomenon and shed light on the contingent performance implications of R&D cooperation.

7.4. Method

The procedure we followed to perform the literature review is organized in three main steps: data collection, paper selection, and information processing and categorization. The above procedure is comparable to the one followed in earlier literature reviews (e.g. de Man and Duysters, 2005; Wassmer, 2010).

The first step was to collect academic papers on the relationship between R&D cooperation and innovative performance. We conducted a general search by broad keywords (e.g. R&D alliances, cooperation, collaboration, partnerships, innovation) in multiple academic literature databases such as JSTOR, ISI Web of Science, and EconLit, and in general data sources such as Google Scholar. Next, we performed a keyword search in specific target journals (e.g. *Research Policy*, *Strategic Management Journal*, *Academy of Management Journal*) to ensure an adequate coverage of works published in high-quality journals and to cross-check the accuracy of the list derived from the more general scan.

The second step was to select the material on the basis of a number of criteria. Before discussing in detail the criteria that we have adopted, it is fruitful to clarify which research area constitutes the basis for our literature review. Our interest is in the papers that focus on the effects of R&D collaboration on firm (innovative) performance. Hence, we limit attention to research assessing the performance implications of cooperative activities. A considerable amount of research is devoted to the investigation of the rationale or the motivations behind the decision to cooperate. This domain in the literature aims primarily at understanding the decision process leading to specific strategic choices. Although both streams of research are relevant and connected, only the first research stream is at the centre of our study. In the above context, we have imposed a series of selection criteria. First, we have included in our selection only papers published in peer-reviewed journals in order to guarantee the quality of the material under review. We have focused on papers published in the last ten years, as they are more representative of current trends in the academic literature. Second, we have selected papers dealing with technological innovation, with the implication that most papers focusing on the service sector were excluded. In line with Duysters and Hagedoorn (2000), we have embraced a broad definition of cooperation by considering various partnering modalities (e.g. equity and non-equity agreements). Third, preference was given to studies that used a quantifiable, objective measure of performance. A large body of literature assesses performance by ranking, traditionally on a Likert scale, success as it is perceived by the respondents. The above approach is especially useful when the research aims at clarifying to what extent expectations about a certain outcome were actually met. The disadvantage of the above measurement is that it is very much context-specific and it does not easily allow a meaningful comparison among different contributions. Finally, we have selected only papers based on large-scale empirical studies. Although case studies are able to provide valuable insights on the mechanisms used in successful R&D collaboration, case studies were excluded from our review, because of the difficulty in generalizing the findings. Similarly, we have omitted studies that investigated the effect of cooperation at the project level, as we focus on firm-level performance.

The papers that were relevant for the purpose of our analyses were initially identified on the basis of the title and abstract. The reference section of those papers was carefully scanned to search for relevant papers that may have been excluded by the keyword search. After this phase, an initial 134 papers were considered to meet our requirements. Next, by reading the entire article, an additional selection was performed and a total of 66 papers were finally selected for the review. The papers included in the review are listed in the appendix (Table A7.1). We note that the application of the selection criteria led us to reject a relatively large number of studies. Our objective, however, was to collect material that allows for meaningful comparisons. In this respect, we consider that the rigorous procedure we followed served the purpose.

The third step was to proceed with the categorization of the available material. For this purpose, we have constructed a database summarizing the relevant information provided by each paper. For example, for each contribution we have highlighted the type of data used for the empirical analyses, the operationalization of the dependent and independent variables, the main findings and results. Additionally, we have reported the level of analysis that has been adopted by the study. This distinction is especially relevant as alliances may be approached from a portfolio perspective, where the attention is on the direct relationships of a focal firm, or from a network viewpoint, where the focus is on both the direct and the indirect linkages among firms. This phase aimed at properly processing the large amount of information at our disposal so as to allow more fine-tuned analysis.

There is a considerable richness of conceptual lenses adopted when studying the performance consequences of R&D cooperation. In order to allow a critical discussion of findings and a meaningful comparison of empirical results, it is therefore fruitful to differentiate the main categories we have identified in our review and the associated empirical results. An important distinction in the literature is the level of analysis of alliances: the (dyadic or general) alliance engagement, the alliance portfolio, or the alliance network. Finally, depending on the paper's aim, various dependent variables have been chosen to assess the impact of R&D cooperation. One literature stream has paid attention to the effect of success of R&D cooperation on broader economic outcomes such as share prices, return on assets, and profit margins, while another line of research has focused on more narrowly defined innovation success reflected in patent applications and the introduction of new products or processes. Classifying the empirical results on the basis of the success measures supports a critical discussion of the areas where R&D cooperation is beneficial.

7.5. Results

The relationship between R&D cooperation and innovative performance represents a central research topic in various research disciplines. To provide a complete overview we have included both economics and management perspectives in our study. Although complementary, these perspectives differ with respect to the research focus and variables adopted. In an economics context, the emphasis has been on the internalization of knowledge and technology spillovers, while in a management framework, the challenges associated with organizing the cooperation have been the primary interest. In the present section, we first present the general findings of our review. Next, we refine our analysis by offering a more fine-grained classification of the empirical findings.

The majority of results in the reviewed papers (around 50 per cent) show a positive effect of alliances on (innovative) performance (see Figure 7.3).

Thirty-three per cent of the empirical findings suggest that cooperation has no significant impact while only a minority (around 14 per cent) indicates that cooperation has detrimental consequences for performance. Finally, only few studies (3 per cent) tested and found a curvilinear (inverted-U) relationship between the number of R&D alliances and performance. The above percentages refer to the detailed results in the papers reviewed: if a study tested models with more than one performance variable (e.g. Belderbos, Carree and Lokshin, 2004; Santamaría et al., 2009), each outcome has been taken into consideration separately. The same applies when the model is tested on the same dependent variable but for different classes of companies (e.g. small and medium/large firms), as in Rogers (2004). Our results support the view

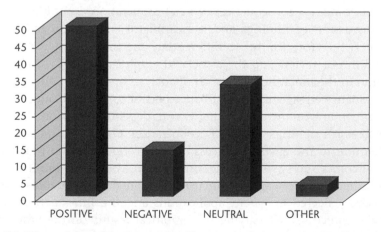

Figure 7.3. The relationship between alliances and innovative performance (in percentages)

that alliances do indeed contribute to firm performance, with positive outcomes dominating.

The review of the literature brings out a number of contingencies that increase the likelihood of successful R&D collaboration. One key finding is that the qualities of the partners chosen for the alliances are critical to determine the success of the cooperation. Partners' qualities (e.g. high network status) are important (Lin et al., 2009), but the relative distance between the company's and the partner's technology bases (Nooteboom et al., 2007; Luo and Deng, 2009) appears to be a key element determining the success of alliances. There is a delicate balance that needs to be achieved: too much cognitive distance between partners hampers the knowledge exchange, but too little leads to redundancy and little innovation (Nooteboom et al., 2007). When the partners are competitors, achieving these common goals is more complicated (Su et al., 2009). Secret agendas and little commitment to the joint interests may prevent the partners from engaging in a cooperation that is fruitful for all the parties involved. Companies with strong internal R&D seem to be in a better position to manage and profit from cooperating with competitors (Tsai and Wang, 2009), although they also have to be aware of free-rider behaviour of R&D partners as they may run a greater risk of spillovers of their technology advantages. The review also suggests that companies with alliance experience and dedicated alliance management functions are generally more successful in their R&D cooperation efforts (Kale et al., 2002).

As it emerged from the papers reviewed, three main levels of analysis have been adopted by the literature: alliance engagement, the alliance portfolio, and the alliance network.

At the first level the effect of dyadic R&D cooperation or the effect of engaging in a particular type of alliance is considered (without detailing the intensity of alliance engagement). In this context, the influence of different qualities of relationship (e.g. partners' characteristics, level of equity involvement) on performance is often assessed. The majority (about 65 per cent) of studies reviewed fall into this category.

As firms are often involved in numerous contemporaneous relationships with external partners, a second research stream has examined alliance performance from a portfolio perspective. A portfolio may be defined as the 'firms' collection of direct ties with partner companies' (Lavie, 2007), and at this level of analysis the challenges associated with multiple simultaneous links are of central importance. The alliance-portfolio management literature adopts a holistic approach where the corporate achievements are determined by the overall portfolio of relationships. Alliances are assessed not in isolation, but in terms of contribution to the success of the entire portfolio. As pointed out by Wassmer (2010), in this context critical tasks include, among others, selecting partners on the basis of their fit with the portfolio, enhancing synergies across knowledge sources, coordinating portfolio activities, and avoiding conflicts among partners. Despite its relevance for managerial implications, there is a clear scarcity of studies of alliance-portfolio performance: in our sample only nine per cent of the papers (six studies) reviewed are included in this category. A potential reason for this limited number of studies may be found in the difficulty of obtaining detailed information on the entire set of alliances in a firm's portfolio and to obtain accurate portfolio performance measures (Wassmer, 2010).

A third level of analysis looks at the entire network of relationships in which the firms are involved. Networks are defined as 'the collection of separate companies linked through agreements', where 'some companies may be linked only by means of common ties with another network company' (Gomes-Casseres, 2004). This stream of literature aims at investigating what specific types of relationship are more beneficial for the network participants, which network configuration (e.g. network density, centrality, etc.) leads to the optimal levels of performance, and how the positioning of the company in the network changes over time (Provan et al., 2007). A total of 17 studies focused on the network level.

Table 7.1 shows the performance effects found for R&D alliance strategies while differentiating the level of analysis that has been adopted by the reviewed studies. Positive effects are prevalent at all levels, confirming our general conclusion about the relationship of R&D cooperation and innovative performance. At the relationship/engagement level the percentage of positive findings is close to 50 per cent but the percentage of neutral findings is rather high, about 40 per cent. This may be partially determined by the data sources used and by the specifications they allow. Many studies in this group use information collected in the European Community Innovation Surveys (CIS). CIS is a survey conducted periodically by countries in the European Union under the auspices of Eurostat to monitor innovative activities in member states. With respect to R&D cooperation activities, this survey indicates the engagement in alliance activity of the firm, but it does not contain count data denoting how many relationships the firm has entered into. As a consequence, little consideration can be paid to the intensity of the cooperative R&D. This limitation may be related to a relatively frequent occurrence of

Table 7.1. The relationship between alliances and (innovative) performance at three levels of analysis: alliance engagement, alliance portfolio, and alliance network

	Positive	Negative	Neutral	Other	Sum
Engagement	49	10	39	2	100
Portfolio	40	32	20	8	100
Network	53	17	28	2	100

ambiguous results. The results of the studies adopting a portfolio perspective are less favourable, with 40 per cent obtaining positive findings and more than 30 per cent showing a detrimental impact. This is likely to be related to the focus of this stream of literature on the entire set of alliances in large firms, which highlights the managerial complexity of portfolio management and potential decreasing returns to portfolio extension. The studies adopting an alliance-network perspective have on average delivered more favourable results. This could suggest that taking into account with which other firms partner firms ally as well is an important consideration for alliance research and alliance practitioners. In particular, this literature has pointed out the influence on performance of the structural aspects of the network, such as size (Thorgren et al., 2009) or density (Schilling and Phelps, 2007; Gilsing et al., 2008), or the specific position the firm occupies in the network (Gilsing et al., 2008) and repeated partnerships with network partners (Goerzen, 2007; Vanhaverbeke et al., 2009). We note that a thorough discussion of the most appropriate level of alliance-strategy analysis, and the related appropriate aspects requiring managerial attention (portfolio relationships or network positioning) will be highly fruitful for further research. At this stage, however, there are too few large-scale empirical studies taking a broader perspective to allow deriving clear conclusions.

Table 7.2 shows the relationship between R&D cooperation and the different output measures. Economic-performance measures (profits and market valuation) were used in 12 studies, patents in 19 studies, sales from new products or new-product counts in 34 studies, and process innovations in five studies.

Among the studies taking patent output as the performance measure, there is a substantial number that find no significant effect of R&D collaboration. One potential explanation is that not all alliances have the purpose of delivering new patentable technologies; alliances may also serve the purpose of keeping the company updated about the current technological developments. In addition, not all technologies that are jointly developed lead to patent applications, as there are alternative appropriation strategies such as secrecy and lead time. For product innovations and sales from new products, the

Table 7.2. The relationship between alliances and (innovative) performance (in percentages)

	Positive	Negative	Neutral	Other	Sum
Patents	46	12	32	10	100
Sales/New products	57	5	37	1	100
Economic indicators	31	30	35	4	100
Process innovation	44	0	56	0	100

particularly high proportion of neutral results seems to indicate that other aspects (e.g. marketing) may be needed as complements to R&D cooperation to generate returns to innovation, but the results may also be related to the use of simple alliance-engagement measures in most of these studies. In terms of economic performance (market valuation, profits), positive, negative, and neutral outcomes appear to be roughly in balance. This may suggest that there is a difficulty in establishing a strong causal and direct relationship between R&D alliance strategies and overall firm performance. Finally, our results indicate that R&D cooperation is not likely to harm process innovations, although there is no predominance of positive effects.

7.6. Discussion and conclusions

In the present chapter, we have provided an overview of the empirical findings on the relationship between R&D collaboration and firms (innovative) performance. Given the attention that R&D cooperation has attracted among economists and management scholars in the last decades, there is an abundant literature on the topic. Without a systematic review of the results however, the variety and the richness of findings do not allow for a solid understanding of the phenomenon. The diversity of approaches and theoretical lenses that have been adopted are likely to hamper a clear insight into the status of extant knowledge and the most important items on the future research agenda. In this context, our study intends to contribute to both managerial practice and the academic debate.

The results of our review of the literature in the last decade indicate that R&D cooperation is, more often than not, beneficial for innovative performance. Our analysis also suggests that specific contingencies need to be taken into consideration. In particular, the choice of the partners in terms of their absolute qualities (e.g. status) or in terms of their relative position with respect to the firm (distance of the companies' reciprocal knowledge bases) seems to be critical. Here emerging evidence suggests that knowledge bases should be complementary but not too distant, as the latter may hamper knowledge exchange. Additionally, the firms developing dedicated alliance functions seem to be in a favourable position to benefit from R&D cooperation. Overall, our review confirms the main conclusions of de Man and Duysters (2005) that cooperating and allying with external partners contributes to innovation. The prevalence of positive effects found in the literature may seem inconsistent with the observation that a notable percentage of alliances (50–60 per cent) fail. Despite relatively high failure rates, the popularity of alliances has remained substantial. Our findings may help to interpret the above apparent contradiction by considering that alliances have neutral effects in a considerable number of cases but that negative outcomes are relatively rare. Our review showed a relatively high percentage of non-significant effects, e.g. compared to prior reviews (see de Man and Duysters, 2005), which suggests that even when alliances fail, this does not generally have major harmful consequences for firms.

Our study found that the relationship between R&D cooperation and performance generally is more positive if the performance measures refer to innovation success: such as the introduction of product innovations, sales due to new products, and patent applications. With respect to overall firm performance (profitability, market valuation, productivity) there is less clarity on the overall effect and on the potential of R&D cooperation to generate economic returns. One reason for this is that, while collaboration may foster innovation success, the returns to the R&D investments will have to be shared with partner firms, reducing the direct impact on (expected) profits of the focal firm (Belderbos et al., 2010). In this respect, companies should be aware that the added value to corporate success is more likely to derive from an efficient and coordinated network of alliance relationships. One salient pattern in our review is that strong alliance networks and positioning therein was most unambiguously related to firm performance. At the same time, the challenges of managing a portfolio of diverse alliances are substantial and may lead to underperformance if not addressed properly.

The literature suggests that a number of key characteristics are relevant for the success of alliances. First, the partner selection represents a critical phase when establishing an external cooperation. Second, increasing experience of alliances and disposing of dedicated functions support the achievement of the goals of alliances. An explanation is that, from repeated experiences, companies develop routines enhancing their collaborative innovative endeavours (Zollo et al., 2002). Third, R&D cooperation should not be considered as a substitution for internal efforts. Investing in internal R&D contributes to develop absorptive capacity and therefore to profit from external relationships (Cohen and Levinthal, 1990).

We note that compared to other governance modalities, such as mergers and acquisitions (M&As), the above finding represents a distinguishing feature. M&As refer to economic transactions where one entity acquires control over the counterpart. Theoretically, a company may decide to obtain technological knowledge to foster innovative endeavours by acquiring a target firm with a complementary knowledge base instead of collaborating with the firm to develop new technologies. M&As, however, require large investments and engage the company in a long-term relationship with an uncertain outcome. The literature has generally found more negative effects of M&As on innovation (de Man and Duysters, 2005). Alliances may be seen as stepping stones towards an acquisition as they allow gathering information on the partner before the M&A (Vanhaverbeke et al., 2002). As the outcome of alliances does not significantly endanger corporate results, a gradual progression from cooperation to acquisition may support the achievement of longer-term innovation goals.

Our study suggests a number of lines of research that deserve to be placed high on the future research agenda. In particular, there appears to be a relative scarcity of interdisciplinary approaches to investigate the link between R&D collaboration and innovative performance. First, we have noted a degree of separation between studies adopting an economics perspective and those with a managerial orientation. Although each discipline provides fruitful insights, there are unexplored opportunities lying at the intersection between the two approaches. Scholars taking an industrial-organization perspective stress the central role of the industry structure to explain corporate outcomes, while those taking a strategic-management perspective focus on firm resources. Obviously, both perspectives matter and future research would benefit from their joint consideration. Studies that systematically evaluate the impact of R&D collaboration from a multidisciplinary point of view would enrich our awareness of the differential consequences on innovative performance. In our review we also noted a separation in the levels of analysis used by empirical studies. Recent contributions (e.g. Hitt et al., 2007) have put forward the view that multilevel research is the most appropriate medium for fully examining this type of research question. This is based on the consideration that it is difficult to identify precise boundaries between levels as 'organizational entities reside in nested arrangements' (Hitt et al., 2007: 1387). Hence, a fruitful path could be to study the performance implication of R&D cooperation at multiple levels of analysis. The above recommendations for further research may provide new insights on how companies may profit from R&D collaboration.

Appendix

Table A7.1. List of reviewed papers

PAPER (ref)

Ahuja, 2000
Anand and Khanna, 2000
Arvanitis and Woerter, 2009
Aschoff and Schmidt, 2008
Bae and Gargiulo, 2004
Baum et al., 2000
Bayona et al., 2006
Becker and Dietz, 2004
Belderbos, Carree and Lokshin, 2004
Belderbos, Carree and Lokshin, 2006
Benfratello and Sembenelli, 2002

Boyd and Spekman, 2008
Caloghirou et al., 2004
Chang, 2003
Cincera et al., 2003
Czarnitzki et al., 2007
Danzon et al., 2005
de Propris, 2002
Duysters and Lokshin, 2011
Faems et al., 2005
Frenz and Ietto-Gilles, 2009
Fritsch and Franke, 2004
George et al., 2001
George et al., 2002
Gilsing et al., 2008
Goerzen and Beamish, 2005
Goerzen, 2007
Janz et al., 2004
Kale et al., 2002
Keil et al., 2008
Kim and Song, 2007
Klomp and van Leeuwen, 2001
Knudsen, 2007
Laursen and Salter, 2006
Lavie, 2007
Lavie and Miller, 2008
Lee et al., 2001
Lin, 2009
Lin et al., 2009
Lööf and Heshmati, 2002
Luo and Deng, 2009
Monjon and Waelbroeck, 2003
Montoya et al., 2007
Negassi, 2004
Nieto and Santamaría, 2007
Nieto and Santamaría, 2009
Nooteboom et al., 2007
Padula, 2008
Rogers, 2004
Rothaermel and Deeds, 2004
Rothaermel and Hess, 2007
Rowley et al., 2000
Sampson, 2007
Santamaría et al., 2009
Schildt et al., 2005
Schilling and Phelps, 2007
Sher and Yang, 2005
Simonen and McCann, 2008
Stuart, 2000
Su et al., 2009
Thorgren et al., 2009
Tsai, 2009
Tsai and Wang, 2008
Tsai and Wang, 2009
Vanhaverbeke et al., 2009
Vega-Jurado et al., 2009

References

Ahuja, G. (2000), 'Collaboration networks, structural holes, and innovation: A longitudinal study', *Administrative Science Quarterly*, 45(3): 425–455.

Anand, B. N. and Khanna, T. (2000), 'Do firms learn to create value? The case of alliances', *Strategic Management Journal*, 21: 295–315.

Arvanitis S. and Woerter M. (2009), 'Firms' transfer strategies with universities and the relationship with firms' innovation performance', *Industrial and Corporate Change*, 18(6): 1067–1106.

Aschoff, B. and Schmidt, T. (2008), 'Empirical evidence on the success of R&D cooperation—Happy together?', *Review of Industrial Organization*, 33: 41–62.

Bae J. and Gargiulo M. (2004), 'Partner substitutability, alliance network structure, and firm profitability in the telecommunications industry', *Academy of Management Journal*, 47(6): 843–859.

Baum, J.A.C., Calabrese, T. and Silverman, B.S. (2000), 'Don't go it alone: Alliance network composition and start-ups' performance in Canadian biotechnology', *Strategic Management Journal*, 21(3): 267–294.

Bayona, C., Corredor, P. and Santamaría, R. (2006), 'Technological alliances and the market valuation of new economy firms', *Technovation*, 26(3): 369.

Becker, W. and Dietz, J. (2004), 'R&D cooperation and innovation activities of firms—Evidence from the German manufacturing industry', *Research Policy*, 33: 209–223.

Belderbos, R., Carree, M., Dideren,B., Lokshin, B. and Veugelers, R. (2004), 'Heterogeneity in R&D cooperation strategies', *International Journal of Industrial Organization*, 8(9), 1237–1264.

———— and Lokshin, B. (2004), 'Cooperative R&D and firm performance', *Research Policy*, 33(10): 1477–1492.

———— and Lokshin, B. (2006), 'Complementarities in R&D cooperation strategies', *Review of Industrial Organization*, 28: 401–426.

——, Faems, D., Leten, B. and van Looy, B. (2010), 'Technological activities and their impact on the financial performance of firms: Exploitation and exploration within and between firms', *Journal of Product Innovation Management*, 27(6): 869–882.

Benfratello, L. and Sembenelli, A. (2002), 'Research joint ventures and firm level performance', *Research Policy*, 31: 493–507.

Boyd, D.E. and Spekman, R.E. (2008), 'The market value impact of indirect ties within technology alliances', *Journal of the Academy Marketing Science*, 36: 488–500.

Caloghirou, Y., Kastelli, I. and Tsakanikas, A. (2004), 'Internal capability and external knowledge sources: Complements or substitutes for innovative performance?', *Technovation*, 24: 29–39.

Cassiman, B., Perez-Castrillo, D. and Veugelers, R. (2002), 'Endogenizing know-how flows through the nature of R&D investments', *International Journal of Industrial Organization*, 20: 775–799.

—— and Veugelers, R. (2002), 'R&D cooperation and spillovers: Some empirical evidence from Belgium', *American Economic Review* 92(4): 1169–1184.

Chang, Y.C. (2003), 'Benefits of co-operation on innovative performance: Evidence from integrated circuits and biotechnology firms in the UK and Taiwan', *R&D Management*, 33(4): 425–437.

Chesbrough, H.W. (2003), *Open Innovation: The New Imperative for Creating and Profiting from Technological Innovation*. Boston: Harvard Business School Press.

Cohen, W.M. and Levinthal, D.A. (1990), 'Absorptive capacity: A new perspective on learning and innovation', *Administrative Science Quarterly*, 35(1): 128–152.

Collins, J.D. and Hitt, M.A. (2006), 'Leveraging tacit knowledge in alliances: The importance of using relational capabilities to build and leverage relational capital', *Journal of Engineering and Technology Management*, 23: 147–167.

Cincera, M., Lieselot, K., van Pottelsberghe, B., Veugelers, R. and Villegas Sanchez, C. (2003), 'Productivity growth, R&D and the role of international collaborative agreements: Some evidence from Belgian manufacturing companies', *Brussels Economic Review/Cahiers Economiques de Bruxelles*, 46(3): 107–140.

Czarnitzki, D., Ebersberger B. and Fier, A. (2007), 'The relationship between R&D collaboration and R&D performance: Empirical evidence from Finland and Germany', *Journal of Applied Econometrics*, 22: 1347–1366.

Danzon, P.M., Nicholson, S. and Sousa Pereira, N. (2005), 'Productivity in pharmaceutical-biotechnology R&D: The role of experience and alliances', *Journal of Health Economics*, 24(2): 317–339.

Das, T.K. and Teng, B. (2000), 'Instabilities of strategic alliances: An internal tensions perspective', *Organization Science*, 11: 77–101.

de Man, A.G., and Duysters, G., (2005), 'Collaboration and innovation: A review of the effects of mergers, acquisitions and alliances on innovation', *Technovation*, 25(12): 1377–1387.

De Propris, L. (2002), 'Types of innovation and inter-firm co-operation', *Entrepreneurship and Regional Development*, 14: 337–353.

Di Masi, J.A., Hansen, R.W. and Grabowsky, H.J. (2003), 'The price of innovation: New estimated of drug development costs', *Journal of Health Economics*, 22: 151–185.

Duysters, G. and Hagedoorn, J. (2000), 'Core competences and company performance in the world-wide computer industry', *Journal of High Technology Management Research*, 11(1): 75–91.

—— and Lokshin, B. (2011), 'Determinants of alliance portfolio complexity and its effect on innovative performance of companies', *Journal of Product Innovation Management*, 28(4): 570–585.

Faems, D., Van Looy, B. and Debackere, K. (2005), 'Interorganizational collaboration and innovation: Toward a portfolio approach', *Journal of Product Innovation Management*, 22: 238–250.

Frenz, M., and Ietto-Gilles, G. (2009), 'The impact on innovation performance of different sources of knowledge: Evidence from the UK Community Innovation Survey', *Research Policy*, 38: 1125–1135.

Fritsch, M. and Franke, G. (2004), 'Innovation, regional knowledge spillovers and R&D cooperation', *Research Policy*, 33: 245–255.

George, G., Zahra, S.A., Wheatley, K.K. and Khan, R. (2001), 'The effect of alliance portfolio characteristics and absorptive capacity on performance. A study of biotechnology firms', *Journal of High Technology Management Research*, 12: 205–226.

—————— and Wood, D.R. (2002), 'The effects of business–university alliances on innovative output and financial performance: A study of publicly traded biotechnology companies', *Journal of Business Venturing*, 17(6): 577–609.

Gilsing, V., Noteeboom, B., Vanhaverbeke, W., Duysters, G. and Van den Oord, A. (2008), 'Network embededdedness and the exploration of novel technologies: Technological distance, betweenness, centrality and density', *Research Policy*, 37(10): 1717–1731.

Goerzen, A. (2007), 'Alliance network and firm performance: The impact of repeated partnerships', *Strategic Management Journal*, 28: 487–509.

—— and Beamish, P.W. (2005), 'The effect of alliance network diversity on multinational enterprise performance', *Strategic Management Journal*, 26(4): 333–354.

Gomes-Casseres, B. (2004), Competing in alliance constellations. In Trick, M.A. (ed.), *Global Corporate Evolution: Looking Inward or Looking Outward?* Carnegie Bosch Institute, International Management Series, Vol. 4. Pittsburgh: Carnegie Mellon Press.

Hagedoorn, J. (1993), 'Understanding the rationale of strategic technology partnering: International modes of cooperation and sectoral differences', *Strategic Management Journal*, 14(15), 371–385.

—— (2002), 'Inter-firm R&D partnerships: An overview of major trends and patterns since 1960', *Research Policy*, 31: 477–492.

Harrison, J.S., Hitt, M.A., Hoskisson, R.E. and Ireland, R.D. (2001), 'Resource complementarity in business combinations: Extending the logic to organizational alliances', *Journal of Management*, 27: 679–690.

Hitt, M.A., Beamish P.W., Jackson, S.E. and Mathieu, J.E. (2007), 'Building theoretical and empirical bridges across levels: Multilevel research in management', *Academy of Management Journal*, 50(6): 1385–1399.

Janz, N., Lööf, H. and Peters, B. (2004), 'Innovation and productivity in German and Swedish manufacturing firms: Is there a common story?', *Problems and Perspectives in Management*, 2: 184–204.

Kale, P., Dyer, J.H. and Singh, H. (2002), 'Alliance capability, stock market response, and long-term alliance success: The role of the alliance function', *Strategic Management Journal*, 23(8): 747–767.

Keil, T., Maula, M., Schildt, H. and Zahra, S.A. (2008), 'The effect of governance modes and relatedness of external business development on innovative performance', *Strategic Management Journal*, 29: 895–907.

Kim, C. and Song, J. (2007), 'Creating new technology through alliances: An empirical investigation of joint patents', *Technovation*, 27: 461–470.

Klomp, L. and van Leeuwen, G. (2001), 'Linking innovation and firm performance: A new approach', *International Journal of the Economics of Business*, 8(3): 343–364.

Knudsen, M.P. (2007), 'The relative importance of interfirm relationships and knowledge transfer for new product development success', *Journal of Product Innovation Management*, 24(2): 117–138.

Laursen, K. and Salter, A., (2006), 'Open for innovation: The role of openness in explaining innovation performance among U.K. manufacturing firms', *Strategic Management Journal*, 27: 131–150.

Lavie, D. (2007), 'Alliance portfolio and firm performance: A study of value creation and appropriation in the US software industry', *Strategic Management Journal*, 28: 1187–1212.

—— and Miller, S.R. (2008), 'Alliance portfolio internationalization and firm performance', *Organization Science*, 19(4): 623–646.

Lee, C., Lee, K. and Pennings, J.M. (2001), 'Internal capabilities, external networks, and performance: A study on technology-based ventures', *Strategic Management Journal*, 22: 615–640.

Lin, L.H. (2009), 'Mergers and acquisitions, alliances and technology development: An empirical study of the global auto industry', *International Journal of Technology Management*, 48(3): 295–307.

Lin, Z., Yang, H. and Arya, B. (2009), 'Alliance partners and firm performance: Resource complementarity and status association', *Strategic Management Journal*, 30: 921–940.

Lööf H. and Heshmati, A. (2002), 'Knowledge capital and performance heterogeneity: A firm level innovation study', *International Journal of Production Economics*, 76: 61–85.

Luo, X. and Deng, L. (2009), 'Do birds of a feather flock higher? The effects of partner similarity on innovation in strategic alliances in knowledge-intensive industries', *Journal of Management Studies*, 46(6): 1005–1030.

Monjon, S. and Waelbroeck, P. (2003), 'Assessing spillovers from universities to firms: Evidence from French firm-level data', *International Journal of Industrial Organization*, 21(9): 1255–1270.

Montoya, P.V., Zarate, R.S. and Martin, L.A.G. (2007), 'Does the technological sourcing decision matter? Evidence from Spanish panel data', *R&D Management*, 37: 161–172.

Narula, R. (1999), 'Explaining the growth of strategic R&D alliances by European firms', *Journal of Common Market Studies*, 37(4): 711–723.

—— and Hagedoorn, J. (1999), 'Innovating through strategic alliances: Moving towards international partnerships and contractual agreements', *Technovation*, 19: 283–294.

Negassi, S. (2004), 'R&D co-operation and innovation a microeconometric study on French firms', *Research Policy*, 33(3): 365–384.

Nieto, M.J. and Santamaría, L. (2007), 'The importance of diverse collaborative networks for the novelty of product innovation', *Technovation*, 27: 367–377.

—— —— (2009), 'Technological collaboration: Bridging the innovation gap between small and large firms', *Journal of Small Business*, 48(1): 44–69.

Nooteboom, B., Van Haverbeke, W., Duysters, G., Gilsing V. and Van den Oord, A. (2007), 'Optimal cognitive distance and absorptive capacity', *Research Policy*, 36: 1016–1034.

NSI (2009), The third state of alliance management study. http://www.duysters.com/Downloads%20managerial

Padula, G. (2008), 'Enhancing the innovation performance of firms by balancing cohesiveness and bridging ties', *Long Range Planning*, 41(4): 395–411.

Park, S.H. and Ungson, G.R. (2001), 'Interfirm rivalry and managerial complexity: A conceptual framework of alliance failure', *Organization Science*, 12(1): 37–53.

Provan, K.G., Fish, A. and Sydow, J. (2007), 'International networks at the network level: A review of the empirical literature on the whole network', *Journal of Management*, 33(3): 479–496.

Rogers, M. (2004), 'Networks, firm size and innovation: Evidence from Australian firms', *Small Business Economics*, 22(6–7): 141–153.

Rothaermel, F.T. and Deeds, D.L. (2004), 'Exploration and exploitation alliances in biotechnology: A system of new product development', *Strategic Management Journal*, 25(3): 201–221.

—— and Hess, A.M. (2007), 'Building dynamic capabilities: Innovation driven by individual-, firm-, and network-level effects', *Organization Science*, 18(6): 898–921.

Rowley, T., Behrens, D. and Krackhardt, D. (2000), 'Redundant governance structures: An analysis of structural and relational embeddedness in the steel and semiconductor industries', *Strategic Management Journal*, 21(3): 369–386.

Sampson, R. (2007), 'R&D alliances and firm performance: The impact of technological diversity and alliance organization on innovation', *Academy of Management Journal*, 50: 364–386.

Santamaría, L., Nieto, M.J. and Barge-Gil, A. (2009), 'Beyond formal R&D: Taking advantage of other sources of innovation in low- and medium-technology industries', *Research Policy*, 38(3): 507–517.

Schildt, H., Maula, M. and Keil, T. (2005), 'Explorative and exploitative learning from external corporate ventures', *Entrepreneurship Theory and Practice*, 29(4): 493–515.

Schilling, M.A. and Hill, C.W.L. (1998), 'Managing the new product development process: Strategic imperatives', *Academy of Management Executive*, 12(3): 67–81.

—— and Phelps, C. (2007), 'Interfirm collaboration networks: The impact of large-scale network structure on firm innovation', *Management Science*, 53(7): 1113–1127.

Sher, P.J. and Yang, P.Y. (2005), 'The effects of innovative capabilities and R&D clustering on firm performance: The evidence of Taiwan's semiconductor industry', *Technovation*, 25(1): 33–43.

Simonen, J. and McCann, P. (2008), 'Innovation, R&D cooperation and labor recruitment: Evidence from Finland', *Small Business Economics*, 31: 181–194.

Stuart, T. (2000), 'Interorganizational alliances and the performance of firms: A study of growth and innovation rates in a high technology industry', *Strategic Management Journal*, 21: 791–811.

Su, Y.-S., Tsang, E.W.K. and Peng, M.W. (2009), 'How do internal capabilities and external partnerships affect innovativeness?', *Asia Pacific Journal of Management*, 26: 309–331.

Thorgren, S., Wincent, J. and Örtqvist, D. (2009), 'Designing interorganizational networks for innovation: An empirical examination of network configuration, formation and governance', *Journal of Engineering and Technology Management*, 26(3): 148–166.

Tsai, K.H. (2009), 'Collaborative networks and product innovation performance: Toward a contingency perspective', *Research Policy*, 38: 765–778.

—— and Wang, J.-C. (2008), 'External technology acquisition and firm performance: A longitudinal study', *Journal of Business Venturing*, 23: 91–112.

—— —— (2009), 'External technology sourcing and innovation performance in LMT sectors: An analysis based on the Taiwanese Technological Innovation Survey', *Research Policy*, 38(3): 518–526.

Vanhaverbeke, W., Duysters, G. and Noorderhaven, N. (2002), 'External technology sourcing through alliances or acquisitions: An analysis of the application-specific integrated circuits industry', *Organization Science*, 13(6): 714–733.

——, Gilsing,V., Beerkens, B. and Duysters, G. (2009), 'The role of alliance network redundancy in the creation of core and non-core technologies', *Journal of Management Studies*, 46(2): 215–244.

Vega-Jurado, J., Gutierrez-Gracia, A. and Fernandez-de-Lucio, I. (2009), 'Does external knowledge sourcing matter for innovation? Evidence from the Spanish manufacturing industry', *Industrial and Corporate Change*, 18(4): 637–670.

Wassmer, U. (2010), 'Alliance portfolios: A review and research agenda', *Journal of Management*, 36(1): 141–171.

Zollo, M., Reuer, J.J. and Singh, H. (2002), 'Interorganizational routines and performance in strategic alliances', *Organization Science*, 13: 701–713.

8

R&D Strategy and Firm Performance: What Is the Long-Run Impact of Persistent R&D?

Hans Lööf, Börje Johansson, Martin Andersson, and Charlie Karlsson

8.1. Introduction

There is a stylized fact in the literature that the level of R&D spending is positively associated with the level of labour productivity across firms (Cohen and Klepper, 1996). In contrast to the overwhelming evidence that productivity increases with R&D in the level dimension, the literature is rather thin and inconclusive on the direction(s) of causality as well as on the significance of the longitudinal relationship and the simultaneous influence from a third factor outside the firm. Three kinds of relationship are possible: (1) investments in R&D influence subsequent productivity, (2) changes in productivity influence subsequent R&D investments, and (3) R&D and productivity are influenced simultaneously by an external factor, for instance the business cycle.

There is also a broad agreement in the literature that firm performance is highly skewed with a fat tail, where high-performing firms tend to retain their position over time. This observation remains valid for several performance measures (Bartelsman and Doms, 2000). In this chapter, we introduce an innovation-strategy variable to show that enduring differences in firm performance can be explained by grouping firms into three categories: (1) persistently R&D active, (2) occasionally R&D active, and (3) persistently R&D inactive. A main result is that persistently R&D active firms outperform other firms with regard to both productivity level and productivity growth.

The lack of congruent results from cross-sectional and time-series data is troublesome. Both methods are expected, in principle, to yield the same results (CBO, 2005). Furthermore, given a high degree of persistence in corporate performance, increasing knowledge about the difference between cross-sectional and time-series estimates is an important challenge for economic research. How can we explain the large and persistent variations in firms' ability to generate added value when the literature does not find a clear long-run link from R&D to productivity and profitability across firms, and in theory R&D is considered a key determinant of competitiveness.

The literature offers several possible explanations for a repeatedly observed fragile, long-run correlation between the level and growth rate of R&D expenditures and productivity growth. One suggestion is that the innovation process is characterized by a large element of randomness, for which the accumulation of new knowledge may not be predictable, steady, or continuous (CBO, 2005). A second view suggests that innovations have only transitory effects on firm performance since other firms can imitate the innovation (Cefis and Ciccarelli, 2005). A third argument is that accumulation of technological knowledge from annual R&D-investments may create a lock-in/lock-out effect, hampering the firm's ability to identify and grasp new technological opportunities (Cabagnols, 2006). Yet another possible explanation might be that a considerable fraction of innovators invest in R&D only occasionally (Malerba and Orsenigo, 1999), and partly as a defensive or reactive strategy to counteract a situation where part of output has become economically obsolete (Schmookler, 1996). Antonelli (1989), for instance, introduces a 'failure inducement hypothesis' where firms make R&D efforts when performance falls below a minimum threshold, resulting in a negative relationship between profitability and R&D expenditure. The literature has also shown that incumbents with high market power and possible monopoly profits are afraid of cannibalizing their current sources of revenues, which reduces the incentive to invest in R&D (Arrow, 1962; Reinganum, 1983).

An additional set of explanations concerns issues such as shortcomings of the data and of measuring a firm's innovation capacity with the narrow concept of R&D. Analyzing French firm-level data, Duguet and Monjon (2002) suggest that formal research expenditures reflect the variation of innovation expenditures over time only in the largest firms. In contrast, the 'not-so-easy to measure' learning-by-doing process dominates the persistent innovation activities in small-sized firms. Cefis and Orsenigo (2001) report overlapping findings. Based on patent data for six large economies (France, Germany, Italy, UK, Japan, and the USA), they suggest that in order to maintain innovative activities, persistence rather than the size of R&D expenditures might be considered. Moreover, a growing number of empirical studies using panel data suggest the presence of a clear time-invariance in firms' R&D: most firms report no R&D over time and the innovative firms can be separated into one group reporting occasional and another reporting persistent R&D

efforts. Such observations suggest alternative ways to examine the association between R&D and growth.

This chapter takes the latter category of possible explanations as its starting point. We introduce the notion of R&D strategy, as captured by the persistence of the firm's commitment to R&D, as an alternative way to assess empirically the relationship between R&D and growth. Our arguments for this are outlined in the following paragraphs.

R&D investments have many faces. Cohen and Levinthal (1990) point out that R&D has two consequences: it results in innovations and it builds up absorptive capacity, where the latter refers to a firm's ability to identify, assimilate, and exploit knowledge from the environment. We emphasize that there is yet another aspect of R&D investments, which is related to the persistence with which firms undertake such investments over time. This aspect is learning-by-doing in the form of routines and capabilities for R&D (Nelson and Winter, 1982). Persistent R&D implies a learning process, in which the firm develops routines for performing R&D as well as experience in how to commercialize R&D results. Such 'R&D skills' are expected to have an influence on the returns to a firm's R&D efforts. The importance of this type of 'R&D skills' is amplified by the fact that they are not expected to depreciate over time, in contradistinction to the R&D stock (Hall, 2007). Skills are the result of 'learning-by-doing', establishing R&D routines. This argument suggests an important distinction between firms with persistent and occasional R&D efforts, where the described learning effects are absent (or considerably weaker) for firms with occasional R&D investments.[1] It is also consistent with Cefis and Orsenigo's (2001) conclusion that persistence rather than the size of R&D expenditures might be the most essential innovation characteristic.

Based on the above arguments, we test whether a firm's long-run economic performance can be predicted by a simple R&D-strategy variable that takes only three values: no, occasional, or persistent innovation efforts, where R&D activities is a main indicator of innovation efforts. This R&D-strategy variable is derived from the harmonized European innovation survey, the Community Innovation Survey (CIS), on Swedish manufacturing and service firms observed in 2002–2004. Firms are classified with regard to their R&D behaviour during the three-year period 2002–2004, as reported in the CIS survey. We separate firms according to three R&D-strategy classes: no, occasional, and persistent R&D efforts.

Similar to what Cefis and Ciccarelli (2005) report for a panel of 267 UK manufacturing firms, in a cross-sectional dimension, we find that persistent-R&D

---

[1] As the saying goes, 'Repetition is the mother of learning.'

firms are different from the two other groups in several respects. They are considerably larger and more export-oriented, they are more skill intensive, have higher sales and value added per employee, and, in contrast to the other two, they typically belong to a multinational company group. The patterns revealed by the descriptive statistics are consistent with the idea that when a firm develops a strategy of persistent R&D engagement, then such a strategic choice also includes decisions to develop the associated resource-base of the firm. Employing a strategy of persistent innovation efforts implies that the firm maintains its heuristics and routines of innovation practice.

By using supplementary data sources we are able to follow the firms in the CIS4 survey over the whole period 1997–2006. Referring to performance differences observed in CIS4, we ask if the same differences in performance can be predicted for the subsequent years 2005 and 2006. Second, we also investigate if the same differences in firm performance can be detected and ascertained for the preceding years 1997–2001. Confirming that this is the case, we assume that the strategy classification of firms for 2002–2004 is valid for the entire ten-year period 1997–2006. Based on this we formulate econometric models in which the three innovation-strategy categories are our prime explanatory variables.

By estimating both level and first-difference dynamic panel models, we find an effect of a firm's R&D strategy on its performance in both the level and growth dimensions. Controlling for differences in past labour productivity, firms with persistent R&D engagement have, on average, a 13 per cent higher labour productivity compared to firms with no R&D, and a 9 per cent higher productivity compared to firms with occasional R&D efforts. In addition, a strategy with persistent R&D commitment corresponds to about a 2 per cent higher growth rate in productivity than for other firms.

The rest of the chapter is organized as follows. Section 8.2 provides a short literature survey and a theoretical background to the role of persistence in knowledge accumulation. We then document some important statistical differences between firms with persistent innovation efforts and other firms in both the cross-sectional dimension and time-series dimension. The empirical model and the estimation strategy are presented in Section 8.4. Section 8.5 confirms that the strong correlation in the descriptive statistics between R&D strategy and economic output holds true in an empirical framework where we use methods which control for past performance, simultaneity, and unobserved heterogeneity. Section 8.6 concludes the study.

8.2. Research on persistent innovation and performance

8.2.1. *Theoretical contributions in the literature*

Contemporary models of innovation and industry dynamics typically suggest that supernormal profitability and productivity is a transitory phenomenon, although the models may differ with regard to the time-sequence of equilibrium adjustments. A source of firm heterogeneity can be the luck of the draw in R&D outcomes, and may offer a temporary monopoly position. However, imitative competition ensures that the temporary increase in market power disappears over time (see e.g. Grossman and Helpman, 1991; Aghion and Howitt, 1992; Roberts 1999). This model structure is also common in the literature on Gibrat-type processes, and various models of real business cycles.

However, empirical observations of firm-level data from different industries, countries, and time-periods provide evidence in favour of a stable skewed distribution reflected as serial correlation in firm performance (Klette and Kortum, 2004). This suggests equilibrium with persistent performance differentials. If the capacity to make persistent innovation efforts is a scarce resource, these differentials could be thought of as a form of economic rent.

The observation of persistent asymmetries among firms in terms of size, innovation, productivity, profitability, and growth has spurred the development of competence-based and other non-equilibrium theories of the firm at the micro level. The literature suggests several different reasons for persistent differences in firms' performance such as 'success breeds success' (Philips, 1971), the cumulative nature of knowledge formation (Nelson and Winter, 1982; Cohen and Levinthal, 1990), and sunk cost in R&D investments (Sutton, 1991). In practice, as Cefis and Orsenigo (2001) suggest, it is very difficult to distinguish between sources of persistent heterogeneity. However, Duguet and Monjon (2002) list some simple empirical tests to determine which of the theoretical models are most relevant and have the best reference to observations.

8.2.2. *Empirical evidence*

Dosi and Nelson (2010) conclude that firms differ over all dimensions one is able to detect. The observed inter-firm heterogeneity has been found to be fairly persistent over time, and the empirical literature on innovation focuses on at least three different aspects of this phenomenon. They are the correlation between: (1) previous and current innovation investments, (2) previous and current innovation-output performance of patents, innovation sales, or major innovations, and (3) persistent innovation activities and economic performance. We briefly summarize some of these studies below.

8.2.2.1. PERSISTENT ENGAGEMENT IN INNOVATION-INPUT ACTIVITIES

Using an innovation panel data set on German manufacturing and service firms for the period 1994–2002, Peters (2009) reports the presence of true state dependence: past innovation experience is an important determinant of current innovation engagements. Malerba and Orsenigo (1999) use patent data from the European Patent Office (EPO) and find that occasional innovators account for a large part of the patenting activities, while there is a smaller core of relatively persistent innovators.

The relevance of these analyses is confirmed by numerous empirical studies in economics, sociology, and managerial science that have demonstrated large and lasting differences in the engagement in innovation activities across firms. Most firms are non-innovators, and a hard core of the innovative firms contains persistent innovators (see e.g. Henderson, 1993; Cohen, 1995; Langlois and Robertson, 1995; Cockburn, Henderson and Stern, 2000; Duguet and Monjon, 2002; Cefis, 2003; Klette and Kortum, 2004; and Raymond et al., 2006).

8.2.2.2. PERSISTENT INNOVATION-INPUT AND INNOVATION-OUTPUT PERFORMANCE

In their seminal paper, Griliches and Pakes (1980) define a theoretical model for relating innovation input to innovation output. Applying a distributed lag approach, they find a significant association between R&D and patents. Regarding the times-series dimension, Griliches (1990) reports literature support in favour of the hypothesis that changes in R&D expenditures correlate with changes in patent numbers. Quantitatively, the elasticity of patents with respect to R&D typically clusters around 0.5 (Blundell et al., 2002). Following the general methodology outlined in Crépon et al. (1998) and simplified by Lööf and Heshmati (2002), a large number of studies have also confirmed a positive relationship across firms between innovation input and sales revenues from new products. However, the impact of a particular R&D strategy—persistent or occasional—on the share of new products in sales is not well documented in the literature. Data availability is one possible explanation for this gap in the literature.

8.2.2.3. PERSISTENT INNOVATION-INPUT AND ECONOMIC PERFORMANCE

It is a stylized fact that firms that are identified as innovators tend to be more productive, profitable, or disposed to export than other firms. See for instance Bernard (2004). However, do they base their success on the ability to continuously bring innovative new products to the market? Applying a Bayesian approach on a panel of 267 UK manufacturing firms over the period 1988–1992, Cefis and Ciccarelli (2005) suggest a difference in profitability between innovators and non-innovators, and a greater difference when the comparison is between persistent innovators and non-innovators. Similar findings have also been reported by Roberts (1999) and others. Few studies, however, have investigated the link between persistent innovation and growth rates regardless of whether it is expressed in terms of employment, sales, exports, productivity, or profitability.

8.2.3. R&D strategy and firm performance: Methodological issues and motivation

There are several issues when trying to assess the impact of persistent R&D. One is the availability of representative time-series data including sufficient and relevant covariates. Another is the reliability of the data. In particular, it is crucial to find an R&D measure that is suitable for both small and large firms, and preferably also for both manufacturing and service firms.

In this chapter, which covers approximately two-thirds of all relevant services and manufacturing firms in Sweden, we identify the R&D strategy of a firm by only one indicator variable. The pragmatic justification is that we do not have a better alternative for the period considered, given that strategy is interpreted as 'a long-term plan for decision-making into the future'. The choice may also be motivated by arguments in the literature. Investigating the prevalence of persistent innovators, Cefis and Orsenigo (2001) found that both 'great innovators' and non-innovators have a strong tendency to remain in their respective categories. Nevertheless, they also reported that, to maintain innovative activities, persistence rather than the size of R&D expenditures might be important. There are two complementary aspects of this finding. One has to do with knowing how to organize R&D efforts and the second is about accumulating knowledge. In both cases, persistence per se is a crucial feature.

As suggested by Nelson and Winter (1982), permanent engagement in innovation efforts makes it possible for the firm to collect experiences through learning-by-doing, and thereby developing innovation skills and establishing routines for carrying out development activities. Such routines also include exploitation of networks for knowledge flows into the firm. The second aspect refers to the argument that the continuity of development efforts facilitates the accumulation of knowledge, and that disruptions of R&D engagement can cause the results from previous efforts to be lost. Continuity ensures maintenance of both routines and knowledge.

A third argument relates to observations in CBO (2005), which contains a discussion of the limitations of the R&D measure for both small and larger firms. Since the R&D budget of a firm only represents a fraction of a firm's total innovation efforts, the presence of persistent R&D efforts may better represent the importance of innovation efforts than the size of R&D spending does (Duguet and Monjon, 2002).

In the Klette-Kortum model (2004) of the innovating firm and productivity, a firm's innovation rate is assumed to depend on both its investment in R&D and its knowledge capital, which the authors define as 'the skills, techniques, and know-how that it draws on as it attempts to innovate' (p. 991). A large literature has shown that human capital, measured by university-educated employees, may be used as a good proxy for knowledge capital. We assume that the significant difference in human capital between persistent innovators and the two other groups of firms gives additional support to the idea that a firm's long-run R&D strategy can be identified by just one indicator variable that can take three different values.

A third issue to be considered is the empirical methodology. Cefis and Orsenigo (2001), Duguet and Monjon (2002), Peters (2009), and others stress the importance of identifying whether the observed persistence in R&D behaviour is the outcome of factors such as (1) observed heterogeneous characteristics of firms, (2) unobserved firm heterogeneity, (3) true state dependence, or (4) spurious state dependence. In addition to these factors, we can add simultaneity and dynamic endogeneity. The latter includes past performance of sales, productivity, and exports, as well as a history of other firm characteristics. However, it excludes the three strategy categories to the extent that the categorization remains invariant over a sequence of years.

8.3. Data and descriptive statistics

We base our econometric analysis on observations from a set of manufacturing and service firms in Sweden with 10 or more employees, making up a representative sample from the Community Innovation Survey (CIS4). The CIS-data survey is a Eurostat/OECD initiative for studying innovative activities of European firms. A growing number of countries outside Europe also employ the survey.

In CIS4 we identify (for the period 2002–2004) three groups of firms: (1) R&D inactive all three years, (2) R&D active occasionally, and (3) R&D active all three years. In CIS4 the total number of firms observed is 3096. The survey (CIS4) that we use to determine the classification of each firm's R&D strategy took place in 2005 and covered the period 2002–2004. The rate of response was close to 70 per cent. The original sample contains 3094 firms and to obtain the full data set we have merged the survey data with information from a database which contains information about all firms in Sweden, including human capital measured as employees with at least three years of university education, physical capital, sales, value added, exports, and corporate ownership. The matching process resulted in a data set containing 2895 firms, which is the data set that we employ in the study.

Table 8.1. Summary statistics for year 2004. Firms observed in the CIS4

	Non R&D	Temporary R&D	Persistent R&D
Number of employees	98 (576)	94 (297)	254 (738)
Innovation exp./sales	0.004 (0.022)	0.015 (0.043)	0.044 (0.076)
Human capital [a]	0.10 (0.14)	0.12 (0.17)	0.20 (0.21)
Physical capital (log)	7.41 (2.88)	7.82 (2.77)	8.86 (2.99)
Sales/emp (log)	7.24 (0.78)	7.31 (0.67)	7.48 (0.71)
Value added/emp (log)	6.24 (0.49)	6.26 (0.56)	6.42 (0.49)
Exporters (fraction)	0.51 (0.49)	0.70 (0.45)	0.80 (0.40)
Export/emp (log)[b]	7.04 (1.56)	7.26 (1.14)	7.48 (1.25)
Manufacturing	0.53 (0.49)	0.72 (0.45)	0.67 (0.47)
Services	0.47 (0.49)	0.28 (0.45)	0.33 (0.47)
Corporate ownership struct.			
Independent	0.34 (0.47)	0.25 (0.43)	0.15 (0.36)
Swedish domestic group	0.33 (0.47)	0.35 (0.48)	0.21 (0.41)
Swedish MNE	0.15 (0.36)	0.21 (0.46)	0.34 (0.47)
Foreign MNE	0.17 (0.37)	0.19 (0.39)	0.29 (0.45)
Number of firms	1,732	474	692

Notes: Mean values and standard deviation between parentheses. [a] Number of employees with three years of university education or more, as a fraction of total employment. [b] Only firms that export.

Table 8.1 presents summary statistics referring to year 2004 from the above data set, where firms are separated into three groups, reflecting their reported type of R&D strategy during the three-year period 2002–2004. The table shows that around 60 per cent of the population consists of firms that do not report any innovation activities, whereas more than 16 per cent report occasional innovation, and 24 per cent are persistent innovators. The entire picture means that we have (1) one group of firms in which the firms remained R&D inactive in 2002–2004, (2) a second group in which firms switched between being R&D active and R&D inactive, and (3) a third group in which firms were R&D active for the entire period 2002–2004. Firms in these three groups remained systematically different during the whole period 1997–2006, which means that they were different both before and after the classification period 2002–2004.

Table 8.1 also reveals substantial differences between firms with persistent R&D efforts and other firms. They have a larger intensity of both human capital and physical capital, and their sales, value added, and export value per employee are higher than for firms without persistent R&D efforts. Moreover, corporate ownership structure makes a difference, and it is shown that firms that do not carry out persistent innovation efforts typically are independent or belong to a group where all firms have a domestic location. In contrast, the vast majority of firms that report a persistent commitment to R&D efforts belong to a multinational company group.

Table 8.2 presents statistics over the ten-year period 1997–2006 for the 2,895 firms observed in the CIS4 survey. The annual number of firms in the

Table 8.2. Summary statistics over the period 1997–2006. Firms observed in the CIS4, year 2005

	Non R&D	Temporary R&D	Persistent R&D
Number of employees	93 (496)	92 (294)	275 (921)
Human capital [a]	0.08 (0.13)	0.10 (0.16)	0.17 (0.20)
Physical capital (log)	7.44 (2.81)	7.77 (2.76)	8.84 (3.02)
Sales/emp (log)	7.18 (0.79)	7.25 (0.69)	7.40 (0.70)
Value added/emp (log)	6.18 (0.51)	6.21 (0.49)	6.34 (0.54)
Export/emp (log)[b]	6.91 (1.59)	7.04 (1.30)	7.15 (1.35)
Manufacturing	0.52 (0.50)	0.70 (0.46)	0.67 (0.47)
Services	0.48 (0.50	0.30 (0.46)	0.33 (0.47)
Corporate ownership struct.			
Independent	0.39 (0.49)	0.31 (0.46)	0.20 (0.40)
Swedish domestic group	0.32 (0.47)	0.32 (0.47)	0.21 (0.41)
Swedish MNE	0.15 (0.36)	0.20 (0.40)	0.34 (0.47)
Foreign MNE	0.14 (0.35)	0.16 (0.37)	0.25 (0.43)
Number of obs firms	15,417	4,350	6,161
Number of obs exporting firms	7,916	3,034	4,978

Notes: Mean values and standard deviation between parentheses. [a] Number of employees with three years of university education or more, as a fraction of total employment. [b] Only firms that export.

Table 8.3. Summary statistics over the period 1997–2006 for firms observed in the CIS4, year 2005. Growth rates

	Non R&D	Occasional R&D	Persistent R&D
∆ Sales/emp (log)	0.044 (0.335)	0.046 (0.350)	0.063 (0.368)
∆ Value added/emp (log)	0.044 (0.496)	0.038 (0.442)	0.059 (0.624)
∆ Exports/emp (log)	0.031 (1.101)	0.045 (0.442)	0.055 (0.909)
Number of obs firms	13,655	3,860	4,505
Number of obs exporting firms	6,339	2,532	4,279

Notes: Mean values and standard deviation between parentheses. Negative values replaced by 0.01 before taking the logs.

unbalanced panel varies between 2,600 and 2,895, with a total of nearly 26,000 observations. The patterns conveyed by the table are remarkably similar to the picture given in Table 8.1: persistent innovators are generically different from other firms regarding both input and output factors. In Table 8.3, we see that persistent R&D firms have an average growth rate that is about 2 per cent larger than the growth rate of the other two groups of firms irrespective of whether we measure in terms of sales, productivity, or exports.[2]

Figures 8.1–8.3 describe the development (in current prices) in sales, value added, and exports expressed in intensity form (per employee) over

---

[2] During the period 1997–2006, the annual change in the Swedish price level was very low. In addition, the analysis is focused on the relative difference between groups of firms. Given this, we have decided to present economic variables at current prices. Moreover, the difference in growth rates remains the same when calculations are based on current and deflated values.

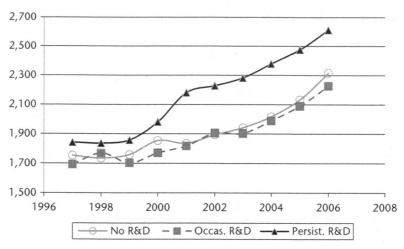

Figure 8.1. Sales per employee 1997–2006. 1,000 SEK. Current prices

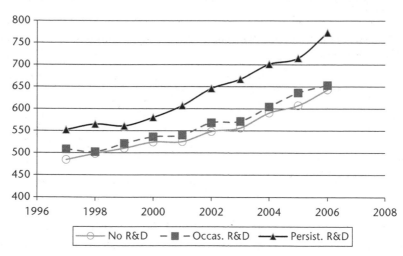

Figure 8.2. Value added per employee 1997–2006. 1,000 SEK. Current prices

the observed period for the three categories of firms. The summary of these findings is that an R&D strategy with persistent R&D engagement strongly predicts a firm's economic output performance, divided into sales performance (sales value per labour input), value added performance (value added per labour input), and export performance (export value per labour input).

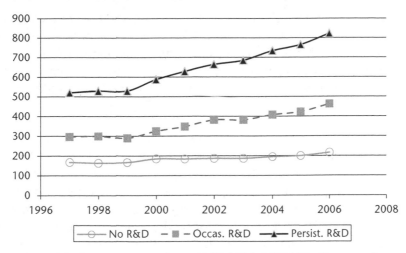

Figure 8.3. Exports per employee 1997–2006. 1,000 SEK. Current prices

8.4. Methodology and empirical strategy

8.4.1. *General framework*

The general model that we use for our empirical analysis is a standard Cobb-Douglas production function. The data are repeated measurements at different points in time for the same firms. Variation in data can be decomposed into variation between firms of different sizes and characteristics, such as industry classification, and variation within firms. Employing a logarithmic transformation, the basic model can be expressed as:

$$Q_{it} = \log \hat{Q}_{it} = X'_{it}\beta + Z'_{i}\alpha + \epsilon_{it} \qquad (1)$$

where $\hat{Q}_{it}$ denotes the output of firm i at time t, X'_{it} are K time-variant regressors, and $Z'_{i}\alpha$ the individual effect where Z includes a set of time-invariant individual-specific variables, of which some, such as R&D-strategy, may be observed and others, such as entrepreneurial culture, are unobserved, and which are taken to be constant over time t. The term ϵ_{it} represents the idiosyncratic errors.

The basic model provides two reasons for correlation in Q over time. The first obtains directly through time-variant observables X and time-invariant variables in Z, and indirectly through the time-invariant individual effect (unobserved heterogeneity).

Our main interest is to investigate the relationship between a persistent R&D strategy and long-run firm performance. The first empirical model that we apply is Hausman and Taylor's (1981) hybrid estimator for random effects, which avoids the problem with the fixed-effects approach in which the within

193

transformation would wipe out the Z_i observations, and therefore would not yield any estimation of the R&D-strategy parameters. At the same time, the strong assumptions that the firm-specific effects are distributed independently of the regressors are mitigated since the model allows for some specified flexibility in the correlation between Z_i and X_{it}. The model takes the form

$$Q_{it} = X'_{1it}\beta_1 + X'_{2it}\beta_2 + Z'_{1i}\alpha_1 + Z'_{2i}\alpha_2 + \epsilon_{it} + u_i \tag{2}$$

where X and Z are observable regressors and the unobserved firm-specific effects are now contained in the random variable u_i. In the model X and Z are split into two sets of variables $X = [X_1; X_2]$ and $Z = [Z_1; Z_2]$. X_1 and Z_1 are assumed exogenous in the sense that they are correlated neither with the unobserved firm effect u_i nor with the idiosyncratic error ϵ_{it}. In contrast, X_2 and Z_2 are correlated with u_i and therefore endogenous. In order to overcome the endogeneity bias a set of instruments are included in the model. The time-invariant variables are by construction exogenous throughout the period of analysis. In particular, the very essence of the R&D-strategy variable is that is should reflect a time-invariant classification.

A third possible determinant of Q is Q in preceding periods, which calls for a dynamic panel data model. In order to control for unobserved heterogeneity, true state dependence, and other firm characteristics when estimating the impact of R&D strategy on firm performance, an autoregressive panel data model is employed:

$$Q_{it} = \gamma_1 Q_{it-1} + \ldots + \gamma_p Q_{it-p} + \beta_1 X'_{it} + \beta_2 X'_{it-1} + Z'_i\alpha + u_i + \epsilon_{it} \quad t = p+1\ldots,T \tag{3}$$

where Z' is a set of time-invariant variables and α the associated key-parameters to be estimated, and where $Q_{i,t-1}\cdots Q_{i,t-p}$ represents a lag structure of the dependent variable, X a set of contemporaneous and lagged variables. The error term includes both unobserved firm effects, μ and the idiosyncratic component ϵ.

In terms of growth rate, the dynamic equation is expressed as

$$\Delta Q_{it} = \gamma_1 \Delta Q_{it-1} + \ldots + \gamma_p \Delta Q_{it-p} + \beta_1 \Delta X'_{it} + \beta_2 \Delta X'_{it-1} + \Delta v_{it} \tag{4}$$

We use a two-step system GMM estimator (Arellano and Bover, 1995; Blundell and Bond, 1998) for estimating equations (3) and (4). In addition to some attractive advantages over alternative estimators regarding the presence of heteroschedasticity, autocorrelation, and potential biased standard errors, the chosen estimator allows the time-invariant variables Z to remain regressors even after the differentiating of equation (3).

An issue with our empirical design is to what extent we should resolve the inherent endogeneity problems associated with analyses of R&D and productivity. We do employ dynamic panel models that can accommodate relevant endogeneity issues. However, it is appropriate to ask whether there can be any endogeneity phenomena associated with the strategy variable when each firm is classified as permanently belonging to one of three possible strategy-category sets.

Since systems dynamics tell us that a variable that changes on an extremely slow time scale can be considered as exogenous (Batten, Casti and Johansson, 1987), a key question is thus whether the innovation strategy that was reported for the period 2002–2004 really can be assumed to be a reliable indicator for the entire period 1997–2006.

The CIS4 data tell us that, during a three-year period, 84 per cent of all firms were either persistently R&D active or persistently R&D inactive. Unfortunately, we have no complete information about R&D strategy for the whole period 1997–2006, but nearly 40 per cent of the firms observed in CIS4 were also observed in the CIS3 in 2000. This overlapping information gives us an indication of the plausibility of our assumption. Together, these two studies give us information on the firms' innovation strategy during six of the ten years studied in this article.

Table A8.1 in the appendix shows a substantial degree of consistency between the two surveys. Three of the four companies that were inactive in terms of R&D over the period 2002–2004 reported the same status for the period 1998–2000. Similarly, it is clear from Table A8.1 that the vast majority (75 per cent) of the companies that claimed to be persistent innovators from 2002 to 2004 also declared the same strategy during a preceding three-year period. Regarding the temporary R&D-active companies in the CIS4, almost half of these companies said that they did not engage in any research at all during the period 1998–2000, while a third were persistent innovators.

8.4.2 Specification of the empirical model

The empirical model we will apply is a Cobb-Douglas firm-level production function for firm i with capital, labour, and skills included as inputs. Our general model looks as follows:

$$\hat{Q}_{it} = A_{it}[F(K_{it}, K_{it}, H_{it}] \tag{5}$$

where in absolute values $\hat{Q}_{it}$ is output, A_{it} is a technology shifter, K_{it} is capital stock, L_{it} is ordinary labour measured as the number of employees, and H_{it} is skill measured as the number of employees with at least three years of university education. At each point in time H reflects the capacity to maintain current and expand future knowledge. The size of H will also reflect the knowledge stock of a firm and its capacity to absorb external knowledge from the local milieu, the company group, national and international suppliers and customers, and other knowledge sources (cf. Bartel and Lichtenberg, 1987; Cohen and Levinthal, 1990).

If we take logs as in (1), we can express value added in levels per employee to obtain the following equation for the log of labour productivity:

$$q_{it} = a_{it} + \beta_1 \log K_{it} + \beta_2 \log L_{it} + \beta_3 \log H_{it} \tag{6}$$

We compare three different categories of output: sales, value added, and export per labour input, and hence q_{it} signifies the log of these three output (or performance) variables. L is assumed to reflect size and it should be noted that β_2 is expected to be negative.[3] The key interest of the study is the internal knowledge accumulation created by a particular R&D strategy. We incorporate the R&D strategy into this framework through the shift-factor in the production function in the following way:

$$a_{it} = a_0 + a_2 R_i + a_3 Z_{it} \tag{7}$$

where R is the firm's R&D variable, which can take three different values: no, occasional, and persistent R&D efforts. Z is a vector of the firm's characteristics that includes ownership status, sector classification of firm i, and a year dummy.

The standard measure of labour productivity is total sales or value added over total employment. An alternative measure was put forward in Griliches and Mairesse (1984). This considers the results of R&D efforts as an input to the basic production process and implies that the return to R&D is reflected by its effect on the productivity of ordinary labour, L, i.e., its effect on $q = \ln(\frac{Q}{L})$. This approach considers the distinction between the production of knowledge and the returns to its use (Geroski et al., 1993), where the latter aspect is reflected by the impact of knowledge on q. We employ this approach here for value added, sales, and exports as well.

In order to reduce the influence of possible errors in our extensive database comprising three sets of firm-level data over the period 1997–2006, we have transformed all observations below the first percentile to be equal to the first percentile and adopted the corresponding procedure for observations above the ninety-ninth percentile.

8.5. Empirical analysis

Taking the anti-log of the descriptive statistics reported in Tables 8.2 and 8.3, persistently R&D-active firms have about 15 per cent higher labour productivity than non-R&D-firms and about 10 per cent higher compared to occasional

---

[3] To see this, observe that $q \equiv Q/L = K^{\beta_1} L^{\beta-1} H^{\beta_3}$ and $\beta < 1$. β_2 in equation (6) is β-1.

innovators. The difference in annual growth rate is 1–2 per cent. The figures are roughly similar for sales productivity (sales per employee) and exports per employee.[4] We now explore these descriptive figures with a macro-econometric analysis.

In our empirical work, we employ three different models. Each of the models reports results for productivity measured in sales and value added and for exports per labour input. The first model is the Hausman-Taylor static panel-data model that allows for time-invariant variables, reported for level values in Table 8.4. Table 8.5 contains the results from the two-step GMM in levels. Table 8.6 presents the estimation results when the dependent variable is the average year-to-year change in the growth rates, using the system GMM-estimator.

The first aim is to consider the observed and unobserved heterogeneity. The estimation results are reported in Table 8.4. We expect these Hausman-Taylor estimates to be overestimated, since the model does not correct for the possible presence of 'success-breeds-success' and this creates omitted variable bias.

Rows 1 and 2 in Table 8.4 report the estimates for the separate R&D strategies. The reference group is firms not conducting any R&D. The estimates

Table 8.4. R&D strategies and economic results 1997–2006. Hausman-Taylor model

	Dep. var.: Log Sales	Dep. var.: Log Productivity	Dep. var.: Log Exports
Occasional Innov. [a]	0.087	0.049	0.229
	(0.039)**	(0.023)**	(0.092)**
Persistent Innov. [a]	0.285	0.171	0.413
	(0.034)***	(0.021)***	(0.081)***
Log Physical capital (K)	0.040	0.028 -	0.049
	(0.002)***	(0.002)***	(0.007)***
Log Human capital (H)	0.003	0.010	−0.003
	(0.003)	(0.003)***	(0.011)
Log Ordinary labour (L)	−0.152	−0.083	−0.114
	(0.005)***	(0.005)***	(0.023)***
Dom. Uninat. [b]	0.060	0.071	−0.059
	(0.009)***	(0.009)***	(0.037)
Domestic MNE [b]	0.084	0.069	0.177
	(0.011)***	(0.012)***	(0.040)***
Foreign MNE [b]	0.120	0.089	0.198
	(0.012)***	(0.012)***	(0.042)***
Observations	25,753	25,753	15,851
Unique firms	2,895	2,895	2,232

*Notes:** Significant at 10%; ** significant at 5%; *** significant at 1%. Standard error within parentheses.
[a] Reference: Noninnovative firms, [b] Reference: Independent domestic firms Year dummies and industry dummies included. Interpretation of the dummy variables: $100 \times (e^{D_i} - 1)\%$

[4] The models have been estimated for variables expressed in both current and deflated values with similar parameter estimates as a result.

Table 8.5. Innovation strategies and economic results 1997–2006. Dynamic GMM

	Dep. var.: Log Sales	Dep. var.: Log Productivity	Dep. var.: Log Exports
Occasional Innov. [a]	0.016	0.039	0.044
	(0.011)	(0.015)**	(0.026)*
Persistent Innov. [a]	0.045	0.125	0.112
	(0.020)**	(0.026)***	(0.038)***
Dep. var. $_{t-1}$	0.699	0.420	0.429
	(0.026)***	(0.038)***	(0.043)***
Dep. var. $_{t-2}$	0.089	0.075	0.053
	(0.017)***	(0.024)***	(0.028)*
Dep. var. $_{t-3}$	0.020	−0.017	0.041
	(0.011)*	(0.015)	(0.011)***
K	0.026	0.027	0.063
	(0.004)***	(0.005)***	(0.058)
K_{t-1}	−0.008	−0.004	0.003
	(0.004)**	(0.003)	(0.008)
HC	0.037	0.036	0.028**
	(0.005)***	(0.006) ***	(0.012)
HC_{t-1}	−0.023	−0.012	−0.010
	(0.004)***	(0.005)	(0.010)
L	−0.313	−0.276	−0.279
	(0.028)***	(0.036)***	(0.060)***
L_{t-1}	−0.349	0.185	0.164
	(0.028)***	(0.028)***	(0.042)***
Dom. Uninat. [b]	0.023	0.067	0.063
	(0.015)	(0.018)***	(0.028)**
Domestic MNE [b]	0.069	0.149	0.167
	(0.040)*	(0.052)***	(0.072)**
Foreign MNE [b]	0.097	0.165	0.205
	(0.047)**	(0.055)***	(0.082)**
Observations	17,157	17,157	9,208
Unique firms	2,813	2,813	1,644
AR (1)	0.000	0.000	0.000
AR (2)	0.353	0.732	0.778
Hansen overid.	0.254	0.107	0.278
Number of instr.	202	202	202

Notes: *Significant at 10%; ** Significant at 5%; *** Significant at 1%. Windmeijer corrected standard error within parentheses. [a] Reference: Noninnovative firms, [b] Reference: Independent domestic firms.
Year dummies and industry dummies included.
Interpretation of the dummy variables: $100 \times (e^{D_i}-1)\%$

for both categories of R&D firms are positive and significant, but there is a substantial difference in size. The estimates shown in column 2 suggest that persistent innovators have 18 per cent higher productivity (value-added performance) than non-R&D firms, while the difference between the occasional group and non-R&D firms is about 5 per cent.[5] This pattern bears a close resemblance to the one observed in the descriptive statistics. The corresponding figures for sales performance and export performance with respect to persistent R&D are 0.33 and 0.51, respectively, compared to 0.09 and

---

[5] Interpretation of the dummy variables, D, is $100 \times (e^{D_i}-1)$ per cent.

Table 8.6. Innovation strategies and economic results 1997–2006. Dynamic GMM

	Dep. var.: ΔSales	Dep. var.: ΔProductivity	Dep. var.: ΔExports
Occasional Innov. [a]	0.000	−0.001	0.018
	(0.004)	(0.006)	(0.015)
Persistent Innov. [a]	0.014	0.023	0.036
	(0.005)***	(0.007)***	(0.015)**
ΔDep. var. $_{t-1}$	−0.173	−0.275	−0.305
	(0.020)***	(0.030)***	(0.036)***
ΔDep. var. $_{t-2}$	−0.042	−0.067	−0.110
	(0.011)***	(0.014)***	(0.031)***
ΔK	−0.003	−0.007	0.022
	(0.014)	(0.017)	(0.056)
ΔK_{t-1}	−0.000	0.001	−0.003
	(0.003)	(0.005)***	(0.011)
ΔHC	0.087	0.062	−0.082
	(0.046)*	(0.065)	(0.079)
ΔHC_{t-1}	0.020	0.016	0.003
	(0.008)**	(0.011)	(0.012)
ΔL	−0.338	−0.061	−0.050
	(0.111)	(0.156)	(0.199)
ΔL_{t-1}	−0.017	−0.022	−0.030
	(0.016)	(0.025)	(0.035)
Dom. Uninat. [b]	−0.006	−0.006	0.003
	(0.006)	(0.007)	(0.020)
Domestic MNE [b]	−0.004	−0.015	0.022
	(0.007)	(0.010)	(0.018)
Foreign MNE [b]	−0.002	−0.012	0.020
	(0.007)	(0.010)	(0.018)
Observations	17,157	17,157	9,208
Unique firms	2,813	2,813	1,644
Lag limits	(2 4)	(2 4)	(2 4)
AR (1)	0.000	0.000	0.000
AR (2)	0.198	0.620	0.966
Hansen overid.	0.234	0.475	0.526
Number of instr.	114	114	114

Notes: Significant at 10%; ** Significant at 5%; *** Significant at 1%. Standard error within parentheses. [a] Reference: Noninnovative firms, [b] Reference: Independent domestic firms.
Year dummies and industry sector included.
Interpretation of the dummy variables: $100 \times (e^{Di}-1)\%$

0.26 for occasional innovators. The estimates for persistent innovators are significant at the highest level and significant at the 5 per cent level for typical firms conducting R&D only occasionally.

The estimates associated with (log) physical capital are positive and significant for sales, productivity, and exports. Looking at the (log) human-capital variable, it is positively associated with productivity, but not statistically different from zero in the sales and export equations. The coefficients of the ownership variables indicate that firms belonging to a multinational or uninational group have superior economic performance compared to non-affiliated firms. These are well-established properties, which remain intact in our model settings.

Next, we consider the results from the dynamic GMM-approach presented in Tables 8.5 and 8.6. In principle, the GMM estimation should be able to correct for bias phenomena due to the presence of both correlated firm-specific effects and endogeneity. The test statistics for the GMM estimates in level are shown at the bottom of the table and reveal how well we have succeeded in reducing these sources of bias. First, to ascertain consistent estimations, the estimators require that the error term $m_{\epsilon_{it}}$ is serially uncorrelated. The Arellano-Bond test for autocorrelation (AR) has a null hypothesis of no autocorrelation. As could be expected, due to the construction of the estimator, the test for the AR (1) process in first difference rejects the null hypothesis. This result can therefore be ignored. More importantly, the test for autocorrelation shows satisfactory values for order 2 ($p<0.05$) in the three equations. Second, we use 202 instruments in order to estimate the 14 parameters reported in Table 8.5, so there are 188 overidentification restrictions. The null hypothesis that the instruments are valid is not rejected in any of the three equations, because the Hansen statistic is larger than the critical value 0.05.

Consider the estimates presented in Table 8.5; we first see that the two R&D coefficients have the expected signs in all three equations. However, there is a clear distinction between persistent and occasional innovators. Starting with the sales equation in column 1, the coefficient is significant only for the group of persistent innovators, showing that they have close to 5 per cent higher sales performance than other firms, everything else being equal.

Column 2 reports that both groups of innovators have significantly higher value-added performance (labour productivity) than non-innovators. According to the size of the estimates, R&D persistence corresponds to a 13 per cent advantage in labour productivity compared to non-R&D firms. An occasional R&D engagement is associated with a 4 per cent higher level of productivity. These results are almost the same for the export equation.

Turning to the covariates, the estimates for the lagged dependent variables indicate a considerable degree of serial correlation and conform to the success-breeds-success hypothesis. The size of the estimates for the first lag is within the range of 0.4–0.7 for the three different equations.

The estimates associated with the current values of physical capital and human capital are positive, significant, and of reasonable sizes (0.03–0.06) for all three equations. The only exception is the capital coefficient in the export equation, which is not significantly different from zero. The two categories of MNE firms enter with more sizeable estimates than other firms do. In concordance with the results from the Hausman-Taylor equation, the MNE firms (those belonging to a multinational enterprise) perform better than other firms, irrespective of whether the results are expressed in sales, value added, or exports.

We now turn from the level dimension to the link between R&D and productivity growth. Although research and development is widely recognized as a main determinant of productivity growth, the empirical confirmation of this convention is rather thin (Griliches, 1990; Klette and Kortum, 2004). It has been suggested that the data available for measuring the size of a firm's current innovation input might explain the fragile link between R&D and productivity growth (CBO, 2005). This argument, which is at the heart of evolutionary theory, suggests that the conception of 'R&D' only captures a fraction of a firm's innovation efforts. A firms' ability to continuously bring innovative new products to the market and to develop methods for producing them more efficiently can largely be linked to its knowledge capital. The firm's knowledge capital comprises skills, techniques, and know-how that draw on accumulated experience from its previous attempts to innovate.

Table 8.6 tests whether our R&D-strategy variables can be used as indicators of firms' combined current and accumulated R&D and knowledge capital in a growth model. Thus, the hypothesis we formulate is that the firm's ability to maintain innovative activities should be reflected in its long-run productivity growth rather than in the size of its R&D expenditures. Similar to the approach in Tables 8.4 and 8.5, we also regress the model on sales and export performance.

In order to capture the effect of the ability to maintain innovative activities on the current growth rate of sales, productivity, and exports, we need to control for past growth rates. In the model, we include two lagged periods of growth rates and the coefficient estimates are supposed to be significant and negative. This is confirmed in rows 3–4.

Looking at the two key variables, the first row shows that the coefficients of the occasional R&D variable are not significantly different from zero. However, the coefficients of persistent R&D are significant and fall within the range 0.014–0.036. In firms that persistently conduct research and development activities year after year, and are therefore able to maintain their knowledge capital, the annual growth rate of sales per employee is 1.4 per cent higher than for other firms (column 1). Looking at productivity growth, column 2 describes a shift effect of 0.023 and the reference group is non-R&D firms. This is close to the observed difference reported in the descriptive statistics (1.9 per cent versus 1.5 per cent). Column (3) shows the determinants of the growth of export performance. Controlling for factors such as size, industry, human capital, physical capital, or ownership, the persistence group has an annual growth rate which is 3.6 per cent higher than for other firms. In the descriptive statistics, we observe a difference corresponding to 2.4 per cent.

The results for the controls in first difference are typically insignificant. Notable, however, is that the contemporaneous and lagged growth of human capital has a causal, positive impact on the growth of sales. In the productivity equation, this variable is positive but just outside the 10 per cent level of significance. Everything else being equal, we cannot confirm any difference in growth rate between non-affiliated firms and other firms.

The test statistics for serial correlation indicate no problem for the relevant second-order serial correlation. Likewise, the diagnosis for the overidentification conditions is satisfactory since the p-values are substantially larger than the critical 0.05 level for all three equations.

8.6. Concluding discussion

There is a stylized fact that R&D spending has a significantly positive effect on the level of productivity, whereas productivity growth is not strongly related to differences in firms' R&D spending.

The above issue is illuminated here from a new angle, by disregarding the annual spending on R&D and instead classifying each firm in accordance with the R&D strategy it applies: with no, occasional or persistent R&D efforts. We assume that a firm's choice of strategy (specified by these three categories) is a lasting or endurable choice, where firms that engage in persistent R&D efforts develop a resource-base with a larger share of knowledge workers, while maintaining the R&D skills of the labour force and the R&D routines of the firm. In view of this, the chapter shows that R&D persistence positively affects a firm's labour productivity (value-added performance) and its productivity growth. The chapter also shows that R&D persistence rewards a firm with higher sales and export performance.

In view of the above results, the chapter presents a model, according to which a firm's R&D strategy has similar implications for its performance level and for its growth in the performance indicators, which resolves earlier inconsistencies between how R&D statistically influences the performance level and the performance change.

The statistical analyses suggest that there is a close association between firm performance and choice of R&D strategy, where the performance level and growth are highest for firms with persistent R&D efforts, second highest for firms with occasional R&D efforts and lowest for firms that do not report any R&D efforts. These observations are consistent with the idea that occasional R&D efforts have transitory effects on firm performance. They are also compatible with the suggestions by Nelson and Winter (1982) that a firm can maintain and improve its innovation capability by recurrently making innovation efforts.

Our data support findings reported in Dosi and Nelson (2010): i.e. firm behaviour is typically persistent in many different dimensions, with regard to both input and output properties. Although we only observe a self-declared R&D strategy for a three-year period, we show that firms with an R&D-persistent strategy form a group with distinct characteristics, which remain invariant over the whole ten-year period of this study. The firms in this group are larger, more intense in terms of both human capital and physical capital, more export-oriented, and are typically owned by a multinational enterprise group. In particular, we provide observations indicating that those firms that were persistently R&D active between 2002 and 2004 were also persistently active in the preceding period 1998–2000.

We base our econometric analysis on observations from a set of manufacturing and service firms in Sweden originating from a representative Community Innovation Survey (CIS) sample. The data from the survey, which took place in 2005 and covers the period 2002–2004, are merged with several data sets containing extensive characteristics of close to 2,900 firms over the period 1997–2006.

By employing longer time series of panel-data observations extending beyond the three-year period of ordinary CIS data, our analysis can be used in future studies to further examine the assumption that firms' selection of R&D strategy is a long-term commitment and that the choice of strategy has both level and growth consequences. This observation suggests that future research should be directed towards studies of firms' long-term strategies, with data that allow for comparisons over time of the persistence features of such strategies.

A basic hypothesis tested in this paper concerns measurement issues. Can a firm's long run economic performance be predicted by a simple discrete strategy variable with three alternative values: no R&D, occasional R&D, or persistent R&D efforts. The econometric analyses, based on both static panel-data models and dynamic GMM-models, reveal a systematic association between the performance of firms and their respective R&D strategies. Controlling for past performance, simultaneity and unobserved heterogeneity, the association is positive and significant in both the level and growth dimensions. Controlling for differences in past labour productivity, firms with persistent R&D commitment have, on average, 13 per cent higher labour productivity compared with non-R&D firms, and 9 per cent higher productivity than firms which make occasional R&D efforts. Furthermore, a persistent R&D strategy corresponds to about a 2 per cent higher growth rate in productivity. The results are similar when firm performance is measured as total sales and exports.

What are the conclusions for policy? Innovation policy may have to reconsider goals that are primarily oriented towards enhancing R&D expenditures, and to contemplate measures that can support sustained and enduring innovation efforts. This may include support that enables a firm to develop its resource-base in a steadfast way. A firm's adoption of a strategy of persistent innovation engagement may, for example, benefit from an environment that can offer it a supply of R&D-experienced workers.

Appendix

Table A8.1. Consistency of R&D strategies across CIS surveys. Comparison of the R&D strategy of unique firms observed years 2000 and 2004

R&D-strategy CIS 2004	CIS 2000: Non R&D	CIS 2000: Occasional R&D	CIS 2000: Persistent R&D
Non R&D	74.7%	13.3%	12.0%
Occasional R&D	46.7%	23.0%	30.3%
Persistent R&D	17.6%	7.1%	75.3%

Notes: The total number of firm observations in CIS 2000 is 2,164 and in CIS 2004 it is 3,096. The number observed in both surveys is 830.

References

Aghion, P. and Howitt, P. (1992), 'A model of growth through creative destruction', *Econometrica*, 60(2): 323–351.

Arellano, M. and Bover, O. (1995), 'Another look at instrumental variable estimation of error component models', *Journal of Econometrics*, 68: 29–51.

Arrow, K.J. (1962), 'Economic welfare and the allocation of resources for invention'. In Nelson, R. (ed.), *The Rate and Direction of Inventive Activity*. Princeton: NBER, Princeton University Press.

Bartel, A.P. and Lichtenberg, F.R. (1987), 'The comparative advantage of educated workers in implementing new technology', *The Review of Economics and Statistics*, 69(1): 1–11.

Bartelsman, E. and Doms, M. (2000), 'Understanding productivity: Lessons from longitudinal microdata', *Journal of Economic Literature*, 38(3): 569–594.

Batten, D., Casti, J. and Johansson, B. (1987), Economic dynamics, evolution and structural adjustment. In Batten, D., Casti, J. and Johansson, B. (eds), *Economic Evolution and Structural Adjustment. Lecture Notes in Economics and Mathematical Systems 293*. Berlin: Springer-Verlag.

Bernard, A.B. (2004), 'Exporting and productivity in the USA', *Oxford Review of Economic Policy*, 20(3): 343–357.

Blundell, R.S. and Bond, S. (1998), 'Initial conditions and moment restrictions in dynamic panel data models', *Journal of Econometrics*, 87(1): 115–143.

——, Griffith, R. and Windmeijer, F. (2002), 'Individual effects and dynamic in count data models', *Journal of Econometrics* 108(May): 113–131.

Cabagnols, A. (2006), 'Technological learning and the persistence of innovation: A France–UK comparison based on a Cox model of duration', *Revue d'economie politique*, 114(2): 263–292.

CBO, (2005), 'R&D and productivity growth', Congressional Budget Office Background Paper.

Cefis, E. (2003), Persistence in innovation and profitability, *Rivisita internationale di scienze sociali*, 110: 1937.

——and Ciccarelli, M. (2005), 'Profit differentials and innovation', *Economics of Innovation and New Technologies*, 14(1–2): 43–61.

——and Orsenigo, L. (2001), 'The persistence of innovative activities: A cross-countries and cross-sectors comparative analysis', *Research Policy*, 30(7): 1139–1158.

Cockburn, I.M., Henderson, R.M. and Stern, S. (2000), 'Untangling the origins of competitive advantage', *Strategic Management Journal*, 21(October/November): 1123–1145.

Cohen, M. and Klepper, S. (1996), 'A reprise of size and R&D', *The Economic Journal*, 106 (437): 925–951.

Cohen, W. (1995), Empirical studies of innovative activitiy. In Stoneman, P. (ed.), *Handbook of Economics of Innovation and Technological Change*. Oxford: Blackwell.

——and Levinthal, D. (1990), 'Absorptive capacity: A new perspective on learning and innovation', *Administrative Science Quarterly*, 35(1): 128–158.

Crépon, B., Duguet, E. and Mairesse, J. (1998), 'Research, innovation and productivity: An econometric analysis at the firm level', *Economics of Innovation and New Technology* 7(2): 115–158.

Dosi, G., and Nelson, R.R. (2010), 'Technical change and industrial dynamics as evolutionary processes'. In Hall, B. and Rosenberg, N. (eds), *The Economics of Innovation*. New York: Elsevier.

Duguet, E. and Monjon, S. (2002), 'Les fondements microéconomiques de la persistance de l'innovation. Une analyse économétrique', *Revue économique, programme national persée*, 53(3): 625–636.

Geroski, P., Machin, S. and van Reenen, J. (1993), 'The profitability of innovating firms', *RAND Journal of Economics*, 24(2): 198–211.

Griliches, Z. (1990), 'Patent statistics as economic indicators: A survey', *Journal of Economic Literature*, 28: 1661–1707.

——and Mairesse, J. (1984), 'Productivity and R&D at the firm level'. In Griliches, Z. (ed.), *R&D, Patents and Productivity*. Chicago: University of Chicago Press.

——and Pakes, A. (1980), 'The estimation of distributed lags in short panels', NBER Technical Working Papers 0004, National Bureau of Economic Research.

Grossman, G. and Helpman, E. (1991), *Innovation and Growth in the Global Economy*. Cambridge, MA: MIT Press.

Hall, B.H. (2007), 'Measuring the returns to R&D: The depreciation problem', NBER Working Papers 13473, National Bureau of Economic Research.

Hausman, J.A. and Taylor, W.E. (1981), 'Panel data and unobservable individual effects', *Econometrica*, 49(6): 1377–1398.

Henderson, R. (1993), 'Underinvestment and incompetence as responses to radical innovation: Evidence from the photolithographic alignment equipment industry', *RAND Journal of Economics*, 24(Summer): 248–270.

Klette, T.J. and Kortum, S. (2004), 'Innovating firms and aggregate innovation', *Journal of Political Economy* 112(5): 986–1018.

Langlois, R.N. and Robertson, P.L. (1995), *Firms, Markets and Economic Change: A Dynamic Theory of Business Institutions*. New York: Routledge.

Lööf, H. and Heshmati, A. (2002), 'Knowledge capital and performance heterogeneity: A firm-level innovation study', *International Journal of Production Economics*, 76(1): 61–85.

Malerba, F. and Orsenigo, L. (1999), 'Technological entry, exit and survival: An empirical analysis of patent data', *Research Policy*, 28(6): 643–660.

Nelson, R. and Winter, S. (1982), *An Evolutionary Theory of Economic Change*. Cambridge, MA: Harvard University Press.

Peters, B. (2009), 'Persistence of innovation: Stylised facts and panel data evidence', *Journal of Technology Transfer*, 34: 226–243.

Philips, A. (1971), *Technology and Market Structure: A Study of the Aircraft Industry*. Lexington: D.C. Heath.

Raymond, W., Mohnen, P., Palm, F. and van der Loeff, S.S. (2006), 'Persistence of innovation in dutch manufacturing: Is it spurious?' UNU-Merit Working Paper 2006-011, Maastricht.

Reinganum, J.F. (1983), 'Uncertain innovation and the persistence of monopoly', *American Economic Review*, 73(4): 741–748.

Roberts, P.W. (1999), 'Product innovation, product-market competition and persistent profitability in the U.S. pharmaceutical industry', *Strategic Management Journal*, 20(7): 655–670.

Schmookler, J. (1996), *Invention and Economic Growth*. Cambridge, MA: Harvard University Press.

Sutton, J. (1991), *Sunk Cost and Market Structure*. Cambridge, MA, and London: MIT Press.

Part III
Beyond the Firm: Economy-Wide Effects of R&D Strategies

9

Technological Congruence and Productivity Growth[1]

Cristiano Antonelli

9.1. Introduction

This chapter aims to make three contributions: first, to establish a direct relationship between the literatures on induced technological change and the economics of knowledge; second, to present a model of localized technological change that stresses the role of local factors both in learning and in factor markets in shaping the direction of technological change; third, to identify the effects of technological congruence, as defined by the matching between the ratio of output elasticities and the relative abundance of production factors, brought about by the introduction of biased technological changes, and disentangle them from the effects of the introduction of neutral technological changes that increase the overall efficiency of the production process.

The rest of the chapter is organized as it follows. Section 9.2 summarizes the main acquisitions of the recent return of interest on the direction of technological change. Section 9.3 implements a simple model of localized technological change that frames the dynamic conditions for the occurrence of increasing technological congruence. Section 9.4 elaborates the basic methodology to distinguish the effects of absolute and congruence efficiency for the empirical analysis of the changing levels of the absolute and relative efficiency. Building upon these bases, section 9.5 highlights the role of the

[1] The comments of Martin Andersson and many colleagues are acknowledged, as well as the funding of the European Union D.G. Research with the grant number 266959 to the research project 'Policy Incentives for the Creation of Knowledge: Methods and Evidence' (PICK-ME), within the context Cooperation Program/Theme 8/Socio-economic Sciences and Humanities (SSH), and of the research project IPER in progress at the Collegio Carlo Alberto.

direction of technological change in affecting congruence and absolute efficiency. This section presents a novel methodology to disentangle empirically the shift effects of neutral technological change on the levels of absolute efficiency from the bias effects of directed technological change on congruence efficiency so as to identify correctly the actual effects on the total efficiency of the production process. The conclusions wrap up the analysis carried out in the chapter.

9.2. The direction of technological change and the quest for efficiency

The empirical evidence shows that significant changes in the distribution of revenue across production factors have been taking place in the last thirty years in the major OECD economies. Specifically, in many countries the share of labour has been falling and the share of capital increasing. These changes in the distribution of income can be considered the consequence of the introduction of biased technological changes directed towards labour-saving innovations aimed at reducing the use of labour after the increase of unit wages so as to make the most efficient use of capital, by now the most abundant production factor.

Hall and Jones (1999) note that output per worker varies enormously across countries. Their analysis, based upon standard accounting methodology, shows that differences in physical capital and educational attainment can only partially explain the variation in output per worker and that total factor productivity accounts for a large amount of variation in the level of output per worker. Yet Hall and Jones note that the effects of technological change differ widely across countries and some are more able to benefit from it than others. Institutional differences are claimed to be the main cause of the variance. Differences in factor endowments seem to play a role, although no clues are provided to account for their effects.

Caselli and Coleman (2006) find that higher-income countries use skilled labour more efficiently than lower-income ones. Lower-income countries use unskilled labour relatively and, possibly, absolutely, less efficiently. According to their interpretation, rich countries, which are skilled-labour-abundant, are able to introduce technologies that are best suited for the local factor markets. Lower-income countries, which are unskilled-labour-abundant, adopt these skill-intensive technologies while their factor endowments should induce them to choose technologies more appropriate to unskilled workers.

Jerzmanowski (2007), uses a frontier analysis to show that the world technology frontier is shifting out faster at input combinations that match the relative factor abundance of the R&D leader, and as a consequence countries with different factorial endowments are less able to exploit the new technologies efficiently and less able to access them. New technologies may lead adopting countries to the inefficient use of inputs according to their relative costs.

Crafts (2009) provides an excellent synthesis of this debate, focusing on the distinction between input efficiency and technological efficiency and relating it to the well-known models of induced technological change. The induced-technological-change approach in fact is able to relate the direction of technological change to the relative factor intensity of countries that are able to generate it.

The contributions by Abramovitz and David (1996 and 2001) may be considered a starting point for opening a new phase in the debate. They identified in the notion of technological congruence a major factor in the uneven capability of countries to participate in the exploitation of the benefits of technological change. They provided the definition of technological congruence as the matching between the relative abundance of production inputs in local factor markets and the characteristics of the technology of the production process, and explored both its effects and determinants.

This line of enquiry has received little attention, so far. Yet it seems very promising as it can be reinforced and strengthened, building upon the opportunities provided by the localized-technological-change approach that builds upon the Cobb-Douglas specification to explore jointly the determinants and the effects of changing ratio of output elasticity.

9.3. The bias of localized technological change

The induced-technological-change approach suffered from the divide between the original approach, outlined by Hicks (1932) and articulated by Binswanger and Ruttan (1978), and the Kennedy-von Weiszacker argument implemented by Samuelson (1965). According to the original approach, both the rate and the direction of technological change are explained by the conditions of factor markets. Technological change is introduced to cope with changes in factor costs and directed to reduce the use of the input whose cost increased. In the induced approach synthesized by Samuelson (1965), technological change is instead biased towards the reduction of the factor that is more expensive in absolute terms, but there is no clue about the determinants of the introduction of new technologies. Acemoglu (1998, 2002, 2010) has enriched the induced-technological-change approach stressing the role of factor complementarity. According to his argument, firms have an incentive to make the most efficient use of locally abundant factors, such as skills, and specifically to increase the use of skilled labour when the size of the market, and hence the profits to innovations, are associated with the relative abundance of complementary production factors such as, in the specific case, capital.

The induced-technological-change approach can be further implemented when the advances of the economics of knowledge and specifically the appreciation of the central role of learning processes in the generation of technological knowledge and in the introduction of technological innovations are integrated so as to provide a theoretical content and an empirical reference to the notion of frontier of possible innovations that is at the heart of the induced-technological-change approach (Arrow, 1969; Braunerhjelm, Chapter 12, this volume).

The localized-technological-change approach provides a suitable starting point to account for the introduction of biased technological changes. In the localized-technological-change approach, the notion of localized learning enables us to understand how and why a dynamic process, induced by changing levels of factor costs, can engender the introduction of directed technological changes that are consistent with the changing levels of factor endowments and hence increase the technological congruence of the production process (Antonelli, 1995, 2003, 2008).

According to its original formulation, technological change is localized by the source of competence and knowledge that is acquired mainly if not exclusively by means of learning-by-doing, learning-by-using, and learning-by-interacting. Firms are able to learn and to build a technological competence upon their learning processes. Such learning processes, however, can take place only in the range of techniques that they have been practising: firms cannot learn about techniques that they have never used. The very notion of learning precludes the assumption that the full map of techniques can be implemented (Arrow, 1969).

The localized origins of such 'tacit' knowledge limit the mobility of firms and the array of possible techniques that firms can use. As Atkinson and Stiglitz (1969: 574) note, 'knowledge acquired through learning by doing will be located at the point where the firm (or economy) is now operating'. In this approach, in order to introduce technological innovations such firms rely mainly, if not exclusively, upon a form of localized technological knowledge based upon the skills of the workforce active at the plant level, implemented by the interactions with current customers and clients and transformed in accumulated competence by means of internal routines. Localized technological knowledge has been built out of learning activities. It is the result of bottom-up processes of induction based upon tacit knowledge that is eventually implemented and codified. Firms can improve only the technologies they have been able to practise and upon which they have acquired a distinctive competence that is characterized by an idiosyncratic and narrow scope of application. Localized technological knowledge cannot be easily stretched and applied far away from its original locus of accumulation. Firms are not able to fully command a broad and codified base of scientific knowledge and to extract out of it, with the typical top-down deductive procedure, a wide range of new possible applications that can characterize all the range of production techniques represented on the full isoquant (Atkinson and Stiglitz, 1969; Antonelli, 1995).

The introduction of biased technological innovations stems from the historic accumulation of competence in a limited portion of the range of techniques and enables more efficient production processes with a strong bias. Firms can learn about the techniques that they have chosen in equilibrium conditions at each point in time. The latter reflect the relative abundance of inputs and their relative prices. In other words, firms can learn about the techniques that make intensive use of the production factors that are locally more abundant. Techniques chosen at time t because of the relative abundance of a production factor are likely to be intensive in that production factor. The relative intensity becomes the locus of the accumulation of the competence. Competence based upon localized learning makes possible the introduction of technological change biased in favour of more intensive use of that factor. This in turn makes possible further accumulation of localized learning: the process has clearly a strong recursive and non-ergodic character. The achievement of higher levels of congruence efficiency keeps firms in a technical region that is intensive of the production factor locally abundant, directs their technological change within a narrow corridor of biased technological change and reinforces the dynamics.

A feedback dynamic pushes the new technologies to reflect the specific conditions of the local factor markets because they are the result of the specific historic path of growth of each firm in terms of acquired competence and the stock of intangible production factors. The localized-technological-change approach provides the basis to build a non-ergodic path-dependent dynamic process where historic conditions can account for a variety of outcomes according to the changing conditions of factor markets and the introduction of new technologies at each step in the process. Localized learning processes enable firms to associate the idiosyncratic characteristics of the tacit knowledge and competence to the characteristics of the techniques in use at each point in time.

In capital-abundant countries, where at time t $K/L>1$, localized learning processes, consisting of learning-by-doing and learning by using capital-intensive techniques, favour the accumulation of idiosyncratic and specific technological knowledge that feeds the introduction of capital-intensive technological change. The localized generation of technological knowledge based upon learning processes takes place in a circumscribed and restricted technical space in which firms have actually been practising, and enables them to increase mainly the output elasticity of capital and hence to introduce capital-intensive technologies (Antonelli, 2003).

By the same token, it is clear that firms based in labour-abundant regions that have selected labour-intensive techniques are learning to use labour-intensive technologies and will be able to better implement labourintensive technologies rather than capital- intensive ones. Hence the factor intensity of the production process at each point in time has non-ergodic effects on the direction of technological change. The bias in technological change is both the result of the circumscribed competences of the firms and of the structure of incentives determined by the local structure of factor markets (Antonelli, 2008).

In the global economy we can also identify countries and regions that have a distinctive comparative advantage in the relative abundance of human capital and skilled labour. Once again, in these countries, firms will find it more convenient to use skill-intensive techniques that are likely to lead to the accumulation of skill-intensive competence and hence eventually will favour the introduction of skilled-biased new technologies. Here the recursive character of the process is even more evident and stronger. The local abundance of skills is in fact fully endogenous to the economic system, as it is clearly the result of the localized capabilities to generate and manage high levels of human capital (Antonelli and Colombelli, 2011; Antonelli and Fassio, 2011).[2]

Let us now try to synthesize the arguments presented so far. There is a direct and clear relationship between the relative endowments in each factor market, the techniques defined in terms factor intensity of the production process at each point in time and the direction of technological change. The relevance of localized learning processes, as the main source of technological knowledge, explains the relationship between endowments, techniques, and technologies. When the inducement mechanism is put to work by changes in factor markets, firms in equilibrium in capital-intensive techniques that have had more opportunities to learn about capital-intensive techniques will favour capital-intensive technologies and firms in equilibrium in labour-intensive technologies that have had better opportunities to learn about labour-intensive techniques will favour a labour-intensive bias.

---

[2] As soon as we abandon the simplified analysis of a production function in added value and we consider a broader array of intermediary inputs for a production function in sales, we see that the relative abundance of a given input can be considered as the result of previous choices. Countries that specialized at time *t* in the production of a commodity and became able to deliver it at prices that were below international standards can experience an endogenous process of increasing specialization in downstream sectors built upon the sequence of relative abundance-factor intensity-localized learning and finally biased technological change aimed at making even more efficient uses of that original production factor in the filiere (production chain) of downstream sectors.

Let us now formalize the argument. Although much recent literature (Acemoglu, 1998, 2002, 2010) relies on the CES production function, the standard Cobb-Douglas production function seems a suitable and effective starting point. The Cobb-Douglas specification, in fact, accommodates explicitly, with α and β, the output elasticities of the production factors, and enables us to analyze their changes. The standard Cobb-Douglas takes the following format:

$$Y(t) = (K^{(\alpha)} L^{(\beta)}) \tag{1}$$

where K denotes the amount of capital and L the amount of labour.

The cost equation is:

$$C = rK + wL \tag{2}$$

Firms select the traditional equilibrium mix of inputs according to the slope of the isocosts given by ratio of labour costs (w) and capital-rental costs (r) and the slope of isoquants. The equilibrium condition is:

$$w/r = (\beta/\alpha)(K/L) \tag{3}$$

In standard textbooks the output elasticity of inputs is given or exogenous. In the induced-technological-change approach the output elasticity of inputs is endogenous, but it is not specific to the learning conditions of firms. Here, learning conditions play a central role in the accumulation of the tacit knowledge and competence that is necessary to introduce new technologies. Firms, localized in capital-intensive techniques, have more opportunities to learn about capital-intensive techniques and eventually introduce capital-intensive technological changes. With given investments in R&D activities, in other words, firms localized in capital-abundant countries where capital user costs are lower than wages, and hence in equilibrium in capital-intensive techniques, are better able to increase the output elasticity of capital.[3] This means that:

$$\alpha = f(Z\frac{K}{L}, \text{R\&D}) \quad \text{with } Z > 0 \text{ for } K/L > 1 \tag{4}$$

Assuming the usual constraint of constant returns to scale ($\alpha + \beta = 1$), this amounts to a postulate that firms in equilibrium in labour-intensive techniques will have more opportunities to learn and hence eventually introduce labour-intensive technologies so as to increase the output elasticity of labour. The specific conditions of learning processes exert a historic effect upon the

---

[3] R&D activities cum learning processes localized in the production techniques currently used can lead to the actual introduction of total factor productivity enhancing technological innovations only if, when, and where firms have access to knowledge externalities.

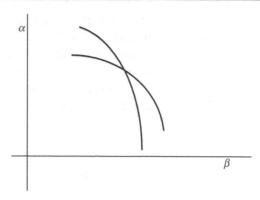

Figure 9.1. Frontier of possible innovations in capital- and labour-abundant countries

possibilities to introduce directed technological change biased towards the introduction of new technologies that are more intensive in the factors that are used more intensively at each point in time.

The appreciation of the effects of learning processes enables us to specify a Frontier of Possible Innovations (FPI), along the lines of the induced-technological-change approach (Samuelson, 1965). Our approach differs from Samuelson's on three counts. First, our FPI confronts possible changes in the output elasticity of production factors, while Samuelson's FPI confronts different factor-augmenting innovations. Second, our isorevenue is based directly upon a Cobb-Douglas production function rather than the factor shares. Third, the FPI is no longer symmetric. The introduction of capital-intensive technologies, consisting in the increase of the output elasticity of capital, will be easier in capital-abundant countries with high levels of equilibrium capital intensity. Conversely, the direction of technological change towards higher levels of labour intensity, with an increase of the output elasticity of labour, will be easier in labour-abundant countries with lower levels of capital intensity.

Figure 9.1 shows how the asymmetric shape of the FPI exhibits the effects of the learning processes. The appreciation of localized learning processes enables us to substantiate the insights about the limits of the symmetric FPI. The asymmetric shape of FPI expresses the different localized conditions of factor markets upon which learning agents can accumulate their competence: in capital-abundant countries the intercept on the vertical axis is much larger than the intercept on the horizontal axis and vice versa in labour-abundant countries.

Assuming the usual constraint of constant returns to scale, this amounts to a postulate that firms in equilibrium in labour-intensive techniques will have more opportunities to introduce labour-intensive technologies so as to increase the output elasticity of labour.

Formally the FPI considers the relationship between attainable levels of output elasticities, as follows:

$$\alpha = g(\beta) \tag{5}$$

The isorevenue is identified by the substitution of the equilibrium condition (3) into the production function (1), as follows:

$$Y = L(w/r \ \alpha/\beta)^\alpha \tag{6}$$

Equation (7) makes clear the interaction effects between the bias of the technology as identified by the ratio of the output elasticity of capital and the output elasticity of labour and the ratio of factor costs on the levels of output. It is well known that the larger the output, the larger is the output elasticity of capital (or labour) and the lower is the user cost of capital (or wages). The Cobb-Douglas specification in fact makes clear that it is convenient to use more intensively the production factor that is cheaper: clearly the larger the output gets, for a given budget, the larger is the intensity of the factor that is locally more abundant and hence cheaper.[4] This static condition becomes a powerful incentive to direct technological change so as to take advantage of the matching between the relative cost of an input and its output elasticity.

The differentiation of equation (6) with respect to the w/r enables us to identify the effects of the changing slope of the isocost for given levels of α and β:

$$\delta Y/\delta(w/r) = \alpha(w/r)Y \tag{7}$$

The maximization of output requires that α and β are chosen so that the slope of the FPI equals equation (7), i.e. the slope of equation (6):

$$g'(\beta) = \alpha(r/w)Y \tag{8}$$

According to equilibrium condition (8), the larger the output elasticity of capital, the more abundant is capital with respect to labour, and the lower are the relative capital user costs with respect to wages. When wages (capital user costs) increase, the incentives to increase the output elasticity of capital (labour) also increase. This result, however, is balanced by the shape of the FPI that reflects the history of learning processes. In a capital-abundant country where firms have had the opportunity to learn more about capital-intensive techniques than labour-intensive ones, the effects of the increase of wages and hence of the relative decline of capital user costs will be sharp. Conversely, for the same increase of wages and relative reduction of capital user costs, the direction of technological change in labour-abundant countries, where wages

---

[4] See more on this in Section 9.4 below.

are lower than capital user costs, and the shape of the FPI reflects the prevalence of learning processes in labour-intensive techniques, the bias in favour
of a larger output elasticity of capital will be smaller. This result is quite
important as it enables us to fully appreciate the effects of the local condition
of factor markets and of the role of historic forces represented here by the non-
ergodic character of learning processes in the selection of the direction of
technological change.

The direction of technological change is influenced both by: (1) the learning
opportunities accumulated through time that in turn reflect the factor intensity, as represented by the slope of FPI, and (2) the relative abundance of
production factors as represented by the slope of the isorevenue. It accommodates the effects of possible changes in factor costs under the constraints of the
non-ergodic effects of learning processes that reflect the original endowments.

This approach to the FPI contrasts with the Kennedy–von Weiszacker–
Samuelson tradition where the slope of the isorevenue is defined by the ratio
of factors share. Factors share however measures the output elasticity of
production factor. Hence the slope of the isorevenue in the Kennedy–von
Weiszacker–Samuelson tradition is nothing other than the ratio of output elasticities. Hence the Kennedy–von Weiszacker–Samuelson tradition leads to the
necessary convergence of the output elasticities to equality (Samuelson, 1965).

This approach provides a formalization of the argument advanced by Paul
David (1975) and confirms that agents have an incentive to direct technological change towards the most intensive use of the factors that are locally more
abundant. From equation (8) we know firms that have acquired their technological competence by means of localized learning processes will try and cope
with the changes in factor markets with the introduction of labour-intensive
technologies, until the slope is <1 and capital-intensive technologies when
the slope of the isocost is >1. The new technology is biased and more congruent with the relative abundance of production factors in local factor markets.

This result can be further refined so as implement a fully dynamic process as
soon as we consider the role of the irreversibility of the production factors that
are already in place. Let us consider the effects of an increase of wages and
decline in the capital user cost. The irreversibility will engender switching
costs that limit the substitution process and push firms to cope with the
increase of wages by means of both a standard substitution process along
the existing isoquants and the induced introduction of a new superior technology. The capital intensity of the production process will be increased by
the working of the standard substitution process, albeit affected by the effects
of introduction of a new labour-intensive technology.

In order to get a formal representation of the biased dynamics of directed
technological change building upon the localized-technological-change

approach, we can start from equation (3) and make the following steps. First, we rearrange equation (3) as follows:

$$K/L = (W/L)(\alpha/\beta) \tag{9}$$

Then we investigate the changes in the equilibrium conditions of factor intensity:

$$\delta K/L = d(w/r)(\alpha/\beta) + d(\alpha/\beta)(w/r) \tag{10}$$

Next we divide both sides by K/L and we use its equivalence on the right-hand side, so as to get:

$$((\delta K/L)/K/L))_t = ((\delta w/r)/(w/r))_t + (\delta(\alpha/\beta)/(\alpha/\beta))_\tau \tag{11}$$

Inspection of equation (11) shows that the new capital intensity depends upon the combined effects of both technical change that feeds the standard substitution process on the existing map of isoquants and localized technological change that changes the shapes of the isoquants. The former consists in the changes of capital intensity, the second in the changes of the output elasticity of production factors.

Following the localized-technological-change approach, the extent to which firms will rely upon substitution and innovation respectively—and hence the combination of technical and technological change—will depend upon the relative costs of switching with respect to the actual costs of introducing directed changes in the technology (Antonelli, 2008).

After the increase of wages a labour-abundant system will remain in technical regions characterized by high levels of labour intensity, yet the new labour intensity will be lower than the original one. As long as the capital intensity of the production process remains lower than 1 and the slope of the isocost is also lower than 1, the dynamics of induced technological change, based upon localized learning processes, and biased towards the more intensive use of labour, the locally abundant production input, will yield the increase of technological congruence and hence congruence efficiency.

As soon as the rate of increase of wages and the contemporary decline of capital cost pushes firms towards equilibrium techniques that are actually capital-intensive, the dynamic is reversed. The continual rate of increase of wages and reduction of capital user costs associated with the increase in savings, in countries that are becoming more and more capital-abundant, will push the capital intensity beyond the threshold of 1 and favour the accumulation of competence in capital-intensive techniques. Now localized learning processes provide the accumulation of competence that directs firms towards the introduction of biased technological changes that are now characterized by the increase in the output elasticity of capital. The new technology is biased because it is pushed by the same dynamics of factor markets, but it is now directed towards the introduction of capital-intensive technologies. The technological congruence is augmented and hence the congruence efficiency.

The model shows that the dynamics of localized technological change, based upon the tight non-ergodic and path-dependent relationship between the characteristics of the production process in terms of factor intensity and hence the specific conditions for the accumulation of competence and tacit knowledge, is able to account for the introduction of biased technological changes that are directed towards the most intensive use of most abundant production factors, hence favouring the increase of the technological congruence and the congruence efficiency of the production process. The shape of the FPI keeps changing as a consequence of the changes in factor markets and its effects upon the changes of the capital intensity of the production processes.

Countries characterized by a specific structure of endowments and idiosyncratic factor markets, with a relative abundance of a specific production factor, have both the incentives and the opportunities to increase their efficiency with the systematic pursuit of a directed technological change that is able to make an ever-increasing and efficient use of the factors that are locally abundant. The appreciation of the notion of congruence efficiency enables us to grasp the incentives: countries can build up higher levels of efficiency if and when they are able to identify the production factors that are locally abundant and scarce elsewhere and to increase the output elasticity of that specific factor with the introduction of biased technological change. The appreciation of the notion of localized learning and its application to the implementation of a directed technological change provides the opportunities to achieve higher levels of congruence efficiency. Opportunities and incentives require intentional action on the part of firms and public research units and competent execution of research activities that are organized and conducted with a clear awareness of the desired direction of technological change.

The well-known argument elaborated by Habakkuk (1962) and implemented by Paul David (1975) finds here a new application and support. The sequence of localized technological changes along a narrow corridor of capital- and land-intensive technologies that characterized the US economy in the nineteenth and twentieth centuries can be interpreted as the effect of the strong command of the idiosyncratic and specific technological knowledge that relied upon learning by using capital-intensive techniques. The latter were determined by the local abundance of land ever since the origins of the US economic growth. The relative abundance of capital and the large endowments of other intermediary inputs provided the opportunity to learn about capital- and land-intensive techniques, and to implement a dedicated technological competence that enabled the introduction of capital-intensive technologies so to keep the trajectory of technological change straight along high levels of capital and intermediary-input intensity indifferent to the transient declines of wages due to strong immigration flows. The UK economy, on the other hand, as characterized by the relative abundance of labour and the fast rate of introduction of new technologies biased towards the intensive use of the locally abundant production factor was able to implement labour-intensive technologies and grow over time keeping a much lower capital intensity. The character of technological change experienced in Italy in the second part of the twentieth century, based upon the generation of localized technological knowledge, acquired by means of the systematic implementation and appreciation of user-producer interactions along vertical filieres (production chains), confirms that importance of the local conditions in directing technological change (Antonelli and Barbiellini Amidei, 2011).

The non-ergodic character of technological change becomes fully apparent as soon as we see how and why the characteristics of the local endowments and the structure of the local factor markets can become, via the dynamics of localized learning, characteristics of the specific technological competence. Localized learning is an opportunity for growth and technological change that countries and regions need to identify and valorize with research and innovation policies that build upon the localized competence.

The microeconomic exploration of the determinants of technological change within the framework of the localized-technological-change approach enables us to implement a consistent interpretation of the broad array of factors that cause the rate and the direction of technological change. The localized-technological-change approach builds upon the tradition of the induced technological change, but, building upon the path-dependent dynamics between techniques and technological changes, enables us to accommodate in a single frame both the Marx-Hicks and the David arguments, taking into account the role of technological congruence.

9.4. The analysis of technological congruence as a neglected source of efficiency

9.4.1. *The theoretical frame*

Technological congruence is a neglected source of efficiency. Congruence efficiency is quite distinct from absolute efficiency. Congruence efficiency consists in the alignment between the structure of local factor endowments and the type of technology in use, as defined by in terms of factor intensity, or, more precisely, composition of output elasticity of the production factors in the production function. For a given level of total costs, output will be larger in labour-abundant countries, the larger is the output elasticity of labour. By the same token, output will be larger in capital-abundant countries, the larger is the output elasticity of capital. The sum of congruence efficiency and absolute efficiency identifies the level of total efficiency. All changes in the production function and hence in the levels of both congruence and absolute efficiency are merely the result of the introduction of localized technological changes.

9.4.2. *The inclusion of absolute and congruency efficiency in the production function*

The understanding of the full array of characteristics of technological change is necessary to grasp the dynamics of growth and change as far as the detailed analysis of the growth of output and inputs is necessary to understand the characteristics of technological change.

Let us start again with the standard Cobb-Douglas production function where K denotes the amount of capital and L the amount of labour. Our production function now includes the notion of total efficiency (ATOT) stemming from the sum of absolute efficiency (ASHIFT) and congruence efficiency (ABIAS). Let us outline the main passages in what follows. The standard Cobb-Douglas now takes the following format:

$$Y(t) = \text{ATOT}(t)(K^{(\alpha)}L^{(\beta)}) \tag{12}$$

Firms select the traditional equilibrium mix of inputs provided by equation (3).

The growth of output through time and its relationship with the changing levels of input can be understood only if the dynamic specification of the production function includes the changing levels of total efficiency (ATOT)(t) that depends upon the sum of the levels of absolute and congruence efficiency:

$$\text{ATOT}(t) = (\text{ASHIFT}(t) + \text{ABIAS}(t)) \tag{13}$$

ASHIFT(t) measures the levels of absolute efficiency defined as the effect of the introduction of Hicks-neutral technological change. A Hicks-neutral technological change simply consists in a pure shift effect and accounts for the leftward change in the position of the map of isoquants. A Hicks-neutral technological change has no effects on the slope of the isoquants: the new map of isoquants can be defined a radial contraction of the previous one. ASHIFT coincides with the measure of total factor productivity (TFP) measured with the methodology first introduced by Solow (1957). The Solow procedure to measure the efficiency effects of technological change in fact grasps only the shift effects of the new technologies independently, whether they were actually Hick-neutral or not. In fact, in the Solow methodology for measuring the effects of the introduction of technological changes output elasticities are allowed to change through time, so that the effects of their changes do not affect the index of efficiency. The numerator Y is the actual output, at time $(t + 1)$, the denominator is the expected output, in equilibrium conditions, with given levels of (w) and (r) and the actual levels of a as they happen to be in the year of observation. Hence we can write it as it follows:

$$\text{ASHIFT} = \text{TFP} = Y/(K^{a(t)}L^{\beta(t)}) \tag{14}$$

ABIAS(t) measures the changing levels of congruence efficiency. It depends on the levels of technological congruence. Technological congruence increases when, in equilibrium, firms can make the most efficient use of the inputs that are locally more abundant. In other words, technological congruence is highest when the output elasticity of capital is high in a capital-abundant country and vice versa. With such a technology in use and a slope of isocosts > 1 it is in fact clear that the production process will be most intensive of the most abundant production factor. For given levels of (w) and (r) and for a given level of total production costs, the congruence efficiency (ABIAS) measures the effects, upon equilibrium levels of the output (Y^*), of the changing ratio of the output elasticities taking into account the slope of the isocost. This effect is in fact influenced by the interaction between the slope of the isocost and the ratio of the output elasticities. When the slope of the isocost = 1 the ratio of output elasticities has no effects on (Y^*). The ratio of output elasticities affects (Y^*) positively when the slope of the isocost is either larger or smaller than 1.

For the sake of clarity, let us consider a simple numerical example that makes extreme assumptions to grasp the basic point. Let us assume that in a region characterized by an extreme abundance of capital and an extreme scarcity of labour, a firm uses a labour-intensive technology:

$$Y_t = K^\alpha L^\beta, \text{ where } a = 0.25 \tag{15}$$

$$C = rk + wL, \text{ where } r = 1; w = 5; C = 100 \tag{16}$$

Standard optimization tells us that the firm will be able to produce in equilibrium at best $Y^* = 17$. Let us now assume that the firm, at time $t + 1$, is able to introduce a technological innovation with a strong capital-intensive bias so as to take advantage of the relative abundance of capital and the relative scarcity of labour in the local factor markets. Specifically let us assume that the new production function will be:

$$Y_{t+1} = K^\alpha L^\beta K^\alpha, \text{ where } \alpha = 0.75 \tag{17}$$

$$C = rK + wL, \text{ where } r = 1; w = 5; C = 100 \qquad (18)$$

The introduction of a new biased capital-intensive technology, characterized by a much larger output elasticity of capital and hence, assuming constant returns to scale, a much lower output elasticity of labour, with the same budget and the same factor costs, will now enable the output maximizing firm to increase its output so that $Y^* = 38$.

This is the effect of the introduction of a new technology. The new technology differs from the previous one only in terms of the slope of the isoquants. No shift has been taking place, but just a change in the form of the isoquants. After and because of the change in technology, Y^* is 2.2 times larger than the old one. If we reverse the time arrow and we assume that the original technology was capital-intensive with an output elasticity of capital 0.75 and hence a labour elasticity of 0.25 we can easily understand that the introduction of a labour-intensive technology might actually reduce output.

In this extreme case it is clear that technological change consists only of a bias and yet has powerful consequences on the levels of output in equilibrium. This strong effect of technological change, clearly distinct from any shift effect, has rarely been considered in the literature. The numerical example shows clearly that, when the slope of the isocost differs from unity, equilibrium levels of output change, albeit at a less than proportionate rate, with the changes of a. When the changing levels of $(a)(t)$ and $(1-a)(t)$ and their ratio $(1-a/a)$ (t) are taken into account, the equilibrium level of output Y^* changes. Hence we can identify the following relationship where, for given levels of w/r different from 1, the effects of all changes in the technological congruence of the production function brought about by the introduction of biased technological changes on the equilibrium levels of Y are specified:

$$\text{ABIAS} = (K^{\alpha(t=n)}L^{\beta(t=n)}/K^{\alpha(t=1)}L^{\beta(t=1)}) \qquad (19)$$

Figure 9.2 helps us to grasp the point. We see clearly that when the slope of the isocost = 1, the ratio of output elasticities has no effect on equilibrium output. When instead the slope of the isocost is < 1 and hence production takes place in a labour-abundant country, it is clear that the levels of technological congruence are low. The lower they become for each level of isocost slope, such as $(w/r)_C < 1$, for and the larger is the capital, the larger is the capital intensity of the technology of the production function and hence the larger the ratio of (β/α) and the lower will be the actual output. With even lower levels of the isocost slope, such as for $(w/r)_E < (w/r)_C$ the effect of the same ratio of output elasticities will be even stronger, with clear negative effects on the levels of output. Conversely, when the slope of the isocosts > than 1, such as for $(w/r)_A$ and hence production takes place in a capital abundant-country,

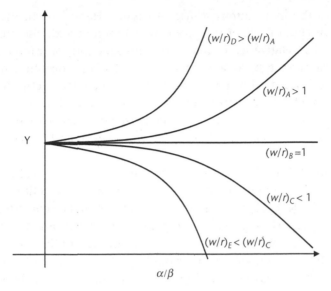

Figure 9.2. Output elasticity and congruence efficiency

the larger is the ratio of output elasticities and the larger will be the output. Additional increases in the slope of the isocosts, such as for $(w/r)_D < (w/r)_A$, will have additional positive effects on output levels with the same range of possible ratios of output elasticities.

9.5. Technological change and congruence efficiency

All changes in total efficiency stem from the introduction of technological changes. Changes in absolute efficiency are engendered by the introduction of neutral technological change. All changes in the congruence efficiency stem from the introduction of biased technological change. The efficiency effects of technological change are supposedly positive when total efficiency is considered. No technology with negative effects in terms of total efficiency could be introduced and adopted by rational agents. A positive result in total efficiency, however, may be the product of an algebraic sum where absolute efficiency associated with a new technology increases and the congruence efficiency declines or vice versa.

Biased technological change simply consists in a change in the slope of the map of isoquants that, for given levels of factor costs, enhances the use of either input. The introduction of new biased technologies will affect the efficiency of the production process provided that the slope of the isocosts differs from unity. Capital-intensive technological changes in a capital-abundant country consist of a change in the slope of the map of isoquants that leads to the more intensive use of capital. Hence it will increase the technological congruence of the production function and will engender an increase in its relative efficiency. The introduction of capital-intensive technological change in a capital-scarce country, on the other hand, will reduce the technological congruence and hence the relative efficiency of the production function. The introduction of either capital-intensive or labour-intensive technologies in a country characterized by even factor endowments will not affect the levels of technological congruence and hence of relative efficiency.

By the same token, the introduction of neutral technological change will not modify the congruence efficiency of the production function, but rather the absolute efficiency. Neutral technological change in fact consists merely of a shift effect that pushes the map of isoquants towards the origins without any effects on the slope of the isoquants. The identification of the notions of shift and bias as distinct components of technological change enables the analysis to grasp the general effect of technological change—that is, the effects on the total efficiency, as defined in terms of both absolute and congruence efficiency.

While neutral technological change consists merely of a shift effect that has direct consequences in terms of the increase of the absolute efficiency, and biased technological change consists only of a change in the slope of the map of isoquants, there is a large spectrum of intermediate forms of technological change, that consist both of a shift and a bias effect. In these cases we may distinguish between complementarity and substitution effects. The latter takes place when the shift effect is positive and the change in the slope of the map of isoquants increases the technological congruence of the production function: the bias effect adds on to the shift effect. The increase in the total efficiency is engendered both by the increase of absolute and congruence efficiency. The former takes place when, instead, the introduction of directed technological change consists in a positive shift effect and in a change in the slope of the map of isoquants that leads to the more intensive use of locally scarce production factors, the increase in the total efficiency is the algebraic result of the decline of the congruence efficiency compensated by an increase of the absolute efficiency. In this case the increase in the absolute efficiency stemming from the shift effect is sufficient to compensate for the decline of the congruence efficiency. The alternative case may take place when a negative shift effect is compensated by a strong positive bias effect that enhances the levels of congruence efficiency. This takes place when the shift effects cannot be separated from a change in the slope of the new map of isoquants that has positive effects on the levels of congruence efficiency. The higher output elasticity of capital will favour the use of capital in a capital-abundant country. In this case the increase in the total efficiency will be lower than the increase in the congruence efficiency: the absolute efficiency in fact will decline.

This analysis has important implications for comparative analysis and to understand the dynamics of the international diffusion of new technologies. The introduction of the same technology with the same shift effect in two different countries will have different effects according to the effects on the relative efficiency. Consider a new technology designed for a capital-abundant country. When this technology is adopted by firms active in a labour-abundant country the adoption may deploy a lower positive effect because of the interplay between the increase in absolute efficiency and the decrease in the relative one. Hence profitability of adoption is lower and technological resilience may be fully justified as the consequence of a rational choice (Johansen, 1972).

9.5.1. A methodology for empirical investigation

To elaborate a measure of the total effect of the features of the technology on the efficiency of the production process we elaborate upon the so-called 'growth accounting' methodology, which draws upon the seminal contribution by Solow (1957) implemented by OECD (2001) and the so-called CDM approach (described by Mairesse and Robin in Chapter 6, this volume).

Our goal is to elaborate a comprehensive empirical measure of both the relative and absolute efficiency engendered respectively by the absolute efficiency effects engendered by the introduction of shift-neutral technological change, the pure congruence effects engendered by the introduction of fully biased technological changes, and the wide array of new directed technologies that consist both in a change in the position and in the slope of the map of isoquants with the consequent combination of bias and shift effects (Antonelli, 2003; Antonelli and Quatraro, 2010).

Output Y of each unit of analysis (agent, industry, region, or country) i at time t, is produced from aggregate factor inputs, consisting of capital services (K) and labour services (L). ASHIFT is defined as the effect of the introduction of a pure Hicks-neutral technological change. Let us outline the main passages in what follows. If we take logarithms of equation (4), we can write ASHIFT = TFP as follows:

$$\ln \text{ASHIFT} = \ln Y(t,i) - \alpha(t,i) \ln k(t,i) - \beta(t,i) \ln L(t,i) \qquad (20)$$

Where $\alpha_{i,t}$ and $\beta_{i,t}$ represent respectively the output elasticity of capital and labour for each unit of analysis at each year.

Next, following Euler's theorem as in Solow (1957), we assume that output elasticities equal the factors' shares in total income, as we consider constant returns to scale and perfect competition in both factor and product markets.

In view of this, the output elasticity of labour and capital represent the shares of respective production factors on income:

$$\beta(t,i) = wL_{(t,i)}/Y_{(t,i)} \tag{21}$$

$$\alpha(t,i) = rK_{(t,i)}/Y_{(t,i)} \tag{22}$$

The measure of ASHIFT obtained in this way, accounts for 'any kind of shift in the production function' (Solow, 1957: 312), and it might be considered a rough proxy of TC (Link, 1987). By means of it Solow intended to propose a way of 'segregating shifts of the production function from movements along it'. Solow is right if and when technological change is neutral, and/or factors are equally abundant. Instead, the effects of biased technological innovations introduced in countries where factors are not equally abundant, are made up of two elements. Besides the shift effect one should also account for the bias effect, i.e. the direction of technological change.

Once we obtain the ASHIFT accounting for the shift in the production function, we can investigate the impact of the bias effect with a few analytical steps. First of all we get a measure of the TFP which accounts for the sum of both effects (for this reason we called it ATOT), by assuming output elasticities unchanged with respect to the first year observed. At each moment in time the log of total-TFP is equal to the difference between the log of the output and the log of inputs weighted by their elasticities fixed at the first observed year:

$$\ln \text{ATOT} = \ln Y(t,i) - \alpha(t=0,i) \ln K(t,i) - \beta(t=0,i) \ln L(t,i) \tag{23}$$

Once the coefficients have been calculated, it is possible to estimate the expected output in value added, which would have been produced each year, after the increase in input levels had the output elasticity of factors remained unchanged.

Next we get the relative-efficiency index that measures the effect of both the shift and the bias effect as the difference between the total effect of technological change (ATOT) and the shift effect (ASHIFT):

$$\text{ABIAS} = (\text{ATOT} - \text{ASHIFT}) \tag{24}$$

Finally we measure (R) as the ratio between the two indices, i.e. ASHIFT, the Solow index and the total TFP (ATOT) we introduced above:

$$R = \text{ATOT}/\text{ASHIFT} \tag{25}$$

The indices obtained from Equations (24) and (25) are straightforward and easy to interpret. Assuming that the slope of isocosts differs from unity, it is clear that when ABIAS in a country is 0 and $R = 1$, technological change is typically neutral. When R in one case is above (below) one, then its technological activity is characterized by a high (low) directionality. When ABIAS and R are large and positive, technological change is directed and has both a strong positive shift effect and a positive bias effect. When ABIAS is negative and ASHIFT is positive, we grasp the case of a unit of analysis that has introduced a superior technology with low(er) levels of technological congruence.

9.6. Conclusion

The understanding of all the characteristics of technological change is necessary to grasp the dynamics of growth and change as much as the detailed analysis of the growth of output and inputs and their changing relations is necessary to understand the characteristics of technological change. Much attention has been paid to the changes in the efficiency of the production process brought by the changes in the position of the map of isoquants, but much less attention has been paid, so far, to the effects of the changes in the slope of the maps of isoquants.

In the recent years there has been a renewed and growing interest in the analysis of the bias of technological change and its effects on the actual efficiency of production processes after the introduction of non-neutral technological changes. The induced-technological-change approach has, after years in the shadows, returned under the spotlight of the contemporary debates (Ruttan, 1997).

This chapter builds upon the induced-innovation perspective and articulates the hypothesis that technological change is endogenous and its direction is the result of the incentive to make the most efficient use of locally abundant production factors. When input prices change, agents within countries have a clear incentive to try to innovate and to search for new technologies that are consistent with the relative local endowments.

In the search for total efficiency, technological congruence becomes a major factor that requires to be considered. Technological congruence consists in the matching between the relative abundance of production factors locally available and the factorial characterization of the technology used in the production. Capital-intensive technologies yield much a smaller output when they are applied in labour-abundant countries rather than in capital-abundant ones. Technological congruence directly affects the relative efficiency of the production process and has important consequences on the relative profitability of introducing and adopting new technologies. Its effects have been substantially ignored in the literature, as well as its causes. The identification of the consequences and the causes of technological congruence can shed new light upon the analysis of the rate and the direction of technological change.

When the notion of technological congruence is taken into account we see that the effects of technological change are much deeper and wider than currently acknowledged, as they consist both of a shift and a bias effect. The latter has rarely been taken into account. The relation between the two effects can be both additive and substitutive. The bias effect can magnify the shift effect as well as reduce it. The interaction between the bias of technological change and the characteristics of local factor markets favours some actors and reduces the actual performance of others.

The identification of absolute and congruence efficiency as the distinct outcomes of different forms of technological change and the analysis of the process of accumulation of competence based upon localized technological knowledge contribute a better understanding of the causes and consequences of technological change and provide a useful frame for implementing effective innovation policies. It is clear that the results of our analysis, built upon a simple two-factor Cobb-Douglas production function, can be easily generalized to all production inputs that qualify a broader production function in sales. The implications of the notion of technological congruence are most important in the global economy.

The results of our analysis stress the role and the need for technological pluralism: countries and regions with heterogeneous endowments and specific characteristics of their internal factor markets have a clear incentive and opportunity to direct technological change towards the intensive use of the factors that are locally most abundant. The appreciation of the notion of congruence efficiency enables us to identify the incentives and the notion of localized learning enables us to identify the opportunities. The pursuit of an idiosyncratic and specialized technological competence is both necessary and possible. Both within the global economy at large, and within large continental economies there is a clear message: technological pluralism should be pursued instead of a generic notion of technological advance which is homogeneous across all countries and regions.

First, countries have a clear and strong interest in increasing the output elasticity of the factors that are locally abundant. This confirms, once more, the need for a localized technological competence and a local R&D policy aimed at valorizing and using most intensively the production factors that are locally abundant. Each country and region should pursue a clear technological strategy based upon the identification and appreciation of the factors that are actually locally abundant.

Second, the ranking of technologies is no longer unequivocal. A new technology can be qualified as superior only after taking into account the local endowments. Higher levels of absolute efficiency and lower levels of congruence efficiency may qualify a new technology. Its actual, total efficiency clearly depends upon their algebraic sum. A new capital-intensive technology with low levels of higher absolute efficiency may be less efficient if it is characterized by strong negative congruence efficiency in a different factor market.

Thirdly, and consistently, the bias of new technologies plays a key role in determining their rate of diffusion in heterogeneous factor markets. The adoption of capital-intensive technologies in labour-abundant ones may be far less profitable than is currently assumed. It is rational for their adoption to be delayed. The lack of congruence between countries limits diffusion and transfer of technology.

Fourth, the lack of technological congruence of new technologies may contrast with the convergence towards common, shared levels of economic efficiency. Users of capital-intensive technologies based in labour-abundant countries may find their adoption profitable and yet experience persisting differences in efficiency due to their different factor endowments.

Fifth, adoption cannot be passive, but rather must be creative. Adopters must try to change the technological bias of new technologies conceived and originally introduced in countries with different factor endowments so as to adjust them to their local factor-market conditions. Hence, each country and region cannot rely upon international technology transfer without the systematic implementation of local and localized technological competence.

References

Abramovitz, M. and David, P.A. (1996), Convergence and delayed catch-up: Productivity leadership and the waning of American exceptionalism. In Landau, R., Taylor, T. and Wright, G. (eds), *The Mosaic of Economic Growth*. Stanford: Stanford University Press.

—— ——(2001), 'Two centuries of American macroeconomic growth: From exploitation of resource abundance to knowledge-driven development', Stanford Institute for Economic Policy Research Discussion Paper No. 01–05.

Acemoglu, D. (1998), 'Why do new technologies complement skills? Directed technical change and wage inequality', *Quarterly Journal of Economics*, 113: 1055–1089.

——(2002), 'Directed technical change', *Review of Economic Studies*, 69: 781–809.

——(2010), 'When does abor scarcity encourage innovation?', *Journal of Political Economy*, 118: 1037–1078.

Antonelli, C. (1995), *The Economics of Localized Technological Change and Industrial Dynamics*. Boston: Kluwer Academic Publisher.

——(2003), *The Economics of Innovation New Technologies and Structural Change*. London: Routledge.

——(2008), *Localized Technological Change. Towards the Economics of Complexity*. London: Routledge.

Antonelli, C. and Barbiellini Amidei, F. (2011), *The Dynamics of Knowledge Externalities. Localized Technological Change in Italy*. Cheltenham: Edward Elgar.

——and Colombelli, A. (2011), 'Globalization and directed technological change at the firm level. The European evidence', *Advances in the Study of Entrepreneurship, Innovation and Economic Growth*, 22.

——and Fassio, C. (2011), 'Globalization and innovation in advanced economies', *Advances in the Study of Entrepreneurship, Innovation and Economic Growth*, 22.

——and Quatraro, F. (2010), 'The effects of biased technological change on total factor productivity. Empirical evidence from a sample of OECD countries', *Journal of Technology Transfer*, 35: 361–383.

Arrow, K.J. (1969), 'Classificatory notes on the production and transmission of technical knowledge', *American Economic Review*, 59: 29–35.

Atkinson, A.B. and Stiglitz, J.E. (1969), 'A new view of technological change', *Economic Journal*, 79: 573–578.

Binswanger, H.P. and Ruttan, V.W. (1978), *Induced Innovation. Technology Institutions and Development*. Baltimore: The Johns Hopkins University Press.

Caselli, F. and Coleman, II., W.J., (2006), 'The world technology frontier', *American Economic Review*, 96(3): 499–522.

Crafts, N. (2009), 'The contribution of new technology to economic growth: Lessons from economic history'. Paper presented as the Figuerola Lecture, Madrid.

David, P.A. (1975), *Technological Choice, Innovation and Economic Growth*. Cambridge: Cambridge University Press.

Eckaus, R.S. (1987), 'Appropriate technology: The movement has only a few clothes on', *Issues in Science and Technology*, 3: 62–71.

Habakkuk, H.J. (1962), *American and British Technology in the Nineteenth Century*. Cambridge: Cambridge University Press.

Hall, R.E. and Jones, C.I. (1999), 'Why do some countries produce so much more output per worker than others?', *Quarterly Journal of Economics*, 114: 83–116.

Hicks, J.R. (1932), *The Theory of Wages*. London: Macmillan.

Jerzmanowski, M. (2007), 'Total factor productivity differences: Appropriate technology vs. efficiency', *European Economic Review*, 51: 2080–2110.

Johansen, L. (1972), *Production Functions*. Amsterdam: North-Holland.

Link, A.N. (1987), *Technological Change and Productivity Growth*. Chur: Harwood.

OECD (2001), *Measuring Productivity. Measurement of Aggregate and Industry-Level Productivity Growth*. Paris: OECD.

Ruttan, V.W. (1997), 'Induced innovation evolutionary theory and path dependence: Sources of technical change', *Economic Journal*, 107: 1520–1529.

Samuelson, P. (1965), 'A theory of induced innovation along Kennedy, Weiszacker Lines', *Review of Economics and Statistics*, 47: 343.

Solow, R.M. (1957), 'Technical change and the aggregate production function', *The Review of Economics and Statistics*, 39: 312–320.

10

Spillover, Linkages, and Productivity Growth in the US Economy, 1958 to 2007

Edward N. Wolff

10.1. Introduction

This study examines whether the contribution of inter-sectoral spillovers to industry productivity growth has increased over time in the USA over the years from 1958 to 2007. There are two potential sources for this. First, the size of the inter-sectoral linkage may have grown over time—that is, linkages may have strengthened over time. Second, the coefficient on the inter-sectoral linkage may have risen over time. With the introduction of information technology (IT) and its widespread adoption beginning in the early 1970s, one would think that the speed of knowledge spillovers would have accelerated over time. Another contribution of the study is that the results of the empirical analysis will make it possible to estimate the direct and indirect return (as well as the social rate of return) to R&D.

In this regard, this chapter extends previous work (Wolff and Nadiri, 1993; Wolff, 1997) on the measurement of R&D spillovers based on computing-embodied R&D using US input-output tables from 1947 to 1987. Throughout the chapter, I will compare the new results to the old ones to see whether the spillover effects found in the older papers still hold true for the more recent period (and whether new relations are found).

The chapter is organized as follows. The next section provides a review of the pertinent literature on spillover effects across industries. Section 10.3 introduces the model to be used in the empirical analysis. Section 10.4 discusses the data sources and methods. Section 10.5 presents the results of the econometric analysis. Concluding remarks are provided in the last part, Section 10.6.

10.2. Review of previous literature

10.2.1. *Domestic R&D spillovers*

R&D spillovers refer to the direct knowledge gains of customers from the R&D of the supplying industry (see Griliches, 1979).[1] There have been several approaches to measuring R&D spillovers. In, perhaps, the earliest work on this subject, Brown and Conrad (1967) based their measure of borrowed R&D on input-output trade flows (purchases and sales) between industries. Terleckyj (1974, 1980) provided measures of the amount of R&D embodied in customer inputs on the basis of inter-industry material and capital purchases made by one industry from the supplying industries. Scherer (1982), using Federal Trade Commission line-of-business data, used product (as distinct from process) R&D, aimed at improving output quality, as the basis of his measure of R&D spillovers.

Another approach is to measure the degree of 'technological closeness' between industries. For example, if two industries use similar processes (even though their products are very different, or they are not directly connected by inter-industry flows), then one industry may benefit from the new discoveries by the other industry. Such an approach is found in the work of Jaffe (1986), where patent data are used to measure technological closeness between industries.

Bernstein and Nadiri (1989) used total R&D at the two-digit Standard Industrial Classification (SIC) level as a measure of intra-industry R&D spillovers and applied this measure to individual firm data within industry. Mairesse and Mohnen (1990) used a similar schema by comparing R&D coefficients based on firm R&D with those based on industry R&D. If there exist intra-industry externality effects of firm R&D, then the coefficient of industry R&D should be higher than those of firm R&D. However, the results of Mairesse and Mohnen did not show that this was consistently the case.

There have been a large number of studies which have followed one or other of these approaches for estimating the spillover effects of R&D (see Mohnen (1990, 1992), Griliches (1992), and Cameron (1996) for reviews of some of the earlier literature). In contrast, the literature on direct productivity spillover is more limited. Some of the earlier literature on this subject was quite suggestive. For the German economy, Oppenlander and Schulz (1981) calculated that only about one-third of new products were derived from technology (that is, process innovation). The remainder are 'market innovations', which are

---

[1] Griliches also identifies a second interpretation of spillovers; namely, that inputs purchased from an R&D-performing industry may embody quality improvements that are not fully appropriated by the supplier. It should be emphasized at the outset that although these two spillover notions are quite distinct, they cannot be distinguished statistically in this work.

used to open up new markets for the producers. Pavitt (1984) estimated that out of 2000 innovations introduced in the UK, only about 40 per cent were developed in the sector using the innovation. The remainder were borrowed from new technologies developed in other sectors.

The work of Nelson and Winters (1982) illustrates another approach. In their evolutionary model, spillovers in technology among firms may occur as firms search or sample from their environment to develop new production techniques. Moreover, Rosenberg (1982) and Rosenberg and Frischtak (1984) suggested the existence of clusters of innovations in industries that occupy a strategic position in the economy in terms of both forward and backward linkages. They speculated that there are certain intra-industry flows of new equipment and materials that have a disproportionate level of technological change in the economy.

A paper by Bartelsman et al. (1991) is also highly suggestive. Using regression analysis, they related the growth in an industry's output to a weighted average of the growth in the outputs of the supplying industries, where the weights are determined by the industry's input coefficients. They concluded that the linkage between an industry and its suppliers appeared to be the dominant factor in accounting for long-term growth externalities. However, they did not directly relate an industry's own productivity growth to the R&D of its suppliers or to its suppliers' rate of productivity advance.

Wolff and Nadiri (1993) provided one of the first investigations of direct productivity spillovers. They used as their measure of embodied technical change a weighted average of the TFP growth of the supplying industries, where the weights are determined by the industry's input-output coefficients. This formulation assumes that the knowledge gained from a supplying industry is in direct proportion to the value of that industry in a sector's input structure. Using US input-output data from 1947 to 1977, they found a statistically significant effect of this index on an industry's own rate of technical change.

Wolff (1997) followed up this work using US input-output data from 1958 to 1987 and found an even stronger effect of embodied TFP growth on an industry's own rate of technical advance, with an elasticity of almost 60 per cent. The return to embodied R&D was estimated at 43 per cent. Direct productivity spillovers from the technological progress made by supplying sectors appeared to be more important than spillovers from the R&D performed by the suppliers. Moreover, changes in the contribution made by direct productivity spillovers to TFP growth accounted for almost half of the slowdown in TFP growth in manufacturing from 1958–1967 to 1967–1977 and for 20 per cent of the TFP recovery in this sector from 1967–1977 to 1977–1987.

Following up the work of Scherer (1982), Ornaghi (2006) considered a model where process-innovation spillovers to other firms raise firms' relative efficiency and technological diffusion of product innovations enhances firms' demand. Using panel data of Spanish manufacturing firms over the period 1990 to 1999, he found technological externalities significantly affect firm-level productivity growth. He also found that technological diffusion of product innovations was larger than the one deriving from process innovations, both in magnitude and pervasiveness.

Several papers have looked at the importance of geographic proximity in explaining R&D spillovers. The usual argument is that firms that are located in the same or proximate locations have greater opportunities to communicate than those further away. Geographic proximity may lead to the formation of social networks that can facilitate learning. Adams and Jaffe (1996) used a panel of manufacturing establishments over time from the Census and Annual Survey of Manufactures, matched by firm and industry to the firm-level R&D survey conducted by the National Science Foundation. The sample period was from 1974 to 1988. They found that the effects of parent-firm R&D on plant-level productivity are diminished by both the geographic and technological distance between the research lab and the plants.

Orlando (2004) looked at firms in SIC 35, Industrial, Commercial Machinery, and Computer Equipment. The primary data were from Standard and Poor's Compustat database from 1970 to 1998. These were supplemented with Bureau of Labor Statistics price deflators for industry input and output, as well as county-level latitude and longitude data from the US Geological Survey. He used a production-function framework to examine the role of geographic and technological proximity for inter-firm spillovers from R&D in SIC 35. He found that spillovers among firms within narrow, four-digit industrial classifications were generally stronger than those identified within the broader, three-digit class. Such spillovers, however, did not appear to be reduced by distance. Geographic distance did appear to attenuate spillovers that cross four-digit boundaries, suggesting that they may play a role in the formation of diverse (but not too diverse) industrial agglomerations.

Lychagin et al. (2010) used US Compustat data for manufacturing firms for the period 1980 to 2000. These were matched with patent data from the US Patent and Trademark Office available from the NBER data archive. Inventor location was taken from the address of the lead inventor of the patent, which is recorded at the city level. Their purpose was to investigate the contributions to productivity of three sources of research and development spillovers: geographic, technology, and product–market proximity. They found that technological proximity (as developed by Jaffe, 1986) was important in explaining R&D spillovers. Moreover, geographical distance also had an effect in accounting for R&D spillovers even after conditioning on horizontal and technological spillovers. However, product–market proximity was less important than these two factors in accounting for R&D spillovers.

10.2.2. *International R&D spillovers*

Over the last 15 years or so, much of the attention in this literature has been directed at international spillovers, and, as a result, there are also quite a few papers that have investigated the presence and importance of cross-national R&D and technological spillovers. Coe and Helpman (1995) were among the first to provide evidence on the importance of trade as a vehicle for the international diffusion of technology. They argued that if there is evidence (as seems to be the case) that innovation or R&D performed in one industry leads to technological gains in using industries, then is it possible that R&D performed in one country leads to technological gains in countries which import products from the first country? Coe and Helpman gathered data for 22 OECD countries covering the period from 1971 to 1990. They constructed measures of (domestic) R&D stock by country and estimated import flows between countries. Their major contribution was to construct a measure of 'foreign R&D capital,' which they defined as the import-share weighted average of the domestic R&D capital stocks of trade partners. Using bilateral import shares to weight foreign R&D expenditures, they calculated the variable S^f_i, which represented the foreign R&D stock of country i, as:

$$S^f_i = \sum_j m_{ik} RD_k$$

where m_{ik} is the share of imports coming from country k as a share of total imports into country i and RD_k is the stock of R&D in country k. Thus, the more R&D-intensive the imports are from other countries, the higher is a country's stock of foreign R&D capital.

They then regressed a country's annual total factor productivity (TFP) growth on both its domestic and foreign R&D capital. They found, like most studies, that domestic R&D was a significant determinant of a country's TFP growth. However, their most important finding was that foreign capital was also a significant determinant of TFP growth within a country. They calculated a domestic R&D elasticity of 23 per cent for the G-7 countries and about 8 per cent for the 15 smaller OECD countries. However, their estimated elasticities for foreign R&D (that is, R&D embodied in imports into these countries) were 6 per cent for the G-7 countries and 12 per cent for the other OECD countries. They concluded that imported R&D was a more important factor in explaining domestic productivity growth in the smaller OECD countries but the converse was true for the larger OECD economies. They also found that the more open a country was, the higher the return to foreign R&D.

They then looked at two additional issues. First, they wanted to determine whether a country's productivity growth was greater to the extent that it imported goods and services from countries with a high (domestic) R&D intensity relative to imports from countries with low R&D expenditures. Second, after controlling for the composition of its imports, they were interested in whether a country's productivity growth would be higher the higher its overall import share. They found support for both predictions. In particular, they found that international R&D spillovers were related to both the composition of a country's imports as well as to its overall import intensity.

This paper stimulated a lot of additional work on the importance of foreign spillovers from trade and R&D. Park (1995), using aggregate data for 10 OECD countries (including the G-7 countries), had similar results. He estimated that foreign R&D accounted for about two-thirds of the total effect of R&D on domestic productivity. He estimated a domestic R&D elasticity of 7 per cent and a foreign R&D elasticity of 17 per cent.

However, Verspagen (1997) challenged the findings of Coe and Helpman. Verspagen constructed a technology-flow matrix based on European patent data which indicated not only in which sector the patent originated but also in which sectors the patent was used. This approach allowed the researcher to identify explicitly the pattern of inter-sectoral spillovers of knowledge. In contrast, Coe and Helpman based their spillover calculations on inter-sectoral trade (import) flows. Another difference was that Verspagen related TFP growth on the *sectoral* level to both direct and indirect R&D capital stocks.

Using a panel dataset of 22 sectors, 14 OECD countries, and 19 years (1974–1992, although there were missing data for some countries, sectors, and years), Verspagen was able to distinguish between R&D effects across sectors (the so-called 'between' effect) and R&D effects over time (the so-called 'within' effect). He found that foreign R&D spillovers were significant only in the 'within' estimation (that is, the time-series effect). Foreign spillovers were positive in the 'between' estimation (that is, between sectors) but not statistically significant. It thus appeared that the Coe and Helpman results overstated the contribution of foreign R&D to domestic productivity growth.

Eaton and Kortum (1999) used a broader approach to calculating the relative importance of domestic and foreign R&D in domestic productivity growth. In their model, they included not only the direct effects on productivity growth but also a contribution from the transitional adjustment path to long-run equilibrium. They estimated that the portion of productivity growth attributable to domestic as opposed to imported R&D was about 13 per cent in Germany, France, and the UK; around 35 per cent for Japan; and upwards to 60 per cent in the USA. Keller (2002) used a more general form of the R&D-productivity function by allowing for multiple channels by which the diffusion of R&D can interact with domestic TFP growth. Using this method, he estimated that over the period from 1983 to 1995, the contribution of technology diffusion from France, Germany, Japan, the UK, and the USA to nine other OECD countries amounted to about 90 per cent of the total R&D effect on TFP growth.

Eaton and Kortum (1996), on the other hand, controlled for both distance and other effects. They found that once these other influences are controlled for, bilateral imports were not significant as a predictor of bilateral patenting activity, which they used as an indicator of international technology diffusion. Moreover, Keller (1998) replicated the set of regressions used by Coe and Helpman (1995) with what he termed 'counterfactual import shares'. These were simulated import shares based on alternative assumptions rather than actual import shares that were used to create the imported R&D variable in the regression equations. Keller argued that for there to be strong evidence for trade-induced international R&D spillovers, one should expect a strong positive effect from foreign R&D when actual bilateral import shares were used but a weaker and probably insignificant effect when the made-up 'import' shares were used. Keller found high and significant coefficients when counterfactual import shares were used instead of actual import shares. The magnitude of the coefficients and the level of significance were similar in the two sets of regression. On the basis of these results, he disputed the claim of Coe and Helpman that the import composition of a country was an important factor in explaining the country's productivity growth.

Xu and Wang (1999) showed that the import-composition effect remained strong when trade in capital goods was used instead of trade in goods produced in total manufacturing. Xu and Wang obtained an R^2 statistic of 0.771 when the weights used in the construction of the imported R&D variable were based on imports of capital goods. In comparison, Keller obtained an R^2 statistic of 0.749 on the basis of his counterfactual import weights, and Coe and Helpman (1995) obtained a R^2 statistic of 0.709 in their original regressions.

Sjöholm (1996) took a different approach by analyzing citations in patent applications of Swedish firms to patents owned by inventors in other countries. Patent citations have been used in a number of studies now as an indicator for knowledge flows either between firms or between countries (see, for example, Jaffe, Trajtenberg and Henderson, 1993). Sjöholm controlled for a number of other variables and found a positive and significant relation between Swedish patent citations and bilateral imports. He concluded that imports contributed to international knowledge spillovers.

Acharta and Keller (2008) looked at two channels by which imports affect productivity. The first is that import competition may lead to market share reallocation among domestic firms with different levels of production. This they called the 'selection effect'. The second is that imports can also improve the productivity of domestic firms through learning externalities or spillovers. They used a sample of 17 industrialized countries covering the period 1973 to 2002. They reported two principal findings. First, increased imports lowered the productivity of domestic industries through selection. Second, if imports embodied advanced foreign technologies (as measured by their R&D intensity), increased imports could also generate technological learning through spillovers that on net raised the productivity of domestic industries.

Madsen (2007) took an even longer perspective on the relationship between trade and productivity growth. His data covered the period from 1870 to 2004. Using data for 16 OECD countries from Maddison (1982), and augmenting this with data on bilateral trade flows and patents for each of the countries, he constructed a measure of knowledge imports from foreign countries. Using a cointegration method, he estimated that as much as 93 per cent of the TFP growth of the average OECD country could be attributed to the international transmission of knowledge through the channel of imports.

10.3. Accounting framework and input-output model

The input-output model can be introduced as follows, where all vectors and matrices are 45-order and in constant (2007) dollars, unless otherwise indicated:

X_t = column vector of gross output by sector at time t.
Y_t = column vector of final output by sector at time t.
A_t = square matrix of technical inter-industry input-output coefficients a_{ij} at time t.

It should be noted that I use the industry-by-industry matrix instead of the commodity-by-industry matrix because R&D data are available by industry of production, not by commodity.

L_t = row vector of labour coefficients ℓ_i, showing employment per unit of output at time t.
K_t = square matrix of capital-stock coefficients k_{ij}, showing the capital stock of each type i per unit of output j at time t.
N_t = square matrix of investment coefficients n_{ij}, showing the new investment of each type i made by sector j at time t.
P_t = row vector of prices at time t, showing the price per unit of output of each industry.

In addition, let us define the following scalars:

w_t = annual wage rate at time t (assumed the same for all workers).

i_t = the rate of profit on capital stock at time t (assumed constant across industries and types of capital).

I will also make use of the so-called inter-industry value matrix A^* defined as:

A^*_t = square matrix of value inter-industry input-output coefficients a^*_{ij} at time t, where $a^*_{ij} = p_i a_{ij}/p_j$.

Another concept that will be used is the sales-coefficient matrix B, which shows the percentage of sector i's output that is sold to sector j and is given by:

B_t = square matrix of inter-industry sales coefficients b_{ij} at time t, where $b_{ij} = a_{ij}x_j/x_i$.

Analogously, the matrix B_n shows the share of total investment of each type i that is sold to sector j:

B_{nt} = square matrix of investment coefficients b_{nij} at time t, where $b_{nij} = n_{ij}x_j/x_i$.

Following Leontief (1953), I can now define a row vector π, where the rate of TFP growth for sector j over period T is given by:

$$\text{TFPGRT}_{jT} \equiv \pi_{jT} = -\left(\sum_i p_{jT}\Delta a_{ijT} + w_T\Delta\ell_{jT} + \sum_i i_T\Delta k_{ijT}\right)/p_{jt0} \qquad (1)$$

where Δ refers to the change over period T, p_{jT} is the average price of sector j over period T, w_T is the average wage over period T, i_T is the average rate of profit over period T, and p_{jt0} is sector j's price at the beginning of the period (t_0).

R&D intensity is introduced into the model as follows. Let

$$\text{RDX}_{jT} \equiv r_{jT} = \text{RD}_{jT}/X_{jT} \qquad (2)$$

which shows the amount of R&D expenditure (RD) in constant US dollars per constant dollar of gross output in sector j.

Forward spillovers from R&D are estimated on the basis of trade flows between sectors. I use two different formulations of R&D spillovers. The first assumes that the amount of information gained from supplier i's R&D is proportional to its importance in sector j's input structure (that is, the magnitude of a_{ij}) and to sector i's R&D intensity:

$$\text{RDINDA}_{jt} \equiv \sum_i a^0_{ijT}\text{RD}_{jt}/\text{GDP}_{jt} \qquad (3)$$

where the matrix A^0 is identical to the matrix A, except that the diagonal of the matrix is set to zero in order to prevent double-counting of R&D expenditures. For period T, the average values of a^0_{ij} and the ratio RD_j/GDP_j are used.

The second approach assumes that the amount of R&D that spills over from sector i to sector j is proportional to the share of output that sector i sells to sector j. This approach was used by Terleckyj (1974, 1980). Then the alternative measure of indirect R&D, RDINDB, is given by:[2]

$$RDINDB_{jt} \equiv \sum_i b^0_{ijT} RD_{jt}/GDP_{jt} \qquad (4)$$

A similar approach was used by Scherer (1982), except that his measure of indirect R&D is distributed proportionally to the number of patents issued by sector i which fall into sector j's industrial classification. In principle, Scherer's measure is identical to RDINDA except that indirect R&D is distributed proportionally to patents instead of sales.

The difference between the two measures, RDINDA and RDINDB, depends on different theories of knowledge transfers. According to RDINDA, if Sector A buys 15 per cent of its total output from Sector B, then 15 per cent of Sector B's R&D is carried forward to Sector A. In this case, knowledge transfer depends on how important B's inputs are in Sector A's input structure. On the other hand, according to RDINDB, if Sector B sells 15 per cent of its output to Sector A, then 15 per cent of Sector B's R&D is carried forward to Sector A.

Another source of borrowed R&D is new investment. In the first case, it is assumed that the information gain is proportional to the annual investment flow per unit of output:

$$RDKINDA_{jt} \equiv \sum_i nij_T RD_{jt}/GDP_{jt} \qquad (5)$$

In the second case, it is assumed that the information gain from the R&D performed in the capital-producing sector i to sector j is proportional to the share of new investment that sector i sells to sector j:

$$RDKINDB_{jt} \equiv \sum_i b_{ijT} RD_{it}/GDP_{jt} \qquad (6)$$

It is also possible to construct estimates of direct productivity spillovers, what I call 'TFP spillovers,' in analogous fashion to the approach for R&D spillovers. The rationale is that TFP growth is an indicator of 'successful' R&D and therefore there may be a 'contagion' effect between industries with a rapid rate of technological gain and those buying from these industries. TFP spillovers are measured by:

$$TFPINDA_{jt} \equiv \sum_i a^0_{ijt} \pi_{it} \qquad (7)$$

which is a measure of sector j's indirect knowledge gain from technological change in its supplying sectors. In this case, it is assumed that the information gained from supplier i's TFP is proportional to its importance in sector j's input structure. An alternative measure is:

---

[2] The matrix B^0 is used instead of B again to avoid double-counting of industry j's own R&D.

$$\text{TFPINDB}_{jt} \equiv \sum_i b^0_{ijt} \pi_{it} \tag{8}$$

where it is assumed that the knowledge gain from sector j's TFP growth is proportional to the percentage of sector i's output that is sold to sector j.

In sum, I have now introduced six different measures of possible inter-sectoral spillover effects. Are there ones that are preferable to others? With regard to RDINDA versus RDINDB (as well as RDKINDA versus RDKINDB), each has its own rationale. As discussed above, with regard to the two measures, RDINDA and RDINDB, each relies on a different theory of knowledge transfers. The selection of a preferred one will depend on the outcome of an empirical investigation of their relative importance and statistical significance in explaining industry-level TFP growth ('the proof of the pudding is in the eating,' as the old expression goes).

In contrast, both inter-industry spillovers (such as RDINDA) and spillovers from new investment (such as RDKINDA) may each contribute separately as factors in accounting for industry-level TFP growth. Here, too, the choice of a preferred measure will depend on the results of an empirical investigation. With regard to the difference between R&D spillovers (such as RDINDA) and direct TFP spillovers (such as TFPINDA) each has its own rationale. If R&D is the medium through which knowledge is transferred between sectors, then the former is to be preferred, but if direct technological change is the medium the latter is to be preferred. Once, again, empirical investigation of the relative importance of each in explaining industry-level TFP growth will lead to a preferred choice.

I also introduce several measures of inter-sectoral linkages. These have been developed in the input-output literature. The first is the average value of the input-output value coefficients, a^*_{ij}:

$$\text{LINK1}_i = \sum_j a^*_{ij}/(v-1), j \neq i \tag{9}$$

where v is the number of sectors. The second index is the row sum of the value inverse matrix:

$$\text{LINK2}_i = \sum_j [(1-A^*)^{-1}]_{ij} \tag{10}$$

This measure shows the total increase in output in sector i that would be forthcoming to meet a dollar increase in the demand for the output of each sector of the economy. This index expresses the extent to which the system of industries in an economy draws upon industry i in order to expand production. The third is given by:

$$\text{LINK3}_i = \Sigma_j [(I-B')^{-1}]_{ij} \tag{11}$$

The column sum of the $(I—B')$ inverse matrix shows the total output of user industries needed to absorb an additional dollar of sector i's output,

10.4. Data sources and methods

The principal data are 85-sector input-output tables for the USA for years 1958, 1967, 1977, 1987, 1997, and 2007. These are produced by the Bureau of Economic Analysis (and are available at: http://www.bea.gov/industry/). I have decided to use ten-year intervals (or approximately ten-year periods) in order to avoid much of the cyclical variation in TFP growth over the business cycle. The last five of these years are near peaks of the business cycle in the USA. However, unfortunately, 1958 is a recession year.[3] The first five of these tables are so-called benchmark tables. However, the 2007 table is one of the annual updates of the 2002 benchmark table. The 1958 table is available only in single-table format.[4] The 1967, 1977, 1987, 1997, and 2007 data are available in separate make-and-use tables.[5]

Two types of employment data are used. The first is full-time equivalent employees (FTEE) and the second is persons engaged in production (PEIP). Both are obtained on the industry level from the US Bureau of Economic Analysis, National Income and Product Accounts (http://www.bea.gov/national/nipaweb/), Tables 6.5 and 6.8 (http://www.bea.gov/bea/dn2/home/annual_industry.htm).

Investment data refer to non-residential fixed investment in constant (2000) dollars. The source is US Bureau of Economic Analysis, National Income and Product Accounts (http://www.bea.gov/bea/dn2/home/annual_industry.htm).

Capital-stock figures are based on chain-type quantity indices for net stock of fixed capital in constant (2000) dollars, year-end estimates. Equipment and structures, including information-technology equipment, are for the private (non-government) sector only. Source: US Bureau of Economic Analysis, CD-ROM NCN-0229, 'Fixed Reproducible Tangible Wealth of the United States, 1925–97' (http://www.bea.gov/bea/dn2/home/annual_industry.htm). For technical details, see Katz and Herman (1997).

Investment flows by industry and by type of equipment or structures are for the private (non-government) sector only. The source is: US Bureau of

---

[3] There is also little that can be done to correct for the business-cycle trough in 1958.

[4] The single-table format relies on the so-called BEA transfer method. See Kop Jansen and ten Raa (1990) for a discussion of this method and its associated methodological difficulties.

[5] Details on the construction of the input–output tables can be found in the following publications: 1967—US Interindustry Economics Division (1974); 1977—US Interindustry Economics Division (1984); and 1987—Lawson and Teske (1994). See also Lawson (1997).

Economic Analysis, CD-ROM NCN-0229, 'Fixed Reproducible Tangible Wealth of the United States, 1925–97' (http://www.bea.gov/bea/dn2/home/annual_industry.htm).

R&D expenditures performed by industry include company, federal, and other sources of funds. Company-financed R&D performed outside the company is excluded. 'Private' refers to privately-funded R&D performed in company facilities including all sources except federally financed R&D. 'Basic' refers to basic research performed in company facilities; 'applied' refers to applied research performed in company facilities; and 'development' refers to development R&D performed in company facilities. Series on the industry level run from 1957 to 2008. The sources are: National Science Foundation, *Research and Development in Industry* (Arlington: National Science Foundation), various years (http://www.nsf.gov/sbe/srs/nsf01305/htmstart.htm).

Data on full-time equivalent scientists and engineers engaged in R&D per 10,000 full-time equivalent employee, SCIENG, are also available. Series on the both the aggregate and industry level run from 1957 to 2008. The sources are: National Science Foundation, *Research and Development in Industry* (Arlington: National Science Foundation), various years (http://www.nsf.gov/sbe/srs/nsf01305/htmstart.htm).

These data are used to construct labour coefficients, capital coefficients, sectoral price deflators, and R&D coefficients. In addition, the deflator for transferred imports is calculated from the NIPA import deflator, that for the Rest of the World industry is calculated as the average of the NIPA import-and-export deflator, and the deflator for the inventory-valuation adjustment is computed from the NIPA change-in-business-inventory deflator. The source is US Bureau of Economic Analysis, National Income and Product Accounts (see above for Internet address).

Altogether, five different data sources are used in the empirical implementation of the work: (1) input-output tables, (2) industry capital stock, (3) industry employment, (4) industry-level price deflators, and (5) industry-level R&D expenditures. In order to make the various data sources consistent, I aggregated the original input-output data to 45 sectors (see Table A10.1 in the appendix for a listing of the sectors).

10.5. Regression models and results

The basic regression model used in the empirical analysis is:

$$\text{TFPGRT}_{jT} = \beta_0 + \beta_1 \text{RDX}_{jT} + \beta_2 \text{IND}_{jT} + \Sigma_k \zeta_k D_{kT} + \epsilon_{jT} \tag{12}$$

245

where β_0, β_1, β_2, and ζk are coefficients, D_{kT} are time dummy variables, and ϵ_{jT} is a stochastic error term. IND refers to the various measures of indirect or embodied R&D and TFP (RDINDA, RDINDB, TFPINDA, TFPINDB, etc.). I assume that the terms ϵ_{jT} are independently distributed but may not be identically distributed. The regression results reported below use the White procedure of a heteroschedasticity-consistent covariance matrix. It is also assumed that $a_{.j}$ are independent—that is, the technology of each industry is independent of that of other industries. In both cases, the sample is a pooled cross-section time-series data set that consists of 45 industries in four time periods (1958–1967, 1967–1977, 1977–1987, and 1987–1997) and 33 sectors in 1997–2007.[6] Although ideally it would be useful to separate out a between-sector effect from a within-sector effect, as in Verspagen (1997), this is not possible in the present application because of the different sector scheme in the 1997–2007 period.

The coefficient b_1 is normally interpreted as the rate of return to R&D under the assumption that the (average) rate of return to R&D is equalized across sectors.[7] The coefficient b_2 is, correspondingly, usually interpreted as the indirect return to R&D and the sum of the two is considered to be the total or social rate of return to R&D.

Another set of regressions will look at the effects of industry-level productivity growth and industry-level R&D expenditures on linkage structure per se. The regression specifications are of the form:

$$LINK1_{jT} = \gamma_0 + \gamma_1 RDX_{jT} + \gamma_2 TFPGRT_{jT} + \Sigma_k \zeta_k D_{kT} + \epsilon_{jT} \tag{13}$$

The descriptive statistics, shown in the appendix in Table A10.2, are, first, of interest. Average TFP growth across sectors shows the familiar pattern, with a marked slowdown between 1958–1967 and the next two periods and then an acceleration in the 1987–1997 and the 1997–2007 periods. R&D intensity remained relatively stable over the five time periods, averaging 0.012. The mean value of SCIENG, on the other hand, trended upwards over the five time periods, particularly in the 1997–2007 period. RDINDA shows no clear time trend, although there is a sharp dip in the 1997–2007 period. RDINDB likewise shows no clear pattern of time, although in this case there is sharp increase in its value in the last period.

---

[6] The reason for the smaller number of industries in the last period is due to the adoption of the North American Industrial Classification System (NAICS) after 1997, as opposed to the Standard Industrial Classification (SIC) system in the preceding years. Moreover, as noted in the footnote to Table 10.3, since investment by kind is not available for public administration for the computation of RDKINDA and RDKINB, the number of sectors is reduced by one when these variables are used in the regression.

[7] See, for example, Griliches (1980) or Mansfield (1980).

The time path for TFPINDA and TFPINDB generally follows the same trend as TFPGRT, with a fall-off in value in the 1967–1977 and the 1977–1987 periods and then a pick-up in the last two periods. In contrast, the mean value of RDKINDA and that of RDKINDB both tend to trend downwards over time. The linkage measures, LINK1, LINK2, and LINK3, are generally stable over time, although LINK1 does show a rise in the 1997–2007 period while the other two linkage measures fall off in the last period.

I next present the results on embodied R&D from Wolff and Nadiri (1993) and Wolff (1997). In the first paper, we found a rate of return to R&D of about 10 per cent among manufacturing industries alone and about 20 per cent among all industries over the period from 1947 to 1977 (see Table 10.1). Fifty industries were used in the full sample. The coefficient of RDX was significant at the five per cent level in all specifications. RDINDA did not prove statistically significant but had a positive coefficient in both specifications. RDKINDA was not statistically significant in the manufacturing sample (in fact, its coefficient was negative) but its coefficient was positive and significant at the five per cent level among all sectors. The coefficient of TFPINDA was positive and significant at the five per cent level among manufacturing industries but was positive though not significant among all industries. The variables RDINDB and RDKIND were not statistically significant.

Wolff (1997), using a sample of 68 industries over the period 1958 to 1987, estimated a rate of return to R&D of about 11 per cent among all industries (see Table 10.2). The variable RDX was significant at the five per cent level. RDINDA was significant at the 10 per cent level and its coefficient, the indirect return to R&D, was estimated to be 0.43. The social rate of return was therefore estimated to be 53 per cent. The alternative form of embodied R&D, RDINDB, was also significant at the ten per cent level, with an estimated coefficient of 0.41. In these regressions, the dominant variable was TFPINDA, whose estimated coefficient was 1.30 and was significant at the one per cent level. The size of the effect and the significance level of the coefficient of TFPINDA were found to be greater in Wolff (1997) than in Wolff and Nadiri (1993). In contrast, the estimated coefficient of TFPINDB was 0.15 but not significant. The R^2 statistic ranged from 0.060 to 0.096 (with TFPINDA) and the adjusted R^2 statistic from 0.045 to 0.078 (again with TFPINDA).

Regression results from the current study are shown in Table 10.3, based on pooled cross-section data covering the period from 1958 to 2007. The estimated coefficients of RDX range from 0.22 to 0.25, about twice the level of Wolff (1997), and are uniformly significant at the one per cent level. The estimated coefficient of RDINDA is 0.366 and is significant at the one per cent level (see Specification 2). As a result, the direct rate of return to R&D is 22 per cent, the indirect rate of return to R&D is 37 per cent, and the social rate

Table 10.1. Pooled time-series cross-industry regressions of industry TFP growth on R&D intensity, embodied R&D, and embodied TFP growth, 1947–1977

Independent variables	Specification							
	(1)	(2)	(3)	(4)	(5)	(6)	(7)	(8)
Constant	0.0041	0.0084*	0.0047	0.0029	0.0000	-0.0030	-0.0010	-0.0003
	(1.33)	(2.07)	(1.42)	(0.99)	(0.01)	(0.07)	(0.27)	(0.07)
RDX	0.106*	0.103*	0.111*	0.106*	0.188*	0.173*	0.208*	0.189*
	(2.21)	(2.39)	(2.26)	(2.28)	(2.31)	(2.13)	(2.53)	(2.31)
RDINDA		0.143				0.076		
		(1.59)				(1.23)		
RDKINDA			-0.008				0.092#	
			(0.51)				(1.73)	
TFPINDA				0.889*				0.114
				(2.48)				(0.25)
R^2	0.222	0.244	0.224	0.273	0.062	0.070	0.075	0.063
Adjusted R^2	0.179	0.193	0.172	0.224	0.041	0.049	0.049	0.037
Standard error	0.0125	0.0124	0.0126	0.0122	0.0243	0.0243	0.0242	0.0244
Sample	Manuf.	Manuf.	Manuf.	Manuf.	All	All	All	All
Sample size	95	95	95	95	250	250	250	250

Source: Wolff and Nadiri (1993).

Notes: The sample consists of pooled cross-section time-series data, with observations on each of 19 (or 50) industries in 1947–1958, 1958–1963, 1963–1967, 1967–1972, and 1972–1977. Time dummy variables for the last four periods are included but the coefficient estiamtes are not shown. The estimation uses the White procedure for a heteroschedasticity-consistent covariance matrix. The absolute value of the *t*-statistic is in parentheses below the coefficient.
Significance levels: # - 10% level; * - 5% level; ** - 1% level.

Table 10.2. Pooled time-series cross-industry regressions of industry TFP growth on R&D intensity, embodied R&D, and embodied TFP growth, 1958–1987

Independent variables	Specification				
	(1)	(2)	(3)	(4)	(5)
Constant	0.004#	0.002	−0.001	0.002	0.004
	(1.84)	(0.62)	(0.37)	(0.67)	(1.62)
RDX	0.126**	0.101**	0.112**	0.102**	0.124**
	(3.32)	(2.50)	(3.00)	(2.51)	(3.28)
RDINDA		0.429#			
		(1.76)			
TFPINDA			1.300**		
			(2.80)		
RDINDB				0.408#	
				(1.66)	
TFPINDB					0.146
					(0.91)
DUM6777	−0.003	−0.003	0.002	−0.003	−0.003
	(1.10)	(0.89)	(0.48)	(0.91)	(0.99)
DUM7787	0.000	0.001	0.004	0.001	0.000
	(0.06)	(0.32)	(1.19)	(0.29)	(0.07)
R^2	0.060	0.074	0.096	0.073	0.064
Adjusted R^2	0.046	0.056	0.078	0.054	0.045
Standard error	0.0168	0.0167	0.0166	0.0168	0.0168
Sample size	204	204	204	204	204

Source: Wolff (1997).

Notes: The sample consists of pooled cross-section time-series data, with observations on each of 68 industries in 1958–1967, 1967–1977, and 1977–1987.
The estimation uses the White procedure for a heteroschedasticity-consistent covariance matrix. The absolute value of the *t*-statistic is in parentheses below the coefficient.
Significance levels: # - 10% level; * - 5% level; ** - 1% level.

of return to R&D is 59 per cent in this specification. This compares to a 53 per cent estimated social rate of return in Wolff (1997).

The coefficient of RDINDB is now only 0.022 and insignificant. This result contrasts with Wolff (1997), where the coefficient of RDINDB was 0.41 and statistically significant. It now appears that the input measure of embodied R&D, as reflected in RDINDA, overwhelming dominates the sales-embodied R&D measure RDINDB, as originally proposed by Terleckyj. In other words, it appears that the knowledge transmitted by the R&D embodied in an industry's inputs depends on the importance of that input in the production structure of the industry rather than the share of the output of the supplying industry sold to that industry.

The estimated coefficient of TFPINDA is 0.713, smaller than its coefficient in Wolff (1997), and its significance level is 10 per cent, compared to one per cent in Wolff (1997). In contrast, the estimated coefficient of TFPINDB is only 0.064 and not statistically significant.

Table 10.3. Pooled time-series cross-industry regressions of industry TFP growth on R&D intensity, embodied R&D, and embodied TFP growth, 1958–2007

Independent variables	Specification							
	(1)	(2)	(3)	(4)	(5)	(6)	(7)	(8)
Constant	0.0111**	0.0096*	0.0110*	0.0066	0.0107*	0.0059	0.0092#	0.0049
	(2.64)	(2.33)	(2.25)	(1.37)	(2.45)	(1.14)	(1.96)	(0.98)
RDX	0.227**	0.222**	0.227**	0.202*	0.227**	0.254**	0.235**	0.248**
	(2.91)	(2.93)	(2.85)	(2.56)	(2.90)	(3.17)	(2.96)	(3.17)
RDINDA		0.366**						0.350**
		(3.42)						(3.24)
RDINDB			0.022					
			(0.04)					
TFPINDA				0.713#				
				(1.84)				
TFPINDB					0.064			
					(0.42)			
RDKINDA						0.849*		0.768#
						(2.01)		(1.86)
RDKINDB							0.222	
							(1.26)	
DUM6777	−0.0079	−0.0196#	−0.0078	−0.0044	0.0076	−0.0045	−0.0063	−0.0075
	(1.35)	(1.85)	(1.34)	(0.73)	(1.29)	(0.73)	(1.04)	(1.24)
DUM7787	−0.0068	−0.0095#	−0.0067	−0.0047	−0.0067	−0.0045	−0.0053	−0.0075
	(1.16)	(1.66)	(1.10)	(0.80)	(1.15)	(0.75)	(0.88)	(1.26)
DUM8797	−0.0015	−0.0047	−0.0014	−0.0011	0.0016	0.0003	0.0000	−0.0035
	(0.26)	(0.82)	(0.23)	(0.19)	(0.03)	(0.04)	(0.00)	(0.60)
DUM9707	0.0011	0.0012	0.0011	0.0008	0.0013	0.0067	0.0019	0.0052
	(0.18)	(0.20)	(0.18)	(0.13)	(0.20)	(0.81)	(0.29)	(0.79)
R^2	0.0564	0.1070	0.0564	0.0717	0.0573	0.0743	0.0631	0.1205
Adjusted R^2	0.0336	0.0810	0.0290	0.0446	0.0298	0.0466	0.0351	0.0897
Standard error	0.0276	0.0269	0.0276	0.0274	0.0276	0.0276	0.0278	0.0270
Sample size	213	213	213	213	213	208	208	208

Notes: The sample consists of pooled cross-section time-series data, with observations on each of 45 industries in 1958–1967, 1967–1977, 1977–1987, and 1987–1997, and on each of 33 industries in 1997–2007.

Investment by type is not available for the public-administration sector. As a result, the number of sectors is reduced by five when RDKINDA and RDKINDB are used in the regression.

The estimation uses the White procedure for a heteroschedasticity-consistent covariance matrix. The absolute value of the *t*-statistic is in parentheses below the coefficient.

In contrast to Wolff and Nadiri (1993) and Wolff (1997), the coefficient of RDKINDA is 0.849, and is now statistically significant at the 5 per cent level among all industries. On the other hand, the coefficient of RDKINDB is not statistically significant. When both RDINDA and RDKINDA are included together, both remain statistically significant, the former at the 1 per cent level and the latter at the 10 per cent level. The direct rate of return to R&D is now 25 per cent, the indirect return is 35 per cent, and the social rate of return is 60 per cent. However, there is an added return to R&D from that embodied in investment goods. It is perhaps best to think of this added return as the productivity gain per dollar of investment. On the basis of the average investment over the period, this added return to R&D works out to be 0.23 per dollar of investment.

The constant term, which might be interpreted as the pure rate of technological progress, varies from 0.0049 to 0.0110. In my preferred regression, Specification 8, its value is 0.0049, about half a percentage point per year. The period dummy variables are generally not significant. In comparison to the period 1958–1967, the excluded period, the dummy variables generally increase over time. In Specification 8, they rise from -0.0075 for period 1967–1977 to 0.0052 for period 1997–2007. The R^2 statistic ranges from 0.056 to 0.121 and the adjusted R^2 statistic from 0.034 to 0.090. The best fit is provided by Specification 8.

In Table 10.4, the sample of industries is restricted to the 21 manufacturing industries in the data. Whereas in Wolff and Nadiri (1993), both RDX and TFPINDA were found to be statistically significant, in the present application neither RDX nor any of the spillover variables are statistically significant. However, the estimated direct return to R&D is about 11 per cent, about the same as was found in Wolff and Nadiri (1993) within manufacturing.

I next look at whether there is any evidence that the indirect effects of embodied R&D or TFP have increased over time, as speculated in the introduction to the chapter. I use five approaches to analyze this issue. In the first, I use single-period data to estimate the effects of R&D on TFP growth. As shown in the first five columns of Table 10.5, no clear pattern emerges, with the estimated coefficient of RDINDA falling and then rising between subsequent periods. Likewise, the estimated coefficient of RDKINDA also falls and then rises between adjacent periods. In most cases, the coefficients of RDINDA and RDKINDA are insignificant in the single-period estimations. These results, by the way, suggest that for the full pooled time-series cross-industry regressions, most of the explanatory power lies 'within sector' as opposed to 'between sector'.

In the second method, I divide the sample into two periods: 1958–1987 and 1987–2007 (last two columns of Table 10.5). Here, the results are much clearer. The coefficients of both RDINDA and RDKINDA are both larger in the second

Table 10.4. Pooled time-series cross-industry regressions of industry TFP growth on R&D intensity, embodied R&D, and embodied TFP growth, manufacturing industries, 1958–2007

Independent variables	Specification						
	(1)	(2)	(3)	(4)	(5)	(6)	(7)
Constant	0.0190**	0.0181*	0.0121	0.0172*	0.0167*	0.0191#	0.0145#
	(2.77)	(2.59)	(1.42)	(2.09)	(2.37)	(1.80)	(1.76)
RDX	0.110	0.111	0.066	0.112	0.113	0.110	0.103
	(1.15)	(1.15)	(0.65)	(1.16)	(1.18)	(1.13)	(1.07)
RDINDA		0.141					
		(0.60)					
RDINDB			1.469				
			(1.33)				
TFPINDA				0.191			
				(0.38)			
TFPINDB					0.267		
					(1.28)		
RDKINDA						−0.047	
						(0.02)	
RDKINDB							1.744
							(0.97)
DUM6777	−0.0052	−0.0062	−0.0046	−0.0042	−0.0033	−0.0054	−0.0027
	(0.58)	(0.67)	(0.51)	(0.45)	(0.36)	(0.52)	(0.29)
DUM7787	0.0063	−0.0072	−0.0019	−0.0057	−0.0064	−0.0064	−0.0042
	(0.70)	(0.79)	(0.20)	(0.63)	(0.71)	(0.66)	(0.46)
DUM8797	−0.0088	−0.0100	−0.0030	−0.0088	−0.0098	−0.0088	−0.0068
	(0.98)	(1.80)	(0.31)	(0.97)	(1.09)	(0.94)	(0.73)
DUM9707	0.0049	0.0040	0.0064	0.0038	0.0052	0.0037	0.0058
	(0.41)	(0.42)	(0.67)	(0.40)	(0.56)	(0.34)	(0.61)
R^2	0.0363	0.0399	0.0539	0.0378	0.0528	0.0363	0.0458
Adjusted R^2	−0.0139	−0.0207	−0.0059	−0.0229	−0.0070	−0.0245	−0.0144
Standard error	0.0291	0.0292	0.0290	0.0292	0.0290	0.2925	0.0291
Sample size	102	102	102	102	102	102	102

Notes: The sample consists of pooled cross-section time-series data, with observations on each of 21 industries in 1958–1967, 1967–1977, 1977–1987, and 1987–1997, and on each of 18 industries in 1997–2007.

The estimation uses the White procedure for a heteroschedasticity-consistent covariance matrix. The absolute value of the *t*-statistic is in parentheses below the coefficient. Significance levels: # -

Table 10.5. Pooled time-series cross-industry regressions of industry TFP growth on R&D intensity and embodied R&D by selected period, 1958–2007

Independent Variables	Period						
	1958–1967	1967–1977	1977–1987	1987–1997	1997–2007	1958–1987	1987–2007
Constant	0.0071	0.0059	−0.0077	0.0027	−0.0004	0.0072	−0.0051
	(1.35)	(1.05)	(1.14)	(0.35)	(0.03)	(1.57)	(0.65)
RDX	0.120	0.117	0.276	0.073	1.151**	0.157#	0.436**
	(1.15)	(0.73)	(1.49)	(0.39)	(4.14)	(1.89)	(2.69)
RDINDA	0.523	−0.182	0.553**	0.490*	−1.771	0.251*	0.489*
	(0.54)	(0.91)	(2.93)	(2.69)	(0.82)	(2.03)	(2.47)
RDKINDA	0.548	0.448	1.444	0.591	5.409	0.657	1.222
	(1.59)	(0.28)	(1.18)	(0.61)	(1.19)	(1.61)	(1.19)
DUM6777						−0.0073	
						(1.37)	
DUM7787						−0.0071	
						(1.36)	
DUM9707							0.0115
							(1.38)
R^2	0.1000	0.0314	0.2398	0.1621	0.3829	0.0953	0.1642
Adjusted R^2	0.0325	−0.0412	0.1828	0.0992	0.3168	0.0594	0.1171
Standard error	0.0173	0.0239	0.0267	0.0296	0.0320	0.0234	0.0323
Sample size	44	44	44	44	32	93	76

Notes: The sample consists of pooled cross-section time-series data, with observations on each of 45 industries in 1958–1967, 1967–1977, 1977–1987, and 1987–1997, and on each of 33 industries in 1997–2007.
Investment by type is not available for the public-administration sector. As a result, the number of sectors is reduced by one when RDKINDA and RDKINDB are used in the regression.
The estimation uses the White procedure for a heteroschedasticity-consistent covariance matrix. The absolute value of the *t*-statistic is in parentheses below the coefficient.
Significance levels: # - 10% level; * - 5% level; ** - 1% level.

period, as is the coefficient of RDX. The results suggest that spillover effects were stronger in the 'IT period' of 1987–2007 in comparison to 1958–1987. The goodness of fit is also better for the second period, with the R^2 statistic and the adjusted-R^2 statistic considerably higher. However, a Chow test does not indicate that the econometric results of the two periods are statistically different, with a *F*-value of 1.33, significant at only the 0.26 level.

The third method consists of successively adding new periods to the 1958–1967 sample to reach the 1958–2007 sample. As shown in the first five columns of Table 10.6, the coefficient estimates as well as the significance levels of RDX, RDINDA, and RDKINDA generally increase with the addition of each new period. The R^2 statistic and the adjusted-R^2 statistic also tend to increase. These results also suggest a strengthening of the R&D spillover effect over time. The fourth method is to include interactive terms between RDINDA and period dummy variables. As shown in the last column of Table 10.6, the results are inconclusive as to whether the R&D spillover effect has risen over time.

In the fifth method, I decompose average TFP growth over both the 1958–1987 and the 1987–2007 periods using the coefficient estimates shown in the

Table 10.6. Pooled time-series cross-industry regressions of industry TFP growth on R&D intensity and embodied R&D by selected period and with interactive terms, 1958–2007

Independent variables	Period					
	1958–1967	1958–1977	1958–1987	1958–1997	1958–2007	1958–2007
Constant	0.0071	0.0102*	0.0072	0.0071	0.0049	0.0062
	(1.35)	(2.42)	(1.57)	(1.53)	(0.98)	(0.80)
RDX	0.120	0.139	0.157#	0.134#	0.248**	0.257**
	(1.15)	(1.63)	(1.89)	(1.74)	(3.17)	(3.21)
RDINDA	0.523	−0.168	0.251*	0.353**	0.350**	0.022
	(0.54)	(1.01)	(2.03)	(3.54)	(3.24)	(0.02)
RDKINDA	0.548	0.505	0.657	0.637#	0.768#	0.776#
	(1.59)	(1.30)	(1.61)	(1.66)	(1.86)	(1.89)
RDINDA x DUM6777						−0.215
						(0.16)
RDINDA x DUM7787						0.549
						(0.40)
RDINDA x DUM8797						0.472
						(0.35)
RDINDA x DUM9707						0.291
						(0.14)
DUM6777		−0.0048	−0.0073	−0.0082	−0.0075	−0.0024
		(0.99)	(1.37)	(1.46)	(1.24)	(0.27)
DUM7787			0.0071	−0.0079	−0.0075	−0.0115
			(1.36)	(1.45)	(1.26)	(1.33)
DUM8797				−0.0037	−0.0035	−0.0069
				(0.68)	(0.60)	(0.80)
DUM9707					0.0052	0.0039
					(0.79)	(0.35)
R^2	0.1000	0.0890	0.0953	0.1140	0.1205	0.1568
Adjusted R^2	0.0325	0.0451	0.0594	0.0825	0.0897	0.1095
Standard error	0.0173	0.0205	0.0234	0.0249	0.0270	0.0267
Sample size	44	88	132	176	208	208

Notes: The sample consists of pooled cross-section time-series data, with observations on each of 45 industries in 1958–1967, 1967–1977, 1977–1987, and 1987–1997, and on each of 33 industries in 1997–2007.
Investment by type is not available for the public-administration sector. As a result, the number of sectors is reduced by one when RDKINDA and RDKINDB are used in the regression.
The estimation uses the White procedure for a heteroschedasticity-consistent covariance matrix. The absolute value of the *t*-statistic is in parentheses below the coefficient.
Significance levels: # - 10% level; * - 5% level; ** - 1% level.

last two columns of Table 10.5 and the average values of each of the explanatory variables over their respective periods. There is a noticeable increase of average TFP growth between the two periods from 0.89 to 1.39 per cent per year. However, there was a relatively small change in the average values of the explanatory variables between the two periods. The mean value of RDX rose slightly from 0.118 to 0.128, that of RDINDA fell slightly from 0.0093 to 0.0085, and that of RDKINDA also fell somewhat from 0.0039 to 0.0031. The main changes were the sizeable increases in the coefficient values, as we saw above. As a result, whereas RDX accounted for 20.7 per cent of TFP growth in the 1958–1987 period (computed by multiplying the mean value of RDX by its coefficient estimate and then dividing by the mean value of TFP growth), its contribution almost doubled to 40.3 per cent in the 1987–2007 period. In contrast, the contribution of RDINDA rose much less, from 26.0 to 30.1 per cent, and that of RDKINDA actually slipped a bit, from 28.4 to 27.5 per cent. The total contribution of R&D spillovers (the sum of RDINDA and RDKINDA) increased somewhat, from 54.3 to 57.6 per cent.

The first set of regressions as shown in Table 10.3 is now repeated with the variable SCIENG, the number of full-time equivalent scientists and engineers engaged in R&D per 10,000 full-time equivalent employees, substituted for RDX. The results are even stronger with SCIENG. The coefficients of SCIENG are all significant at the one per cent level, with higher t-statistics than the corresponding RDX variable (see Table 10.7). The coefficient estimates and t-statistics of RDINDA and RDKINDA are higher than the corresponding ones in the first set of regressions. In Specification 8, in particular, the coefficient of RDKINDA is now significant at the five per cent level, as opposed to the 10 per cent level in the original regression. The R^2 statistic and the adjusted-R^2 statistic are all substantially higher than the corresponding statistics in the original set of regressions. In the case of Specification 8, the R^2 is now 0.159 as opposed to 0.121. One reason for the better fit provided by SCIENG in comparison to RDX is that there are fewer missing values in the manufacturing industries.[8]

10.5.1. *Linkage measures*

In the last piece of analysis, I consider the effects of TFP growth and R&D intensity on the size of forward linkages. The rationale is that more technologically active industries should acquire new customer industries and expand their ties with existing customer industries. This should show up as both increased values of input coefficients from the innovating industry and a greater number of positive input coefficients from this industry.

Results from Wolff and Nadiri (1993), covering the period from 1947 to 1997, are first shown in Table 10.8. Within the manufacturing sector itself, neither RDX nor TFPGRT showed any statistically significant effect on the size of their industry's LINK1 index. However, among all sectors of the economy,

---

[8] I repeated the same analysis to determine whether there is any evidence that R&D spillover effects had increased over time using SCIENG instead of RDX. The results were virtually the same. The individual period regressions showed no clear pattern. A comparison of regression results from periods 1958–1987 with 1987–2007 showed much higher and more significant coefficients on RDINDA and RDKINDA for the later period. However, once again, the Chow test did not indicate that the two sets of regressions were statistically different. Adding data from successive periods to the 1958–1967 period to reach the full 1958–2007 sample generally showed successively greater and more significant coefficients on RDINDA and RDKINDA as the sample was expanded. Including interactive terms between RDINDA and period dummy variables revealed no clear pattern.

Table 10.7. Pooled time-series cross-industry regressions of industry TFP growth on SCIENG, embodied R&D, and embodied TFP growth, 1958–2007

Independent variables	Specification							
	(1)	(2)	(3)	(4)	(5)	(6)	(7)	(8)
Constant	0.0080*	0.0095*	0.0111*	0.0069	0.0109*	0.0054	0.0092*	0.0043
	(2.27)	(2.36)	(2.22)	(1.45)	(2.58)	(1.10)	(2.03)	(0.89)
SCIENG	0.0332**	0.0394**	0.0389**	0.0361**	0.0388**	0.0423**	0.0394**	0.0427**
	(3.77)	(4.23)	(4.00)	(3.74)	(4.02)	(4.28)	(4.00)	(4.43)
RDINDA		0.378**						0.364**
		(3.61)						(3.44)
RDINDB			0.007					
			(0.01)					
TFPINDA				0.654#				
				(1.72)				
TFPINDB					0.029			
					(0.19)			
RDKINDA						0.925*		0.850*
						(2.23)		(2.10)
RDKINDB							0.223	
							(1.29)	
DUM6777	−0.0047	−0.0110#	−0.0082	−0.0050	−0.0081	−0.0046	−0.0067	−0.0077
	(0.90)	(1.97)	(1.43)	(0.84)	(1.40)	(0.76)	(1.12)	(1.29)
DUM7787	−0.0042	−0.0107#	−0.0079	−0.0059	−0.0078	0.0056	−0.0065	−0.0086
	(0.81)	(1.91)	(1.32)	(1.02)	(1.37)	(0.94)	(1.09)	(1.48)
DUM8797	−0.0047	−0.0073	−0.0040	−0.0034	−0.0040	−0.0029	−0.0025	−0.0063
	(0.81)	(1.29)	(0.65)	(0.59)	(0.70)	(0.49)	(0.42)	(1.09)
DUM9707	−0.0090	−0.0100	−0.0100	−0.0095	−0.0099	−0.0067	−0.0098	−0.0071
	(1.52)	(1.52)	(1.47)	(1.40)	(1.45)	(0.96)	(1.40)	(1.03)
R^2	0.0805	0.1441	0.0900	0.1029	0.0902	0.1090	0.0944	0.1588
Adjusted R^2	0.0628	0.1192	0.0635	0.0768	0.0637	0.0824	0.0674	0.1294
Standard error	0.0272	0.0263	0.0271	0.0269	0.0271	0.0271	0.0273	0.0263
Sample size	213	213	213	213	213	208	208	208

Notes: The sample consists of pooled cross-section time-series data, with observations on each of 45 industries in 1958–1967, 1967–1977, 1977–1987, and 1987–1997, and on each of 33 industries in 1997–2007.

Investment by type is not available for the public-administration sector. As a result, the number of sectors is reduced by five when RDKINDA and RDKINDB are used in the regression.

The estimation uses the White procedure for a heteroschedasticity-consistent covariance matrix. The absolute value of the t-statistic is in parentheses below the coefficient.

Table 10.8. The effect of R&D intensity and productivity growth on forward-linkage structure, 1947–1977

Independent variables	Dependent variable						
	LINK1	LINK1	LINK1	LINK1	LINK2	LINK2	LINK3
Constant	0.0122*	0.0123**	0.0093**	0.0094**	1.957**	1.986**	2.437**
	(13.01)	(6.78)	(16.17)	(7.76)	(31.52)	(15.14)	(32.43)
RDX	0.031		0.081*		6.594*		6.835#
	(1.09)		(2.86)		(2.15)		(1.84)
TFPGRRT		−0.011		0.042*		3.961**	
		(0.02)		(2.59)		(2.24)	
R^2	0.013	0.007	0.032	0.028	0.018	0.021	0.013
Adjusted R^2	0.002	0.000	0.028	0.008	0.014	0.017	0.010
Standard error	0.0075	0.0077	0.0085	0.0086	0.921	0.927	1.114
Sample	Manuf.	Manuf.	All	All	All	All	All
Sample size	95	95	250	250	250	250	250

Source: Wolff and Nadiri (1993).

Notes: The sample consists of pooled cross-section time-series data, with observations on each of 19 (or 50) industries in 1947–1958, 1958–1963, 1963–1967, 1967–1972, and 1972–1977.
Significance levels: # – 10% level; * – 5% level; ** – 1% level.

Table 10.9. The effect of R&D intensity and productivity growth on forward-linkage structure, 1958–2007

Independent variables	Dependent variable					
	LINK1	LINK1	LINK2	LINK2	LINK3	LINK3
Constant	0.0105**	0.0097**	1.608**	1.574**	2.137**	2.180**
	(13.41)	(12.86)	(36.72)	(36.89)	(26.11)	(27.51)
RDX	−0.033		−0.022		0.017	
	(1.19)		(1.43)		(0.59)	
TFPGRT		0.025		0.430		−1.698
		(1.00)		(0.31)		(0.65)
R^2	0.007	0.005	0.010	0.001	0.002	0.002
Adjusted R^2	0.002	0.000	0.005	−0.005	−0.003	−0.003
Standard error	0.0097	0.0968	0.5437	0.5464	1.016	1.015
Sample size	213	213	213	213	213	213

Notes: The sample consists of pooled cross-section time-series data, with observations on each of 45 industries in 1958–1967, 1967–1977, 1977–1987, and 1987–1997, and on each of 33 industries in 1997–2007.
See text for definitions of LINK1, LINK2, and LINK3.
Significance levels: # - 10% level; * - 5% level; ** - 1% level.

both RDX and TFPGRT were positively and significantly associated with higher values of both LINK1 and LINK2, and RDX (although not TFPGRT) was positively and significantly related to LINK3. The early results clearly indicated a positive relation between the degree of technological activity of a sector and its degree of forward linkage.

New results, for the 1958–2007 period, are shown in Table 10.9. Neither RDX nor TFPGRT have a significant relation to LINK1. Indeed, the estimated coefficient of RDX is negative. Results are quite similar for the linkage measure LINK2. In the case of LINK3, both RDX and TFPGRT are again statistically insignificant but in this case the estimated coefficient of RDX is positive and that of TFPGRT is negative. The apparent reason why neither RDX nor TFPGRT bear any significant relationship to forward linkages is that the forward linkages themselves remain almost unchanged over time (see Table A10.2 in the appendix).

10.6. Conclusion

I speculated at the outset of the study that technological spillover effects may have become more important over time as IT penetrated the US economy. The rationale is that IT may speed up the process of knowledge transfer and make these knowledge spillovers more effective.

I estimated first of all that the direct rate of return to R&D is 22 per cent and the indirect rate of return to R&D (RDINDA) is 37 per cent. The rate of return to R&D estimates are higher than in my previous studies. The indirect rate of

Table 10.10. Summary of findings from earlier studies and current study on R&D intensity, embodied R&D, and embodied TFP growth, 1947–1977

Independent variables	Wolff and Nadiri (1993)[a]	Wolff and Nadiri (1993)[a]	Wolff (1997)[b]	Current Study[c]	Current Study[d]
RDX	Signif. at 5% level	Signif. at 5% level	Signif. at 1% level	Signif. at 1% or 5% level	Not Signif.
SCIENG			Signif. at 1% level	Signif. at 1% level	
RDINDA	Not Signif.	Not Signif.	Signif. at 10% level	Signif. at 1% level	Not Signif.
RDKINDA	Not Signif.	Signif. at 10% level		Signif. at 5% or 10% level	Not Signif.
TFPINDA	Signif. at 5% level	Not Signif.	Signif. at 1% level	Signif. at 10% level	Not Signif.
RDINDB			Signif. at 10% level	Not Signif.	Not Signif.
TFPINDB			Not Signif.	Not Signif.	Not Signif.
RDKINDB				Not Signif.	Not Signif.
Sample	Manufacturing	All Industries	All Industries	All Industries	Manufacturing
Sample size	95	95	204	213	102

Notes: [a] The sample consists of pooled cross-section time-series data, with observations on each of 19 (or 50) industries in 1947–1958, 1958–1963, 1963–1967, 1967–1972, and 1972–1977. [b] The sample consists of pooled cross-section time-series data, with observations on each of 68 industries in 1958–1967, 1967–1977, and 1977–1987. [c] The sample consists of pooled cross-section time-series data, with observations on each of 45 industries in 1958–1967, 1967–1977, 1977–1987, and 1987–1997, and on each of 33 industries in 1997–2007. [d] The sample consists of pooled cross-section time-series data, with observations on each of 21 industries in 1958–1967, 1967–1977, 1977–1987, and 1987–1997, and on each of 18 industries in 1997–2007.

return to R&D is now significant at the one per cent level, in comparison to insignificant coefficients in Wolff and Nadiri (1993) and a 10 per cent significance level in Wolff (1997). (See also Table 10.10 for a comparison of results from the current study with those from the older two studies.) The newly estimated social rate of return to R&D is 59 per cent, and this compares to a 53 per cent social rate of return estimated in Wolff (1997).

In contrast to Wolff and Nadiri (1993) and Wolff (1997), the coefficients of R&D embodied in new investment (RDKINDA) are now statistically significant at the 5 per cent level among all industries and the coefficient estimates are higher. When both RDINDA and RDKINDA are included together, both remain statistically significant, the former at the 1 per cent level and the latter at the 10 per cent level. The direct rate of return to R&D is now 25 per cent, the indirect return is 35 per cent, and the social rate of return is 60 per cent. There is also an added return to R&D from that embodied in investment goods, which I estimate at 0.23 per dollar of investment. All in all, the direct and indirect returns to R&D are at least as high in the later period as estimated here as in the earlier periods as estimated in Wolff and Nadiri (1993) and Wolff (1997).

Separate regressions on the 1958–1987 and the 1987–2007 periods and the addition of successive periods to the sample also suggest a strengthening of the R&D-spillover effect over time, particularly as between the 1958–1987 and the 1987–2007 periods. The coefficient estimates as well as the significance levels of RDX, RDINDA, and RDKINDA generally increase with the addition of each new period, as do the R^2 and the adjusted-R^2 statistics. A decomposition of TFP growth in the two periods also indicated a higher contribution from R&D spillovers in the later period than the earlier one. These results suggest a strengthening of the R&D-spillover effect over time, as I speculated in the introduction to the study.

Direct TFP spillovers (TFPINDA) now appear to be less important than in Wolff and Nadiri (1993) and Wolff (1997). The coefficient estimates and significance levels are smaller than in the prior work. Moreover, in contrast to the earlier work, R&D spillovers now appear to be more important than direct TFP spillovers (as gauged by the significance level of the respective coefficients).

In contrast to Wolff and Nadiri (1993), no statistically significant relation now appears between forward linkages and either RDX or TFPGRT. The apparent reason is that in this application, measures of forward linkages are relatively unchanged over time.

Appendix

Table A10.1. Classification of 45-sector schema and concordance with the BEA 85-order input-output sectors

45-Sector Classification		BEA 85-Order Codes[a]	1987 SIC Codes
Number	Name		
1	Agriculture, forestry, and fishing	1–4	01–09
2	Metal mining	5–6	10
3	Coal mining	7	11,12
4	Oil and gas extraction	8	13
5	Mining of nonmetallic minerals, except fuels	9–10	14
6	Construction	11,12	15–17
7	Food and kindred products	14	20
8	Tobacco products	15	21
9	Textile mill products	16–17	22
10	Apparel and other textile products	18–19	23
11	Lumber and wood products	20–21	24
12	Furniture and fixtures	22–23	25
13	Paper and allied products	24–25	26
14	Printing and publishing	26	27
15	Chemicals and allied products	27–30	28

16	Petroleum and coal products	31	29
17	Rubber and miscellaneous plastic products	32	30
18	Leather and leather products	33–34	31
19	Stone, clay, and glass products	35–36	32
20	Primary metal products	37–38	33
21	Fabricated metal products, including ordnance	13,39–42	34
22	Industrial machinery and equipment, except electrical	43–52	35
23	Electric and electronic equipment	53–58	36
24	Motor vehicles and equipment	59	371
25	Other transportation equipment	60–61	37
26	Instruments and related products	62–63	38
27	Miscellaneous manufactures	64	39
28	Transportation	65	40–42,44–47
29	Telephone and telegraph	66	481,482,489
30	Radio and TV broadcasting	67	483,484
31	Electric, gas, and sanitary services	68	49
32	Wholesale trade	69A	50–51
33	Retail trade	69B,74	52–59
34	Banking: credit and investment companies	70A	60–62,67
35	Insurance	70B	63–64
36	Real estate	71B	65–66
37	Hotels, motels, and lodging places	72A	70
38	Personal services	72[part]	72
39	Business and repair services except Auto	73C, 72[part]	73,76
40	Auto services and repair	75	75
41	Amusement and recreation services	76	78–79
42	Health services, including hospitals	77A	80
43	Educational services	77B[part]	82
44	Legal and other professional services and non-profit organizations	73A,73B, 77B[part]	81,83,84,86 87,89
45	Public administration	78,79,84	43[b]

Notes: [a] Bureau of Economic Analysis 85-sector industrial classification system for input-output data (1987 version).
[b] US postal service only.

Table A10.2. Mean values and standard deviations of variables by time period

Variables	Time period					
	1958–2007	1958–1967	1967–1977	1977–1987	1987–1997	1997–2007
TFPGRT						
1. Mean	0.0107	0.0140	0.0058	0.0071	0.0126	0.0151
2. Std. Dev.	0.0280	0.0175	0.0232	0.0292	0.0309	0.0383
3. (Sample size)	(213)	(45)	(45)	(45)	(45)	(33)
RDX						
1. Mean	0.0122	0.0124	0.0111	0.0119	0.0131	0.0125
2. Std. Dev.	0.0243	0.0287	0.0232	0.0225	0.0249	0.0221
3. (Sample size)	(213)	(45)	(45)	(45)	(45)	(33)
SCIENG						
1. Mean	13.8	7.3	7.5	9.9	14.0	36.0
2. Std. Dev.	21.8	11.4	11.5	15.5	22.5	33.3

(Continued)

Table A10.2 Continued

Variables	Time period					
	1958–2007	1958–1967	1967–1977	1977–1987	1987–1997	1997–2007
3. (Sample size)	(213)	(45)	(45)	(45)	(45)	(33)
RDINDA						
1. Mean	0.0092	0.0043	0.0117	0.0118	0.0131	0.0040
2. Std. Dev.	0.0177	0.0032	0.0186	0.0217	0.0245	0.0028
3. (Sample size)	(213)	(45)	(45)	(45)	(45)	(33)
RDINDB						
1. Mean	0.0033	0.0049	0.0037	0.0017	0.0011	0.0056
2. Std. Dev.	0.0040	0.0053	0.0025	0.0012	0.0008	0.0060
3. (Sample size)	(213)	(45)	(45)	(45)	(45)	(33)
TFPINDA						
1. Mean	0.0051	0.0068	0.0019	0.0039	0.0062	0.0072
2. Std. Dev.	0.0053	0.0048	0.0045	0.0047	0.0047	0.0064
3. (Sample size)	(213)	(45)	(45)	(45)	(45)	(33)
TFPINDB						
1. Mean	0.0060	0.0071	0.0023	0.0062	0.0090	0.0054
2. Std. Dev.	0.0128	0.0104	0.0108	0.0146	0.0148	0.0121
3. (Sample size)	(213)	(45)	(45)	(45)	(45)	(33)
RDKINDA						
1. Mean	0.0037	0.0062	0.0021	0.0034	0.0047	0.0016
2. Std. Dev.	0.0049	0.0078	0.0024	0.0035	0.0048	0.0013
3. (Sample size)	(208)	(44)	(44)	(44)	(44)	(32)
RDKINDB						
1. Mean	0.0048	0.0096	0.0021	0.0025	0.0027	0.0080
2. Std. Dev.	0.0115	0.0213	0.0024	0.0023	0.0023	0.0128
3. (Sample size)	(208)	(44)	(44)	(44)	(44)	(32)
LINK1						
1. Mean	0.0100	0.0095	0.0095	0.0096	0.0095	0.0128
2. Std. Dev.	0.0097	0.0084	0.0084	0.0086	0.0090	0.0141
3. (Sample size)	(196)	(41)	(41)	(41)	(41)	(32)
LINK2						
1. Mean	1.557	1.573	1.578	1.576	1.562	1.493
2. Std. Dev.	0.546	0.499	0.507	0.523	0.535	0.671
3. (Sample size)	(205)	(41)	(41)	(41)	(41)	(41)
LINK3						
1. Mean	2.114	2.244	2.185	2.126	2.105	1.910
2. Std. Dev.	1.019	1.152	1.075	1.016	0.990	0.856
3. (Sample size)	(205)	(41)	(41)	(41)	(41)	(41)

Notes: The sample consists of pooled cross-section time-series data, with observations on each of 45 industries in 1958–1967, 1967–1977, 1977–1987, and 1987–1997, and on each of 33 industries in 1997–2007. Investment by type is not available for the public-administration sector. As a result, the number of sectors is reduced by five when RDKINDA and RDKINDB are used in the regression.

References

Acharta, R.C. and Keller, W. (2008), 'Estimating the productivity selection and technology spillover effects of imports', NBER Working Paper No. 14079, October.

Adams, J.D. and Jaffe, A.B. (1996), 'Bounding the effects of R&D: Investigation using matched establishment-firm data', *RAND Journal of Economics*, 27: 700–721.

Bartelsman, E.J., Cabbalero, R.J. and Lyons, R.K (1991), 'Short and long run externalities', NBER Working Paper No. 3810, August.

Bernstein, J.I. and Nadiri, M.I. (1989), 'Research and development and intra-industry spillovers: An empirical application of dynamic duality', *Review of Economic Studies*, 56: 249–269.

Brown, M. and Conrad, A. (1967), 'The influence of research on CES production relations'. In Brown, M. (ed.), *The Theory and Empirical Analysis of Production, Studies in Income and Wealth*, Vol. 3. New York: Columbia University Press for the NBER.

Cameron, G. (1996), 'Innovation and economic growth', London School of Economics Centre for Economic Performance Discussion Paper No. 277.

Coe, D.T. and Helpman, E. (1995), 'International R&D spillovers', *European Economic Review*, 39: 859–887.

Eaton, J. and Kortum, S. (1996), 'Trade in ideas: Patenting and productivity in the OECD', *Journal of International Economics*, 40: 251–278.

—— (1999), 'International patenting and technology diffusion: Theory and measurement', *International Economic Review*, 40: 537–570.

Griliches, Z. (1979), 'Issues in assessing the contribution of research and development to productivity growth', *Bell Journal of Economics*, 10: 92–116.

—— (1980), 'R&D and the productivity slowdown', *American Economic Review*, 70: 343–347.

—— (1992), 'The search for R&D spillovers', *Scandinavian Journal of Economics*, 94: 29–47.

Jaffe, A.B. (1986), 'Technology opportunity and spillovers of R&D: Evidence from firms' patents, profits, and market value', *American Economic Review*, 76: 984–1001.

——, Trajtenberg, M. and Henderson, R. (1993), 'Geographic localization of knowledge spillovers as evidenced by patent citations', *Quarterly Journal of Economics*, 108: 577–598.

Katz, A.J. and Herman, S.W. (1997), 'Improved estimates of fixed reproducible tangible wealth, 1929–95', *Survey of Current Business*, May: 69–92.

Keller, W. (1998), 'Are international R&D spillovers trade related? Analyzing spillovers among randomly matched trade partners', *European Economic Review*, 42: 1469–1481.

—— (2002), 'Geographic localization of international technology diffusion', *American Economic Review*, 92(1): 120–142.

Kop Jansen, P. and ten Raa, T. (1990), 'The choice of model in the construction of input-output matrices', *International Economic Review*, 31: 213–227.

Lawson, A.M. (1997), 'Benchmark input-output accounts for the U.S. economy, 1992', *Survey of Current Business*, 77: 36–83.

—— and Teske, D.A. (1994), 'Benchmark input-output accounts for the U.S. economy', *Survey of Current Business*, April 1: 73–115.

Leontief, W. (1953), *Studies in the Structure of the American Economy, 1919–29*. New York: Oxford University Press.

Lychagin, S., Pinske, J., Slade, M.E. and Van Reenen, J. (2010), 'Spillovers in space: Does geography matter?' NBER Working Paper No. 16188, July.

Maddison, A. (1982), *Phases of Capitalist Development*. Oxford: Oxford University Press.

Madsen, J.B. (2007), 'Technology spillover through trade and TFP convergence: 135 years of evidence for the OECD countries', *Journal of International Economics*, 72: 464–480.

Mairesse, J. and Mohnen, P. (1990), 'Rechereche-développement et productivité: Un sorvol de la littérature économétrique', *Economie et Statistique*, 237–238: 99–108.

Mansfield, E. (1980), 'Basic research and productivity increase in manufacturing', *American Economic Review*, 70(5): 863–873.

Mohnen, P. (1990), 'New technology and interindustry spillovers', *Science/Technology/ Industry Review*, 7: 131–147.

—— (1992), *The Relationship between R&D and Productivity Growth in Canada and Other Major Industrialized Countries*. Ottawa: Canada Communications Group.

Nelson, R.R. and Winters, S.G. (1982), *Evolutionary Theory of Economic Change*. Cambridge, MA: Harvard University Press.

Oppenlander, K.M. and Schulz, L. (1981), 'Innovation test: A new survey of the IFO Institute', paper presented at the 15th CIRET Conference, Athens, Greece.

Orlando, M.J. (2004), 'Measuring spillovers from industrial R&D: On the importance of geographic and technological proximity', *RAND Journal of Economics*, 35: 777–786.

Ornaghi, C. (2006), 'Spillovers in product and process innovation: Evidence from manufacturing firms', *International Journal of Industrial Organization*, 24: 349–380.

Park, W.G. (1995), 'International R&D spillovers and OECD economic growth', *Economic Inquiry*, 23: 571–591.

Pavitt, K. (1984), 'Sectoral patterns of technical change: Towards a taxonomy and theory', *Research Policy*, 13: 343–373.

Rosenberg, N. (1982), *Inside the Black Box: Technology and Economics*. Cambridge: Cambridge University Press.

—— and Frischtak, C.R. (1984), 'Technological innovation and long waves', *Cambridge Journal of Economics*, 8: 7–24.

Scherer, F.M. (1982), 'Interindustry technology flows and productivity growth', *Review of Economics and Statistics*, 64: 627–634.

Sjöholm, F. (1996), 'International transfer of knowledge: The role of international trade and geographic proximity', *Weltwirtschaftliches Archiv*, 132: 97–115.

Terleckyj, N.W. (1974), *Effects of R&D on the Productivity Growth of Industries: An Exploratory Study*. Washington, DC: National Planning Association.

—— (1980), 'Direct and indirect effects of industrial research and development on the productivity growth of industries'. In J.W. Kendrick and B. Vaccara (eds), *New Developments in Productivity Measurement*. New York: National Bureau of Economic Research.

US Interindustry Economics Division (1974), 'The input-output structure of the U.S. economy, 1967', *Survey of Current Business*, 54(2): 24–56.

—— (1984), 'The input-output structure of the U.S. economy, 1977', *Survey of Current Business*, 64(5): 42–84.

Verspagen, B. (1997), 'Estimating international technology spillovers using technology flow matrices', *Weltwirtschaftliches*, 133(2): 226–248.

Wolff, E.N. (1997), 'Spillovers, linkages, and technical change', *Economic Systems Research*, 9(1): 9–23.

—— and Nadiri, M.I. (1993), 'Spillover effects, linkage structure, and research and development', *Structural Change and Economic Dynamics*, 4(2): 315–331.

Xu, B. and Wang, J. (1999), 'Capital goods trade and R&D spillovers in the OECD', *Canadian Journal of Economics*, 32: 1258.

11

R&D Spillovers, Entrepreneurship, and Growth[1]

Zoltan J. Acs

11.1. Introduction

The purpose of this chapter is to catalogue the contribution of Jaffe-Feldman-Varga that simultaneously and independently sparked a search for the mechanism of knowledge spillovers. David B. Audretsch and Zoltan J. Acs were attracted to the economics of technological change by innovative prowls of new technology-based firms in the 1980s. While the conventional wisdom held that large firms had an innovative advantage over small firms, in a 1988 article in the *American Economic Review* they discovered an anomaly instead of solving a problem:

> A perhaps somewhat surprising result is that not only is the coefficient of the large-firm employment share positive and significant for small-firm innovations, but it is actually greater in magnitude than for large firms. This suggests that, *ceteris paribus*, the greater extent to which an industry is composed of large firms, the greater will be the innovative activity, but that increased innovative activity will tend to emanate more from the small firms than from the large firms. (Acs and Audretsch, 1988: 686)

The anomaly of where new technology-based start-ups acquire knowledge was unresolved. Building on the work of Griliches (1979), Adam Jaffe (1989) was the first to identify the extent to which university research spills over into the generation of commercial activity. Building on Jaffe's work, Maryann Feldman

[1] Originally published as Zoltan J. Acs (2011), 'Innovation, Entrepreneurship and the Search for Knowledge Spillovers'. In Audretsch, D., Falck, O., Heblich, S. and Lederer, A. (eds), *Handbook of Research on Innovation and Entrepreneurship*. Cheltenham: Edward Elgar. With kind permission of Edward Elgar.

(1994) at Carnegie Mellon University expanded the knowledge production function to innovative activity and incorporated aspects of the regional knowledge infrastructure. Attila Varga (1998) at West Virginia University extends the Jaffe-Feldman approach by focusing on a more precise measure of local geographic spillovers. Varga approaches the issue of knowledge spillovers from an explicit spatial econometric perspective. The Jaffe-Feldman-Varga spillovers (henceforth JFV) go a long way towards explaining the role of knowledge spillovers in technological change. Building on this foundation, the model was recently extended to identify entrepreneurship as a conduit through which knowledge spillovers take place (Acs, Audretsch, Braunerhjelm and Carlsson, 2009). Finally, the role of agglomerations in knowledge spillovers represents the frontier in this scientific revolution (Clark, Feldman and Gertler, 2000). The purpose of this chapter is to catalogue the contribution of JFV—two of them my students—that simultaneously and independently sparked a search for the mechanism of knowledge spillovers.

Section 11.2 outlines the main contributions of Jaffe, Feldman, and Varga. Section 11.3 examines extensions of the model by Jaffe, Trajtenberg, and Henderson as well as recent criticisms of the model by Thomson and Fox-Kean. Section 11.4 examines spatialized explanations of economic growth by Acs and Varga; Fujita, Krugman, and Venables; and Romer. Section 11.5 presents work on the knowledge-spillover theory of entrepreneurship. Section 11.6 discusses agglomerations with policy discussed in Section 11.7. Conclusions are in the final section.

11.2. Jaffe-Feldman-Varga

In his 1989 paper in the *American Economic Review*, Adam Jaffe extended his trailblazing 1986 study measuring the total R&D pool available for spillovers to identify the contribution of spillovers from university research to commercial innovation. Jaffe's findings were the first identifying the extent to which university research spills over into the generation of inventions and innovations by private firms. In order to relate the response of this measure to R&D spillovers from universities, Jaffe modifies the 'knowledge-production function' introduced by Zvi Griliches (1979) for two inputs: private corporate expenditures on R&D and research expenditures undertaken at universities.

Essentially, this is a two-factor Cobb-Douglas production function that relates an output measure for 'knowledge' to two input measures: research and development performed by industry; and research performed by universities. Formally, this is expressed as:

$$\log(K) = \beta_{k1}\log(R) + \beta_{k2}\log(U) + \epsilon_k \tag{1}$$

where K is a proxy for knowledge measured by patent counts, R is industry R&D, and U is university research, with ϵ_K as a stochastic error term. The analysis is carried out for US states for several points in time and disaggregated by sector. The potential interaction between university and industry research is captured by extending the model with two additional equations that allow for simultaneity between these two variables:

$$\log(R) = \beta_{R1}\log(U) + \beta_{R2}Z_2 + \epsilon_R \tag{2}$$

and

$$\log(U) = \beta_{U1}\log(R) + \beta_{U2}Z_1 + U \tag{3}$$

where U and R are as before, Z_1 and Z_2 are sets of exogenous local characteristics, and ϵ_R and ϵ_U are stochastic error terms.

Jaffe's statistical results provide evidence that corporate patent activity responds positively to commercial spillovers from university research. The lack of evidence that geographic proximity within the state matters clouds results concerning the role of geographic proximity in spillovers from university research. According to Jaffe (1989: 968), 'there is only weak evidence that spillovers are facilitated by geographic coincidence of universities and research labs within the state'. In other words, we know very little where knowledge spillovers go.

Maryann Feldman expands on the work of Jaffe in two ways (Acs, Audretsch and Feldman, 1992, 1994; Feldman 1994; Feldman and Florida, 1994). First, she uses a new data source—a literature-based innovation-output indicator developed by the US Small Business Administration that directly measures innovative activity (Acs and Audretsch, 1988) and extends the knowledge-production function (Jaffe, 1989) to account for tacit knowledge and commercialization linkages.

Griliches (1979) introduced a model of technological innovation which views innovative output as the product of knowledge-generating inputs. Jaffe (1989) modified this production-function approach to consider spatial and technical area dimensions. However, Jaffe's model only considers what were previously defined as the elements of the formal knowledge base. Such a formulation does not consider other types of knowledge inputs, which contribute to the realization of innovative output. This is important since innovation requires both technical and business knowledge if profitability is to be the guide for making investments in research and development. Following the innovation-knowledge-base conceptual model, a more complete specification of innovative inputs would include

$$\log(K) = \beta_{K1}\log(R) + \beta_{K2}\log(U) + \beta_{K3}\log(BSERV) + \beta_{K4}\log(VA) + \epsilon_K \qquad (4)$$

where K is measured by counts of innovations, and R and U are as before. VA is the tacit knowledge embodied by the industry's presence in an area $BSERV$ stands for the presence of business services that represents a link to commercialization.

The last input in the knowledge-base model is the most evasive. There are a variety of producer services that provide knowledge to the market and the commercialization process. For example, the services of patent lawyers are a critical input to the innovation process. Similarly, marketing information plays an important role in the commercialization process.

Substitution of the direct measure of innovative activity for the patent measure in the knowledge-production function generally strengthens Jaffe's (1989) arguments and reinforces his findings. Most importantly, use of the innovation data provides even greater support than was found by Jaffe: as he predicted, spillovers are facilitated by the geographic coincidence of universities and research labs within the state. In addition, there is at least some evidence that, because the patent and innovation measures capture different aspects of the process of technological change, results for specific sectors may be, at least to some extent, influenced by the technological regime. Thus, it is found that the importance of university spillovers relative to private-company R&D spending is considerably greater in the electronics sector when the direct measure of innovative activity is substituted for the patent measure.

However, the relative importance of industry R&D and university research as inputs in generating innovative output clearly varies between large and small firms (Acs, Audretsch and Feldman, 1994). That is, for large firms, not only is the elasticity of innovative activity with respect to industry R&D expenditures more than two times greater than the elasticity with respect to expenditures on research by universities, but it is nearly twice as large as the elasticity of small-firm innovative activity with respect to industry R&D. By contrast, for small firms the elasticity of innovative output with respect to expenditures on research by universities is about one-fifth greater than the elasticity with respect to industry R&D. Moreover, the elasticity of innovative activity with respect to university research is about fifty per cent greater for small enterprises than for large corporations.

These results support the hypothesis that private-company R&D plays a relatively more important role in generating innovative activity in large corporations than in small firms. By contrast, spillovers from the research activities of universities play a more decisive role in the innovative activity of small firms. Geographic proximity between university and corporate laboratories within a state clearly serves as a catalyst to innovative activity for firms of all sizes. However, the impact is apparently greater on small firms than on large firms.

There were two limitations of the Jaffe-Feldman research. First, the unit of analysis at the state level was too aggregate, requiring a geographical coincidence index to control for co-location. Second, the research did not take into consideration the potential influence of spatial dependence that may invalidate the interpretation of econometric analyses based on contiguous cross-sectional data.

Attila Varga mitigates these limitations examining both the state and the metropolitan statistical area (MSA) levels and using spatial econometric techniques[2] (Anselin, Varga and Acs, 1997, 2000a, 2000b; Varga, 1998, 2000; Acs, Anselin and Varga, 2002). These extensions yielded a more precise insight into the range of spatial externalities between innovation and R&D in the MSA and university research both within the MSA and in surrounding counties. He was able to shed some initial light on this issue for high-technology innovations measured as an aggregate across five two-digit SIC industries and also at a more detailed industrial-sector level. He found a positive and highly significant relationship between MSA innovations and university research indicating the presence of localized university research spillovers in innovation. In comparison to the effect of industrial knowledge spillovers (i.e. knowledge flows among industrial research laboratories), the size of the university effect is considerably smaller as it is one-third of the size of the industrial research coefficient. University knowledge spillovers follow a definite distance-decay pattern as shown by the statistically significant albeit smaller size university research coefficient for adjoining counties within a 50-mile distance range from the MSA center.

There are notable differences among sectors with respect to the localized university effect as studied at the MSA level. Specifically, for the four high-technology sectors machinery, chemicals, electronics, and instruments, significant localized university spillover impact was found only for electronics and instruments, while for the other two industries the university research coefficient remains consistently insignificant.

Acs, Anselin and Varga (2002) test whether the patent data developed by the United States Patent and Trademark Office is, in fact, a reliable proxy measure of innovative activity at the regional level as compared to the literature-based innovation-output indicator developed by the US Small Business Administration. This is important, since the patent data are readily available over time and can be used to study the dynamics of localized knowledge flows within

---

[2] When models are estimated for cross-sectional data on neighboring spatial units, the lack of independence across these units (or, the presence of spatial autocorrelation) can cause serious problems of model misspecification when ignored (Anselin, 1988). The methodology of spatial econometrics consists of testing for the potential presence of these misspecifications and of using the proper estimators for models that incorporate the spatial dependence explicitly (for a recent review, see Anselin, 2001).

regional innovation systems. Before this study, there was some evidence that patents provide a reliable measure of innovative activity at the industry level (Acs and Audretsch, 1989) and some evidence that patents and innovations behave similarly at the state level (Acs, Audretsch and Feldman, 1992). However, this had not been tested at the sub-state level.

The correlation between the PTO patent and SBA innovation counts at the MSA level is reasonably high (0.79) and this could be taken as a first indication that patents might be a reliable measure of innovation at the regional level. However, this correlation coefficient value is not high enough to guarantee that the role of different regional actors in knowledge creation would turn out to be similar with both measures if applied in the same empirical model. Varga proceeds by replacing innovation counts with the patent measure in the same model as in Anselin, Varga and Acs (1997) in order to directly compare the results of the two measures of new technological knowledge and assess the extent to which patents may be used as a reliable proxy.

Sizes of all the parameters in the estimated knowledge-production function are smaller for innovation than for patents, suggesting that firms in the product-development stage rely on localized interactions (with universities as well as with other actors) less intensively than in earlier stages of the innovation process. The other important finding of this comparative study is that the importance of university knowledge spillovers (measured by the size of the university research parameter) compared to that of R&D spillovers among private firms is substantially less pronounced for patents than for innovations. Since patenting reflects more the earlier stages of innovation whereas the direct innovation measure accounts for the concluding stage of the innovation process, the relatively higher weight of local universities in innovation than in patenting appears to reflect the different spatial patterns of basic and applied research collaboration. To collaborate with universities in applied research, firms tend to choose local academic institutions, whereas basic research collaboration can be carried out over larger distances.

11.3. Extensions of the JFV model

Jaffe, Trajtenberg and Henderson (1993, 2005) expand on the above work to answer the question of whether knowledge externalities are localized. This is important since growth theory assumed that knowledge spills over to agents within the country, but not to other countries. This implicit assumption poses the question to what extent knowledge externalities are localized. Jaffe, Trajtenberg, and Henderson extend the search for knowledge spillovers by using a matching method that found that knowledge spillovers are strongly localized. Their method matches each citing patent to a non-citing patent intended to control for the pre-existing geographic concentration of production. Using patent data, they came to two conclusions: that spillovers are particularly significant at the local level, and that localization fades slowly over time. These results and the large research issue are reproduced in Jaffe and Trajtenberg (2002).

Audretsch and Feldman (1996) explore the question of the geography of innovation and production. They provide evidence concerning the spatial dimension of knowledge spillovers. Their findings suggest that knowledge spillovers are geographically bounded and localized within spatial proximity to the knowledge source. Feldman and Audretsch (1999) further examine the question of knowledge spillovers by looking into the question of specialization versus industrial diversity in cities. Their research supports the idea that diversity leads to more innovation.

Recently, Thompson and Fox-Kean (2005a and 2005b) challenged the findings of Jaffe, Trajtenberg, and Henderson. They suggest that Jaffe, Trajtenberg, and Henderson's method—matched case-control methodology—included a serious spurious component. Controlling for unobservables using matching methods is invariably a dangerous exercise because one can rarely be confident that the controls are doing their job. In some cases, imperfect matching may simply introduce noise and a corresponding loss of efficiency. They suggest at least two reasons why the matching method may not adequately control for existing patent activity. First, the level of aggregation might not be fine enough. Second, patents typically contain many distinct claims, each of which is assigned a technological classification. These two features of the control selection process mean that there is no guarantee that the control patent has any industrial similarity with either the citing or originating patent. Of course, their conclusion that spillovers stop at the country level also needs explaining.

Empirical research done within the JFV framework and the extensions introduced so far were established and originally carried out in the United States with the use of state, MSA, and county-level data sets. However, the issue of the geographic extent of knowledge spillovers has definite international validity. The JFV model has been replicated and continually refined in the search for the geographical boundaries of knowledge flows in Europe, South America, and Asia. Varga (2006) provides an assessment of the international literature.

11.4. The 'spatialized' explanation of economic growth

Building on the JFV model of knowledge spillovers, Acs and Varga (2002) suggest that a 'spatialized' theoretical framework of technology-led economic growth needs to reflect three fundamental issues. First, it should explain why knowledge-related economic activities concentrate in certain regions, leaving others relatively underdeveloped. Second, it needs to answer the questions of how technological advances occur and what are the key processes and institutions involved with a particular focus on the geographic dimension. Third, it must present an analytical framework where the role of technological change in regional and national economic growth is clearly explained. In order to answer these three questions Acs and Varga examine three separate and distinct literatures: the new economic geography, the new growth theory, and the new economics of innovation.

Although the three approaches focus on different aspects, the three are at the same time complements. The 'new' theories of growth endogenize technological change and as such interlink technological change with macroeconomic growth. However, the way technological change is described is strongly simplistic and the economy investigated is formulated in an aspatial model. On the other hand, systems of innovation frameworks are very detailed with respect to the innovation process but say nothing about macroeconomic growth. However, the spatial dimension has been introduced into the framework in the recently developed 'regional innovation systems' studies (Braczyk, Cooke, and Heidenreich, 1998).

The idea behind the innovation systems approach is quite simple but extremely appealing. According to this in most cases, innovation is a result of a collective process and this process is shaped in a systematic manner. The elements of the system are innovating firms and firms in related and connected industries (suppliers, buyers), private and public research laboratories, universities, supporting business services (such as legal or technical services), financial institutions (especially venture capital), and the government. These elements are interconnected by innovation-related linkages where these linkages represent knowledge flows among them. Linkages can be informal in nature (occasional meetings in conferences, social events, etc) or they can also be definitely formal (contracted research, collaborative product development, etc). The effectiveness (i.e. productivity in terms of number of innovations) of the system is determined by both the knowledge already accumulated by the actors and the level of their interconnectedness (i.e. the intensity of knowledge flows). Ability and motivations for interactions are shaped largely by traditions, social norms, values, and the countries' legal systems.

New economic geography models investigate general equilibrium in a spatial setting (Krugman, 1991). This means that they provide explanations not just for the determination of equilibrium prices, incomes, and quantities in each market but also the development of the particular geographical structure of the economy. In other words, new economic geography derives economic and spatial equilibrium simultaneously (Fujita, Krugman and Venables, 1999; Fujita and Thisse, 2002). Spatial equilibrium arises as an outcome of the balance between centripetal forces working towards agglomeration (such as increasing returns to scale, industrial demand, and localized knowledge spillovers) and centrifugal forces promoting dispersion (such as transportation costs). Until the latest developments, new economic geography models did not consider the spatial aspects of economic growth. However, models of technological change follow the same pattern as endogenous growth models and fail to reach the complexity inherent in innovation-systems studies.

As emphasized by Acs and Varga (2002), although each of the above three approaches has its strengths and weaknesses, each could serve to create the building blocks of an explanatory framework of technology-led economic growth. The three suggest that a specific combination of the Krugmanian theory of initial conditions for spatial concentration of economic activities with the Romerian theory of endogenous economic growth complemented with a systematic representation of interactions among the actors of Nelson's innovation system could be a way of developing an appropriate model of technology-led regional economic development.

Following Acs and Varga (2002), Varga (2006) develops an empirical modelling framework of geographical growth explanation. This framework is the spatial extension of the endogenous growth model in Romer (1990) and it integrates elements of the innovation systems and the new economic geography literature. For a more formal treatment, Varga (2006) applies the generalized version of the Romer (1990) equation of macroeconomic level knowledge production developed in Jones (1995):[3]

$$dA = \delta H_A^\lambda A^\phi \tag{5}$$

where H_A stands for human capital in the research sector working on knowledge production (operationalized by the number of researchers), A is the total stock of technological knowledge available at a certain point in time whereas dA is the change in technological knowledge resulting from private efforts to invest in research and development; δ, λ, and ϕ are parameters.

Technological change is generated by research and its extent depends on the number of researchers involved in knowledge creation (H_A). However, their efficiency is directly related to the total stock of already available knowledge (A). Knowledge spillovers are central to the growth process: the higher A is, the larger the change in technology produced by the same number of researchers. Thus, macroeconomic growth is strongly related to knowledge spillovers.

---

[3] The functional form corresponds to the Jones (1995) version, however, the interpretation of λ and ϕ is different in Varga (2006).

Parameters in the Rômer knowledge-production function play a decisive role in the effectiveness of macro-level knowledge production. The same number of researchers with a similar value of A can raise the level of already existing technological knowledge with significant differences depending on the size of the parameters. First, consider δ $(0<\delta<1)$ which is the research productivity parameter. The larger δ the more efficient H_A is in producing economically useful new knowledge.

The size of ϕ reflects the extent to which the total stock of previously established knowledge impacts knowledge production. Given that A stands for the level of codified knowledge (available in books, scientific papers, or patent documentations), ϕ is the parameter of codified knowledge spillovers. The size of ϕ reflects the portion of A that spills over and, as such, its value largely influences the effectiveness of research in generating new technologies.

The research-spillover parameter is λ. A larger λ indicates a stronger impact on technological change with the same number of researchers. In contrast to ϕ and δ that are determined primarily in the research sector (and as such their values are exogenous to the economy), λ is endogenous. Its value reflects the diffusion of (codified and tacit) knowledge accumulated by researchers. Technological diffusion depends on three interactions: first, on the intensity of interactions among researchers (H_A); second, on the quality of public research, and the extent to which the private research sector is connected to it (especially to universities) by formal and informal linkages; and third, the development level of supporting/connected industries and business services and the integration of innovating firms into the system. The extensive innovation-systems literature evidences that the same number of researchers contribute to different efficiencies depending on the development of the system. In the Romer equation, this is reflected in the size of λ.

Within the JFV framework, a series of papers demonstrate that a significant fraction of knowledge spillovers is bounded spatially. These findings imply that the geographic structure of R&D is a determinant of technological change and ultimately economic growth. *Ceteris paribus*, in an economy where R&D institutions are highly concentrated, intensive knowledge spillovers will result in a higher level of innovation than in a system where research is more evenly distributed over space. Thus λ is also sensitive to the spatial structure of H_A. Even with the same number of researchers, λ can have different values depending on the extent to which research and development is spatially concentrated.

Finally, λ depends on the interaction of researchers and entrepreneurs. The distribution of entrepreneurs is also not evenly distributed over space. The more entrepreneurs are concentrated in a region where knowledge is produced, the greater the impact of knowledge spillovers on economic growth.

11.5. A knowledge-spillover theory of entrepreneurship

In this section, the JFV model of knowledge spillovers is extended by Acs and Audretsch who develop the knowledge-spillover theory of entrepreneurship in order to answer the question, 'What is the conduit by which knowledge spillovers occur'? As a first step in this direction, the theory incorporates two of the above literatures: new growth theory (Romer, 1990) and the new economics of innovation (Nelson, 1991) to explain how entrepreneurship facilitates the spillover of knowledge.

A modern synthesis of the entrepreneur is someone who specializes in making judgmental decisions about the coordination of scarce resources (Lazear, 2005). In this definition, the term 'someone' emphasizes that the entrepreneur is an individual. Judgmental decisions are decisions for which no obvious correct procedure exists—a judgmental decision cannot be made simply by plugging available numbers into a scientific formula and acting based on the resulting number. In this framework, entrepreneurial activity depends upon the interaction between the characteristics of opportunity and the characteristics of the people who exploit them. Since discovery is a cognitive process, it can take place only at the individual level. Individuals, whether working in an existing organization or not, are the entities discovering opportunities. The organizations employing people are inanimate and cannot engage in *discovery*. Therefore, any explanation for the mode of opportunity discovery must be based on choices made by individuals about how they would like to exploit the opportunity that they have discovered (Hayek, 1937).

So where do opportunities come from? Today we know that the technology opportunity set is endogenously created by investments in new knowledge. The new growth theory, formalized by Romer (1986), assumes that firms exist exogenously and then engage in the pursuit of new economic knowledge as an input into the process of generating endogenous growth. Technological change plays a central role in the explanation of economic growth, since on the steady-state growth path the rate of per capita GDP growth equals the rate of technological change.

However, not only does new knowledge contribute to technological change, it also creates opportunities for use by third party firms, often entrepreneurial start-ups (Shane, 2001). The creation of new knowledge gives rise to new opportunities through knowledge spillovers, and therefore entrepreneurial activity does not involve simply the arbitrage of opportunities (Kirzner, 1973) but also the exploitation of new opportunities created but not appropriated by incumbent organizations (Hellmann, 2007). Thus, while the entrepreneurship literature considers opportunity to exist exogenously, in the new economic growth literature, opportunities are endogenously created through the purposeful investment in new knowledge. The theory, as suggested by Audretsch (1995: 48), 'proposes shifting the unit of observation away from exogenously assumed firms to individuals—agents confronted with new knowledge and the decision whether and how to act upon that new knowledge'.

The theory relaxes two central (and unrealistic) assumptions of the endogenous-growth model to develop a theory that improves the microeconomic foundations of endogenous-growth theory (Acs, Audretsch, Braunerhjelm and Carlsson, 2009). The first is that knowledge is automatically equated with economic knowledge. In fact, as Arrow (1962) emphasized, knowledge is inherently different from the traditional factors of production, resulting in a gap between knowledge (K) and what he called economic knowledge (K^c). The second involves the assumed spillover of knowledge. The existence of the factor of knowledge is equated with its automatic spillover, yielding endogenous growth. In the knowledge-spillover theory of entrepreneurship, *institutions* impose a filter between new knowledge and economic knowledge ($0 < K^c / K < 1$) that results in a lower level of knowledge spillovers.

The model is one where new product innovations can come either from incumbent organizations or from entrepreneurial start-ups (Schumpeter, 1934). According to Baumol (2004: 9):

> The bulk of private R&D spending is shown to come from a tiny number of very large firms. Yet, the revolutionary breakthroughs continue to come predominantly from small entrepreneurial enterprises, with large industry providing streams of incremental improvements that also add up to major contributions.

We can think of incumbent firms that rely on the *flow* of knowledge to innovate as focusing on incremental innovation, i.e. product improvements (Acs and Audretsch, 1988). Entrepreneurial start-ups that have access to knowledge spillovers from the *stock* of knowledge and entrepreneurial talent are more likely to be engaged in radical innovation that leads to new industries or the complete replacement of existing products (Acs, Audretsch and Feldman, 1994). Start-ups play a major role in radical innovations such as software, semiconductors, biotechnology (Zucker, Darby and Brewer, 1998), and the information and communications technologies (Jorgenson, 2001). The presence of these activities is especially important at the early stages of the life cycle when technology is still fluid.

Equation (6) suggests that entrepreneurial start-ups (E) will be a function of the difference between expected profits (π^*) minus wages (W). Expected profits are conditioned by the knowledge stock (K) that positively affects start-ups and is negatively conditioned by knowledge commercialized by incumbent firms. Yet a rich literature suggests that there is a compelling array of financial, institutional, and individual barriers to entrepreneurship, which results in a modification of the entrepreneurial choice equation:

$$E = \gamma\left(\pi(K^{\xi}) - w\right)/\beta \tag{6}$$

where β represents those institutional and individual barriers to entrepreneurship, spanning factors such as risk aversion, financial constraints, and legal and regulatory restrictions (Acemoglu, Simon and Robinson, 2004). The existence of such barriers explains why economic agents might choose not to enter into entrepreneurship, even when confronted with knowledge that would otherwise generate a potentially profitable opportunity. Thus, this mode shows how local differences in knowledge stocks, the presence of large firms as deterrents to knowledge exploitation, and an entrepreneurial culture might explain regional variations in the rates of entrepreneurial activity. The primary theoretical predictions of the model are:

- An increase in the stock of knowledge positively affects the level of entrepreneurship.
- The more efficient incumbents are at exploiting knowledge flows, the smaller the effect of new knowledge on entrepreneurship.
- Entrepreneurial activities decrease in the face of higher regulations, administrative barriers, and governmental market intervention.

Thus, entrepreneurship becomes central to generating economic growth by serving as a conduit, albeit not the sole conduit, by which knowledge created by incumbent organizations spills over to agents who endogenously create new firms. The theory is actually a theory of *endogenous entrepreneurship*, where entrepreneurship is a response to opportunities created by investments in new knowledge that was not commercialized by incumbent firms. The theory suggests that, *ceteris paribus*, entrepreneurial activity will tend to be greater in contexts where investments in new knowledge are relatively high, since the start-ups will benefit from knowledge that spills over from the source actually producing that new knowledge. In a low-knowledge context, the lack of new ideas will not generate entrepreneurial opportunities based on potential knowledge spillovers. A series of studies link entrepreneurship and economic growth at the regional level (Acs and Armington, 2006; Audretsch, Keilbach and Lehmann, 2006) and at the national level (Acs, Audretsch, Braunerhjelm and Carlsson, 2009) finding that entrepreneurship does in fact offer an explanation for how knowledge spillovers occur.

Acs and Varga (2005) empirically test the theory within the JFV framework. They build their modelling approach on the interpretation of the Romerian equation (equation (5)) provided in Section 11.4. They start with the assumption that the value of λ bears the influence of the level of entrepreneurship because the value of new economic knowledge is uncertain. While most R&D is carried out in large firms and universities, it does not mean that the individuals who discover the opportunity will carry out the subsequent exploitation. An implication of the theory of firm selection is that new firms may enter an industry in large numbers to exploit knowledge spillovers. The higher the rate of start-ups, the greater should be the value of λ because of knowledge spillovers.

The empirical model in which the parameter λ in equation (5) is endogenized has the following form:

$$\log(NK) = \delta + \lambda\log(H) + \varphi\log(A) + \epsilon \tag{7}$$

$$\lambda = \left(\beta_1 + \beta_2 lpg(\text{ENTR}) + \beta_3\log(\text{AGGL})\right) \tag{8}$$

where NK stands for new knowledge (i.e. the change in A), $ENTR$ is entrepreneurship, $AGGL$ is agglomeration, A is the set of publicly available scientific-technological knowledge and ϵ is a stochastic error term. Implementation of (7) into (8) results in the following estimated equation:

$$\log(NK) = \quad \delta + \beta_1\log(H) + \beta_2\log(\text{ENTR})\log(H) + \beta_3\log(\text{AGGL})\log(H) \\ +\varphi\log(A) + \epsilon \tag{9}$$

In equation (9), the estimated value of the parameter β_2 measures the extent to which research in interaction with entrepreneurship contributes to knowledge spillovers. Applied to European data, Acs and Varga (2005) find a statistically significant value of β_2 that is taken as evidence supporting the knowledge-spillover theory of entrepreneurship.

11.6. Agglomeration: The final frontier

The JFV model is extendable for empirically testing agglomeration effects in knowledge spillovers. Agglomeration forces are crucial in technological change and as such in the explanation of economic growth. Varga (2006) points out that in equation (5) the size of λ is also influenced by agglomeration. Insights from the new economic geography can help understand the dynamic effects of the spatial structure of R&D on macroeconomic growth (Baldwin and Forslid, 2000; Fujita and Thisse, 2002; Baldwin et al., 2003). If spatial proximity to other research labs, universities, firms, and business services matters in innovation, firms are motivated to locate R&D laboratories in those regions where actors of the system of innovation are already agglomerated in order to decrease innovation costs.

Thus, spatial concentration of the system of innovation is a source of positive externalities and, as such, these externalities (as centrifugal forces in

R&D location) determine the strength of the cumulative process that leads to a particular spatial economic structure. However, agglomeration effects can be negative as well. Increasing housing costs and travel time make innovation more expensive and might motivate labs to move out of the region. The actual balance between centrifugal and centripetal forces determines the geographical structure of the system of innovation. Through determining the size of λ in equation (5), this also influences the rate of technological progress (dA/A) and, eventually, the macroeconomic growth rate (dy/y).

Within the JFV framework Varga (2000 and 2001) estimates the magnitude of agglomeration effects. Based on a data set of 125 US metropolitan areas, he finds that spatial concentration of high-technology production and business services has a definite positive relationship with the intensity of local academic knowledge transfers. Increasing returns resulting from the spatial concentration of economic activities is clearly demonstrated in the study. It is shown that the same amount of local expenditure on university research yields dramatically different levels of innovation output depending on the concentration of economic activities in the metropolitan area. A critical mass of agglomeration is found to be necessary for regions to experience substantial local economic effects of academic research spending. This critical mass is characterized by a city population of around three million, with employment in high-technology production facilities and business service firms about 160,000 and 4,000, respectively. In Varga (2001), agglomeration effects in university knowledge spillovers for two 'high-technology' sectors (electronics and instruments) are also demonstrated.

How can the JFV framework contribute to studying empirically the dynamism of agglomeration (i.e. the dynamism of λ) described in detail by the new economic geography? To model empirically the effects of centripetal and centrifugal forces on spatial structure, researchers develop spatial computable general equilibrium (SCGE) models (e.g. Thissen, 2003). These models are empirical counterparts of the new economic geography and are extremely powerful tools for explaining spatial distribution of economic activities under different starting assumptions.

Now it is technically possible to integrate the JFV approach into SCGE modelling in order to study the dynamic effects of knowledge spillovers on geography, technological change, and growth. With this step the JFV model becomes a crucial bridge between academic research on the geography of innovation and policy analysis for studying different scenarios of economic development. Varga (2007a) demonstrates that incorporating the lessons of the JFV framework into development policy analysis opens up the possibility of building 'new generation models' with such simulations where both regional, inter-regional, and macro effects of different policy scenarios can be studied and compared to each other. The GMR-Hungary model (Varga, 2007b) is the first one in this field.

11.7. Public policy

Policy-makers are interested in promoting economic growth at the national and the regional level. Politicians look to academia to help them understand the process of economic development and inform their decisions. Academics long ago identified technical change through innovation as a key process for generating long-term stable economic growth. However, that poses the question, 'What causes innovation in a region or economy?' (Acs and Sanders, 2007).

In accordance with the evidence, the entrepreneur is the agent with whom the buck stops. The creation of the knowledge he or she commercializes is not (necessarily) motivated by the rents that the entrepreneur receives for commercialization. Rents reward the act of commercialization, and as such should not be destroyed, to enhance static efficiency. However, the claim to these rents should also not be transferred to the generators of knowledge, who may have had no intent of commercializing and/or require no incentive to create such knowledge in the first place.[4] It is not the generation of new knowledge that is valuable to society at large but rather its utilization and subsequent economic growth. Knowledge creation, of course, is a necessary but insufficient condition for innovation and growth, and creation without implementation is clearly a waste of resources. We argue, therefore, that policy-makers should stop and think about the bottlenecks in the innovative process before committing large amounts of public money and/or entitlements to profits and rents to the (formal) knowledge-generation process.

These results also carry over to the regional level if one considers the impact of limited geographical labour mobility, transport costs, and communication costs. As the knowledge spillovers that drive economic growth are likely to be regionalized, regional policies should aim to facilitate spillovers. A first requirement is that sufficient resources are available for both knowledge creation and knowledge commercialization. And as entrepreneurial talent is a key resource in the innovation chain, regional policies should try to develop it. Moreover, the impediments to knowledge spillovers from creators to commercializers deserve attention. Legal impediments such as non-competition clauses in labour contracts should be abandoned. By investing in physical and communication infrastructures and by stimulating or enabling the exchange of knowledge,

---

[4] This may well be the effect of stronger patent and IPR-protection.

local and regional governments can support the entire innovation chain. Direct support to new entrants or R&D should be given only as long as that does not reduce the incentives to create or commercialize new knowledge.

The model outlined in this paper has important policy implications at the aggregate and regional level but also raises important questions. The presence of knowledge spillovers is well documented in the literature. But the exact channels through which such spillovers arise are a challenging arena for further research. The three propositions predicting regional clustering are empirically indistinguishable in most studies due to data-availability issues. The detailed case studies by Klepper (2008) provide support for the first channel that was identified with evidence on the importance of physical support infrastructure. Florida (2002) presents evidence in support of the third channel we have discussed, but to our knowledge, studies that try to distinguish between them have not yet been done. In addition, at the aggregate level, the theory and its underlying assumptions require further empirical scrutiny. The available evidence supports the claim that knowledge spillovers are important for (regional) economic growth but much more can be done to test the model predictions. This empirical research agenda will hopefully inspire other researchers.

11.8. Conclusions

In this review, the Jaffe-Feldman-Varga model is introduced and an assessment as to its relevance for economics research is made. It is highlighted that this approach has become a widely applied tool for testing the spatial extent of knowledge spillovers in different countries, different sectors, and at different spatial scales. In addition, this model became a workhorse of empirical studies of entrepreneurship, agglomeration, and growth. The JFV approach has also proved to be a crucial element in 'new-generation development-policy modelling'. Thus the JFV model of knowledge spillovers and its extensions offer an avenue to re-explain the mechanism by which knowledge spillovers operate and open the door for a new understanding of regional and macroeconomic development. If this indeed happens, we will have experienced a paradigm shift in economic science.

References

Acemoglu, D., Johnson, S. and Robinson, J. (2004), 'Institutions as the fundamental cause of long-run growth'. In Aghion, P. and Durlauf, S. (eds), *Handbook of Economic Growth*, Vol. 1. New York: Elsevier North Holland.

Acs, Z.J. and Armington, C. (2006), *Entrepreneurship, Geography and American Economic Growth*. Cambridge: Cambridge University Press.

——and Audretsch, D.B. (1988), 'Innovation in large and small firms: An empirical analysis', *The American Economic Review*, 78(4): 678–689.

————(1989), 'Patents as a measure of innovative activity,' *Kyklos*, 42: 171–180.

——and Sanders, M. (2007), *Intellectual Property and the Knowledge Spillover Theory of Entrepreneurship*. Jena: Max Planck Institute of Economics.

——and Varga, A. (2002), 'Geography, endogenous growth and innovation', *International Regional Science Review*, 25: 132–148.

————(2005), 'Entrepreneurship, agglomeration and technological change', *Small Business Economics*, 24(3): 323–334.

————and Feldman, M.P. (1992), 'Real effects of academic research: Comment', *American Economic Review*, 82: 363–367.

——————(1994), 'R&D spillovers and recipient firm size', *Review of Economic Statistics*, 99: 336–340.

——Anselin, L. and Varga, A. (2002), 'Patents and innovation counts as measures of regional production of new knowledge', *Research Policy*, 31: 1069–1085.

——Andretsch, D.B. Braunerhjelm, P. and Carlsson, B. (2009), 'The knowledge spillover theory of entrepreneurship', *Small Business Economics*, 32: 15–30.

Anselin, L. (1988), *Spatial Econometrics: Methods and Models*. Boston: Kluwer Academic Publishers.

——(2001), 'Spatial econometrics'. In Baltagi, B. (ed.), *A Companion to Theoretical Econometrics*. Oxford: Basil Blackwell.

——,Varga, A. and Acs, Z.J. (1997), 'Local geographic spillovers between university research and high technology innovation', *Journal of Urban Economics*, 42: 422–448.

——————(2000a), 'Geographic and sectoral characteristics of academic knowledge spillovers,' *Papers in Regional Science*, 79: 435–445.

——————(2000b), 'Geographic spillovers and university research: A spatial econometric approach', *Growth and Change*, 31: 501–515.

Arrow, K.J. (1962), 'Economic welfare and the allocation of resources for invention'. In Nelson, R. (ed.), *The Rate and Direction of Inventive Activity*. Princeton: NBER, Princeton University Press.

Audretsch, D. (1995), *Innovation and Industry Evolution*. Cambridge, MA: MIT Press.

——and Feldman, M.P. (1996), 'R&D spillovers and the geography of innovation and production,' *American Economic Review*, 8: 630–640.

——,Keilbach, M.C. and Lehmann, E.E. (2006), *Entrepreneurship and Economic Growth*. Oxford: Oxford University Press.

Baldwin, R.E. and Forslid, R. (2000), 'The core-perihpery model and endogenous growth: Stabilising and de-stabilizing integraion,' *Economica*, 67: 307–324.

————,Martin, P., Ottaviano, G. and Robert-Nicoud, F. (2003), *Economic Geography and Public Policy*. Princeton: Princeton University Press.

Baumol, W. (2004), 'Entrepreneurial enterprises, large established firms and other components of the free-market growth machine', *Small Business Economics*, 23(1): 9–21.

Braczyk, H., Cooke, P. and Heidenreich, M. (1998), *Regional Innovation Systems: The Role of Governances in a Globalized World*. London: UCL Press.

Clark, G.L., Feldman, M.P. and Gertler, M.S. (2000), *The Oxford Handbook of Economic Geography*. Oxford: Oxford University Press.

Feldman, M.P. (1994), *The Geography of Innovation*. New York: Kluwer Academic Publishers.

——and Audretsch, D.B. (1999), 'Innovation in cities: Science-based diversity, specialization and localized competition', *European Economic Review*, 43: 409–429.

——and Florida, R. (1994), 'The geographic sources of innovation: Technological infrastructure and product innovation in the United States', *Annals of the Association of American Geographers*, 84: 210–229.

Florida, R. (2002), *The Rise of the Creative Class*. New York: Basic Books.

Fujita, M. and Thisse, J. (2002), *Economics of Agglomeration. Cities, Industrial Location, and Regional Growth*, Cambridge, MA, and London: Cambridge University Press.

——, Krugman, P. and Venables, A. (1999), *The Spatial Economy*. Cambridge, MA: MIT Press.

Griliches, Z. (1979), 'Issues in assessing the contributions of research and development to productivity growth', *The Bell Journal of Economics*, 10: 92–116.

Hayek, F.A. von (1937), 'Economics and knowledge', *Economica* (New Series), 4: 33–54.

Hellmann, T. (2007), 'When do employees become entrepreneurs?' *Management Science*, 53(6): 919–933.

Jaffe, A. (1989), 'The real effects of academic research', *American Economic Review*, 79: 957–970.

——and Trajtenberg, M. (2002), *Patents, Citations and Innovations: A Window on the Knowledge Economy*. Cambridge, MA: MIT Press.

———and Henderson, R. (1993), 'Geography, location of knowledge spillovers as evidence of patent citations', *Quarterly Journal of Economics*, 108: 483–499.

————(2005), 'Patent citations and the geography of knowledge spillovers: A reassessment: Comment,' *American Economic Review*, 95(1): 461–465.

Jones, C. (1995), 'R&D based models of economic growth', *Journal of Political Economy*, 103: 759–784.

Jorgenson, D.W. (2001), 'Information technology and the U. S. Economy', *American Economic Review*, 91: 1–32.

Kirzner, I.M. (1973), *Competition and Entrepreneurship*. Chicago: University of Chicago Press.

Klepper, S. (2008), 'Industry life cycles and market dominance'. In Collins, W.D. (ed.), *Issues in Competition Law and Policy*. Chicago: ABA Press.

Krugman, P. (1991), 'Increasing returns and economic geography', *Journal of Political Economy*, 99: 483–499.

Lazear, E.P. (2005), 'Entrepreneurship', *Journal of Labor Economics*, 23(4): 649–680.

Nelson, J.R. (1991), *National Innovation Systems*. Cambridge, MA: Harvard University Press.

Romer, P. (1986), 'Increasing returns and economic growth', *Journal of Political Economy*, 94: 1002–1037.

——(1990), 'Endogenous technological change', *Journal of Political Economy*, 98: S71–S102.

Schumpeter, J.A. (1934) [1911], *The Theory of Economic Development*. Cambridge, MA: Harvard University Press.

Shane, S. (2001), 'Technological opportunity and new firm creation', *Management Science*, 47(2): 205–220.

Thissen, M. (2003), 'RAEM 2.0: A regional applied general equilibrium model for the Netherlands'. Manuscript. 19.

Thompson, P. and Fox-Kean, M. (2005a), 'Patent citations and the geography of knowledge spillovers: A reassessment', *American Economic Review*, 95(1): 450–461.

——––(2005b), 'Patent citations and the geography of knowledge spillovers. A reassessment: Reply', *American Economic Review*, 95(1): 465–467.

Varga, A. (1998), *University Research and Regional Innovation: A Spatial Econometric Analysis of Academic Technology Transfers*. Boston: Kluwer Academic Publishers.

——(2000), 'Local academic knowledge spillovers and the concentration of economic activity', *Journal of Regional Science*, 40: 289–309.

——(2001), 'Universities and regional economic development: Does agglomeration matter?' In Johansson, B., Karlsson, C. and Stough, R. (eds), *Theories of Endogenous Regional Growth—Lessons for Regional Policies*. Berlin: Springer.

——(2006), 'The spatial dimension of innovation and growth: Empirical research methodology and policy analysis', *European Planning Studies*, 9: 1171–1186.

——(2007a), 'From the geography of innovation to development policy analysis: The GMR-approach', *Annales d'Economie et de Statistique*, ENSAE, 87–88: 1–5.

——(2007b), 'GMR-HUNGARY: A complex macro-regional model for the analysis of development policy impacts on the Hungarian economy'. Final Report, Project No. NFH 370/2005.

Zucker, L.G., Darby, M.R. and Brewer, M.B. (1998), 'Intellectual human capital and the birth of U.S. biotechnology enterprises', *American Economic Review*, 88(1): 290–306.

12

Innovation and Growth: A Technical or Entrepreneurial Residual?

Pontus Braunerhjelm

12.1. Introduction

Innovation is increasingly viewed as the key to elevate prosperity and secure sustainable long-run growth. The last decades have witnessed a refinement of previous growth models to include also investments in education by individuals and R&D by firms. Better educated individuals and increased expenditure on R&D is then shown to result in innovations and accelerated growth. Also policy-makers, most recently the OECD, the EU commission, as well as other organizations, have presented innovation strategies to combat future growth and welfare challenges. Similarly, a number of countries have designed policy measures that are currently being implemented in order to upgrade and strengthen their innovation capacities.

The issues discussed in this chapter include how innovative opportunities arise and are exploited, whether the normative conclusions of contemporary growth models are derived from a realistic micro-economic setting, and suggestions as to how these models can be improved in order to provide appropriate guidance for policy-makers.[1]

Going back a few decades, the dominating view would be that innovation occurs as firms invest in R&D to generate new knowledge and new ideas, where the returns to those investments are appropriated through commercialization (Griliches, 1979; Cohen and Levinthal, 1989, 1990; Chandler, 1990; Warsh 2006). Apparently this contradicts at least part of the entrepreneurship literature, where the opportunity space is assumed to be given, not created by

---

[1] This chapter builds on Braunerhjelm (2008, 2011) and Braunerhjelm and Thulin (2003).

the entrepreneur, and where innovation is primarily an outcome of the entrepreneurs' abilities to exploit such opportunities (Acs et al., 2004b, 2009). Also, the literature on endogenous growth deviates, at least partly, from a linear perception of the innovation process, modelling innovation and growth as a combination of firms' in-house R&D and access to externally produced R&D, i.e. spillovers.

Empirical observations have piled up suggesting that irrespective of modest R&D investments, small and entrepreneurial firms contribute substantially to aggregate innovation (OECD, 2010). The interpretation is that they exploit existing knowledge in different ways than older and more established incumbents and increasingly emanate from industries traditionally considered less innovative, i.e. the service sector. This process also generates new knowledge of a type that does not appear in aggregate R&D figures but does spill over to other firms. Apple, Google, Ikea, Starbucks, and Ryanair are some obvious examples of innovative firms that have had a strong impact on the organization of other companies without being heavily committed to research, albeit some of them have sizeable design and development departments. This new knowledge is sometimes produced independently, sometimes in conjunction with other firms. But the process differs radically as compared to large, R&D-investing firms (Carlsson et al., 2009). As shown by Almeida and Kogut (1997) and Almeida (1999), small firms also innovate in relatively unexplored fields of technology.[2]

The institutional design has been advanced as the most important factor in obtaining a sustainable long-run growth trajectory. Even though there is no simple explanation for the 'mystery of growth', proper institutions that encourage private ownership and openness seem to be the most important explanatory variable. Other factors, such as the size of the public sector, and even the level of human capital (with the exception of basic education), give more ambiguous results according to the last 15–20 years of research (Sala-i-Martin 2002). Copying institutions that have worked well in one country is no guarantee for success in others, as shown by Easterly (2001). Also North (1990) is sceptical since institutional set-ups are driven by vested interest and traditions, while Lucas (2000) believes that per-capita income will converge over time because good institutions will be copied. Hence, with perhaps the exception of property rights, openness and the imposition of a trustworthy rule of law, there is little evidence as to which particular institutions matter. This is also obvious from the fact that growth and innovation varies considerably within countries exposed to the same basic institutional framework.

---

[2] See also Rothwell and Zegveld (1982); Baumol (2004); Ortega-Argilés, Vivarelli and Voight (2009). See Braunerhjelm (2011) for a survey.

In addition, measurement problems are manifold and influenced by the level of growth analysis. More aggregated measures fail to capture the dynamics on the micro-level, and evaluations of institutions are by and large restricted to those observed in legislation, disregarding the fact that informal tacit and non-codifiable rules and traditions may be just as important. The meso-level that forms institutions and rules is claimed to be neglected (Foster, 2011). Before going into the analysis I will present some background facts on the mystery of growth.

12.1.1. *The background: Some illustrations*

At the firm- or industry-levels most studies confer a positive effect of R&D investments on productivity. As reported by Wieser (2005) and Hall et al. (2010), the average estimated firm-level return on R&D investments is in the range of 25–30 per cent, while R&D elasticity is around 0.10 per cent (productivity).[3] At the national level the empirical analyses become more intricate as variation at the micro-level may be concealed at more aggregate levels, together with endogeniety and causality issues that make the interpretation of the results considerably harder. Since policy-makers are predominantly concerned with observations at the macro-level, instruments to propel growth are designed—and implemented—at that level. Increased expenditures on R&D in relation to GDP and the share or numbers of the population with a tertiary education are obvious examples. Figures 12.1a and 12.1b illustrate the increase of numbers of students in China, the EU, Japan, and the USA with a tertiary and research education, respectively.

They all display a positive trend, with China and Japan representing the extremes among the four. Still, in terms of growth effects the results of these policy efforts seem ambiguous or even non-existent at the national level, as shown in Figure 12.2.

There is simply no correlation between growth and outlays on R&D in relation to GDP among the OECD countries. Some countries with modest R&D spending manage to obtain a high level of growth while countries spending considerably more perform much worse in terms of growth. The pattern does not change if we extend the data back a decade or if we use different lag structures. Hence, R&D by itself does not seem to be the solution to enhancing growth performance, even though that seems to be the normative conclusion of most contemporary growth models.

---

[3] See also Adams (1990), Caballero and Jaffe (1993), Lichtenberg (1993), Coe and Helpman (1995), Baumol (2007), LeSage and Fischer (2008), and Naudé (2008) for related empirical and theoretical analyses.

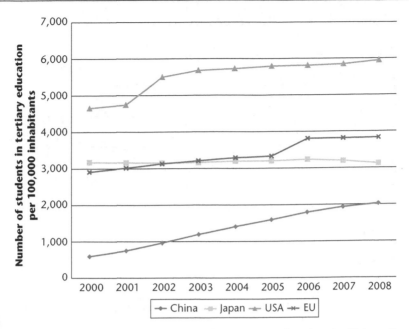

Figure 12.1a. The number of students with a tertiary education in China, the EU, Japan, and the USA, 2000–2008

Sources: Data on the EU from Eurostat; data on China, Japan and USA from Unesco and Penn world table 7.0.

On the other hand, R&D is just an input in the production of innovations and we may be looking at the wrong variable. To pinpoint innovations, patents are the most frequently used indicator, in particular quality-adjusted. They perform somewhat better than R&D in relation to GDP growth per capita, indicating a weak positive correlation (Feldman, 2004). Even so, patents are at best a partial measurement of innovation since most of the business sector—i.e. services—is excluded. In addition, there is an ongoing discussion about the problems with depreciating requirements which is claimed to have inflated patents. Too many patents are granted where novelty is claimed to be questionable. Patents have also developed into a strategic asset used by large firms, whereas smaller firms and entrepreneurs find it hard to protect themselves from patent infringement.

An alternative measure to patents is provided by various innovation indices that are composed of a number of underlying variables. These are supposed to capture a more extensive part of an economy's innovation capacity. One example is the EU's innovation-capacity index based on six input dimensions and two output dimensions, which in turn are composed of a large number of observable variables. In Figure 12.3 the relationship between GDP per capita and EU's innovation-performance index is shown. A distinct positive

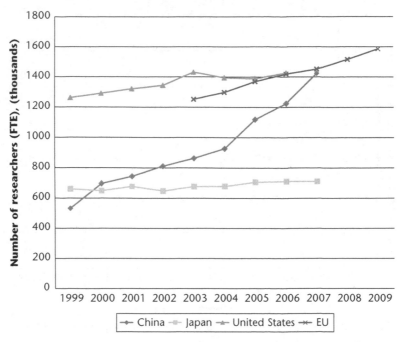

Figure12.1b. The number of students with a research education in China, the EU, Japan, and the USA, 2000–2008

Sources: Data on the EU from Eurostat; data on China, Japan, and the USA from Unesco and Penn world table 7.0.

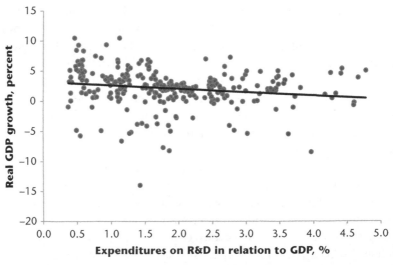

Figure 12.2. R&D expenditures in relation to GDP and annual growth in 33 OECD countries, 2001–2009

Source: Data OECD via Internet.

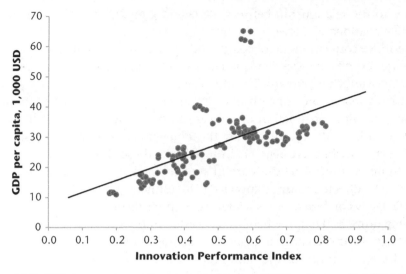

Figure 12.3. EU's innovation performance index and GDP level per capita, 2006–2010
Source: Data EU—Pro Inno Europe, 2011 and OECD.

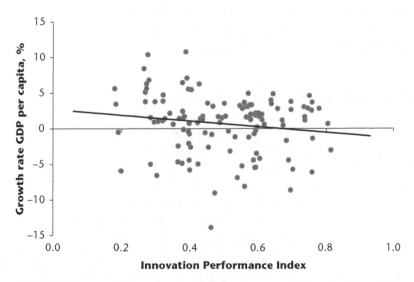

Figure 12.4. EU's innovation performance index and annual growth, 2006–2010
Source: Data EU—Pro Inno Europe, 2011, and OECD.

relationship characterizes these two variables, i.e. wealthier countries seem to innovate more.

The relationship between the GDP level and innovation is expected but of limited interest for understanding how innovation affects growth. In Figure 12.4 innovation is instead related to annual growth in the EU countries.

Similar to the relationship between R&D and growth, the figures suggest a negative relationship between the two.[4]

The above correlations do of course not capture any causal relationship and there are several conceivable explanations to the negative relations between R&D/innovation and growth. The initial level of GDP, the institutional set-up, and other variables are not controlled for, the time horizon may be too short, the weights and construction of indices can be challenged. All of these are valid remarks. Still, together with the ambiguous econometric results as knowledge variables are regressed on growth, these illustrations hint that something is missing in the current growth models. Too much emphasis seems to be directed towards knowledge investments, too little on how such knowledge is converted into societal value in terms of innovation, new and growing firms, and employment and investment opportunities.

The rest of the chapter is organized in the following way. Section 12.2 provides an overview of the dominant growth models and discusses their microeconomic foundation. Section 12.3 presents a simple model of the occupational choice that individuals face, i.e. whether to engage in innovative entrepreneurship or remain an employee. In Section 12.4 the modelling of innovation in mainstream growth models are discussed in some detail, while Sections 12.5 and 12.6 discuss improvement of current models and policy implications. Finally, Section 12.7 concludes.

12.2. Modelling growth and innovation

Before examining the micro foundation of the knowledge-based-growth models, it may be useful to recapitulate the building blocks of the neoclassical model, constituting the dominant growth paradigm between the 1930s and the mid 1980s. One of the model's obvious advantages was transparency and intuitive logic. Supply of labour, capital investments and a 'shift' factor constituted the backbone of the model (complemented with human capital in its later versions). The dynamics were constrained by the 'golden rule' which implied that investments were determined by the increase in the labour supply: too much capital in relation to labour would drive down the return to the owner of capital below the equilibrium interest-rate level, and thus halt further investments, whereas too little capital in relation to labour would

---

[4] Enlarging the set of countries to include less developed countries, Fagerberg and Srholec (2009) find a positive correlation between GDP per capita and technological capacity, education, financial markets, and regulation.

lead to an upward pressure on returns that would spur investments.[5] Hence, policies to foster growth focused on optimizing the relationship between investments and labour in order to obtain steady-state equilibrium growth.

Despite its obvious advantages with regard to tractability and clarity, the model suffered from a major disadvantage: empirical support was weak. There was little explanatory power attributed to the capital and labour variables, and rather a third, unidentified, factor was driving growth. Even though this factor remained unidentified, it became known as the 'technical residual', since it was assumed to pick up new knowledge, both technological and organizational (Solow, 1956, 1957; Denison, 1962).

It is in that perspective that the seminal contribution of the knowledge-based (endogenous) growth models, appearing in the mid 1980s, should be viewed. Basically these models demonstrated how investments in knowledge and human capital were undertaken by profit-maximizing firms in a dynamic general equilibrium setting (Romer, 1986, 1990; Lucas, 1988; Rebelo, 1991; and others).[6] Savings were transformed to investments in R&D which firms undertook to get a competitive edge, and part of that knowledge spilled over to a societal knowledge stock that impacted productivity of all other firms. Hence, growth was disentangled from investments in capital and increases in the labour supply: even if those remained constant, increases in knowledge meant that growth could increase.

Notwithstanding that this was a major contribution, the model failed to picture how knowledge might spill over to other agents in the economy. Hence, while knowledge production was kept exogenous in the traditional neoclassical growth model, knowledge diffusion—the critical mechanism in generating growth—is exogenous in the endogenous growth models. And that remains a puzzle, i.e. even though an economy invests heavily in R&D, the mechanisms by which this knowledge spills over and is converted into goods and services, is basically unknown (Acs et al., 2004a, 2004b, 2009; Braunerhjelm et al., 2010). It is likely to be non-uniform across regions and countries and influenced by different traditions, norms, and institutions.

The contributions of Segerstrom (1991, 1995), Aghion and Howitt (1992, 1998) and Cheng and Dinopoulos (1992), to mention a few, aimed at introducing innovation more explicitly into the endogenous growth model. More

---

[5] The equilibrium rate is related to the rate of time preferences in consumption, i.e. the changes of consumer prices over time that would induce intertemporal shifts in consumption (see Braunerhjelm, 2005).

[6] As pointed out in a previous section, the difference between this vein of the literature and the entrepreneurship literature is striking. Whereas the latter considers opportunity to exist exogenously, in the new economic growth literature opportunities are systematically and endogenously created through the purposeful investment in R&D.

precisely, innovation was modeled as a R&D race between firms, turning a fraction of R&D into successful innovations. Firms compete with innovations rather than price, and firms have to innovate in order to survive (Hicks, 1950; Porter, 1990). This was no doubt a step forward, but again the essence of the Schumpeterian entrepreneur is missing. Rather, these models seem to picture large incumbents where the winner takes the major part of the market (e.g. a new and better drug).

More recent contributions follow an industrial-organization tradition that examines the effects of preemption, entry regulation, strategic interaction, etc., on innovation (Gilbert and Newbery, 1982; Tirole, 1988; Laffont and Tirole, 1993; Nickell, 1996; Berry and Pakes, 2003; Aghion et al., 2006). Apparently these models are more sophisticated than the previous ones, incorporating the effects of competition and innovation of incumbents and new firms in the analysis. Competition is one vital component in fostering growth, hence keeping entry barriers low is strategically important (Howitt, 2007). For instance, Aghion et al. (2006) show that entry—or entry threats—has positive effects on the innovative behaviour by incumbents close to the technological frontier, while no such effects could be found for technological laggards. They coin these effects as the 'escape-entry' effect and the 'discouragement effect' and draw policy conclusions related to the diverse effects across industries (Aghion and Griffith, 2005).

A growing number of smaller and new firms also seem to induce more heterogeneous and firm-specific performance, measured in terms of profits and stock value of firms (Fink et al., 2005; Pastor and Veronesi, 2005). Such firm-specific performance is interpreted as a sign of creative destruction, enhanced efficiency, and higher productivity and growth (Acemoglu et al., 2003, 2006; Durnev et al., 2004; Aghion et al., 2004, 2005; Chun et al., 2007). Jovanovic and Rosseau (2005) conclude that young firms are more prone to exploit new technologies or knowledge. Hence, the knowledge-based growth models have ameliorated our understanding of the growth process, but empirical support is, however, weak, indicating that knowledge about the underlying factors driving growth is only partial (Jones 1995a, 1995b, 2006).[7] The crucial mechanism generating growth—i.e. knowledge spillovers—is basically assumed to be in place without specifying how and by whom. An essential component seems missing in contemporary growth models which may have important normative implications: if the microeconomic setting of the model is mis-specified then the policy conclusions may also be flawed.

---

[7] See also Antonelli (2007) on the 'economics of complexity'.

12.2.1. *The microeconomic foundation of contemporary growth models*

Knowledge externalities, increasing returns in production at the aggregate level, and decreasing returns in the production of knowledge at the firm level, are the three main pillars of endogenous growth models. I will argue that present knowledge-based growth theories need to be redefined in order to better capture the true entrepreneur who recognizes an opportunity but does not necessarily get involved in R&D-investments.

There are several concerns as regards the present endogenous growth models.[8] First, the ability to exploit and absorb knowledge spillovers has been shows to be contingent on previous knowledge accumulation, both with regard to type and volume (Cohen and Levinthal, 1990). Moreover, since such previous experience sets the condition for current knowledge-absorption capacity, forces like path dependence and lock-in also set in.

Second, even though knowledge can be transmitted across national borders (Coe and Helpman, 1995), there is a virtual consensus that spillovers are locally bounded.[9] The distance decay effect has also been established in a large number of studies. Knowledge spillovers tend to be stronger for more technologically sophisticated production, and in more fluid and early stages of production of new knowledge. Innovative processes assessed by either patents, or a quality-adjusted measure of patents, indicate that innovation is more concentrated than inventive or production activities (Paci and Usai, 1999; Ejermo, 2009). Note also that the adoption of an innovation seems to diffuse slowly (Rosenberg, 1972).

Third, the potential for organizational learning together with internal incentive structures in incumbents also tends to ring-fence firms' dynamic capabilities, i.e. invention and innovation. As shown by, for instance, Aldrich and Auster (1986) and Christensen (1997), the intertemporal dynamics within large enterprises to attain established growth targets tend to make incumbents less likely to adapt to change a system that may affect the usefulness or value of an existing production structure. Hence, incumbents are geared towards less risky and incremental innovations.

Fourth, new ventures which are more inclined towards radical innovations (Casson, 1990, 2002a, 2002b; Baumol, 2007) are not being constrained by path dependencies, lock-in effects, and previous organizational structures. In addition, even though R&D remains important, many highly innovative firms do not engage in R&D at all. Increasingly, firms in services and manufacturing create value through a wide range of complementary technological and non-technological changes and innovations (OECD, 2010).

---

[8] See also Durlauf (2001) and Durlauf et al. (2008) for an account of methodological problems associated with the enedogenous growth model.

[9] Anselin et al. (1997, 2000). See also Braunerhjelm (2008).

Fifth, the policy conclusions derived from mainstream endogenous growth models may be flawed because of too rudimentary a modelling of the microeconomic dynamics. Without a proper understanding and modelling of the microeconomic setting and the way firms are affected by institutions and norms, policy measures may not be well targeted to attain an optimal growth trajectory.

Entrepreneurial ventures, as well as incumbents searching for new discoveries, draw on existing knowledge which together with individual abilities is likely to play an important role in the transformation and growth of knowledge-based economies. Thus, both the individuals and the contexts in which agents operate have to be integrated in the model. In other words, the individual-opportunity nexus has to be operationalized and combined with pure R&D-driven innovation efforts. The next section will address the individual's choice between different occupations, while subsequent sections will discuss how the entrepreneur is introduced in the endogenous (knowledge-based) growth models, and point at possible ways to better integrate the entrepreneur.

12.3. The occupational choice: Wage earner or entrepreneur?

Suppose the economy consists of a population of $\bar{S}$ individuals and that each individual differs in inborn (exogenous) entrepreneurial ability $\bar{e}$. Assume that entrepreneurial ability is normally distributed across individuals, that each individual has full access to the common stock of knowledge, K, and that individuals with high entrepreneurial ability are able to identify more opportunities to commercially exploit K than individuals with low ability. Finally, the aggregate entrepreneurial ability is assumed to be composed of the sum of each individual's ability,

$$\sum_{i=1}^{s} \overline{e_i} = \overline{E,E} \subset K, e_i = f(\overline{e}, K) \tag{1}$$

where individual entrepreneurial ability is increasing in given $\bar{e}$ and K, and $\bar{E}$ is a subset of K. Given those assumptions, Figure 12.5 illustrates each individual's total entrepreneurial ability (ranked by ability):

Next, suppose that each individual calculates the net expected payoff (*NEP*) of becoming an entrepreneur, as shown in Figure 12.6.[10]

---

[10] We can think of the horizontal line segment as a welfare system that guarantees that all individuals receive some payoff. We don't consider negative expected payoffs, since an individual with negative expected entrepreneurial payoff will never engage in entrepreneurial activity.

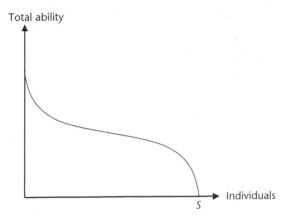

Figure 12.5. Total entrepreneurial ability

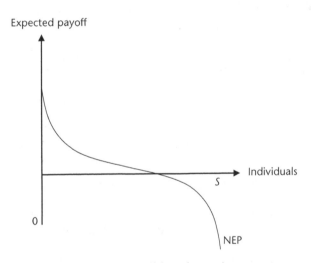

Figure 12.6. Expected net payoff from becoming an entrepreneur

Those individuals who decide to remain employees receive a wage based on their individual skill. More precisely, individuals with higher entrepreneurial ability are also paid a higher wage than those with low ability, i.e. a higher net working payoff (NWP). The choice to become an entrepreneur consequently depends on the expected utility of that option as compared to remaining an employee. Suppose that the individuals' preferences admit a strictly increasing utility representation of the expected utility form (normally referred to as the von Neumann-Morgenstern utility function). Moreover, assume that individuals are risk-averse and that $u(0) = 0$. The decision whether to become an entrepreneur or not is illustrated in Figure 12.7.

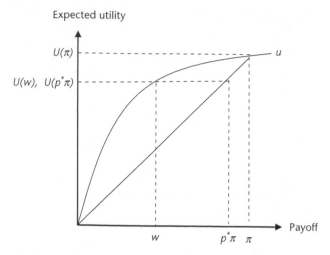

Figure 12.7. Expected utility of becoming an entrepreneur

If the individual chooses not to become an entrepreneur, he will receive a wage (w) with certainty, yielding the following utility:

$$U^{Worker} = 1u(w) + (1 - 1)u(0) = u(w). \tag{2}$$

If, on the other hand, he chooses to become an entrepreneur, his expected utility is dependent on the probability of success, P_ϵ [0,1], and the expected payoff, π, which equals

$$U^{Entrepreneur} = pu(\pi) + (1 - p)u(0) = pu(\pi). \tag{3}$$

If $\pi \geq w$, then there exists a probability, p^*, such that the choice of being an entrepreneur is optimal for the individual for all $p > p^*$. If $\pi < w$, no such p^* exists.

By introducing the NWP curve into Figure 12.5, we can identify two segments of S individuals willing to become entrepreneurs (Figure 12.8). First, those between 0 and s', and, second, those between s'' and s'''. Whether they actually become entrepreneurs or not depends on whether their probability of success is high enough.[11]

Factors influencing the expected net entrepreneurial payoff (NEP)—and the NWP—are the exogenously given entrepreneurial ability ($\bar{e}$), the economy's total stock of knowledge (K), together with other factors (institutional setting, culture, demographics, etc.) which presently are disregarded.

---

[11] The curve can be drawn in several ways and Figure 12.8 is just one illustration. The downward sloping segment is of course a simplification. However, it is likely that the NEP curve is more volatile than the NWP curve.

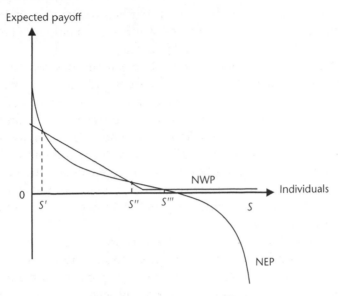

Figure 12.8. Potential entrepreneurs

The issue to be addressed concerns how the occupational choice, based on expected payoffs and a subjective evaluation of the individual's ability, will influence diffusion of knowledge, innovation, and growth. The above set-up shares some similarities with the epidemic technological diffusion models, where diffusion is a function of individual characteristics, uncertainty, profits, and the number of users, as well as the time sequence of the adoption of a new technology.[12] In the following Section 12.4 the structure of a growth model based on R&D-generated innovation as well as innovations stemming from entrepreneurs not involved in research activities will be outlined.

12.4. A simple model involving genuine entrepreneurs and growth

12.4.1. The Romer structure

To illustrate the role of entrepreneurs in growth I take the model of Romer (1990) as the departure point.[13] I will outline the basic structure of the knowledge-based growth model and then introduce the 'genuine' entrepreneur into this model. There will be two methods of developing new products, either in research labs of incumbent firms or by entrepreneurs. Some individuals are inherently better at undertaking entrepreneurial ventures. The economy then hosts three factors of production—labour, capital goods, and

---

[12] Stoneman (2001). See Hall (2005) for a survey.
[13] This is based on the model presented in Braunerhjelm et al. (2010). To simplify, physical investments are disregarded.

entrepreneurship—employed at markets characterized by monopolistic competition (due to heterogeneity imposed by different valuations of knowledge) and firms compete with differentiated products.

Just as in the traditional growth model, researchers develop new varieties of new goods or ways of organizing business activities by investing in R&D. However, in addition, entrepreneurs may also introduce new goods or business models, but they differ from incumbents since the entrepreneurs will not be involved in R&D activities. Rather, entrepreneurial activity is the sum of inherited and different abilities across individuals, the knowledge stock, and how conducive the economy is to entrepreneurial activities (institutions).[14] As entrepreneurs introduce a new product, process, or business model, they will also contribute with new knowledge that spills over to other agents in the economy.

An economy's labour force ($S = L_E+L_R+L_F$) can then be distributed across three sectors: R&D-staff, final goods production, and those engaged in entrepreneurial activities. We disregard the final-goods section and focus on the distribution between knowledge-producing segments of the labour market, i.e. researchers and entrepreneurs.

Assume the economy is endowed with a stock of knowledge (K) at a given point in time. Due to the assumption of decreasing returns to scale ($\gamma < 1$) in entrepreneurial activities—doubling the number of people engaged in entrepreneurial activities will not double the output of new knowledge and varieties—the aggregate production function (Z) for entrepreneurs can be written as

$$Z_E(L_E) = \sigma_E L^\lambda{}_E K \qquad (4)$$

where σ_E represents efficiencies in an economy that impact on entrepreneurship.[15] Similarly, in its simplest form, the aggregate production function for research activities can be written as

$$Z_R(L_R) = \sigma_R L_R K \qquad (5)$$

where research production is positively influenced by a larger knowledge stock and higher efficiency. As a side-effect of their efforts, researchers and entrepreneurs produce new knowledge that will be publicly available for future use, positively influencing coming research and entrepreneurial activities.

---

[14] To some extent this links to the recombinant growth literature (Olsson and Frey, 2002).

[15] Undisputedly an economic development characterized by innovations and exit and entry of firms depends on the presence of a wide set of factors, ranging from a proper design of the legal framework and institutions (property rights, taxes, etc.), access to venture capital, relevant networks to complementary competencies, to culture, etc. (North and Thomas, 1973; Nelson and Winter, 1982; Nelson, 1994, 2002; Feldman and Audretsch, 1999; Acs and Audretsch, 2003; Shane, 2003; Braunerhjelm, 2011). Here we assume that these factors are captured in σ.

Equation (6) describes the production of new knowledge, i.e. the evolution of the stock of knowledge, in relation to the amount of labour channelled into R&D (L_R) and entrepreneurial activity (L_E):

$$\dot{K} = Z_R(L_R) + Z_E(L_E) \tag{6}$$

where $\bar{K}$ represents the time derivative. Substituting from equations (4) and (5),

$$\dot{K}/K = \sigma_R L_R + \sigma_E L_E^{\gamma} \tag{7}$$

the rate of technological progress increases in R&D, entrepreneurship, and the efficiency of these two activities.

Implementing the same theoretical modelling devices as in the standard growth model, it can be shown that an equilibrium steady-state growth rate (g) is attained for a certain distribution of employment between entrepreneurs and R&D-staff,

$$g = \frac{\dot{K}}{K} = \sigma_R L_R + \sigma_E L_E \tag{8}$$

and that equilibrium steady state growth is characterized by

$$\frac{\dot{Y}}{Y} = \frac{\dot{C}}{C} = \frac{\dot{K}}{K_1} \tag{9}$$

implying that output, consumption, and knowledge all grow at the same rate. Moreover, a sub-optimal distribution between entrepreneurs and R&D employees can be shown to lower growth below its optimal, long-run steady-state level. Consequently, this simple model of knowledge-based growth includes 'genuine' entrepreneurs and incumbents, providing a more realistic microeconomic foundation for growth that can be exposed to empirical testing.

12.4.1.1. THE NEO-SCHUMPETERIAN VERSION OF ENDOGENOUS GROWTH

There are two competing versions (sharing several similar features) of the neo-Schumpeterian growth model, albeit one is rooted in the evolutionary tradition (Nelson and Winter, 1982) whereas the other is more closely linked to the Romer (1986, 1990) general equilibrium models. The former is characterized by heterogeneous firms applying Leontief production functions, search and imitation activities to acquire new techniques, R&D routines, and collective learning. Simulation techniques are used to analyze these models.[16] Here I will however focus on the general equilibrium type of endogenous neo-Schumpeterian growth models. As compared to the Romer models the entry

---

[16] See Verspagen (2005).

of new firms (and innovations) is more explicitly modelled, yet in a quite restricted way.[17]

The typical endogenous neo-Schumpeterian growth model is based on the following key characteristics.[18] On the production side, one final good is produced, where entry is measured as quality improvements through the introduction of new products. Production technology only uses labour—assumed to be inelastic in supply and fixed over time—which can either be employed in the production of existing products or in R&D-intensive activities that may result in new products (qualities). Inter-industry mobility assures that wages are equalized in these two production sectors.

Innovation is thus endogenized through R&D races, and innovation draws on previous research efforts—referred to in the literature as 'standing on the shoulders of giants'. A firm that invests more in R&D has a higher probability of discovering new products and temporary monopoly prices can be charged. At the same time, a negative externality is created since the new product sweeps away the market for previous innovations, the so-called business stealing effect (Aghion and Howitt 1998). The net effect of these two forces determines the extent of the R&D-generated spillover.

A crucial assumption is that the introduction of new qualities/products—innovations—is assumed to follow a Poisson process. A Poisson distribution means that innovations occur randomly and independently over time, and the intensity of those events are constant but could be influenced by multiple factors. The time interval between such events could in an innovation context be viewed as 'patents'. Thus, a Poisson process is convenient since its properties comply well with the discovery of new products, and can also be shown to take into account that increased investments in R&D increase the possibilities for innovations, which in turn yields higher growth.

At the firm level, competition is driven by the introduction of a new product in the coming period. This is accomplished by investing in R&D, i.e. hiring labour to undertake research (L_R). At the aggregate level of the economy, the Poisson distributed probability (μ) of a new discovery is then

$$\mu(L_R)dt = L_R^\gamma dt, 0<\gamma<1 \tag{10}$$

where, as in the Romer model outlined above, the parameter γ captures the standard assumption of decreasing returns to scale in R&D production.

Firms' probability of success increases with the firm's share of R&D, $\mu_j dt = \mu_j(L_{jR}/L_R)dt$, where each firm (j) assumes itself to be too small to influence aggregate R&D. The factor (labour) market equilibrium, disregarding

---

[17] See also Braunerhjelm (2008).
[18] See for instance Aghion and Howitt (1992, 1998) and Dinopoulos (1996). The Schumpeterian characteristics of these models has been questioned, e.g. by Alcouffe and Kuhn (2004).

entrepreneurs for the moment, simply requires that total employment does not exceed the supply of labour (S),

$$L_R + L_M = \bar{S} \tag{11}$$

Proceeding with the demand side of the economy, consumers strive to maximize intertemporal utility,

$$U = \int_0^\infty e^{-\rho t} \ln[h(x)]dt, \tag{12}$$

where $\rho t > 0$ equals the consumer's rate of time preferences (discount rate) and h is a sub-utility function,

$$h(x_0, x_1, x_2 \ldots \ldots) = \sum_{I=0}^\infty v^I x_I, v > 1$$

and products (x's) are assumed perfect substitutes and v represents a quality improvement.

Applying standard dynamic maximization techniques, the solution to this intertemporal consumer-maximization problem given an income constraint is

$$C/C = Y/Y_* = r(t) - \rho \tag{13}$$

i.e. balanced growth equilibrium requires consumption expenditure to be constant over time and interest rates to equal consumers' rate of time preferences.

This expression, together with the labour market condition, can be used to derive equilibrium in R&D production, which also shows that consumer expenditure is increasing in R&D investment (L_R). If expected aggregate utility is represented by $G(t,Y)$ in the economy at t, and the occurrence of innovations (I) follows a Poisson distribution, $Exp(I) = tL_R^\gamma$, then the long-run Schumpeterian growth is

$$g = dG(t, Y)/dt = L_R^\gamma \ln v \tag{14}$$

The expected growth rate increases in quality increment (v), in the amount of investment in R&D ($L^\gamma{}_R$), and is exposed to decreasing returns to R&D ($\gamma < 1$).

Despite being an improvement as compared to the original endogenous growth model, insofar as it takes—at least partly—innovative entry into account, this model still suffers from some substantial weaknesses. For instance, the model seems to equalize inventions and innovations. That implies that all successful innovators have exhausted the potential commercial applications of aggregate R&D investments. In order to more accurately capture real-world behaviour, the model should also entail 'pure' Schumpeterian entrepreneurs—i.e. individuals using their skill and the stock of K to innovate—and not only participants of R&D races.

To account for entrepreneurs in the model, simply postulate—exactly as has been done for the probability of successful innovators of the R&D race—that a subset L_E of the population of S individuals will randomly appear as entrepreneurs over time in the economy, governed by a Poisson procedure. Between periods we would have some probability η that entrepreneurs not participating in the R&D race will enter the market in the next period through innovations as they draw on their own given entrepreneurial ability and the common stock of knowledge (K),

$$\eta dt = \sum_{i=1}^{S} e_i S dt = E^{\gamma} dt \quad 0 \leq \gamma \propto 1, \quad e_i = f(\overline{e}, K, X) \tag{15}$$

where, for simplicity, we assume that also the share of entrepreneurs in the aggregate economy is exposed to decreasing returns to scale (γ) of the same magnitude as in R&D.

Hence, doubling the numbers of entrepreneurs does not mean that production is doubled, and at some point it is even conceivable that increasing the numbers of entrepreneurs may have a negative effect on production. Assuming the independence of two events occurring over time—such as winners of R&D race and the prevalence of successful 'pure' entrepreneurs—then the probability that both of them will occur is additive.

$$g = L^{\gamma} \ln v < (L + E)^{\gamma} \ln v = g^{*} \tag{16}$$

From a policy view, as discussed in the paper, this implies a substantial change as compared to the traditional endogenous growth model.

12.5. Policy 1: A technical or an entrepreneurial residual?

The empirical analyses based on the neo-classical model concluded that the overwhelming share of growth was explained by the so called 'technical residual' (Solow, 1956, 1957). Ensuing growth-accounting exercises corroborated those findings. The technical residual picked up all factors that influenced growth, once the effects of increased labour and additions to the capital stock had been taken into account. The interpretation was that new knowledge in one or another way was contained in the technical residual: new technology, better educated employees, product and process innovations, organizational change, entry and exit of firms, etc. In short, much of what Schumpeter ascribed to be the core of the forces behind creative destruction.

In the Schumpeterian (1911) world the evolutionary change originated in entrepreneurial endeavours that basically introduced new knowledge to the market, be it in terms of new scientific discoveries or be it in new combinations of already existing knowledge. The ultimate experiment implied taking the new idea to the market. Only then could its value be tested through competitive selection and only then could it be confirmed or rejected as an innovation. Hence, an innovation is defined by the market value it attains which appears either in the price of the new product or service, or in the value of the firm.

Schumpeter did not view knowledge as such, or a technical discovery, as important for economic development. The crucial actor was the entrepreneur, not the scientist or the inventor. With a few notable exceptions that prediction also seems to be correct. The inventor rarely succeeds without support of an entrepreneur; the most successful outcome seems to be when the inventor and the entrepreneur cooperate (Braunerhjelm and Svensson, 2010). What Schumpeter did not recognize was that the cooperation of smaller entrepreneurs and larger firms may also help to create markets for ideas (Norbäck and Persson 2010). Rather, Schumpeter (1942) feared that large firms would crowd out small entrepreneurial firms, leading to a market structure dominated by the former. The findings of Norbäck and Persson suggest that a complementary and symbiotic relationship prevails, where large firms constitute a market for more radical ideas introduced by smaller firms. As larger firms acquire those ideas and integrate them into their own organizations, the possibilities of extending sales and market shares increases.

The question is whether the technical residual more adequately should have been coined the 'entrepreneurial residual'? A number of empirical analyses support that allegation, albeit the issue of causality—is entrepreneurship causing growth or the other way around—is still unsettled. Block et al. (2009) empirically test the knowledge spillover theory introduced by Acs et al. (2004b, 2009), i.e. that entrepreneurs convert knowledge into innovations without engaging in R&D themselves, thereby substantiating spillovers. According to Block et al. R&D outlays positively influence growth, but the impact of such expenditures displays large variance across countries. Based on an empirical analysis of 21 countries from 1986 to 2006, they conclude that the differences are explained by impediments to entrepreneurial activities, i.e. red tape and regulations.

Acs et al. (2004a) and Braunerhjelm et al. (2010) find a positive relationship between entrepreneurship and growth at the country level, examining 20 OECD countries for the period 1981–2002. The impact is considerably stronger in the 1990s than in the 1980s, while the importance of R&D seems to diminish in the latter time period. Salgado-Banda (2005) implements a measure of innovative entrepreneurship based on quality-adjusted patent data for

22 OECD countries, which is reported to positively influence growth while no such effect could be established for self-employment.[19] Other recent studies report similar results (van Stel and Storey, 2004; Baptista et al., 2008; van Stel and Suddle, 2008).

Glaeser and Kerr (2009) show how a 10 per cent increase in the number of firms per worker increases employment growth by 9 per cent, while a 10 per cent increase in average size of firms is claimed to result in a 7 per cent decrease in employment growth due to new start-ups.[20] Numerous studies of the regional level indicate that not only regional entrepreneurship but also knowledge are significantly related to regional prosperity.[21]

According to Klapper et al. (2010) entrepreneurship is essential for the continued dynamism of the modern market economy and a greater entry rate of new businesses can foster competition and economic growth.[22] They also stress that divergence in economic growth between developed and less developed countries narrows down to differences in entrepreneurial activity (see also Galor and Michalopoulos, 2006). Research on Canadian data suggests that the impact on growth of entry of new firms outpaces growth in existing firms (Brander et al., 1998), which is corroborated in the more recent study of Haltiwanger et al. (2010).

The lesson to be learned is that our understanding of how entrepreneurs work, and how innovations are generated and new ventures emerge, is only partial. Moreover, this is aggravated by the fact that lack of policy data prevents analyses of how economic and political factors affect entrepreneurship.

12.6. Policy 2: At which level should policies be implemented?

The evolutionary and complex feature of the growth process is far from new. Marshall had earlier advocated an evolutionary approach to growth (Raffaelli, 2003). Harrod (1948) claimed that growth dynamics to a large extent depended on investors' expectations, as did Keynes, introducing animal spirits as an irrational behavioural factor while Schumpeter attributed creative destruction—which is basically identical to competitive selection—as the

[19] See Braunerhjelm (2011) for a survey.

[20] The results are corroborated by McMillan and Woodruff (2002) and Audretsch et al. (2006).

[21] See Ashcroft and Love (1996); Fritsch (1997); Audretsch and Fritsch (2002); Acs and Armington (2002); Carree et al. (2002); van Stel and Storey (2004); and Klapper et al. (2006). A number of studies report a positive correlation between knowledge and regional prosperity. However, as stressed by several scholars, these studies suffer from numerous problems, e.g. the complex dynamics between R&D and its commercial applications (Scarpetta et al., 2002; Disney et al., 2003; Erken et al., 2008), and they fail to account for physical and human capital factors/ stocks (Holtz-Eakin and Kao, 2003; Heden, 2005; Foster et al., 2006). Thus, much of the variation in productivities may have little to do with differences in knowledge or technology.

[22] See also Djankov et al. (2002); Klapper, Laeven and Rajan (2006).

major explanation for growth. Also, Fabricant (1940) and Kuznets (1953) stressed that the rise and fall of firms and industries was an outcome of entrepreneurial forces, innovation, and degree of competition. As discussed above, the major modelling contribution in the evolutionary strand has been provided by Nelson and Winter (1974, 1982).

Current theoretical growth models do, however, largely neglect the evolutionary factors; instead the micro-foundations are still based on the representative individual agent, combined with firms that optimize along well-behaved utility and production functions. Evolutionary economics has since long rejected the idea that an averaging out of heterogeneous individual behaviour can be used to construct a representative agent. It is claimed that competitive selection, even in the absence of optimizing the neoclassical case, can result in growth provided that technological and organizational variety, from which heterogeneous innovations can be drawn, exists. The empirical evidence to support traditional growth models is, at best, ambiguous. And without empirical evidence it is a dire task to design economic policies and select effective instruments to attain higher productivity and growth.

As discussed by, for example, Foster (2011), there are techniques available, such as replicator-dynamic mathematics, to demonstrate how competitive selection operates. Yet this approach is hard to apply empirically since it can only reach an identifiable stationary state if variety is fixed. That is rarely, if ever, the case with economic systems. Rather, variety and competitive selection take place at the same time and affect each other, i.e. it is a dynamic adaptive system with positive and negative feedbacks. Moreover, empirical analyses at the macro-level are hampered by the fact that aggregate economic data remove most of the variety through which selection occurs. That makes it even more difficult to observe evolutionary patterns. Hence, the question remains of how to link aggregate economic growth with underlying patterns of variety generation and dynamic replication, even if the processes can be identified at the microeconomic level.

Taking variety and competitive selection as the point of departure in understanding growth carries considerable consequences for the way growth is modelled. In particular, equilibrium and steady-state patterns are exceptions to dynamics characterized by non-equilibrium. These non-equilibrium paths tend to change slowly and will also generate dynamic processes aiming at equilibrating the system around the given paths.[23] Such systems contain elements of structural irreversibility, though associated with some kind of order, and strong elements of path dependence.

---

[23] Known as homeostasis in physics, see Foster (2011).

If structural irreversibility is present due to a set-up of norms, traditions, and the legal framework, and if the evolution of such structures is unobservable or unpredictable, growth trajectory cannot be presumed to yield a final equilibrium in the sense used in standard economics. In the present context that would mean death to a dynamic system. Such complex structures imply that various control mechanisms will be adopted along non-equilibrium trajectories, and stability is limited to relatively short periods. Structures, on the other hand, are connective networks that function through explicit or implicit adaption of a set of rules. When these rules change, evolution sets in. If those rules and the dynamics that influence them are understood, then the growth process can also be better perceived.

This may constitute a superior way of describing and understanding how an economy works, but it builds on the recognition of a complex and adaptive system, characterized by self-organization and competitive selection. A merger—or at least a bridging of the gap—between evolutionary and standard macroeconomic models of growth, taking structural development and change into account, should improve the microeconomic foundation from which normative conclusions are drawn.

Apparently the model becomes considerably more complicated. Not only are meso-level structures and forces hard to observe, but they are also difficult to quantify since they may emerge and appear slowly in the economic system. They also originate in an extremely heterogeneous microeconomic setting, consisting of a complex system expressed in a range of institutions, i.e. customs, norms, routines, laws, etc. Such rules have been adopted and applied to generate economic value, often in a hierarchical framework. Some rules are longer lived and more general in character, others are short-lived and specialized. They may also differ across sectors and industries, i.e. an economy's average growth position depends on the distribution of the position of its industries on the diffusion curve in downward or upward phases.

There is no doubt that in order to understand the forces that propel growth, changing institutions, technologies, and organizational structures become critically important.[24] In the current analysis, these forces appear ex post, giving little or no guidance for the ex ante actions to take, particularly if they are governed by dynamic feedback. Hence, a more complete theory of growth needs to incorporate the co-evolutionary dynamics that results not only in knowledge growth, but also the creative destruction of meso-level rules and the implication for agents converting knowledge to societal value in terms of innovations, entry and exit of firms, investment, and employment. Still, the increased analytical rigor that may be attained through

---

[24] See also Malerba et al. (1999).

incorporating more institutional layers must be traded off against analytical clarity and transparency.

12.7. Conclusion

In this chapter I have reviewed the mainstream endogenous growth models, focusing on their microeconomic foundation and the mechanisms that generate innovation, spillovers, and productivity. Notwithstanding that endogenous growth models imply a considerable step forward in our understanding of growth, empirical support at the aggregate level is ambiguous. I have emphasized the risk of drawing normative conclusions from a model based on simplifying assumptions and too rudimentary a microeconomic setting. Whereas the neoclassical growth model attributed knowledge production to an exogenous 'technical residual', current knowledge-based growth models assume the diffusion of knowledge to take place exogenously. Hence, there seems to be a missing link between the production of knowledge and its conversion to societal economic value.

One conceivable candidate is the entrepreneur, taking us back to Schumpeter's growth-propelling forces of creative destruction. Indeed, empirical evidence increasingly suggests that there is an 'entrepreneurial residual' attached to endogenous growth models, much of the same type as Solow's 'technical residual' in neoclassical models. But there may also be other missing components, such as labour mobility, or different institutions supporting the bridges between knowledge-producing entities and producers of goods and services.

If creative destruction and competitive selection account for the dynamics, then policies to promote growth should be designed in a different manner as compared to the standard recipe derived from endogenous growth models, i.e. subsidizing R&D and education. Competition policies, low entry and exit barriers, and mobility of factors then become strategic policy areas in order to leverage measures to strengthen R&D and human-capital policies. Those are contained not only in legislation but also in other formal and informal institutions, often present at the meso-level and often country- or region-specific. Hence, understanding how those institutions emerge, adapt, and change becomes critically important in designing growth-enhancing policies.

References

Acemoglu, D., Agion, P. and Zillibotti, F. (2003), 'Distance to frontier, selection and growth', *Journal of the European Economic Association*, 1: 630–638.

—— —— —— (2006), 'Distance to frontier, selection and economic growth', *Journal of European Economic Association*, 4: 37–74.

Acs, Z. and Armington, C. (2002), *Economic Growth and Entrepreneurial Activity*. Center for Economic Studies, U. S. Bureau of the Census, Washington, DC.

—— and Audretsch, D. (eds) (2003), *Handbook of Entrepreneurship Research: An Interdisciplinary Survey and Introduction*. Boston, Dordrecht, and London: Kluwer Academic Publishers.

—— ——, Braunerhjelm, P. and Carlsson, B. (2004a), 'The missing link. The knowledge filter and entrepreneurship in endogenous growth', CEPR Discusson Paper 4783.

—— —— —— —— (2004b), 'The knowledge spillover theory of entrepreneurship', Cesis Working Papers 77, Royal Institute of Technology, Stockholm.

—— —— —— —— (2009), 'The knowledge spill-over theory of entrepreneurship', *Small Business Economics*, 32: 15–30.

Adams, J. (1990), 'Fundamental stocks of knowledge and productivity growth', *Journal of Political Economy*, 98: 673–703.

Aghion, P., Bloom, N., Blundell, R., Griffith, R. and Howitt, P. (2005), 'Competition and innovation: An inverted U relationship', *Quarterly Journal of Economics*, 120: 701–728.

——, Blundell, R., Griffith, R., Howitt, P. and Prantl, S. (2006), 'The effects of entry on incumbent innovation and productivity', NBER WP 12027, Cambridge, MA.

——, Burgess, R., Redding, S. and Zilibotti, F. (2004), 'Entry and productivity growth: Evidence from microlevel panel data', *Journal of the European Economic Association*, 2: 265–276.

—— and Griffith, R. (2005), *Competition and Growth: Reconciling Theory and Evidence*. Cambridge, MA: MIT Press.

—— and Howitt, P. (1992), 'A model of growth through creative destruction', *Econometrica*, 60: 323–351.

—— —— (1998), *Endogenous Growth Theory*. Cambridge, MA: MIT Press.

Alcouffe, A. and Kuhn, T. (2004), 'Schumpeterian endogenous growth theory and evolutionary economics', *Journal of Evolutionary Economics*, 14: 223–236.

Aldrich, H. and Auster, E. (1986), 'Even dwarfs started small: Liabilities of age and size and their strategic implications', *Research in Organizational Behavior*, 8: 165–198.

Almeida, P. (1999), 'Small firms and economic growth'. In Acs, Z., Carlsson, B. and Thurik, R. (eds), *Small Business in the Modern Economy*. Oxford: Blackwell.

—— and Kogut, B. (1997), 'The exploration of technological diversity and the geographic localization of innovation', *Small Business Economics*, 9: 21–31.

Anselin, L., Varga, A. and Acs, Z., (1997), 'Local geographic spillovers between university research and high technology innovations', *Journal of Urban Economics*, 42: 422–448.

—— —— —— (2000), 'Geographic and sectoral characteristics of academic knowledge externalities', *Papers in Regional Science*, 79: 435–443.

Antonelli, C. (2007), *The Path Dependent Complexity of Localized Technological Change: Ingredients, Governance and Processes*. London: Routledge.

Ashcroft, B. and Love, J. (1996), 'Firm births and employment change in the British counties:1981–1989', *Papers in Regional Science*, 75: 483–500.

Audretsch, D. and Fritsch, F. (2002), 'Growth regimes over time and space', *Regional Studies*, 36: 113–124.

——, Keilbach, M. and Lehmann, E. (2006), *Entrepreneurship and Economic Growth*. New York: Oxford University Press.

Baptista, R., Escária, V. and Madruga, P. (2008), 'Entrepreneurship, regional development and job creation: The case of Portugal', *Small Business Economics*, 28: 49–58.

Baumol, W. (2004), 'Entrepreneurial enterprises, large established firms and other components of the free-market growth machine', *Small Business Economics*, 23: 9–21.

—— (2007), 'Small firms: Why market-driven innovation can't get along without them', Paper presented at the IFN conference in Waxholm.

Berry, S. and Pakes, A. (2003), 'Empirical models of entry and market structure'. In Schmalensee, R. and Willig, R. (eds), *Handbook of Industrial Organization*. Amsterdam: North Holland.

Block, J., Thurik, R. and Zhou, H. (2009), 'What turns knowledge into growth? The role of entrepreneurship and knowledge spillovers', Research Paper ERS -2009–049, ERIM.

Brander, J., Hendricks, K., Amit, R. and Whistler, D. (1998), 'The engine of growth hypothesis: On the relationship between firm size and employment growth work', mimeo, University of British Columbia.

Braunerhjelm, P. (2005), 'Knowledge capital and economic growth: Sweden as an emblematic example'. In Curzio, A. and Fortis, M. (eds), *Research and Technological Innovation*. Heidelberg and New York: Physica-Verlag.

—— (2008), 'Entrepreneurship, knowledge and growth', *Foundations and Trends in Entrepreneurship*, 4: 451–533.

—— (2011), 'Entrepreneurship, innovation and economic growth: Interdependencies, irregularities and regularities'. In Audretsch, D., Falck, O. and Heilbach, P. (eds), *Handbook of Innovation and Entrepreneurship*. London: Edward Elgar.

——, Acs, Z., Audretsch, D., and Carlsson, B. (2010), 'The missing link. Knowledge diffusion and entrepreneurship in endogenous growth', *Small Business Economics*, 34: 105–125.

—— and Svensson, R. (2010), 'The inventor role. Was Schumpeter right?', *Journal of Evolutionary Economics*, 20: 314–344.

—— and Thulin, P. (2003), 'A note on entrepreneurship and endogenous growth', mimeo, Royal Institue of Technology, Stockholm.

Caballero, R. and Jaffe, A. (1993), 'How high are the giants' shoulders? An empirical assessment of knowledge spillovers and creative destruction in a model of economic growth', *NBER Macroeconomics Annual*, 8: 15–74.

Carlsson, B., Acs, Z., Audretsch, D. and Braunerhjelm, P. (2009), 'Knowledge creation, entrepreneurship, and economic growth: A historical review', *Industrial and Corporate Change*, 18: 1193–1229.

Carree, M., van Stel, A., Thurik, R. and Wennekers, S. (2002), 'Economic development and business ownership: An analysis using data of 23 OECD countries in the period 1976–1996', *Small Business Economics*, 19: 271–290.

Casson, M. (1990), *Entrepreneurship*. London: Edward Elgar.

Casson, M. (2002a), 'Entrepreneurship, business culture and the theory of the firm'. In Acs, Z. and Audretsch, D. (eds), *The International Handbook of Entrepreneurship Research*. Berlin and New York: Springer Verlag.

—— (2002b), *The Entrepreneur: An Economic Theory*. Northampton, MA: Edward Elgar.

Chandler, A. (1990), *Scale and Scope: The Dynamics of Industrial Capitalism*. Cambridge, MA: Harvard University Press.

Cheng, L. and Dinopoulos, E. (1992), 'Schumpeterian growth and international business cycles', *American Economic Review*, 82: 409–414.

Christensen, C. (1997), *The Innovator's Dilemma*. Boston: Harvard Business School Press.

Chun, H., Kim, J.-W., Morck, R. and Yeung, B. (2007), 'Creative destruction and firm-specific performance heterogeneity', NBER WP 13011, Cambridge, MA.

Coe, D. and Helpman, E. (1995), 'International R&D spillovers', *European Economic Review*, 39: 859–887.

Cohen, W. and Levinthal, D. (1989), 'Innovation and learning: The two faces of R&D', *Economic Journal*, 99: 569–596.

—— —— (1990), 'Absorptive capacity: A new perspective on learning and innovation', *Administrative Science Quarterly*, 35: 128–152.

Denison, E. (1962), *The Sources of Economic Growth in the United States and the Alternatives Before Us*. Washington, DC: Committee for Economic Development.

Dinopoulos, E. (1996), 'Schumpeterian growth theory: An overview'. In Helmstädter, E. and Perlman, M. (eds), *Behavioral Norms, Technological Progress, and Economic Dynamics*. Ann Arbor: The University of Michigan Press.

Disney, R., Haskel, J. and Heden, Y. (2003), 'Restructuring and productivity growth in UK manufacturing', *Economic Journal*, 113: 666–694.

Djankov, S., La Porta, R., Lopes de Silanes, F. and Schleifer, A. (2002), 'The regulation of entry', *Quarterly Journal of Economics*, 117: 1–37.

Durlauf, S. (2001), 'Econometric analysis and the study of economic growth: A skeptical perspective'. In Backhouse, R. and Salanti, A. (eds), *Macroeconomics and the Real World*. Oxford: Oxford University Press.

——, Kourtellos, A. and Tan, C. (2008), 'Are any growth theories robust?', *Economic Journal*, 118: 329–344.

Durnev, A., Morck, R. and Yeung, B. (2004), 'Value-enhancing capital budgeting and firm-Specific stock return variation', *Journal of Finance*, 59: 65–105.

Easterly, W. (2001), 'The lost decades: Developing countries' stagnation in spite of policy reform 1980–1998', *Journal of Economic Growth*, 6: 135–157.

Ejermo, O. (2009), 'Regional innovation measured by patent data—Does quality matter?', *Industry and Innovation*, 16: 141–165.

Erken, H., Donselaar, P. and Thurik, R. (2008), 'Total factor productivity and the role of entrepreneurship', Jena Economic Research Paper 2008–019, Max Planck Institute of Economics, Jena.

Fabricant, S. (1940), *The Output of Manufacturing Industries: 1899–1937*. New York: NBER.

Fagerberg, J. and Srholec, M (2009), 'Innovation systems, technology and development: Unpacking the relationships'. In Lundvall, B.-A., Joseph, K., Chaminades, C. and

Vang, J. (eds), *Handbook of Innovation Systems and Developing Countries*. Cheltenham and Northampton: Edward Elgar.

Feldman, M. (2004), 'The significance of innovation', Swedish Institute for Growth Policy Studies, Stockholm.

―― and Audretsch, D. (1999), 'Innovation in cities: Science-based diversity, specialization and localized competition', *European Economic Review*, 43: 409–429.

Fink, J., Fink, K., Grullon, G. and Weston, J. (2005), 'IPO vintage and the rise of idiosyncratic risk'. Paper presented at the Seventh Annual Texas Finance Festival (http://papers.ssrn.com/sol3/papers.cfm?abstract_id=661321).

Foster, J. (2011), 'Evolutionary macroeconomics: A research agenda'. In Pyka, A. and de Graca Derengowski Fonseca, M. (eds), *Evolutionary Macrocononomics: A Research Agenda*. Heidelberg, Dordrecht, London, and New York: Springer.

Foster, L., Haltiwanger, J. and Krizan, C. (2006), 'Market selection, reallocation, and restructuring in the U.S. retail trade sector in the 1990s', *Review of Economics and Statistics*, 88: 748–758.

Fritsch, M. (1997), 'New firms and regional employment change', *Small Business Economics*, 9: 437–447.

Galor, O. and Michalopoulos, S. (2006), 'The evolution of entrepreneurial spirit and the process of development', CEPR Discussion Paper No. 6022.

Gilbert, R. and Newbery, D. (1982), 'Preemptive patenting and the persistence of monopoly', *American Economic Review*, 72: 514–526.

Glaeser, E. and Kerr, W. (2009), 'Local industrial conditions and entrepreneurship: How much of the spatial distribution can we explain?', *Journal of Economics and Management Strategy*, 18: 623–633.

Griliches, Z. (1979), 'Issues in assessing the contribution of R&D to productivity growth', *Bell Journal of Economics*, 10: 92–116.

Hall, B. H. (2005), Innovation and diffusion. In Fagerberg, J., Mowery, D. and Nelson, R. (eds), *The Oxford Handbook of Innovation*. Oxford and New York: Oxford University Press.

――, Mairesse, J. and Mohnen, P. (2010), 'Measuring the returns to R&D'. In Hall, B.H. and Rosenberg, N. (eds), *Handbook of the Economics of Innovation*. Amsterdam: North-Holland.

Haltiwanger, J., Jarmin, R. and Miranda, J. (2010), 'Who creates jobs? Small vs. large vs. small', Working Paper CES 10–17, August.

Harrod, R. (1948), *Towards a Dynamic Economics*. London: MacMillan.

Heden, Y. (2005), 'Productivity, upskilling, restructuring, entry and exit: Evidence from the UK and Swedish micro data', University of London.

Hicks, J. (1950), *A Contribution to the Theory of the Cycle Trade*. London: Oxford University Press.

Holtz-Eakin, D. and Kao, C. (2003), *Enterpreneurship and Economic Growth: The Proof is in the Productivity*. Syracuse: Syracuse University Press.

Howitt, P. (2007), 'Innovation, competition and growth: A Schumpeterian perspective on Canada's economy'. C.D. Howe Institute Commentary No. 246, Ottawa.

Jones, C. (1995a), 'R&D-based models of economic growth', *Journal of Political Economy*, 103: 759–784.

Jones, C. (1995b), 'Time series test of endogenous growth models', *Quarterly Journal of Economics*, 110: 495–525.

—— (2006), 'Knowledge and the theory of economic development', mimeo, Department of Economics, Berkeley.

Jovanovic, B. and Rosseau, P.L. (2005), General purpose technologies. In Aghion, P. and Durlauf, S. (eds), *Handbook of Economic Growth*. Amsterdam: Elsevier.

Klapper, L., Amit, R. and Guillén, M. (2010), 'Entrepreneurship and firm formation across countries'. In Lerner, J. and Schoar, A. (eds), *International Differences in Entrepreneurship*. Chicago: University of Chicago Press.

—— Laeven, L. and Rajan, R. (2006), 'Entry regulation as a barrier to entrepreneurship', *Journal of Financial Economics*, 82: 591–629.

Kuznets, S. (1953), *Economic Change*. New York: Norton.

Laffont, J.-J. and Tirole, J. (1993), *A Theory of Incentives and Regulation*. Cambridge, MA: MIT Press.

LeSage, J. and Fischer, M. (2008), 'The impact of knowledge stocks on regional total factor productivity' (http//:ssrn.com/abstract=1088301).

Lichtenberg, F. (1993), 'R&D investments and international productivity differences', NBER WP 4161.

Lucas, R. (1988), 'On the mechanisms of economic development', *Journal of Monetary Economics*, 22: 3–42.

—— (2000), 'Some macroeconomics for the 21st century', *Journal of Economic Perspectives*, 14: 451–479.

Malerba, F., Nelson, R., Orsenigo, L. and Winter, S. (1999), 'History friendly models of industrial evolution: The computer industry', *Industrial and Corporate Change*, 8: 3–40.

McMillan, J. and Woodruff, C. (2002), 'The central role of entrepreneurs in transition economies', *Journal of Economic Perspectives*, 16: 153–170.

Naudé, W. (2008), 'Entrepreneurship in economic development'. Research Paper 2008/20, UNU-Wider, Helsinki.

Nelson, R. (1994), 'What has been the matter with neoclassical growth theory?'. In Silverberg, G. and Soete, L. (eds), *The Economics of Growth and Technical Change—Technologies, Nations, Agents*. Cambridge, MA, and London: Harvard University Press.

—— (2002), 'Bringing institutions into evolutionary growth theory', *Journal of Evolutionary Economics*, 12: 17–28.

—— and Winter, S. (1974), 'Neoclassical vs. evolutionary theories of growth: Critique and prospectus', *Economic Journal*, 84: 886–905.

—— —— (1982), *An Evolutionary Theory of Economic Change*. Cambridge: Cambridge University Press.

Nickell, S.J. (1996), 'Competition and corporate performance', *Journal of Political Economy*, 104: 724–746.

Norbäck, P.J. and Persson, L. (2010), 'The organization of the innovation industry: Entrepreneurs, venture capitalists, and oligopolists', *Journal of the European Economic Association*, 7: 1261–1290.

North, D. (1990), *Institutions, Institutional Change and Economic Performance*. Cambridge: Cambridge University Press.

—— and Thomas, R.T. (1973), *The Rise of the Western World: A New Economic History*. Cambridge: Cambridge University Press.

OECD (2010), *Ministerial Report on the OECD Innovation Strategy, Key Findings*. Paris: OECD.

Olsson, O. and Frey, B. (2002), 'Entrepreneurship as recombinant growth', *Small Business Economics*, 19: 69–80.

Ortega-Argilés, R., Vivarelli, M. and Voight, P. (2009), 'R&D in SMEs: A paradox', *Small Business Economics*, 33: 3–11.

Paci, R. and Usai, S. (1999), 'Externalities, knowledge spillovers and the spatial distribution of innovation', *GeoJournal*, 49: 381–390.

Pastor, L. and Veronesi, P. (2005), 'Technological revolutions and stock prices', mimeo, University of Chicago.

Porter, M. (1990), *The Competitive Advantage of Nations*. Cambridge, MA: Harvard University Press.

Raffaelli, T. (2003), *Marshall's Evolutionary Legacy*. London: Routledge.

Rebelo, S. (1991), 'Long-run policy analysis and long-run growth', *Journal of Political Economy*, 99: 500–521.

Romer, P. (1986), 'Increasing returns and long run growth', *Journal of Political Economy*, 94: 1002–1037.

—— (1990), 'Endogenous technological change', *Journal of Political Economy*, 98: 71–S102.

Rosenberg, N. (1972), 'Factors affecting the diffusion of technology', *Explorations in Economic History*, 10: 3–33.

Rothwell, R. and Zegveld, W. (1982), *Innovation and the Small and Medium Sized Firm*. London: Pinter Publishers.

Sala-i-Martin, X., (2002), '15 years of new growth economics: What have we learnt?', Columbia University, NY.

Salgado-Banda, H. (2005), 'Entrepreneurship and economic growth: An empirical analysis'. Direction de Estudios Económicos, Banco de México.

Scarpetta, S., Hemmings, P., Tressel, T. and Woo, J. (2002), 'The role of policy and institutions for productivity and firm dynamics: Evidence from micro and industry data'. OECD Economics Department WP no. 329.

Schumpeter, J. (1911), *The Theory of Economic Development*. Cambridge, MA: Harvard University Press.

—— (1942), *Capitalism, Socialism and Democracy*. New York: Harper and Row.

Segerstrom, P. (1991), 'Innovation, imitation and economic growth', *Journal of Political Economy*, 99: 190–207.

—— (1995), 'A quality ladders growth model with decreasing returns to R&D', mimeo, Michigan State University.

Shane, S. (2003), *A General Theory of Entrepreneurship*. Cheltenham: Edward Elgar.

Solow, R., (1956), 'A contribution to the theory of economic growth', *Quarterly Journal of Economics*, 70: 65–94.

Solow, R. (1957), 'Technical change and the aggregate production function', *The Review of Economics and Statistics*, 39: 312–320.

Stoneman, P. (2001), *The Economics of Technological Diffusion*. Oxford: Blackwell.

Tirole, J. (1988), *The Theory of Industrial Organization*. Cambridge, MA: MIT Press.

van Stel, A. and Storey, D. (2004), 'The link between firm birth and job creation: Is there an upas tree effect?', *Regional Studies*, 38: 893–909.

—— and Suddle, K. (2008), 'The impact of new firm formation on regional development in the Netherlands', *Small Business Economics*, 30: 31–47.

Verspagen, B. (2005), 'Innovation and economic growth'. In Fagerberg, J., Mowery, D. and Nelson, R. (eds), *The Oxford Handbook of Innovation*. Oxford and New York: Oxford University Press.

Warsh, D. (2006), *Knowledge and the Wealth of Nations*. New York: W.W. Norton & Company.

Wieser, R. (2005), 'Research and development productivity spillovers—Empirical evidence at the firm level', *Journal of Economic Surveys*, 19: 587–621.

13

Framework Conditions for High-Potential Entrepreneurship: A Theoretical Structure and its Implications[1]

David M. Hart

13.1. Introduction

This volume is devoted to the relationship between R&D strategies at the firm level and their broader economic consequences. Entrepreneurship, conceived of here as the creation of new businesses, is, along with the commercialization of innovative products and the refinement of production routines within existing firms, one of the key processes that mediate this relationship. Existing firms are able to draw on a range of resources to convert the knowledge that they create into value, which in turn leads to growth and employment; these resources include managerial talent, lines of credit, and relationships with other firms. Entrepreneurs have a much more challenging task: they may bring good ideas to the new enterprise, but they have to find and organize the kinds of resources that existing firms take for granted in order to take advantage of those ideas and have an effect on the broader economy.

Yet, they do. Recent research, referenced in more detail below, shows that new businesses are responsible for most of the net employment and growth in at least some high-income economies, notably the USA. Thus, even though the task of the entrepreneur is so challenging that it results quite often in failure, the impact of the minority of entrepreneurs who are successful is profound. Sometimes their success occurs along precisely the strategic lines

[1] An early version of this paper was prepared for the 2007 Shibusawa North American Seminar. The author thanks Jack High, Emilia Istrate, Haifeng Qian, Erik Stam, Amanda Elam, and participants at the CESIS workshop in Jönköping for helpful comments and encouragement.

that existing firms have considered and rejected or tried and failed. Where this is the case, entrepreneurs may be seen (at least to some degree) as completing the translation of existing firms' R&D investments into societal value. In other cases, they may be working with ideas drawn from academic research, again, converting the investment that generated that research (in this case, typically made by a government or a philanthropy, rather than an existing firm) into results that are very important to society.

Societies with too few entrepreneurial ventures, or perhaps too few successful entrepreneurial ventures, then, do not reap the benefits from R&D that they might like. While R&D and even innovation may be of value for their own sake, providing satisfying work for a few experts and adding to the global sum of human knowledge, their larger value comes when they get put to practical use. In addition to employment and growth, the value comes from improved consumer welfare, as people are able to do things that they want to do more cheaply than in the past or become able to do things that they could not do in the past.

So the question of what causes entrepreneurship is quite appropriate for a volume like this one. Or, to put it more sharply, the question of what causes a certain kind of entrepreneurship is quite essential for a volume like this one. Because only a certain kind of entrepreneurship, which I will call 'high-potential entrepreneurship', really matters for society. The causes of such entrepreneurship have been explored in some depth but too often in a fragmented fashion. In this chapter, I seek to pull the various threads together into a unified framework.

The chapter begins by reviewing what the literature tells us about the sources of high-potential entrepreneurship and its impact on society. It then advances a set of 'framework conditions' that seek to explain variation in rates of high-potential entrepreneurship over time and across societies. These conditions operate at three levels—the individual, the organization, and the society—and are interconnected, so that a society's capacity to generate high-potential entrepreneurship cumulates over time. The analysis offers, I conclude, important insights for public policy-makers, implying these rates of high-potential entrepreneurship will tend to change slowly and that policy leverage is difficult to exert.

13.2. The importance of high-potential entrepreneurship

Entrepreneurship is, of course, a word with many meanings. One wit (Pozen, 2008) has gone so far as to entitle an article 'We Are All Entrepreneurs Now'. While this sort of semantic flexibility may be a virtue in politics, where being seen as entrepreneurial is sometimes an asset, it creates challenges for analysts. In this chapter, my purpose is to shed light on the role of entrepreneurship in linking R&D strategies to their economic impacts and, more specifically, exploring linkages outside the context of existing firms. That means that I can adopt a straightforward definition of entrepreneurship—the founding of a new business.

This decision also allows me to rely on others' work over the past decade that uses a similar definition, such as research that draws on cross-national data from the Global Entrepreneurship Monitor (GEM). Although the central question of whether and how much entrepreneurship contributes to economic growth has not been fully resolved, the evidence points to the value of decomposing entrepreneurship into several components. Of these components, the most important seems to be high-potential entrepreneurship—new businesses that have grown very rapidly.

A casual review of early GEM data suggested that there was no clear relationship between the level of development of a country and its rate of total entrepreneurial activity. However, once a distinction was made between 'necessity' entrepreneurs, who have no other employment options, and 'opportunity' entrepreneurs, who undertake entrepreneurship for motives other than sheer desperation (Reynolds et al., 2002), a clearer pattern emerged. Higher rates of opportunity entrepreneurship seemed to be associated with better economic performance.

Within the high-income countries, most entrepreneurship is opportunity entrepreneurship. In data restricted to these countries, researchers also found that total rates of entrepreneurship at the regional and national level were closely associated with economic growth (Wennekers and Thurik, 1999; Acs, Audretsch, Braunerhjelm and Carlsson, 2006). Haltiwanger (2008), for instance, provides evidence that firms that are less than five years old account for nearly all net job creation in the USA.

This finding set the stage for a further decomposition of the data. Even within the high-income countries, most entrepreneurs create few jobs and often none at all. This outcome is the logical result of their aspirations; most entrepreneurs do not want to build a business that goes beyond their basement or a single office or a small establishment. A tiny fraction of aspiring entrepreneurs (Autio 2007), on the other hand, dream of emulating Bill Gates or Richard Branson by building a big and durable business. While their dreams do not often come true, those that do achieve success have important consequences for the societies in which these entrepreneurs live.

Turning from the literature on entrepreneurial aspirations to actual firm performance, we find that a small number of young firms have a hugely disproportionate impact on the broader economy. Wong, Ho and Autio (2005) and Autio (2005), for instance, summarize a variety of studies showing that 1–10 per cent of new firms generate 40–75 per cent of new jobs. The literature reviewed by Henrekson and Johansson (2010: 240), reaches the same 'clear-cut' conclusion: 'A few rapidly growing firms generate a disproportionately large share of all new net jobs.' Acs, Parsons, and Tracy (2008) show that just 2.2 per cent of all firms in the USA accounted for the bulk of net job creation and economic growth in the United States between 1994 and 2006.

The precise definitions and terminology in this growing literature vary. The GEM literature, such as Autio (2005), labels these aspirants 'high-expectation', because they are identified by a question that asks them how many jobs they expect that their firms will eventually create. Acs, Parsons, and Tracy (2008) use the term 'high-impact' and the definition that the firm has doubled in size and revenue in a four-year period. Following Autio (2003), I will use the term 'high-potential', which is also common in the literature, because I am concerned with prospective as well as realized opportunities.

One key reason for this disproportionate impact is that new firms are more able than established businesses to create and to absorb radical technological innovations that open up new markets and support new business models (Christensen and Rosenbloom, 1995). Competition from successful new entrants, in turn, forces their older rivals to adapt or face extinction (Fritsch and Mueller, 2004). This dynamic can drive productivity growth across the broader economy, as it seems to have done in the USA in the decade prior to the current recession (Cotis, 2007). While it is true that this competition destroys jobs in older firms, the literature cited above focuses on net job creation, showing that the additions outweigh the subtractions.

High-potential entrepreneurship is likely to become even more important in the future for high-income nations. Production processes are more easily standardized and modularized than in the past and therefore more easily offshored and imitated. A steady stream of high-potential start-ups may allow these nations to cope with the outflow of economic activity that these trends imply. Like the Red Queen in Lewis Carroll's *Alice in Wonderland*, the rich will have to run faster just to stay in the same place. High-potential entrepreneurship is one crucial way to do so.

13.3. Explaining high-potential entrepreneurship

The importance of high-potential entrepreneurship to economic growth in the high-income countries compels us to seek to understand better the conditions under which it is more or less likely to occur. Entrepreneurship scholars have recently begun to explore these issues, building on research that focuses on total entrepreneurial activity. However, because the individuals, opportunities, and institutions involved in high-potential entrepreneurship are different from those involved in other forms of entrepreneurship, the received wisdom must be modified somewhat to suit our needs.

GEM and other projects have given entrepreneurship scholars more data than they had to work with ten years ago. In parallel with the expansion of data availability has come a revolution in scholarly perspective. Thornton, writing in 1999 (p. 19), concluded that in work prior to that date, 'the supply-side perspective, which focuses on the individual traits of entrepreneurs, has been the dominant school of research'. That is no longer the case. Entrepreneurship journals these days are more likely to feature studies of the 'demand-side' than the 'supply-side' (to use Thornton's terms).

The stage was set for this turn by the broader focus on institutions within economics. Baumol (1990), surveying many centuries of history on a global scale, organized entrepreneurship into productive, unproductive, and destructive categories, and made the case that the rules of the game in society induce potential entrepreneurs to select one or the other of these. Murphy, Shleifer and Vishny (1991) similarly distinguished between rent-seeking and entrepreneurship and considered which societal institutions might make equally talented people select one rather than other.

As the focus on the demand for entrepreneurs sharpened, a set of relatively narrow but very productive research streams emerged. The financial environment for new businesses, for instance, has captured enormous scholarly energy (e.g. Lerner, 2009). The availability of knowledge and information to entrepreneurial ventures, too, has been of great interest to researchers (e.g. Acs et al., 2009). The ways in which entrepreneurs draw on social networks constitutes a third aspect of the context for entrepreneurship about which we know much more now than we did a decade ago (e.g. Casson, 2010).

Somewhat less effort has gone into synthesizing these threads into a broader fabric of explanation. Levie and Autio (2008) advance the GEM model, which includes a very broad range of national framework conditions and entrepreneurial framework conditions that in turn shape individual capacities to perceive and act on opportunities. This impressive effort produces a model that is comprehensive, but is also somewhat static. In a recent working paper, Autio (2009) takes this work a step further in trying to explain what he calls 'the curious absence of high-growth entrepreneurship in Finland'. The conclusion is nuanced but suggests that 'experience matters', which points to the need for a more dynamic conceptualization of the process.

Henrekson and Johansson (2009) introduce the idea of a 'competence bloc' into their effort to synthesize an explanation for variations in high-potential entrepreneurship. They identify a range of actors and institutions that contribute to the entrepreneur's ability to generate and exploit high-growth opportunities. Many of these overlap with the GEM model, but envisioning them as a bloc suggests interactions and system-level properties that are not present in that model.

Shane's 'individual/opportunity nexus' (2003) provides the third and most important pillar of a synthesis. This work conceives of the entrepreneurial process as occurring sequentially through time, characterized by the phases of discovery, evaluation, and exploitation (Shane and Venktaraman, 2000). Although somewhat less comprehensive than the GEM model, and more oriented to the individual entrepreneur than to the entrepreneur's social context, the dynamic nature of Shane's treatment is striking.

My effort is focused on a particular set of opportunities, those with the potential for rapid growth, as well as a particular set of individuals who have the requisite capabilities to perceive these opportunities. These individuals are available to become entrepreneurs thanks to the kinds of framework conditions identified by the GEM model, which interact in the systemic fashion of competence blocs. In addition, the time horizon for understanding framework conditions is extended for a much longer period.

13.4. Framework conditions: The general argument

High-potential entrepreneurship is a complex phenomenon. This complexity undermines single-factor theories and should dissuade policy-makers from the temptation to search for a 'magic bullet' to stimulate it. For instance, secure property rights, including intellectual property rights, embedded in a well-functioning legal system, may be necessary but are not sufficient to explain high-potential entrepreneurship. Among other things, property rights do not necessarily provide adequate incentives for knowledge creation.

On the other hand, a thriving system of non-proprietary academic and governmental research may make a society knowledge-rich, but its presence may not be sufficient to ensure that the high-potential opportunities it generates will be exploited. A ready supply of high-risk venture funding, to pick a third possible 'magic bullet,' may be necessary if start-ups are to be scaled up rapidly, but cheap finance alone may not be sufficient to induce would-be entrepreneurs to shoulder non-pecuniary risks to their social status or career prospects that 'taking the leap' would entail.

Rather than searching for single factors, we need to adopt a comprehensive framework for explaining variation in high-potential entrepreneurship across countries and over time. Multiple institutional systems—cultural, political, economic, and educational—interact to produce a social context that is propitious for it. These institutional systems interact over time through the adaptive work of various agents, not just entrepreneurs, but also policy-makers, financial decision-makers, managers, and others.

These actors adjust their behaviour, including their routines for making and enforcing institutional norms and rules themselves, in order to reduce conflicting institutional influences. Institutions thus tend to fit together harmoniously from the agents' point of view. In such a setting, simultaneous change in multiple-institutional systems, as seems to be required to alter something as complex as the rate of high-potential entrepreneurship in a society, may be very difficult to motivate and coordinate. The future is strongly conditioned by the past.

This approach draws on work by scholars seeking to explain similarly complex phenomena. Pierson (2004), for instance, considers the historical process by which welfare states come to have stability: they create the conditions for their own perpetuation and are 'locked in' by a complex web of beliefs, commitments, incentives, and habits. Murmann (2003) explores technological innovation in a similar fashion, as does the work of Greif (2006) on an even grander scale on market-based economic institutions. High-potential entrepreneurship is complex enough and important enough to society to fit comfortably in such company.

Of course, we should bear in mind that this process of institutional self-reinforcement is a matter of dependence, not determinism. Especially when powerful external pressures are present, the trajectory of institutional change may deviate from its historical path. And sometimes small changes accrete over time to produce tensions among institutions that can lead to conflict and disruption (Thelen and Mahoney, 2010).

Inspired by this work on path dependence and cumulative institutional capacity, and drawing particularly on Shane (2003), I advance a framework for understanding high-potential entrepreneurship in the next three sections. If high-potential opportunities are to be created, society must be rich in intellectual and economic resources and open to innovation. These are fundamentally questions of political economy. If such opportunities are to be recognized, society must possess a diverse array of sophisticated and ambitious individuals. This set of conditions has mainly to do with culture and human resources. If high-potential opportunities are to be exploited, society must value risk-taking and be able to redirect substantial resources to particularly promising new enterprises. These issues lie in the realm of management and organizations.

To put it another way, we can productively group high-potential entrepreneurship framework conditions into three clusters that correspond with three levels of analysis. *Societies* create opportunities for high-potential entrepreneurship through the operation of political-economy framework conditions. *Individuals* recognize opportunities for high-potential entrepreneurship when enabled by socio-cultural framework conditions. *Organizations* exploit opportunities for high-potential entrepreneurship if resource-mobilization framework conditions permit them to do so.

323

13.5. Political economy and the creation of high-potential opportunities

My detailed argument begins with a discussion of political economy. In order for high-potential opportunities to be created, much less recognized and exploited, the social context for entrepreneurship must be changing more rapidly or profoundly than existing businesses can respond to. Firms, like other agents, tend to continue doing what they have done in the past. The more a new opportunity would require changing existing routines, the less likely incumbents are to seize it. The prospect of new competition, moreover, may prompt them to seek protection through the political system. Opportunities for high-potential entrepreneurship will appear more frequently in highly dynamic economic systems where political protection for existing businesses is scarce.

If established businesses were so perceptive and so nimble that they recognized and seized all the available opportunities, new businesses would be unnecessary. In practice, the standard operating routines of established businesses make it difficult for them to recognize and act on new opportunities, especially high-potential opportunities (Nelson and Winter, 1982; Christensen, 1997).

The emergence of new markets, either through the introduction of new customers or as a result of changing tastes, is one source of change with which existing businesses may have trouble coping. For example, the opening of a large new foreign market could be a powerful stimulus to high-potential entrepreneurship, especially if the demands of the new customers are different from those at home. Changing tastes in the domestic market, especially sudden and dramatic ones, are likely to be even more powerful stimuli for high-potential entrepreneurship. Such changes in taste may arise for a variety of reasons, such as saturation of existing demand, the whims of fashion, and, perhaps most important, product and process innovation.

Innovation, in turn, stems in large part from the creation of new knowledge. The extent and location of knowledge creation depends significantly on economic and political institutions. These institutions (such as financial markets and tax law) may provide incentives for existing businesses to create new knowledge even as their established routines (such as the 'wall' that often separates R&D from production within firms) interfere with these businesses' ability to recognize the value that they have created. The greater the tension between knowledge creation and opportunity recognition within existing businesses, the more likely it is that disgruntled employees will depart to pursue high-potential entrepreneurship based on ideas rejected by their employers (Auerswald and Branscomb, 2003).

Opportunities based on new knowledge created by non-business organizations, such as academic or government laboratories, tend to be even more difficult for existing businesses to recognize. These organizations are supported primarily by political institutions, either directly through government appropriations or indirectly through tax incentives for charitable contributions. The routines of laboratory researchers are distinct from most business routines, and communication between the world of research and that of business is often fraught with barriers. Entrepreneurs may be better positioned than existing businesses to recognize high-potential opportunities drawing on laboratory-based science and engineering (Rosenberg, 2003).

Opportunities for high-potential entrepreneurship, however promising, are far less likely to be pursued if government agencies or existing businesses, however clumsy, are perceived by potential entrepreneurs to be likely to place a 'thumb on the scales' and alter market outcomes arbitrarily to suit their interests. Such a bias in favour of existing businesses may be caused by onerous taxes on entrepreneurs, by regulations that protect incumbents, by unfair trade practices of incumbents against which new entrants have no recourse, or by collusion between government and incumbents. Effective systems of real- and intellectual-property rights, policies that control excessive market power, and political practices that allow potential and new interests to be expressed in the policy process limit the chances that the economic system will be rigged against start-ups.

13.6. Culture, human resources, and the recognition of high-potential opportunities

While the economic and political institutions of nations shape the relative availability of opportunities for high-potential entrepreneurship, the extent to which entrepreneurial individuals recognize and seize them depends on cultural factors as well. High-potential opportunities, especially those resulting from the development of new knowledge, are more likely to be recognized by people with high levels of education and experience. Cultural diversity also enhances recognition by widening the range of evaluations placed on uncertain opportunities. A society with a strong and diverse human-resource base might nonetheless experience relatively low rates of high-potential entrepreneurship if potential high-potential entrepreneurs perceive financial disincentives and discouraging cultural cues about risk-taking.

High-potential entrepreneurship marries extreme ambition with technical expertise and market savvy. While the scale of an individual's ambition may not depend closely on his or her education and experience, his or her level of expertise and savvy are likely to. Education allows a potential entrepreneur to access and appreciate new knowledge; business experience provides insights into how it might be applied. GEM finds, not surprisingly, that high-potential entrepreneurs are better educated, better off, and better connected than other entrepreneurs (Bullvaag et al., 2006). The educational and occupational mix of a society thus shapes its capacity for high-potential entrepreneurship. These demographic patterns tend to change only slowly over time, shaped by a society's collective resources and commitments.

Cultural diversity, too, tends to be relatively fixed in the short-run, due to historic patterns of immigration and social mobility. Holding education and experience constant, diversity affects high-potential entrepreneurship by increasing the likelihood that unexploited market niches and technical combinations will be perceived as opportunities, rather than ignored. As Carlsson and Jacobson (1997) put it in a different context, the blending of cultures enlarges the 'search space' in which opportunities are sought. People holding diverse values will resolve uncertainties about these opportunities differently, driving disagreements that lead to spin-offs and start-ups. Florida (2003, 2005) provides evidence of a strong association between diversity and high-potential entrepreneurship at the regional and, to a lesser extent, national levels.

High-potential entrepreneurs typically risk more than other entrepreneurs. Their education and experience make it likely that they have reasonably secure and remunerative career options within existing businesses as alternatives to going out on their own. The cost of entrepreneurial failure to these individuals involves more than the loss of a salary and any capital invested. They stand to lose in addition organization-specific human and social capital if a return to their prior career track is prohibited in the case of failure. Where the individual opportunity costs of entrepreneurial behaviour are low, high-potential entrepreneurship will thrive.

High-potential entrepreneurship involves non-pecuniary as well as financial risks and payoffs. The non-pecuniary benefits of high-potential entrepreneurship might include the esteem of family and friends, the expansion of social networks, and the pleasures of acquiring new knowledge and tackling a challenge—even if the venture fails in the end. Whether such rewards can be expected depends in the first place on the values that potential entrepreneurs have absorbed throughout their lives. These expectations may be shaped as well by cultural cues, including the status accorded entrepreneurs in the media.

13.7. Organizations, managers, and the exploitation of high-potential opportunities

The exploitation of high-potential opportunities requires that entrepreneurs draw on more substantial and more diverse outside resources—including money, talent, connections, and knowledge—than other forms of entre-preneurship. High-potential entrepreneurship is defined by rapid and extended growth, driving demands for these resources on a scale that quickly outstrips the personal capacities of even the most experienced and well-heeled founders. Scaling up brings qualitative as well as quantitative changes in resource requirements, particularly managerial skills. In societies with high rates of high-potential entrepreneurship, entrepreneurs are embedded in an institutional framework that nurtures organizations and individuals—in addi-tion to the entrepreneurs themselves—who are able to evaluate high-potential opportunities well and to leverage their control of critical resources to enhance exploitation.

The most obvious resource required by high-potential start-ups is money. The 'burn rate' (monthly or quarterly spending) varies substantially across sectors and over time, but regardless of the initial level, it accelerates quickly when these firms are successful. Manufacturing firms that move from proto-typing to production, for instance, typically face a step change in costs. When the pockets of the founders and their 'family and friends' are emptied, new investors must be solicited. This solicitation process must overcome substan-tial transaction costs, especially negotiating an appropriate valuation for the firm and control rights over it (Gompers and Lerner, 2001). National financial institutions, including private and public markets and government grant and loan programs, may be more or less effective in surmounting these obstacles.

High-potential start-ups also need to recruit a rapidly-changing array of high-level technical and managerial talent. Skills and strategies that are critical in a firm's earliest phases tend to become less so as it grows and may even become irrelevant or counterproductive. The decision to join such a firm once it is already up and running is similar to that of engaging in high-potential entrepreneurship, as discussed in the previous section, albeit with more infor-mation and perhaps lower risk. A deep and mobile talent pool will make high-potential entrepreneurship easier. Well-developed social networks that may involve entrepreneurs, investors, and specialized service providers can facili-tate recruitment as well.

Knowledge, beyond that brought to the firm by new employees, is a third external resource upon which high-potential entrepreneurship is dependent. Social networks are a crucial means to access such knowledge. For instance, highly-competitive and rapidly-moving technical fields in which many start-ups are involved rely more heavily on such networks for information exchange than formal vehicles such as conferences and publications. Current business information, too, is transferred through informal relationships as well as through specialized media. Other things being equal, societies rich in social capital, particularly among elites, will probably give rise to more high-potential entrepreneurship.

13.8. A little bit of evidence

I have argued, then, that societies create opportunities for high-potential entrepreneurship, individuals recognize them, and organizations exploit them, and that there are institutional framework conditions that operate at each of these three levels. I am not able in this space to provide a comprehensive test of this framework. Elsewhere, I have made a first pass at an application to the history of the United States, which has maintained a relatively high level of high-potential entrepreneurship (Hart, 2011). Although there are no consistent data of the quality of GEM, I believe that this has been a characteristic of the US economy for decades and helps to account for the nation's economic success.

I will briefly, however, explore empirically one of the major implications of my argument. I have suggested that high-potential entrepreneurship is the outcome of a complex set of interactions among a number of major institutional systems in society. These institutional systems are interactive, co-evolving, and typically self-reinforcing. That suggests that the level of high-potential entrepreneurship will change slowly, if at all, in the absence of a major disruption in society, such as a war or economic depression.

I will use GEM data in order to look at this issue. GEM operationalizes high-potential entrepreneurship as the entrepreneur's expectation that his or her business will employ 20 or more people within five years. Obviously, entrepreneurial expectations are not always fulfilled; indeed, entrepreneurs of all stripes fail more often than they succeed. On the other hand, some start-ups succeed well beyond their founders' expectations. Nonetheless, as Wiklund and Shepherd (2003) and Autio (2005) show, there is a correlation, albeit imperfect, between initial expectations and eventual growth.

High-potential entrepreneurship is, of course, a rare occurrence. In fact, it is so rare that it is necessary to aggregate data across a number of years, even in a survey as large as GEM, in order to study it. About 1.5 per cent of the surveyed population in the USA, for instance, fell into this category between 2000 and 2004. That share was roughly three times the rate of major continental European and highly-developed Asian countries for which data were available in these years. As Bullvaag et al. (2006: 6) put it, this rate puts the USA 'in a league of its own'.

More countries have been added to the GEM project over time, and the US position appears less exceptional when this broader perspective is available. New Zealand, Iceland, and Canada nearly match the US level, while China exceeds it. Still, when the data from 2000 to 2006 are aggregated, the major countries (including the UK, Germany, Sweden, and Spain) for which the full data are available remain in the same positions and at roughly the same levels

(Autio 2007). By 2009, it became possible to do a comparison of two separate five-year periods, and the result is unchanged (Bosma and Levie, 2010).

Of course, by the lights of my argument, even a decade is a relatively short time. As the GEM data cumulate longitudinally and in a wider range of countries, the hints from this cursory effort might be followed up more carefully. It may also be possible to examine the impact of social disruption with the most recent data, as a result of the financial crisis of 2008 and resulting economic downturn. Iceland, for instance, which was forced to secure assistance from the International Monetary Fund very early in the global crisis, would be an interesting candidate for such a project, along with the USA, where the 'great recession' still lingers, with unemployment rates over 9 per cent in mid-2011.

13.9. Possible futures

The bottom line of my argument for policy-makers is that they must be patient as well as determined. They might also need to be a little lucky in the sense that, while they may be able to shape the broad conditions within which entrepreneurs operate, the internal dynamics are not in their direct control. Leadership firms, which become role models and spawn spin-offs, for instance, cannot be created by fiat. Self-reinforcing feedbacks must develop within the entrepreneurial system, often in ways that policy-makers cannot anticipate.

An impressionistic scan around the world suggests that there are some nations that have been successful in carrying through a high-potential entrepreneurship policy, although perhaps not under that name. China is the most obvious and biggest. A few smaller, wealthier countries, such as Ireland, Singapore, and Israel (along with Iceland) stand out in recent GEM data, but were hardly known as hotbeds of high-potential entrepreneurship twenty or thirty years ago.

As my argument would suggest, each of these countries has followed a different evolutionary path to its present position (Breznitz, 2007). For countries considering what to do, much can be learned from experiences elsewhere, but there is no point in slavish imitation. Institutional endowments differ and so do the external conditions at any point in time. The words of Gerschenkron (1962: 4), though written for a different purpose, still ring true: 'No past experience, however rich, and no historical research, however thorough, can save the living generation the creative task of finding their own answers and shaping their own future.'

Looking forward, it will be ever more important for high-potential entrepreneurship policy to be attuned to the globalization process, which may provide a means to short-cut some aspects of indigenous institutional development. Not only can markets increasingly be found globally, but so too can knowledge, talent, and money. The 'micro-multinational' (Copeland, 2006) start-up can assemble resources and exploit opportunities in ways that were not available to start-ups in years past. Policy-makers may want to consider easing access to such resources, whether through R&D collaboration, migration policy, or capital-access rules.

At the same time, however, the globalization process may sap away some of the benefits that have historically been associated with high-potential entrepreneurship. Just as resources can be gathered offshore, so too can jobs flow offshore. The folk wisdom of Silicon Valley for some time has been that every start-up there needs to have an offshoring strategy. Difficult trade-offs as well as opportunities lie ahead.

References

Acs, Z.J., Audretsch, D.B., Braunerhjelm, P. and Carlsson, B. (2006), 'Growth and entrepreneurship: An empirical assessment'. Discussion paper 5409, Centre for Economic Policy Research, London.

———————(2009), 'The knowledge spillover theory of entrepreneurship', *Small Business Economics*, 32:15–30.

——, Parsons, W. and Tracy, S. (2008), 'High impact firms: Gazelles revisited', U.S. Small Business Administration Office of Advocacy Working Paper no. 328, Washington, DC.

Auerswald, P.E. and Branscomb, L.M. (2003), 'Start-ups and spin-offs: Collective entrepreneurship between invention and innovation'. In Hart, D.M. (ed.), *The Emergence of Entrepreneurship Policy*. New York: Cambridge University Press.

Autio, E. (2003), *High-Potential Entrepreneurship*. New York: United Nations Global Entrepreneurship Symposium.

—— (2005), *Global Entrepreneurship Monitor 2005 Global Report on High Expectation Entrepreneurship*. Wellesley, MA: Babson College and London Business School.

—— (2007), *Global Entrepreneurship Monitor 2007 Global Report on High-Growth Entrepreneurship*. Wellesley, MA: Babson College and London Business School.

—— (2009),'The Finnish paradox: The curious absence of high-growth entrepreneurship in Finland', ETLA working paper #1197. Helsinki: ETLA.

Baumol, W.J. (1990),'Entrepreneurship: Productive, unproductive, and destructive', *Journal of Political Economy*, 98: 893–921.

Bosma, N. and Levie, J. (2010). *Global Entrepreneurship Monitor 2009 Executive Report*. Wellesley MA: Babson College.

Breznitz, D. (2007), *Innovation and the State*. New Haven: Yale University Press.

Bullvaag, E., Acs, Z.J., Allen, I.E., Bygrave, W.D. and Spinelli Jr, S. (2006). *Global Entrepreneurship Monitor, National Entrepreneurship Assessment, U.S.A., 2004–2005 Executive Report*. New York: Babson College and George Mason University.

Carlsson, B., and Jacobson S. (1997), 'Diversity creation and technological systems: A technology policy perspective'. In Edquist, C. (ed.), *Systems of Innovation*. London: Pinter.

Casson, M. (2010), *Entrepreneurship: Theory, Networks, History*. Cheltenham: Edward Elgar.

Christensen, C. (1997), *The Innovator's Dilemma*. Boston: Harvard Business School Press.

—— and Rosenbloom, R.S. (1995), 'Explaining the attacker's advantage: Technological paradigms, organizational dynamics, and the value network', *Research Policy*, 24: 233–257.

Copeland, M.V. (2006), 'The mighty micro-multinational', *Business 2.0*, July 1.

Cotis, J.-P. (2007), 'Entrepreneurship as an engine for growth: Evidence and policy challenges'. Paper presented to GEM Forum, London, January, available at http://www.oecd.org/dataoecd/4/51/38031895.pdf (accessed 14 June 2011).

Florida, R. (2003), *The Rise of the Creative Class*. New York: Basic.

—— (2005), *The Flight of the Creative Class*. New York: HarperBusiness.

Fritsch, M. and Mueller, P. (2004), 'Effects of new business formation on regional development over time', *Regional Studies*, 38: 961–975.

Gerschenkron, A. (1962), *Economic Backwardness in Historical Perspective*. Cambridge, MA: Belknap.

Gompers, P. and Lerner, J. (2001), 'The venture capital revolution', *Journal of Economic Perspectives*, 15(2): 145–168.

Greif, A. (2006), *Institutions and the Path to the Modern Economy*. New York: Cambridge University Press.

Haltiwanger, J. (2008), 'Entrepreneurship and job growth'. In Acs, Z.J., and Audretsch, D.B. (eds), *Entrepreneurship, Economic Growth, and Public Policy*. New York: Cambridge University Press.

Hart, D.M. (2011), 'The social context for high-potential entrepreneurship in the U.S.: An historical-institutional perspective'. In Usui, C. (ed.), *Comparative entrepreneurship initiatives*. Houndmills, Basingstoke: Palgrave Macmillan.

Henrekson, M. and Johansson, D. (2009), 'Competencies and institutions fostering high-growth firms', *Foundations and Trends in Entrepreneurship*, 5: 1–80.

—— —— (2010), 'Gazelles as job creators: A survey and interpretation of the evidence', *Small Business Economics*, 35: 227–244.

Lerner, J. (2009), *Boulevard of Broken Dreams: Why Public Efforts to Boost Entrepreneurship and Venture Capital Have Failed and What to Do about It*. Princeton: Princeton University Press.

Levie, J. and Autio, E. (2008), 'A theoretical grounding and test of the GEM model', *Small Business Economics*, 31: 235–263.

Murmann, J.P. (2003), *Knowledge and Competitive Advantage*. New York: Cambridge University Press.

Murphy, K.M., Shleifer, A. and Vishny, R.W. (1991), 'Allocation of talent: Implications for growth', *Quarterly Journal of Economics*, 106: 503–530.

Nelson, R.R. and Winter, S.G. (1982), *An Evolutionary Theory of Economic Change*. Cambridge, MA: Harvard University Press.

Pierson, P. (2004), *Politics in Time*. Princeton: Princeton University Press.

Pozen, D. (2008), 'We are all entrepreneurs now', *Wake Forest Law Review*, 43: 283–340.

Reynolds, P.D. et al. (2002), *GEM Global Summary Report 2001*. Wellesley, MA: London Business School and Babson College.

Rosenberg, N. (2003), America's entrepreneurial universities. In Hart, D.M. (ed.), *The Emergence of Entrepreneurship Policy*. New York: Cambridge University Press.

Shane, S. (2003), *A General Theory of Entrepreneurship: The Individual/Opportunity Nexus*. Cheltenham: Edward Elgar.

—— and Venktaraman, S. (2000), 'The promise of entrepreneurship as a field of research', *Academy of Management Review*, 25: 217–226.

Thelen, K. and Mahoney, J. (2010), *Explaining Institutional Change: Ambiguity, Agency, and Power*. New York: Cambridge University Press.

Thornton, P.H. (1999), 'The sociology of entrepreneurship', *Annual Review of Sociology*, 25: 19–46.

Wennekers, S. and Thurik, R. (1999), 'Linking entrepreneurship and economic growth', *Small Business Economics*, 13: 27–55.

Wiklund, J. and Shepherd, D. (2003), 'Aspiring for and achieving growth: The moderating role of resources and opportunities', *Journal of Management Studies*, 40: 1919–1941.

Wong, P.K., Ho, Y.P. and Autio, E. (2005), 'Entrepreneurship, innovation, and economic growth: Evidence from GEM data', *Small Business Economics*, 24: 335–350.

Part IV
Reflections

Someone who has made a journey has something to reflect upon. One way of appreciating the journey of this book is to view it as a passage through a set of inquiries into innovation strategies, continuing over alternative perspectives on how firm-level performance is influenced by innovation strategies and associated R&D efforts, further on to deliberations on economy-wide aspects of innovation and R&D investments across industries or sectors of an entire economy.

Another way of describing the journey is the following.

First, it emphasizes the importance of separating fast processes of change from those that evolve on a slow time scale. This distinction helps to illuminate the causes behind the lasting heterogeneity of firms in each industry.

Second, it suggests that the permanency of an industry's composition in terms of high-performance and low-performance firms can be associated with the difference between innovation strategies employed by individual firms.

Third, several of the studies presented in the book examine multinational company groups (MNEs) over long time periods. Other contributions recognize that subsidiaries of multinational corporations often comprise small and medium-sized firms with above average innovation results. One fundamental lesson from the analyses of MNE firms is that networks for innovation flows play a substantial role in the overall growth process of an economy. Many observations indicate that such knowledge flows have become a more frequent phenomenon in recent decades, providing multinationals with a knowledge-flow advantage due to new technologies for network control and governance (Karlsson, Johansson and Stough, 2010).

The fourth and a most significant contribution in the book is the observation that it is not enough to study the knowledge assets and knowledge creation of the innovating firm. Innovation activities benefit substantially from a firm's capacity to combine opportunities in the conjunction of internal and external knowledge sources. In this context there are also spatial externalities to consider, such as knowledge flows in industrial clusters in local economies as well as in diversity-rich metropolitan regions. An associated phenomenon is the uneven distribution of localized entrepreneurship cultures, and this may call for policies aiming at reshaping relevant institutions. These spatial aspects of innovation processes are not a focal point in the book, although they are present in contributions in Part III where entrepreneurship is analysed as an economy-wide element.

Strategy

In decision- and game-theory models strategy means a plan specifying which decisions to make in response to information that becomes available at each point in time. This notion of strategy is important in contexts with strategic uncertainty, where the result of the individual decision-maker's choice depends on decisions made by rivals. The contributions in this book primarily adhere to a strategy concept of a pro-active nature, thereby sharing common ground with the management literature, where strategy refers to firms' decisions about structure and behaviour with long-term consequences.

A major element in a pro-active strategy of an innovating firm is its efforts to build up a resource base which comprises investments in innovation skills of employees, routines for orchestration of R&D efforts, and links to other actors for knowledge accession and collaboration. The ambition behind such a strategy that has to be persistent over time in order to ascertain positive results is to establish capabilities such as:

- Absorptive capacity
- Innovation skills
- Innovation routines
- Capacity to exploit in-house knowledge in conjunction with external knowledge, sometimes formalized in alliances
- Capacity to combine various types of knowledge across technology fields.

As emphasized above, the chapters in the book illustrate that both intra- and extra-firm resources are important for a firm's development of these kinds of capabilities. Extra-firm resources include characteristics of the local milieu as well as networks to other firms, customers, and knowledge sources.

An additional observation that is present in a set of the book's chapters can be illuminated by categorizing firms into two groups where S_0 denotes strategies which imply that firms do not engage in innovation efforts or engage only occasionally, and where firms with long-term commitments to innovation efforts apply strategies of type S_1. In a long-term perspective, firms of type S_1 exhibit superior performance in comparison with S_0 firms.

The importance of persistency of innovation efforts implies that overall economic growth is facilitated if the conditions for employing S_1 strategies are favourable. There is, however, a more challenging issue for improved firm performance and economy-wide growth, and that issue is specified in the following question: what causes a firm to transit from S_0 to S_1, and what factors trigger a firm to shift from S_1 to S_0?

The existing literature contemplates why firms tend to maintain an S_1 path, once such a strategy has been adopted, and why so few S_0 firms shift strategy to engage persistently in innovation efforts. These considerations include a variety of suggestions:

- The necessary technological knowledge is partly tacit, and partly embodied in complex organizational practices, and this explains why firms with persistent innovation efforts have much to gain from remaining on their S_1 path, whereas S_0 firms have a lead–lag relation to overcome (Dosi and Nelson, 2010). Leader–laggard rivalry is examined in Aghion et al. (2005), who emphasize the difficulties for an S_0 firm to catch up with leader firms that employ S_1 strategies.
- Philips (1971) refers to feedback mechanisms in knowledge formation, implying that 'success breeds success'.

Lessons to learn from MNEs

Multinational firms, i.e. firms belonging to a multinational company group, are in fundamental ways different from other firms. In the chapter by Almeida and Phene it is observed that managers need to tap external knowledge resources. Obviously, a multinational corporation has its own subsidiaries to tap in the corporation's internal networks for knowledge interaction. This may be assessed as a knowledge-governance advantage of multinational corporations, but there is an additional feature that makes a multinational corporation as well as all its member firms different. The additional advantage is that the corporation can use its different subsidiaries to access localized knowledge from many different places in the world. Moreover, a multinational corporation may strategically select the location of its subsidiaries in a manner that enhances its capability to access external knowledge.

Conjunction of intra-firm and extra-firm knowledge

A recurrent finding across the chapters in the book is that a firm's innovation and growth performance depends critically upon its resource base, its knowledge assets, and the routines for carrying out innovation activities—all factors that influence the firm's capabilities in a dynamic context. However, observations from both firm-level, sector-level, and economy-wide analyses indicate that a firm's internal resources for innovation and renewal combine to represent just one component of a firm's capacity to innovate and grow.

The second factor influencing a firm's innovation behaviour is dependent on the firm's interaction with its environment via networks and contacts in the local and regional milieu as well as via long-distance links or channels for interaction with actors globally. The message is clear: it is the very conjunction of internal and external knowledge sources that makes the difference.

This is also reflected in the suggestion at the very start of the book, where we learn that knowledge-management and knowledge-accession strategies become a vital development factor. It is also claimed that the ability of a firm to integrate technologically diversified knowledge through combination is a factor which affects the performance of the individual firm. Increasingly, new products (goods and services) require a growing number of technologies to be combined, and this expands the demand on an individual firm's capacity to orchestrate multidisciplinary inputs to its innovation efforts.

The above observations have their counterpart in the chapters dealing with economy-wide, inter-sector relations in productivity-enhancing technology development. They are also supported by the suggestions in the entrepreneurship contributions in Part III of the book.

- Conjunction phenomena require an interface between the individual firm and its environment. Interface activities may be positively stimulated by a local cluster formation of firms in the same and related industries, where 'related' may include both inter-sector deliveries and technology similarities of two or several different firms.
- Firms' search for knowledge-complexity conjunctions may get support from an environment which consists of firms and industries that are primarily located in large urban agglomerations, in which knowledge flows are facilitated by short time distances for contacts and by more frequent job mobility between firms, where the mobility of labour causes knowledge to flow between firms in a local labour market.
- Entrepreneurship and birth of new firms is associated with local knowledge spillovers, taking the form of spin-offs and spin-outs, while implying that knowledge may spread more in regions with a high frequency of start-ups. Incumbent firms with persistent innovation efforts may also be an important source for new ideas that are materialized in the form of new firms, and this may be an important economy-wide consequence of firms' innovation efforts.

- Technology impacts associated with inter-sector deliveries are a major vehicle for spreading innovation results in one sector to other sectors of the economy, and diffusion of this kind can also be considered as a conjunction phenomenon. In addition, a firm's interaction with its suppliers and customers provides a mechanism for spillovers which feed the firm with innovation ideas. Furthermore, technology impacts via input-output linkages are influenced by how cleverly the individual firm selects its supplier links, and by how successful it is in developing customer relations. These processes are indeed affected by the economic milieu in which the firm is embedded.

Local economic milieu

The knowledge-conjunction phenomenon has clear connotations to system features of the local/regional economic milieu as emphasized in observations of entrepreneurship culture and labour-force mobility. Policies to contemplate in this context include innovation-enabling and friction-reducing measures. As stressed by Klepper and Sleeper (2002), entrepreneurs who can access existing technological and experience-based knowledge in the pertinent industry enjoy a large advantage.

As emphasized in the third part of the book, there is also an economy-wide aspect of the regional economic milieu which refers to the correspondence between the relative abundance of production factors and the factorial characterization of the technology that firms use in production. A local economic milieu may be characterized by its regional factor prices, e.g. with regard to different categories of knowledge-intensive labour, as well as natural resources. New technical solutions are not adopted by a firm as a new (superior) isoquant, but rather as a point on an isoquant surface. Considering that a new technical solution which is introduced in a region has the form of a specific point on the isoquant surface, this technical solution may be biased to match the regional factor prices. Imitation of such a technique in another region with other relative factor prices will then result in a much less favourable economic outcome. This phenomenon sheds light on why technology may evolve along different paths in different regions (and countries), generating idiosyncratic technology configurations at different places. The phenomenon can also help to explain why technical solutions may diffuse in very selective ways across different regions. The observation also calls for contemplations about the design (when applicable) of regional and national innovation systems.

References

Aghion, P., Bloom, N., Blundell, R., Griffith, R. and Howitt, P. (2005), 'Competition and innovation: An inverted U-relationship', *Quarterly Journal of Economics*, 120: 701–728.

Dosi, G. and Nelson, R.R. (2010), Technical change and industrial dynamics as evolutionary processes. In Hall, B. and Rosenberg, N. (eds), *The Economics of Innovation*. Amsterdam: North Holland, Elsevier.

Karlsson, C., Johansson, B. and Stough, R.R. (2010), Introduction. In Karlsson, C., Johansson, B. and Stough, R.R. (eds), *Entrepreneurship and Regional Development—Local Processes and Global Patterns*. Cheltenham: Edward Elgar.

Klepper, S. and Sleeper, S. (2002), *Entry by Spinoffs, Papers on Economics and Evolution 2002–07*. Jena: Max Planck Institute for Research into Economic Systems, Evolutionary Economics Group.

Philips, A. (1971), *Technology and Market Structure: A Study of the Aircraft Industry*. Lexington: D.C. Heath.

Author Index

Subject Index